ECONOMIC THEORIES OF DEVELOPMENT:

An analysis of competing paradigms

ECONOMIC THEORIES OF DEVELOPMENT:

An analysis of competing paradigms

Diana Hunt

School of African and Asian Studies
University of Sussex

HARVESTER WHEATSHEAF

New York London Toronto Sydney Tokyo Singapore

First published 1989 by
Harvester Wheatsheaf,
Campus 400, Maylands Avenue, Hemel Hempstead
Hertfordshire HP2 7EZ
A division of
Simon & Schuster International Group

Printed in Great Britain by
Antony Rowe Ltd, Chippenham, Wiltshire

British Library Cataloguing in Publication Data

Hunt, Diana, 1942–
    Economic theories of development.
    1. Economics. Theories, history
    I. Title
    330.1

ISBN 0-7450-0132-7
ISBN 0-7450-0237-4 pbk

---

6 7 8 9 98 97 96 95

Reprinted 1998

To my parents

CONTENTS

PREFACE

This book is not intended as a text in development economics but, rather, as a complement to any such text. In it I have sought to outline the main perspectives from which the study of economic development has been approached and, thus, the main intellectual frameworks that have guided the formulation of recommendations for development-oriented action in the economic sphere. In doing so I have assumed that the reader has both a prior grounding in the basic economic tools and concepts which, as Ian Livingstone has pointed out, form the core of economics syllabuses in less developed countries as much as in the more developed ones, and an awareness of the types of issues that have formed the substance of development economics: a branch of study concerned both with the interpretation of processes of resource allocation and economic change in less developed countries and with generating recommendations for development-oriented action, including choice of development strategy and the policies with which to pursue it.

Given the wealth of ideas and theories that have stemmed from the study of economic development during the last half century, any attempt to outline the main intellectual perspectives that have dominated the discipline can only be approached with a serious risk of superficiality and oversimplification. Certainly one cannot enter into the same degree of analytical detail with respect to particular policy issues and policy instruments that one might expect of a conventional text in development economics. Nor can one treat these in the same manner: rather than being discussed in one concentrated block of analysis, the same or linked issues now crop up in different chapters, in the context of the discussion of different perspectives. Furthermore, the very organisation of the material to be covered entails the risk of oversimplification in another sense: that which occurs when ideas are categorised and classified.

With respect to the first of these risks I can only reiterate the above-stated presumption that the present study will be read either as a sequel to, or alongside, both basic texts in economic theory and the more standard texts in development economics. The second risk I have attempted to confront primarily by avoiding the temptation to classify all theoretical and applied work in development economics within as few as two or three main schools of thought. The number of distinct perspectives that have excited a significant influence within the discipline are, it seems to me, greater than this. In Chapter 1, I have attempted to delineate what I understand by a 'dominant perspective' or 'intellectual framework'. This delineation has led me to focus on six such perspectives; fortunately a reasonably manageable number.

Marxist, as opposed to neo-Marxist, scholars may feel that I have underrated the contribution of Marxism to development economics. Marxism is not one of the six perspectives that I have singled out as having dominated this debate, for the following reasons. The criteria of 'dominance' that I have applied (outlined more fully in Chapter 1) include the requirement that an intellectual perspective so described should, once its core has been established, have provided the inspiration and basis both for significant further theoretical development and for more applied work on economic development. Moreover, my interpretation of the core of development economics is that outlined in the first paragraph of this preface. Marxism does not meet these criteria as completely as the other six perspectives. The Marxist contribution has been largely confined to the interpretative aspect of development analysis, applying an existing stock of concepts and beliefs to this exercise (as, for example, in the debates on whether and where a capitalist class is emerging and on the nature and role of the state in developing countries).

Given the hazards, and the already abundant expositional literature, why, the sceptical reader may ask, attempt the present task. The positive reasons for writing the present text are quite straightforward. While standard texts in development economics analyse policy issues and instruments in greater depth than the present one, they generally do so by drawing on the contributions of economists working within a range of different intellectual frameworks whose significance is not always made plain. Here the focus is reversed: it is on these perspectives *per se*, their main features and the nature of the differences between them. This approach is not original: since the mid-1970s there has been a wealth of writing on schools of thought in development economics. However, much of this has been addressed primarily to other development theorists. I hope that the present text will also prove useful both to students and to development practitioners.

As has already been hinted, in preparing this book it has proved impossible to avoid courting a degree of controversy, both in the identification and determination of the dominant perspectives and in the classification of certain well-known contributions to the development debate. However, it seems to me that, for better or for worse, what follows is for the most part uncontentious. In writing these pages it was not my primary intention to enter into a polemic, but to assist in the clarification of thinking about the development process.

ACKNOWLEDGEMENTS

Many people have helped me in the preparation of this book. In particular I should like to acknowledge the contribution of those students on the MA programme in Development Economics at Sussex University who over a number of years attended my lectures on the material covered here, and whose questions and comments were a consistent stimulus. More recently various people have read, and commented on, parts of the text. Ken Cole provided speedy, stringent and stimulating criticism of the whole. Franco Viciani, who originally suggested this project, also commented on Chapters 1–6, 8 and 9, Fred Nixson and an anonymous reader on Chapters 1–6, Jack Grey on Chapter 8 and Hans Singer, Barry Heinman and Mohammed Ahmed on Chapter 9. I am very grateful to all of them for their patience and help. My grateful thanks also go to the various people who undertook the typing and retyping of various drafts, and to the library staff of the British School and of the Universita Gregoriana, both in Rome, who provided for a stranger with no reading rights a tranquil environment in which to work; my thanks too to Professor W. A. Lewis and the Editors of the *Manchester School* for permission to reproduce the diagram on page 90 and to Oxford University Press for permission to reproduce the diagram on page 303.

My thanks also go to the staff of Sussex University Library and of the Institute of Development Studies Library at Sussex, most recently for their help in completing bibliographical references. Sussex University provided me with a sabbatical term in 1984 which enabled me to get this project under way, and a grant towards typing costs,while the lively interest in development issues both of the 1987/88 student intake into the Economics Diploma at Sussex and of members of the Economics BA programme in the School of African and Asian Studies provided some of the stimulus to bring this study to long-delayed conclusion. Finally I should like to thank everyone at Harvester Wheatsheaf for their interest, support and patience throughout. For the remaining errors of omission and commission which you, the reader, will doubtless identify, I am solely responsible.

1 · INTRODUCTION

THE PURPOSE OF THIS BOOK

Every student of development economics can expect to encounter in the literature a number of different perceptions of the processes of development and underdevelopment. The fact that this is so widens the area of debate and the scope for disagreement among students of ostensibly the same range of problems. It also provides an additional potential source of confusion (as, for example, when half-way through a debate it is discovered that the protagonists are arguing from different premises, or indeed, that one protagonist has switched premises in mid-stream). Confusion may be worse confounded by virtue of the fact that the different approaches are associated with different interpretations of development and underdevelopment.

Some of these perceptions of the nature and process of development and/or underdevelopment have come to command, for varying periods of time, widespread support, in the course of which they have both generated significant theoretical developments and informed various types of more practical activity, such as economic planning and policy formation. It is the purpose of this book to elucidate the nature of these dominant perceptions.

THE KEY ELEMENTS OF AN INTELLECTUAL FRAMEWORK OR PARADIGM

The different intellectual frameworks from which both scientific and social scientific enquiry are approached do not consist simply of a body of theory. Each also incorporates a set of values, beliefs and specific assumptions about the object of study. Each also employs distinctive central concepts and a distinctive methodology. Each, that is to say, incorporates the various features that are embodied in the original Kuhnian interpretation of a scientific paradigm. Hence this book's subtitle, for in seeking to identify the dominant intellectual frameworks in development economics the author uses the concept of a paradigm both as a 'sorting device' and as the basis from which the exposition of each framework is developed. It may, therefore, be helpful to offer at the outset a more precise definition of this concept.

For the purposes of this book, a paradigm is defined, following Kuhn (1962), as:

> that constellation of values, beliefs and perceptions of empirical reality, which, together with a body of theory based upon the foregoing, is used by a group of scientists, and by applying a distinctive methodology, to interpret the nature of some aspect of the universe we inhabit.

The concept is a complex one, and each of its component parts is itself an important element in a scientist's professional approach. Furthermore, two additional characteristics are implicit in this definition: i.e. that over time those who adopt a particular paradigm can be expected both to develop its theoretical content and to apply it to the solution of specific problems.

KUHN'S ORIGINAL INTERPRETATION OF SCIENTIFIC PARADIGMS

In *The Structure of Scientific Revolutions* (a study which was addressed to physical scientists but rapidly attracted the attention of social scientists) Kuhn starts from the proposition that all science is governed by a schematic view on the part of the scientist of that aspect of the universe which is his subject of enquiry. Into this schema enter certain fundamental laws that the scientist accepts, certain theories that he likewise accepts, an accepted methodology, and, although the scientist may not always be fully aware of this, certain values which govern his approach to his work. The laws and theories pinpoint certain key variables and relationships which are held to be of fundamental importance in interpreting and explaining the *modus operandi* of the scientist's field of enquiry. The methodology that the scientist applies in seeking to solve outstanding problems will directly reflect them. In order to articulate these laws and theories the scientist needs to use particular concepts, of which the most central are likely to be specific to his schema. His statements are therefore governed by a particular use of language, readily understood by those who share his vision, but not always so by others who may find part of his vocabulary unfamiliar, while being accustomed to interpret other items in it differently. It is to this distinctive intellectual framework – or *gestalt*, as he himself also describes it – that Kuhn (1962) attaches the label 'paradigm'.

In principle every scientist might espouse a distinct vision of the nature of his field of enquiry. This of course would make for considerable difficulty of communication between scientists. It would also tend to impede progress in problem solution as scientists would constantly be engaged in debate about fundamentals, rather than about how to solve problems within a given intellectual framework. While such debate may be expected in the formative years of a new discipline, Kuhn asserted that in a mature science this does not occur: such a science is characterised by the relative scarcity of competing paradigms.[1]

Those familiar with *The Structure of Scientific Revolutions* and the controversy it aroused will be aware of the debate that Kuhn's original interpretation of a scientific paradigm generated,[2] and of the fact that, eight years later, Kuhn abandoned this interpretation, reverting to the conventional definition of a paradigm as an 'exemplar'. In my view, however, Kuhn created a linguistic gap by doing so, for many had found his original interpretation fruitful, albeit complex, and no other fully satisfactory term has yet been found to represent it.[3]

Hence, to recapitulate, in this study the term 'paradigm' is applied to those interpretations of the processes of development and/or underdevelopment which, in the author's view, fulfil the following conditions:

1. They can be clearly seen to have the various components specified in the definition above.
2. They have commanded the support of a significant group of scholars.
3. They have generated further theoretical development following their preliminary articulation.
4. They have also, in one form or another, been applied to practical activity, for example, to policy formation.

CONTEXT AND INTENT AS INFLUENCES ON PARADIGM EMERGENCE AND ADOPTION

When Kuhn developed the concept of a scientific paradigm, he did so in order to focus on the causes of emergence of new paradigms. He identified two of the causes as the emergence of a new discipline, and paradigm failure (inability to solve a key problem) within an existing discipline. However, he also acknowledged that an important omission from his analysis was that of any systematic attempt to identify the influence of external factors — technological, social, economic or intellectual[4] — on the development of particular paradigms. He notes their influence, illustrating the point with reference to the social pressures for calendar reform at the time of Copernicus, but in *The Structure of Scientific Revolutions* he pursues the point no further. Yet for the student who seeks to understand not only the values, beliefs and internal logic of a particular intellectual approach but also the range of conditions and pressures that gave rise to its birth, these factors cannot be ignored. Indeed, the list above could well be extended to include political and religious factors as well.

External factors may help to explain, *inter alia*, the timing of the emergence of a new paradigm. In some instances they may also influence the range of new perspectives considered by the scientist who is confronted with an intractable problem. The impact of such external influences upon scientific endeavour may be both positive and negative, direct and indirect. For example, the influence of church doctrine and belief upon the development of scholarship in Europe throughout the Middle Ages is well known. It is widely agreed that this had a retarding influence upon the development of certain lines of scientific enquiry and theory. Today, in philosophy and the social sciences, perhaps even more than in the physical sciences, it is inevitable that certain lines of thought should prove politically more acceptable than others. Political pressures may influence, both positively and negatively, both the manner of specifying a problem and the identification of different angles of approach to it – as well as the urgency with which these are pursued.

Meanwhile, certain recent developments in the philosophy of social science also emphasise that the content of social theorising directly reflects the *purpose* of the theoriser.[5] The latter in turn is likely to be influenced both by contextual factors and the values of the theoriser.[6]

In what follows, an attempt will be made to give the reader an indication of the broader context in which each of the perspectives under discussion emerged and to outline the main purpose for which they were first articulated.

SELECTED CRITICISMS OF THE PARADIGM CONCEPT

Recent trends in thought concerning the nature of social scientific theorising largely endorse Kuhn's ideas concerning the main components of an intellectual framework. However, some social theorists have found Kuhn's (1962) interpretation of paradigms overly rigid. According to this line of criticism, his rather dramatic emphasis on the nature of differences in 'gestalt' seems to offer no scope for relatively subtle variations in perspective, nor for possible elements of compatibility between paradigms; nor, by implication, does it seem to allow for the possibility that an individual might draw inspiration from more than one intellectual perspective. The second of these criticisms is, however, based on a particular, and contestable, interpretation of Kuhn.[7] The former criticism, too, seems overly harsh if one acknowledges the possibility, as Kuhn did, of intraparadigm theoretical and methodological development. Certainly the purpose of the present study is not to suggest that every development economist holds rigidly to one of the intellectual frameworks reviewed, precisely as it is outlined in the following pages. Rather, while the primary emphasis is on the core elements of the dominant frameworks – those that have exerted the greatest influence – it is acknowledged that debate has taken place within each framework, on their periphery (usually by those growing dissatisfied with a particular intellectual frame-work), and between them – albeit in the latter case often impeded by the communication barriers that derive from differences in value and belief, from the use of different concepts and from differences of purpose.

THE STRUCTURE OF THIS BOOK

The rest of this book is structured as follows. Chapter 2 deals briefly with the origins of development economics, and then provides a synoptic review of the stock of intellectual capital upon which development economists were able to draw, i.e. those elements of already established economic theory that were likely to be of most relevance to the new discipline. Chapter 3 provides a brief account of the evolution of the discipline, outlining the key paradigms that have emerged at different phases in its development and noting certain important features of the broader context in which they emerged. Subsequent chapters analyse each of these paradigms in more detail, paying particular attention to the publications which set out the core of each paradigm, the more important features of each paradigm's subsequent theoretical development, its main policy recommendations and also the main criticisms levelled against it. Chapter 7 reviews the main contribution to development economics of the dependency school, arguing, however, that from these contributions a distinctive new paradigm has not emerged. Chapter 10 provides an account of the use of the neò-classical paradigm within development economics. Finally, the concluding chapter examines the main areas of compatibility and incompatibility between the different paradigms.

CAVEAT

Before proceeding, however, one word of warning is necessary. It is often convenient to refer to particular individuals as espousing particular intellectual perspectives. Yet individuals may switch perspectives. It is the different items of a person's work that are the candidates for classification, and the author will attempt to adhere to this in what follows.

NOTES

1. Originally Kuhn (1962) argued that mature sciences are dominated by a single school of thought, but he later modified this position; see Kuhn, 1970: 209. (A second edition of Kuhn's *The Structure of Scientific Revolutions* was published in 1970. This edition includes a previously unpublished postscript in which Kuhn replies to some of his critics. All references in what follows are to the 1970 edition.)

2. Various critics claimed that the concept was too complex and/or that Kuhn was himself inconsistent in his interpretation of it (see e.g. Masterman in Lakatos and Musgrave, 1970).
3. Kuhn also generated a certain amount of linguistic confusion, for in the literature of the social sciences we now find the term 'paradigm' used in at least two senses: by many in some approximation of Kuhn's original interpretation, by others (e.g. Preston, 1987) as an alternative to 'exemplar'.
4. These are the categories identified by Kuhn (*op.cit.*: x).
5. See e.g. Preston, 1987: Chapter 2.
6. These factors can also be expected to influence subsequent paradigm espousal where scope for choice exists.
7. Kuhn explicitly refers to the possible occurrence of compatibility between the preliminary perspectives that emerge in a new discipline. Furthermore, the fact that a new paradigm emerging in a mature science must be able to resolve the majority of the problems resolvable by the paradigm now to be abandoned may also be interpreted as implying at least a degree of 'lower-level' compatibility even while the overall perspective from which the problem is approached changes.

REFERENCES

Kuhn, T., *The Structure of Scientific Revolutions*, (University of Chicago Press, 1962; second edition, enlarged, 1970).

Masterman, M., 'The nature of a paradigm' in *Criticism and the Growth of Knowledge*, eds. Lakatos, I. and Musgrave, A., (Cambridge, 1970).

Preston, P., *Rethinking Development*, (Routledge and Kegan Paul, 1987).

2 · THE THEORETICAL HERITAGE

In the 1940s and early 1950s some economists began to focus on a body of data and of associated problems that were sufficiently distinctive, and of sufficient importance, to justify, in the opinion of many who turned to them, the search for a new analytical perspective with which to confront them. The focus of their attention was twofold: firstly the causes of the relative poverty of underdeveloped countries, and secondly the potential way forward for these economies, the specification of the route to economic progress in these largely pre-industrial regions.

However, development economics emerged not as a totally new discipline, but as a sub-division of an existing one. The economists who turned to these issues consequently brought with them a certain stock of intellectual baggage. While the problems that they set out to investigate were distinct from those that constituted the contemporary subject matter of mainstream economics, it was inevitable that they should bring to bear on these problems, wherever it seemed appropriate, elements of the intellectual capital of the existing discipline. Furthermore, in so far as there were conflicting analytical approaches associated with the existing discipline, there was also the possibility that these might be reflected in any debate about fundamentals within the new sub-discipline.

Initially the main preoccupations of this emerging group of economists were largely with a dynamic macro-economics: the specification of those variables and relationships which could provide the key to future economic expansion, and the analysis of possible long-term growth paths and strategies. However, the focus of the bulk of mainstream economic theory for the previous seventy years or so had been on a different set of issues: those associated with the maximisation of short-run efficiency in resource allocation, supplemented, since the 1930s, by a preoccupation with short-run macro-economic management. The analytical method used to confront these issues was in both cases comparative statics. We shall see later that these same issues have also become a growing focus of attention in development economics, but they were certainly not the prime concern at the outset.

Within the corpus of mainstream economic theory there were, however, important exceptions to the general rule: instances in which theoreticians had, in the more or less recent past, turned their attention to dynamic issues. Most notable amongst such contributions in the first half of the twentieth century had been, firstly, Schumpeter's seminal work *The Theory of Economic Development* (first published in German in 1911) and, secondly, the work of Harrod and Domar on the conditions needed to sustain long-run economic growth in the industrially advanced countries, published respectively in the late 1930s and 1940s – work which, to paraphrase Harrod, attempted to give a dynamic perspective to Keynesian theory.

Furthermore, for anyone who chose to go back in time, the corpus of literature produced by the classical economists from the late eighteenth to the mid-nineteenth century was concerned to a notable degree with the analysis of long-run economic growth: with its causes, with its impact on other macro-economic variables, and with the prospects for sustaining growth in the long term. There was also a further reason for returning to this literature. It had been generated in a context in which the economies subject to analysis were in certain respects structurally more similar to the underdeveloped economies of the mid-twentieth century than to the industrialised, technologically advanced economies that they themselves had become.[1]

Then, there was also the body of literature that represented Marxist political economy. This was of relatively little influence in the West in the 1940s. However, within that literature there was a dynamic theory in Marx's own work, a subsequent body of analysis of economic imperialism and its implications for colonial development, and another body of analysis debating the route to growth for an independent but initially largely agricultural socialist economy: the Soviet Union.

The core of this chapter provides a brief overview of the main elements of dynamic theory concerned with the causes of, and constraints to, long-run economic growth that had accumulated in the corpus of economic literature by the mid-twentieth century. The summary will be largely chronological, but will also employ an element of thematic grouping. Finally, at the end of the chapter the neo-classical paradigm is reviewed because, although it is not primarily dynamic in orientation, it is also part of the intellectual heritage that, as already noted, has had a considerable influence on development economics.

The primary purpose of this review is not to identify the dominant paradigms of the past, so there will be no attempt to explore systematically the overall intellectual frameworks of which the theories reviewed formed part. The reader interested in a fuller review of these frameworks may find this elsewhere (see e.g. Barber, 1967; Deane, 1978). Rather, the primary purpose of this review is to identify potentially relevant elements of *theory* – chiefly theoretical relationships that may be used to explain aspects of the processes of economic growth and rising labour productivity. We shall also briefly note the context of the development of these theoretical contributions. However, as will be seen in later chapters, specific theoretical models, concepts and analytical techniques originally developed in one context, and as part of a particular intellectual framework, may sometimes be lifted from one intellectual perspective and adapted to the purposes of another.

THE CLASSICAL LEGACY

Among the classical political economists the three most original contributors to dynamic theory were Smith, Ricardo and Marx. The theoretical contribution of Marx was, however, so distinctive that it is customary to single out Marxian theory from the main body of classical political economy. This section will refer chiefly to the pre-Marxian literature on economic growth, while Marxism will be discussed in the section that follows.

Prior to the founding of the classical school, another group of economists had, earlier in the eighteenth century, also studied the process of economic growth. In France the physiocrats analysed the scope for advances in both total output and output per worker, concluding that these could only be generated by the agricultural sector: only labour employed in exploitation of the land was capable of generating surplus output in excess of the value of material inputs and the labour employed. Expanded agricultural output leads in turn to an increased supply of food and raw materials to other branches of the economy, permitting an expansion of manufacturing output also; but manufacturing itself could never generate economic growth, for artisans add to their raw materials only the value of their own labour.

The physiocrats' ideas represented a reaction to contemporary economic policy in France, which discriminated against agriculture while deliberately promoting, and subsidising, the development of manufacturing. This policy was geared to generating national self-sufficiency in manufacturers. In so doing it reflected the mercantilist philosophy of the times.[2]

From the work of Adam Smith – the founding father of the classical school – onwards, there is a recognition that a growth dynamic can be generated in manufacturing as well as agriculture: this sector too can generate advances not only in total output but in labour productivity. The classicals, indeed, perceived the scope for productivity advances to be greater in manufacturing than in agriculture, and some saw in this fact reason for considerable pessimism concerning the prospects for sustained overall advances in productivity and mass welfare.

These developments in perception were associated with the articulation of a number of propositions concerning the causes of growth, some of which were completely new, and with a new elaboration also of the constraints to growth.

Adam Smith

When Adam Smith published the *Wealth of Nations* in 1776, agricultural and industrial revolutions were both already under way in Britain, and the book is written in a tone of optimism concerning the prospects for long-run growth. At the time Smith was writing he also observed that producers in parts of Europe had been, and were, experiencing an extension of both domestic and foreign markets. Two factors, improvements in law and order along actual and potential trade routes, and the expansion of low-cost water-borne transport, were resulting in greater exchange over longer distances. For Smith, the *primum mobile* of expanding national output and labour productivity is this same extension of the market. It is this which both makes growth possible and simultaneously provides the necessary inducement not only to expand production, but to do so in a manner which increases labour productivity. Extension of the market provides opportunities for an increase in the division of labour, and, observes Smith, the division of labour – or specialisation – raises labour productivity for three reasons:

1. Workers become more efficient in the performance of particular tasks.
2. Job specialisation reduces time spent switching tasks.
3. Job specialisation also increases the scope for designing improved tools and machines to raise labour productivity.

However, while market expansion provides the opportunity and inducement for growth in output and productivity, the latter will only occur if firms respond to new opportunities by committing increased resources to production. It is noteworthy that of Smith's three routes to increased labour productivity only the third is necessarily predicated upon investment in capital equipment. All three, however, require that firms mobilise additional working capital in order to take on extra labour. If this happens on a scale that exceeds the rate of growth of the labour force, it will result, at the national level, in a movement of labour away from what Smith classed as unproductive activities such as services towards greater engagement in productive activities (i.e. those which generate a material output).

However, before an expanded outlay on production can occur there must be a prior increase in savings. Increased savings can only be achieved by those groups in society who have sufficient income. Smith identified three such groups: landlords, merchants and manufacturers. However, Smith, as was typical of the classical economists, did not expect the landlord class to constitute a major source of productive investment. Landlords derive their income from the ownership of property, for the right to exploit which others pay them. Being removed from the sphere of production, and generally perceiving little incentive to enter it, the traditional landlord class spends its income on consumption of commodities and on the hiring of unproductive labour (retainers, entertainers, etc.)

In contrast to the landlords, manufacturers and farmers employ labour for productive purposes, while merchants, through their trading activities, may also come to realise the potential profitability of investment in production. Smith did not, however, identify farmers as an important potential source of increased savings. He took the view that most small tenant farmers were left with insufficient income after paying rent to undertake significant savings. Rather, it is merchants and manufacturers who, out of past profits and in pursuit of their own increased gain, can be expected to generate the bulk of the savings that are needed to exploit new markets.

Not only did Smith see manufacturing (together with trade) as a more important source of increased savings than agriculture, but he also saw it as a more important source of increased output. The scope for increasing labour productivity through specialisation is much greater in manufacturing. In agriculture the seasonal sequence of tasks makes it impossible to develop enterprises in which different workers are simultaneously engaged upon the various stages of the production process. However, there is some scope for productivity increase – both of land and labour – in this sector through technical innovations, such as improved rotations and increased use of manure, and through provision of greater incentives to farmers including the break-up of large tenanted estates into more owner-operated units[3] and a reduction in the tax burden.[4] Smith thought too that the purchase of land by innovatory, profit-conscious merchants would help to raise agricultural efficiency.[5]

However, for Smith, unlike his successors, the more limited scope for technical change in agriculture was not a problem. Since physical subsistence is man's first priority, in principle the expansion of agricultural supplies must precede and underpin the development of urban-based manufacture.[6] However, Smith observes that the town 'may not always derive its whole subsistence from the country in its neighbourhood, or even from the territory to which it belongs, but from very distant countries.'[7] While subsistence is necessary, national self-sufficiency is not.

Indeed, Smith further observed that in all the modern states of Europe the natural precedence of agricultural development over manufacturing had been inverted, 'and manufacturers and foreign commerce together have given birth to the principal improvements of agriculture'[8] (via means that included the promotion of improvements in law and order and transport, the consequent enlargement of markets, the concomitant increase in incentives to invest in farm improvements, and also investment in agriculture by profit-minded merchants). Smith, in contrast to the physiocrats, saw the urban sector, with its merchant and manufacturing classes, as the leading, dynamic sector in economic growth in contemporary Europe.

At some distant point in the future, growing economies might reach the point where all scope for the development of their productive capacity would have been exhausted, when they would have reached their 'full complement of riches', given their natural resources and opportunities for international trade.[9] However, Smith did not see the attainment of a stationary state by the growing economies of Western Europe as imminent, nor did he analyse in any detail the factors likely to bring it about (although he observed that a country with economically repressive laws and institutions, such as China, could induce such a state prematurely).[10]

From his analysis of the causes and sources of economic growth, Smith generated policy recommendations geared to sustaining this process. Firstly, governments should eliminate all obstructions to free trade and competition. Controls on international trade and government creation and protection of monopolies should be abolished. Law and order along trade routes should be enforced, and the laws of primogeniture and entail, which served to prevent the break-up of large landed estates, should be rescinded.

A twentieth century reinterpretation of Smith

At the time Smith wrote the *Wealth of Nations* (between 1766 and 1776) the industrial revolution was in its infancy. It is therefore to his credit that he already recognised that in industrialising nations manufacturing and not agriculture would be the main source of growth.

By the beginning of the twentieth century both the structure of production in Western Europe and North America, and the production technologies used, had changed dramatically. It was from this very different perspective that Young, in 1911, published an article that drew its inspiration directly from Smith, but which reinterpreted Smith's analysis in the light of the accumulated evidence of the subsequent 140 odd years.

In Young's view, Smith was correct to emphasise the importance of the extension of the market for economic growth. However, the market does not just expand through an increase in area or population, but because per capita income grows. This increase in per capita income is in turn due to the increasing division of labour and the associated increase in labour productivity, and this latter comes not so much from increases in dexterity and time-saving – the two factors most emphasised by Smith – but from increasing mechanisation. It is mainly the increasing capitalisation of the production process, together with the associated rise in labour productivity, that leads to growth in per capita incomes. The consequent increase in demand induces another round of the virtuous spiral of expansion, with an increase in demand for capital goods to raise labour productivity still more. (Young was writing some 40 years after the expanding British economy had begun to encounter shortages of labour.)

Young identified three possible impediments to this virtuous spiral, but he did not expect them to be overwhelming. They were as follows:

1. Inelastic demand for certain products.
2. Supply inelasticities due to shortages of raw materials.
3. The high investment costs of exploiting new technologies.

These potential constraints could be overcome in two ways. Firstly, even if for certain branches of production demand is inelastic, it is still possible to raise per capita output and income in these branches through technical innovations that cut costs and raise labour productivity. Likewise Young thought that advances in science and technology would make it possible to break raw material supply inelasticities (through reducing extraction costs or development of substitutes) and that similar advances would help to lower the investment costs of exploiting new technologies.

Classical growth theory continued: the problems imposed by agriculture

Not all the classical economists, however, were as sanguine as Smith or Young concerning the prospects for prolonged economic growth and an associated rise in real wages. In the first half of the nineteenth century first Malthus and then Ricardo – two economists whose economic theory in other respects diverged[11] – gave reasons for supposing that the agricultural sector could impose a break on rising real wages and, in the case of Ricardo, on overall economic expansion as well.

Malthus
In *An Essay on the Principle of Population*, written in 1798, Malthus shows himself to be more concerned with what could be expected to happen over time to mass welfare in an economy than with economic growth *per se*. These concerns were probably prompted by contemporary events, in particular the younger Pitt's proposed revision of the Poor Laws to give larger allowances to families with more children, and the poor harvests and food shortages of preceding years (see Barber, 1967: 52).

Malthus' analysis is based on a mixture of argument and factual assertion, the essence of which may be summarised as follows. Economic growth generates increased demand for labour and hence rising wages. Rising wages lead in turn to an increase in population and hence labour supply: with an increase in living standards parents choose to have more children and, in addition, a higher proportion of children survive infancy. These points were commonly made by the classical economists. The distinctive feature of Malthus' thesis is the next step in his analysis.

Malthus asserted that any rise in mass living standards could only be temporary because the increase in population would rapidly outstrip the capacity of the agricultural sector to meet the growing demand for food, for additional land brought into cultivation is generally less fertile than that already cultivated. It is in this context that Malthus made his famous, but unsubstantiated, assertion that while population grows in a geometric progression (i.e. by a constant proportion each time period), agricultural output can only grow in arithmetic progression (i.e. by a constant absolute amount per given time period).

Malthus took the view that a rise in wages and mass living standards, followed by a period of population expansion, could only be succeeded by one of growing food shortages and mass misery. This would in turn result in a decline both in the birth rate and in infant survival until, as a result of the decline in population growth, labour shortages re-emerge, and the cycle repeats itself. The only acceptable way out of this impasse was for the working classes to exert greater restraint on family size, but Malthus did not anticipate this happening. He concluded that only in a society with an unequal distribution of wealth and income could some people – the wealthy minority – persistently enjoy high living standards. In a society with equal income and wealth distribution all would experience periods of fluctuating well-being and misery.

Malthus does not provide any sound justification for his proposition concerning the respective growth rates of population and agriculture. Indeed in later editions of the *Essay* the progressions were no longer insisted on, although the basic thesis is sustained and buttressed with historical material (see Roll, 1961). Ricardo, in contrast, undertook a more sophisticated analysis both of the constraints to agricultural growth and of the impact of these constraints upon the rest of the economy.

Ricardo

Ricardo, like all the classical economists, observed that economic growth is financed out of the profits accruing from productive activity. If growth is to continue, it follows that the share of profits in national income must remain positive. For Smith this was not a problem, because although he thought that during periods of economic expansion wages would tend to rise and the return on capital to fall, he also thought that with the expansion of production the absolute volume of profits accruing to manufacturers would expand, thereby providing the means to finance further growth. Only at some indefinite point in the future would the net profit rate fall to zero. Ricardo, however, foresaw that during a phase of economic growth profits might quite quickly be eroded to such an extent that growth itself would be brought to a halt. (He too was partly motivated in the development of his ideas by the prevailing conditions of the time, including an early nineteenth century amendment to the Corn Laws which gave increased protection to British agriculture at a time of poor harvests and rising food prices.[12])

Ricardo's argument, which begins on the same lines as Malthus', was as follows. Economic growth leads to an increase in demand for labour which in turn leads to a rise in wages and, consequently, an increase in population. Both the latter generate an increase in demand for food. All this is already familiar. Ricardo, however, then introduces his own analysis of the consequences of rising food demand.

Ricardo's starting point is the fact that in every country land supply is fixed. It is also of variable quality. At any point in time farmers meet agricultural demand by cultivating the better land and avoiding the less good as far as possible. However, as demand increases, it is necessary to increase the total area cultivated by bringing less good land under the plough. This has several consequences:

1. On marginal land the costs per unit of output are higher than on intramarginal land. Thus marginal costs rise as output expands.
2. It is the marginal cost of production that determines the price of food. Consequently, since there is no comparable problem of fixed asset quality in manufacturing, the price of food relative to that of manufactured goods rises as food production rises.
3. As a result, money wages in manufacturing must rise to cover workers' subsistence costs. Manufacturers, in other words, have to pay out a higher proportion of their revenue in wages simply to enable workers to buy their subsistence requirements, and profit rates are therefore lowered.
4. It might be assumed that the higher agricultural prices would raise the profits of those farmers who cultivate the more productive, intramarginal land, but Ricardo shows that this cannot occur.
5. Rather, land rents will be bid up as farmers compete with each other for the better. temporarily more profitable,[13] land.
6. As a result of the increasing scarcity value of good land, and the consequent rise of rents, there is a redistribution of national income towards the landowning class, while the share of profits is reduced.
7. This process can be expected to continue until, as a result of steadily rising marginal food production costs, and, hence, wage costs as a proportion of revenue, profits in both farming and manufacturing are squeezed to zero.
8. At this point all economic growth will come to a halt.

Ricardo did, however, identify two possible ways out of this impasse. These were the introduction of technical innovations in agriculture, and the use of international trade to obtain lower cost food in exchange for manufactures. If one or both of these conditions are fulfilled, then growth may continue while real wages remain buoyant as a result of the rising demand for labour.[14]

For Ricardo the main significance of expanded trade lay not so much in the enlargement of the market *per se* as in the fact that it could lead to a decrease in the price of wage goods and greater efficiency in resource use through specialisation according to comparative advantage.

In *The Principles of Political Economy and Taxation* Ricardo's analysis of the reasons why, and the route by which, growing economies might reach a stationary state is quite dispassionate. Yet the amount of space which he devotes to this issue is sufficient to indicate that he took it seriously.

Mill

Ricardo's *Principles* were published in three editions between 1817 and 1821. The Corn Laws were finally repealed in 1846. Two years later J. S. Mill published his *Principles of Political Economy*, perhaps the last great text of the mainstream classical political economists. After two revisions, the third edition appeared in 1852. Mill's analysis of economic growth was not particularly original. To a large extent he articulated what by then were the generally received theories of the classical school, incorporating the theoretical innovations of Ricardo. However, one of the book's most striking features is Mill's optimism concerning the prospects for sustaining long-run growth compared to Ricardo's pessimism. In this respect the wheel seems to have turned full circle, for Mill's optimism is as great as Smith's. The reasons Mill gives for this optimism are a belief in the boundless prospects for improvements in technology,[15] the opportunities for increasing imports of cheap wage goods (including food) and opportunities for capital export.[16]

This greater optimism was probably also partly a response to the changed economic conditions of the time. Not only had the Corn Laws been abolished; the British economy had recovered from the recession that followed the Napoleonic Wars, various institutional reforms, most notably in money and banking, had been implemented, and the Poor Laws had been modified to promote the free movement of labour (Barber, *op.cit.*: 88).

What still preoccupied Mill, however, was a fear, somewhat in the Malthusian tradition, that among the 'labouring classes' increases in real wages would continue to be quickly eroded by population increase.[17] Among the changes that he wanted to see were increased voluntary restraints on population growth amongst working people, which, unlike Malthus, he was confident could be achieved, combined with a more equitable distribution of the fruits of economic growth.[18]

Comment on classical growth theory

Classical growth theory was not a completely monolithic whole. There were disagreements and contradictions within it. There is no such thing as a single classical growth paradigm. Rather, we have a body of increasingly tightly articulated theory, reflecting a range of different perspectives and preoccupations within which there are, as Deane has observed, a number of recurring key factors and relationships. The former include capital accumulation, institutional factors, trade, technology, population growth and natural resources.

The first four of these factors recur in one or more paradigms of economic development and underdevelopment, although, as we shall see, the interpretation of their significance varies. Thus, for example, expansion of international trade according to existing comparative advantage is sometimes seen as a stimulus, and sometimes as a constraint to economic development,[19] while unquestioning adoption of modern technology has also been shown to be problematic.

The agricultural sector in modern development theory

Meanwhile it is notable that none of the paradigms of economic development that are reviewed in later chapters have given the same emphasis as some of the classicals to a possible brake on growth due to diminishing returns in agriculture. In so far as agriculture has been a focus of attention in development economics, the reasons for this interest have been more diffuse. The rising costs of agricultural production do not receive the same emphasis as in the early nineteenth century, but instead the focus is variously upon the role of agriculture in surplus generation, equity and employment creation, demand creation for the industrial sector, and foreign exchange generation.

There are a number of probable reasons for this modern day relative lack of interest in the Ricardian analysis of diminishing returns. They include the following facts:

1. In the past, and in some cases still today, parts of the Third World, particularly in Latin America and Africa, seemed to have abundant land.
2. Land tenure systems in some parts of the Third World, particularly Africa, have been different from those assumed by the classical economists.
3. In some larger (e.g. Brazil, India), and/or more industrialised Third World countries (including countries such as South Korea and Taiwan) agricultural production and productivity have not imposed a long-term brake on growth.
4. Meanwhile enormous breakthroughs in agricultural research and productivity in the industrially advanced countries, already partly transmitted to some developing countries through the 'green revolution', may be interpreted as an indication of what the Third World has in prospect, while simultaneously increasing the supply of agricultural exports to it.

Only in poor semi-arid countries with low irrigation potential do diminishing returns appear to constitute a serious threat to growth.

THE CLASSICAL MARXIST PERSPECTIVE

Karl Marx was only twelve years younger than Mill, but their interpretation of contemporary economic conditions was very different. Mill saw in the beginnings of working class organisation which he observed signs that the contemporary economic system could be reorganised and modified to give a more equitable distribution of wealth and improvements in mass welfare. However, in the 1840s, such improvements were for the most part still to come. The living and working conditions of the working class were, for the majority, exceedingly harsh: a working day of up to fourteen hours, chronically inadequate public health measures, a bare subsistence wage and insecurity of employment, *inter alia*. Marx, observing these phenomena, and exploring their causes, saw his role as that of exposing to the working class the true nature of the capitalist economic system, within which he regarded a genuine shift in the distribution of economic and political power away from the capitalist class as impossible.

Marx chose to take as one of the central features of his analysis of capitalism the nature of the relationship between capital and labour. No prior classical economist had explored this issue in such depth (nor, indeed, had any earlier observations concerning this relationship pointed to the same conclusions). Neither had any prior classical economist explored the implications of the anarchical nature and the internal contradictions of the capitalist mode of production, with its inherent risks of periodic overproduction and its need for cheap labour to sustain profits alongside its simultaneous need for an expanding demand to absorb rising output.

Marx's political economy

The rest of this section briefly sketches the central elements of Marx's political economic theory.[20] Numbered points are used because the Marxist perspective has, since the early 1970s, experienced a revival in development economics. The summary is therefore structured in such a way as to aid comparison with the summaries of the various paradigms of development economics which are presented in the next chapter.

1. The ideal state for all societies is one of material abundance in a context of communal ownership of the means of production, where all individuals work, each according to their ability, for the good of society and are rewarded according to their need.
2. Marx considered that no society had yet achieved this state. To attain it would require the social, political and economic transformation of society.
3. Furthermore, to achieve such a transformation, a society would already have to have reached a certain level of development of the

forces and relations of production (see 7. below), and of the state apparatus necessary to sustain these.

4. However, the study of history revealed that the directions of economic change observable in Western Europe (and impinging on much of the rest of the world) were tending towards the creation of the conditions necessary for a successful transition first to socialism and then to communism.

5. The key impulses in this tendency can be identified through an examination of the essential nature of different modes of production, and, above all, the factors that distinguish the capitalist mode from pre-capitalist ones.

6. An important feature of Marxism is its emphasis upon the close interconnections between the economic, political and cultural aspects of social organisation and activity. Generally the polity and culture of a society reinforce a particular pattern of class dominance associated with a particular mode of production, where the latter is comprised of two main component parts: the forces and relations of production.

7. The 'forces of production' refer to the mode of combination of labour with the instruments of labour and raw materials. These forms of combination vary with the technology employed. Meanwhile production relations comprise the class distribution of control over the means of production, together with associated forms of organisation of production and different modes of appropriation of the output.

8. Marx identified five modes of production: the Asiatic, ancient (or slave), feudal, modern bourgeois (or capitalist) and communist.

9. The distinctive form of the relations of production that characterises each mode is appropriate to, and conditioned by, a given stage in the development of the forces of production.

> The totality of these relations of production constitutes the economic structure of society, the real foundation, on which arises a legal and political superstructure and to which correspond definite forms of social consciousness.[21]

10. In the first four (i.e. pre-communist) modes of production it is possible to distinguish two components of output: the part that is used to sustain the work force, and the surplus, appropriated from the workers by the dominant class. Appropriation is legitimated through the rights of slave ownership, land ownership, ownership of other means of production by non-workers and through taxation and other forced levies.

11. In the pre-capitalist modes of production the object of production is to produce use values: part of the output is retained for direct use by the producers and the surplus appropriators, and part is exchanged in the market (either by the producers or the surplus appropriators) for other use values. This exchange relationship can be summarised by the

formula $C \rightarrow M \rightarrow C$: commodities ($C$) are produced, some of which are exchanged for money (M), which is then transformed by the seller into other commodities.

12. In the pre-capitalist modes, the dominant class after meeting its subsistence needs uses the surplus for luxury consumption, support of the state apparatus and public works of an unproductive nature (e.g. the monuments of ancient Egypt and ancient Rome, the churches and cathedrals of medieval Europe).[22] Given these forms of use of the surplus, there is no inbuilt tendency to economic growth in these modes and, if technical change occurs, it does so very slowly.

13. Capitalism differs from all three pre-capitalist modes in a number of important respects. These include the objective of production, the use made of the surplus by the capitalist class, capitalism's inherent drive to technological progress, its tendency to increase both the socialisation and the alienation of labour, and its inherent tendency to periodic crises of overproduction and underconsumption.

14. In this mode the means of production are owned by the capitalist class whose dominant objective is not to produce use values but to accumulate wealth in the form of exchange value.[23] This objective determines the use of the surplus, which now becomes transformed into surplus value, and it gives to capitalism an in-built dynamic not possessed by previous modes.

15. The capitalist begins each round of the production process with a stock (M) of financial capital (i.e. exchange value). With this he buys raw materials, maintains his existing equipment and hires labour, all in order to produce commodities (C). These he sells in order to realise an augmented exchange value: M'. Thus this process may be summarised by the formula $M \rightarrow C \rightarrow M'$. The difference between M' and M is the surplus value generated in production and realised through exchange.[24]

16. With the augmented exchange value the capitalist adds to his means of production, buys more raw materials and hires more labour, in order to increase his stock of material and financial capital yet further.

17. Meanwhile, the mass of the population, divorced from ownership of the means of production, sell to the capitalists the only commodity that they possess – labour – in order to be able to buy the means of subsistence.

18. It is through the terms of hire of labour that capitalists are able to generate surplus value ($M' - M$).

19. Surplus extraction occurs as follows. The exchange value of a commodity has three components: $c + v + s$. c represents the value of the material capital that is used up in production: wear and tear on equipment, raw materials and semi-finished goods. Clearly the full

value of c must form part of the value of the finished good if production is to be commercially viable. Meanwhile v represents the cost of labour: for the same reason it too must be reflected in the value of the finished good. The value of v is partly physiologically and partly socially determined. Wages must be at least sufficient to permit the survival and physical reproduction of labour. However, social convention may set wages at a somewhat higher level. Finally, s arises as follows. Each worker has to work a certain number of hours to produce the value of his wage. Through requiring labour to work each day for longer than this the capitalist generates surplus value s. The ratio s/v Marx defines as the rate of exploitation of labour.[25]

20. Under capitalism two classes, with opposing interests, dominate economic activity – capitalists and proletariat. The more powerful of these two classes, the capitalists, also dominates the state, and uses state institutions to promote its own interests.[26]

21. The driving need of the capitalist class constantly to enlarge its wealth gives to economies dominated by this mode a dynamic which is not present in pre-capitalist modes. However, the nature of this dynamic is such that it leads inevitably to the creation of the preconditions for the transition to socialism.[27] This occurs in the following manner:

22. The capitalist objective of surplus accumulation through production and exchange leads capitalists to compete against each other for available markets, striving to increase their market shares by undercutting or buying out weaker competitors. There is, thus, an inbuilt tendency towards increasing centralisation of capital.[28]

23. One instrument of competition is the constant search for technical innovations that will lower production costs. Such technical change tends to be associated with enlargement of plant size, combined with increasing specialisation of labour.[29]

24. Meanwhile, the anarchy of capitalist competition, in which individual firms expand output without any central co-ordination, leads to periodic crises of overproduction and underconsumption.[30] Crises may also be caused by a decline in the rate of profit due to capital intensification and/or to increasing labour scarcity and rising wages.[31] During these periods of crisis weaker firms collapse and/or are bought out by the stronger ones.

25. During each crisis of capitalism, labour is laid off and wages tend to fall. Consequently, in the stronger firms which survive the initial rise in costs and/or drop in demand, the rate of profit tends to rise again. Employers may also try to raise the rate of surplus per worker by forcing labour to work longer hours for the same wage.[32]

26. The processes outlined in 22 and 23 lead jointly to the replacement of competitive capitalism by monopoly capitalism.

27. Meanwhile, the development of the productive forces under capitalism, the enlargement of plant size and increasing specialisation of labour lead in turn to increased awareness on the part of the workers of their mutual interdependence in production. However, these developments also lead to increased monotony of work and to increasing alienation of the work force from the work process and from the capitalist class which imposes this process.[33]

28. Ultimately a fresh and particularly deep crisis, with an associated widespread loss of employment, will move the proletariat to rise up and seize both the means of production and state power from the capitalist class, establishing in their stead a socialist workers' state. In this the groundwork will be laid for the transition to a communist society.

29. Not only does the capitalist mode of production prepare the way for this transition through raising the social awareness, and alienation, of the working class, but it also does so in another very practical sense. The development of technology and the increasing concentration of production which capitalism generates, create a context in which the centralised co-ordination of production in the social interest becomes a more practicable proposition.[34]

30. Marx wrote little on the colonial world, but what he did write suggests that he thought capitalism in the colonies would play the same roles, destructive, creative and exploitative, that were already manifest in more industrially advanced economies. With the penetration of capitalism into Asia and Africa, old, stagnant modes of production would be undercut and destroyed, and in their place would be established a new capitalist mode, generating a steady development of the productive forces, but tending in precisely the same directions that we have just reviewed.[35]

The study of political economy is, in the Marxist perspective, geared to the need to unfold this knowledge to those who may ultimately use it: the working class. Economists studying the Third World who work within this perspective hold, unlike the neo-Marxists, that it applies to underdeveloped economies as well as to industrially advanced ones.

Lenin on imperialism

Several decades after Marx's death in 1883, Lenin published, in 1917, a long pamphlet entitled *Imperialism: the Latest Stage of Capitalism*, the aim of which was to explain the First World War in terms of inter-imperialist rivalries. In it, Lenin sought to take account of certain developments in the capitalist mode of production which had become increasingly apparent after Marx's death.

The essence of Lenin's thesis was that monopoly capitalism had reached a new 'over-ripe' phase. Capital had accumulated faster than the outlets for profitable new investment. Consequently large industrial combines, supported by the financial power of the major banks, were using imperialism as a basis for sustaining the rate of profit; the colonies were being used as outlets for surplus finance capital as well as captive markets for the products of industrial capital and as sources of cheap raw materials.

Lenin's analysis contains a significant modification of Marx's sanguine attitude towards capitalist development prospects in the colonies. On the one hand, imperialism was a spur to the development of capitalism in the periphery: 'capitalism is growing with the greatest rapidity in the colonies and in the overseas countries' (Lenin, *op.cit.*: 91).[36] On the other hand, however, this rapidly developing capitalism was imperialist not indigenous, and its development was actively suppressing any scope for the latter to emerge. The undercutting of local producers by cheap manufactured imports from the more advanced centres of industrial capitalism, and foreign (rather than local) investment of equity and loan capital in mines, plantations and infrastructure, with the associated outflow of profits and interest, were stifling indigenous capitalist development. Rather than accumulating surpluses and expanding production, local producers of manufactures were being forced out of production by more advanced capitalist producers elsewhere in the world. Viewed in this light the prospects for the development of indigenous industrial capitalism in the colonies appear much poorer than Marx himself had thought. A substantial part of the inspiration for the neo-Marxist paradigm of underdevelopment is to be found in Lenin's work.[37]

SCHUMPETER ON GROWTH, DEVELOPMENT AND ENTREPRENEURSHIP

We have seen that for the classical economists the *primum mobile* of economic growth was, variously, the expansion of the market, saving and investment out of profits, and the driving determination of the capitalist to accumulate ever-increasing wealth. In all cases, as Deane emphasises, investment, albeit if only in additional working capital and labour, is recognised as an essential precondition for expanded output.

In 1911 Schumpeter published the first German edition of his analysis of economic development. The first English edition – a translation of the second in German – appeared in 1934. In this study Schumpeter breaks with classical growth theories in several key respects.

Firstly, Schumpeter draws a clear distinction between economic growth and development. The former consists of a gradual process of expansion of production – producing more of the same, and using the same methods in order to do so. Economic development, in contrast, is a more dramatic and disruptive process. It consists, in Schumpeter's terminology, of the carrying out of 'new combinations of productive means', such that either the conditions of production of existing goods are transformed, and/or new goods are introduced, or new sources of supply or new markets are opened up, or an industry is reorganised (e.g. the creation of a monopoly position or the breaking up of a monopoly position).[38] In each case innovation is entailed: in production methods, products, markets or industrial organisation.

Schumpeter characterises these five aspects of economic development as giving rise to 'productive revolutions', a phrase that emphasises both the transforming aspect of development, and the fact that changes of this type tend to cluster together, so that development, rather than being a smooth, continuous process, occurs in fits and starts.

A central aspect of Schumpeter's analysis is his specification of the three common features which, in his view, are inherent in most instances of economic development, and without which that development cannot generally occur. Each of these Schumpeter places in opposition to another element which, in his view, has, in earlier theorisation of economic advance, been assigned a misplaced importance. These three essential features are as follows:

1. The mobilisation of existing factors of production and their combination in new ways.
2. Extension of credit, which is generally essential in order to provide the necessary command over these factors in the market.
3. The presence of an economic entrepreneur, which is a *sine qua non* for the initiation of this process of resource mobilisation and for carrying it through to completion.

For Schumpeter the essential feature of economic development is not the incremental accumulation of new capital, but the mobilisation of existing factors for new uses.

> As a rule the new combinations must draw the necessary means of production from some old combinations. . . Different methods of employment and not saving and increases in the available quantity of labour, have changed the face of the economic world in the last fifty years.
>
> (Schumpeter, 1961: 68.)

If new combinations of factors of production are carried out by existing firms, or by individuals with substantial wealth, then a problem of finance may not arise. The initiators of the new combinations may either already have the necessary factors, or be able to buy them. However, Schumpeter argues, the situation is usually different. Firstly, 'new combinations are, as a rule, embodied, as it were, in new firms . . . in general it is not the owner of stage-coaches who builds railways'.[39] Secondly, even large firms usually need extra finance to implement this type of innovation. Some finance comes from other investors, but most is provided by banks, and most of it is generated by bank credit creation. The onlending of savings deposits is, Schumpeter argues, far less significant in the financing of economic advance than the expansion of the money supply by the banking system.[40] The banker, by creating finance capital for particular purposes, has himself become the capitalist *par excellence*.

The capitalist provides the finance, and carries the risk, of economic development, but he does not bring it about. This is done by the entrepreneur – someone who has the foresight to perceive new opportunities and who takes the initiative to pursue them. He persuades the capitalist(s) to provide the necessary finance and uses this to organise a new combination of productive factors. In the absence of individuals who have these innovatory and organisational talents, and the motivation to use them, economic development cannot occur. In the early stages of the industrial revolution the entrepreneur and capitalist were usually one and the same person: the manufacturer. However, in more industrially advanced societies, the two functions are generally separated, the role of entrepreneur often being fulfilled by company managers, or members of boards of directors. Furthermore, entrepreneurship is not a full-time, permanent occupation. It is a function that certain individuals perform at certain points in time:

> everyone is an entrepreneur only when he actually carries out new combinations, and loses the character as soon as he has built up his business, when he settles down to running it as other people run their businesses.
> (Schumpeter, *op.cit.:* 78.)

Thus, for Schumpeter, the crucial features of economic development are not the mobilisation of savings by capitalists to finance the accumulation of more productive capital, but the actions of entrepreneurs in mobilising credit to finance the procurement of existing factors of production in order to combine them in new ways. Innovation lies at the heart of development, and the innovator is the entrepreneur. In emphasising that by the twentieth century the activities of entrepreneur and capitalist, previously conjoined, had become separated, Schumpeter may be interpreted as simply updating one element in classical theory. However, by distinguishing between growth and development, and emphasising the importance of credit creation, as opposed to savings, in financing development, he distanced himself from the classical economists.

Schumpeter's emphasis on the importance of entrepreneurship has a potential relevance in the Third World which has been noted by a number of development economists from Walt Rostow onwards.[41]

THE 'KEYNESIAN REVOLUTION'

The 1930s international economic recession witnessed what is widely known as the 'Keynesian revolution' in economic theory. During the 1930s, first Kalecki and then Keynes identified the role of effective demand in the determination of aggregate output and employment.[42] The suggestions that attempts to increase savings during a recession may exacerbate the downward spiral of output and employment, and that increased public sector spending during a recession might be a virtue not a vice, were indeed largely innovatory.[43] Kalecki's papers on these issues were not widely read in the West until the 1970s, but Keynesian macro-economic theory quickly achieved a wide influence.

Keynesian theory, incorporating the assumption of downward rigidity in money wages, entailed a clean break with the orthodox view that under competitive conditions each resource will be fully employed, as did his argument that economists need two economic models, one for analysing economies operating at full employment, and one for those operating below full employment. The analytical method of Keynesianism, on the other hand, remained based on the comparative statics employed by the neo-classical school. The focus is still on the determinants of equilibrium (in this case the equilibrium levels of aggregate output and employment), and of the determinants of change therein – but now equilibrium may occur at below full employment.

Keynes' major contribution to economic thought – the so-called 'Keynesian revolution' – was his theorisation of the causes of, and policy solutions to, unemployment (Keynes, 1936). However, a subsequent major contribution came in his proposals for the reform of international economic institutions which were partially implemented in the 1940s (see Singer in Thirlwall (ed.), 1987).

Views on the relevance of Keynesian economics to development economics have varied. In the 1950s and 1960s none of the leading early development economists acknowledged the direct inspiration of Keynes in their theoretical work. Indeed Arthur Lewis (1954) explicitly rejects the relevance of Keynes' work for development economics, emphasising the irrelevance of Keynes' assumption that in economies below full employment not only labour but also land and capital are in unlimited supply, and also of Keynes' view that long-run economic expansion is embarrassed not by a shortage but by a superfluity of saving (Lewis, 1954, reprinted in Agarwala and Singh, 1963: 400, 401). As we shall see, most early development economists also rejected the very notion of tendency towards equilibrium and the analytical method of comparative statics which emphasises this.

On the other hand, some economists today detect the influence of Keynesianism in varying aspects of development economics, although views vary on whether this influence has been positive or negative. Suggested areas of influence include the adaptation to analysis of developing economies of the Harrod–Domar growth model (itself based on the Keynesian perspective – see the next section), the structuralist concern with the role of aggregate demand as the engine of growth[44] (see Chapters 3 and 5), and the propensity of early development economists to think in macro-economic terms (see e.g. Lal, 1983: 8).

The views that have been expressed concerning both the relevance and influence of Keynes' work in development economics may be classified in three groups – those that identify an active but negative influence, those that regard Keynesianism as irrelevant, and those that detect a positive influence. Essentially, those that hold the first and third view argue that although certain economists (e.g. Lewis, Myrdal and the Latin American structuralists) may have insisted upon the irrelevance of Keynesian theory to development economics, in fact Keynesianism influenced, albeit subconsciously, the attitude of mind with which they approached the latter.

The negative influence of Keynesianism has been emphasised most forcibly by neoclassical economists such as Harry Johnson and Deepak Lal. The main features of this influence are, they suggest, as follows:

1. Lack of confidence in the ability of the private sector to achieve full utilisation of productive resources (Johnson, 1971).
2. Hence, emphasis upon state interventionism (Johnson, *op.cit.*; Lal, 1983).
3. Overemphasis on the role of investment in the determination of aggregate output and employment (Johnson and Johnson, 1978).
4. A focus on macro-economic policy to the exclusion of micro-economic efficiency issues (Lal, *op.cit.*).

It is noteworthy, however, that points 3 and 4 are also features of classical economic theory, whose influence some development economists (e.g. Arthur Lewis) explicitly acknowledged.

In contrast, amongst the defenders of the Keynesian influence is Hans Singer. Singer lists a number of instances of such influence, each of which he regards as on balance meritorious. They include the following:

1. An attitude of mind which recognises (a) the need for more than one economic model to analyse different types of economic system; (b) the need for macro-economic policy.
2. The inspiration which Keynes gave to the development of national income accounting and hence also the systematic collection of macro-economic data.
3. His recognition of the potential of economic protectionism as a measure for the maintenance of national output and employment (albeit in the United Kingdom in the 1930s).
4. Keynes' proposals on institutional reforms with respect to international trade and finance.

Clearly there is a lack of consensus on both the extent and merit of the Keynesian influence on development economics which derives from the varying points of view of the evaluators. On two points, however, there does appear to be agreement. First, it is an accepted fact that Keynes himself had no particular interest in less developed economies; any relevance that his work has had has been incidental. Secondly, that influence has been, again in

Singer's words, largely upon the 'attitude of mind' of various development economists rather than in terms of specific elements of theory.

HARROD AND DOMAR ON THE CONDITIONS FOR GROWTH WITH FULL EMPLOYMENT

Harrod (1939) states that his purpose is to give a dynamic dimension to Keynesian economics – a purpose that is also implicit in Domar (1947). However, the growth model that these two economists generated also revives two classical themes: the focus is on growth not development, and it is assumed that growth is financed out of savings.

In 'An Essay in Dynamic Theory' Harrod raised once again a question that Schumpeter had answered negatively: that is, whether an economy can sustain a steady rate of growth for an indefinite period, growing at the same rate each year with no digressions into recession or explosive expansion. However, while Schumpeter's analysis represented an attempt to theorise the actual experience of Western Europe, Harrod's was conducted at a much higher level of abstraction. His article was followed a few years later by the publication of an independent analysis by Evsey Domar which reached the same central conclusion.

In Domar's case, the starting point was a concern to establish under what circumstances a growing economy could sustain full employment. Harrod's article is summarised in what follows, since it is the more widely quoted of the two.

Harrod's model of unstable growth

Harrod begins his analysis by introducing the concept of the *warranted rate of growth* (G_w). This is the rate of growth which is sanctioned by the values of two other crucial variables – the planned national rate of savings, and the average value of the capital:output ratio as planned by producers. Planned savings represents the sum of the spending power which individuals and firms plan to withhold from consumption in a given period, and which, if the plans are fulfilled, can be made available to finance new capital formation. The capital:output ratio represents the value of the capital needed to produce a given output divided by the value of that output. It is a stock:flow ratio, whose value depends partly on the time period over which the output flow is measured. (The period conventionally chosen is a year.) If planned savings are represented as a proportion of national income, then this proportion divided by the planned capital:output ratio (c_p) gives the warranted rate of growth of output.

$$G_w = \frac{S}{c_p}$$

For most of his analysis Harrod assumes that savings plans as a proportion of national income are fulfilled. He then focuses his attention on c – its determinants and the consequences of failure by producers to achieve planned c. Harrod observes that c_p is essentially technically determined. It represents the value of all capital (fixed and revolving) required to produce one unit of output in a given time period, when machines are working the optimum time (allowing for maintenance and repair), and when there are no additions to, or reductions from, the stock of working capital; c_p is a weighted average of the individual $c_p s$ for all the different sectors of the economy. This average is assumed to be constant: the marginal capital:output ratio equals the average. The amount of investment that producers plan to undertake in any given period is given by the value of the extra output that they wish to produce, multiplied by the relevant capital:output ratio.

Harrod next makes an arbitrary, and much criticised, assumption as to the basis on which producers plan to expand production: if the rate of growth of output that occurred in the previous period was that which producers had planned that it should be, then they will plan to repeat this growth rate in the next period. Critics have asked why producers should plan to implement the same growth rate of output rather than to achieve the same absolute increase in output, and, equally important, whether they would really adopt such a short time perspective, basing their plans only on the outcome of the previous period. Harrod indicates that he is aware of these difficulties, but assumes them away for the purposes of his analysis.

In Harrod's model output plans may not be fulfilled because aggregate demand may not behave as expected. By the assumption noted above, this is not because savings plans, expressed as a proportion of national income, are either changed or unfulfilled. Presumably therefore, although he is not explicit about this, Harrod is assuming either that foreign demand changes, or that there is a change in the money supply, either of which would permit aggregate demand to rise or fall, without necessarily violating the savings assumption.

Producers adjust immediately to unanticipated changes in demand. At first they do so by working their plant overtime (i.e. at above planned capacity) in the case of an output increase, or by accumulating unsold stocks in the case of a demand decrease. In either event the *actual* capital:output ratio diverges from that which had been planned, and the actual rate of growth of output therefore diverges from the warranted rate. The actual growth rate, G_a, is given by the actual savings rate (which is assumed unaltered) divided by the actual capital:output ratio. Where output growth is above the planned rate, c will be forced below its desired level, and vice versa.

Important consequences flow from this divergence. If producers find that demand in a given period has been higher than anticipated, so that to meet it machines have been worked longer than planned and stocks run down, then in the next period they will increase their investment. However, the rise in investment will, through the multiplier, generate a further increase in demand. Once again capacity will prove inadequate and c_a will again be forced below c_p. The economy, in other words, having once diverged from the state of steady growth, now moves further and further away from that state, along an explosive growth path. In circumstances in which the initial divergence is due to a decline in the rate of growth of demand, exactly the opposite will occur, with net investment falling and eventually becoming negative (as worn-out capital is not replaced).

We are not required to conceive what would happen if these centrifugal forces were to operate indefinitely, because Harrod identifies certain buffers that not only bring both spiralling growth and decline to a halt, but, indeed, reverse each process. In the former case this occurs when the economy reaches full employment. Harrod assumes not only a constant c_p, but also a constant capital:labour ratio, and, given this assumption, the economy cannot, at full employment, grow faster than the rate of growth of the labour force G_n. G_n, which Harrod terms the 'natural rate of growth', is the maximum rate of growth allowed by population growth and labour-saving technical innovation combined. If either current G_a and/or G_w exceed G_n, then at full employment either or both will no longer be realised. If G_a is lowered, then in the next period investment plans will be revised downwards. Through the multiplier the slowing down in investment will lead to a decline in the rate of growth of demand. Investment plans in the next round will be further contracted, and the economy will move into recession. Recession in turn is brought to a halt because, at a certain point, dissaving will slow down the decline in consumption as households try to maintain certain mimimum standards of living. In economies with a welfare state the floor is raised by state welfare payments. With a slowing down, or halt, to the decline in consumption, producers who have been disinvesting once again begin to replace worn-out equipment. With increased employment in the capital goods sector, demand rises still further and once more the process is reversed.

We are now reaching the conclusion of Harrod's analysis. In his view the likelihood that an economy will grow steadily at full employment is extremely low. This would require that, with the economy already at full employment, $G_w = G_a = G_n$. If the economy is below full employment it is not enough for these equalities to hold, unlikely as this is, for if they do full employment will never be reached. For that to occur G_a, which may or may not equal G_w, *must* exceed G_n until the unemployed labour force is absorbed. But if G_a initially exceeds G_n, then when full employment is reached it is extremely unlikely that the triple equality will suddenly hold. It is far more likely that the slowing down in investment will lead the economy into recession. Leaving aside the full employment question, if $G_w = G_a$ below full employment, then steady growth may occur, but it is still a knife-edged process. Any divergence of G_a from G_w will lead the economy away from the steady state growth path.

Harrod observes that the empirical evidence for the United Kingdom suggests that the warranted rate of growth *exceeds* the natural rate. Thus even if G_w equals G_a below full employment, cyclical swings in economic activity are inevitable unless government policy can bring the rates into line at full employment. Harrod therefore advocates lowering the warranted rate. For this he recommends use of a low interest rate policy which should tend both to lower the inducement to save and to raise c_p (by cheapening the price of capital relative to labour). He advocates too an anti-cyclical programme of public works in order to raise the floor of economic recessions. These are not sufficient conditions to achieve steady growth at full employment. They are designed, however, both to raise the possibility of achieving this and to reduce the degree of fluctuation in activity should this not be successful.[45]

In a separate article published in 1947 Evsey Domar reached similar conclusions to Harrod's.[46] Hence the growth rate equation $g = s/v$ is generally referred to as the Harrod–Domar model. In this model the savings rate, together with the capital-output ratio, is reinstated as one of the key determinants of economic growth. Now, however, it is acknowledged that the rate may prove to be too high as well as too low. Subsequently, as we shall see, the Harrod–Domar growth formula was adopted by some development economists in order to estimate the target savings rate needed to achieve a target growth rate, the capital-output ratio now being taken as given.

THE NEO-CLASSICAL PARADIGM

The various theories that have been reviewed so far in this chapter constitute the main attempts to theorise the dynamics of long-run economic change that had accumulated in the corpus of economic literature by the 1940s. This chapter has concentrated upon this stock of theory for the reason given at the outset. That is to say, the first concern, and a continuing one, of development economics has been to identify the route (i.e. the means) to long-run economic progress in less developed countries.

There is, however, one other body of theory to consider. Some development economists have preferred to adhere to the predominantly short-run, efficiency-oriented perspective of the neo-classical paradigm, applying to developing countries both the efficiency-maximising tenets of partial and general equilibrium theory and the linked precepts of the law of comparative advantage. Since the neo-classical paradigm constitutes part of the analytical heritage which was available to development economists in the 1940s, it is appropriate to summarise its core here. A later chapter will examine its actual use by development economists. Once again, since the paradigm is actively applied in development economics, a numbered point-by-point summary is used for purposes of easier comparison with the paradigm summaries in Chapter 3. Following that summary, a brief indication is given of the direction taken by later attempts to use neo-classical theory to analyse economic growth.

By the end of the nineteenth century most economists in Western Europe had ceased to focus their attention upon the analysis of long-run growth. This was now widely taken for granted, and from the last decades of the century attention was increasingly focused instead upon issues of allocative efficiency – how resources come to be allocated to different uses, and the criteria which need to be fulfilled if the value of the output generated from a given stock of resources is to be maximised. Economic analysis focused, in other words, largely upon decision-taking by firms and consumers and upon the role of market forces in resource allocation. Early preoccupation with the issues that are the main focus of the neo-classical perspective may be traced back to the work of Mill and Jevons. However, the core of the neo-classical paradigm was first clearly articulated in Marshall's *Principles of Economics*, which was published in 1890, and soon began to replace Mill's *Principles* as the standard text of mainstream economics. The paradigm, which is today spelled out in all mainstream texts on micro-economic theory, may be summarised as follows:

1. It is desirable to maximise aggregate economic welfare.
2. Welfare maximisation can only be achieved when the market value of goods and services produced at any given point in time is maximised.
3. Neo-classical theory is designed to show how these ends can be achieved through the operation of the free market.
4. In order to demonstrate this, it is necessary to make a number of explicit assumptions about the nature of the economic system. These assumptions include:
    (a) profit maximisation by firms, which face cost structures character-ised by the U-shaped cost curve;
    (b) utility maximisation by consumers, who experience diminishing marginal utility in the consumption of different items;
    (c) an infinite range of production technologies (all of which experi-ence diminishing returns to scale at some point);
    (d) perfectly competitive markets.
    Given these assumptions, neo-classical theorists have generated the following propositions:
5. The prices for goods and services which are generated by the un-impeded operation of the market (i.e. by the forces of supply and demand) are normally the correct prices for the purposes of guiding resource allocation by producers and consumers. This is because free market equilibrium prices will simultaneously reflect marginal con-

sumer preferences and marginal supply costs. However, where a particular form of resource use generates external costs or benefits, prices should be adjusted accordingly. Generators of external benefits should be rewarded and vice versa.

6. Factor prices should also be determined through the operation of the free market. In this way producers will be faced with correct information concerning the relative opportunity costs of different factors of production.

7. Given consumer preferences, firms' production costs, the total value of monetary demand and free markets, there will be one set of equilibrium prices for all factors of production, intermediate products and final goods and services, at which all markets are cleared and the value of output maximised.

8. Given infinite technical choice and factor price flexibility, the maximum value of output and, hence, maximum social welfare, will always be achieved by the full employment of all factors of production. There will be no involuntary unemployment.

9. Relative factor prices determine factor income shares.

10. In the absence of government intervention, factor prices combined with the distribution of asset ownership determine interpersonal income distribution. This in turn determines, together with consumer tastes, the pattern of demand for final goods and services and hence, indirectly, the pattern of demand for factors of production.

11. The following propositions concerning growth can also be derived from the paradigm:
    (a) sustained growth of output with full employment is possible provided there is a positive propensity to save and to invest in excess of the amounts needed for capital maintenance;
    (b) output per worker will grow if the rate of savings and investment exceeds that which is required both for capital replacement and to equip any increase in the work-force;
    (c) investment will occur at a rate determined by the interaction of the social rate of time preference, which will determine the supply of savings for any given rate of interest, and the marginal productivity of capital, which will determine the amount of investment that producers are prepared to undertake at that rate of interest.

12. The main corollary of neo-classical theory is that, in any market, price distortion will lead to a distorted pattern of resource allocation with a consequent reduction in efficiency and welfare.

13. Hence the key policy recommendation of the neo-classical paradigm is to remove all market distortions.

In the 1950s and 1960s the neo-classical perspective generated a distinctive body of highly abstract growth theory. Using the standard neo-classical assumptions, and assuming also no distinction between savers and investors (and hence no need for an investment function) it was shown that an increase in savings can be expected to have a positive, but only temporary, effect on the growth rate (it will be associated with a relative lowering of the price of capital, and consequent increase in capital intensity per worker). The main source of long-run per capita income growth in these models is technical progress.

Neo-classical growth theory is not reviewed here, partly because it did not form part of the intellectual heritage of development economists in the 1940s and early 1950s, since it was developed later, but also because it has had no appreciable influence on development economics. The interested reader is referred to the excellent summary and the bibliography in Hywel G. Jones (1974).

SUMMARY AND CONCLUSION

The purpose of these concluding remarks is firstly to recapitulate the main points to emerge from those dynamic theories that were available to development economists in the 1940s and early 1950s, and secondly to indicate some of the main factors that could be expected to preoccupy development economists looking to these theories as a potential source of insights into economic change in less developed countries. (Later, the whole of Chapter 10 is devoted to the neo-classical paradigm and its use in development economics.)

Amongst the most notable features of classical growth theories – i.e. those given greatest emphasis by the classical theorists themselves – are the following:

1. The importance of market expansion as a stimulus both to expansion of total output and to raising labour productivity.
2. The importance of profits as the source of finance for new investment, in contrast to the unproductive use of land rents and the zero or minimal savings capability of wage-earners.
3. The potential of an agricultural sector dominated by rentier land owners to impose a brake on overall economic growth (Ricardo).
4. The need to liberalise trade as a means of enlarging the market (Smith) and of permitting the exploitation of comparative advantage (Ricardo).
5. The importance of technological change in raising labour productivity and in helping to meet the food and raw material demands of a rising population.

In the early twentieth century Arthur Young took Adam Smith's emphasis on the extension of the market a step further, arguing that technical innovation can itself generate an extension of the market through raising labour productivity and, hence, incomes and demand.

Turning to Marxian dynamic theory, among the basic points that Marx emphasises are the following:

1. The motive force of the capitalist system, and one of the factors that differentiates it from earlier modes of production, is the capitalist's drive to accumulate wealth through productive investment.
2. Capitalism is based on the antagonistic relationship of two classes, capitalist and proletarian. The former own the means of production and use the power derived from this ownership to extract and appropriate surplus value from the workers, the surplus value being used to finance further accumulation.
3. The drive to accumulate leads the capitalist to search constantly for means, including technical innovation, that will enable him to raise his rate of profit and/or undercut his competitors. The consequent development of the productive forces is the positive aspect of capitalism.
4. Meanwhile, capitalist competition also undercuts and destroys all backward pre-capitalist producers (artisans, peasants) as well as the less efficient capitalists.
5. As individual capitals expand, in association with technological advance, plant size rises, and labour becomes more specialised and routinised and also increasingly interdependent. Simultaneously workers become increasingly alienated from the labour process and the capitalist class.
6. The anarchic nature of capitalist competition leads to periodic crises caused by an underlying tendency to a decline in the rate of profit and by recurrent phases of overproduction and underconsumption. In these periods labour is laid off and wages fall.
7. As the scope for further unco-ordinated development of the productive forces approaches exhaustion, a final crisis will lead the working class to appropriate the means of production and instigate the transition to a new, egalitarian mode of production. Lenin, however, provided grounds for doubting whether the colonies would experience the same pattern of capitalist development as the imperial powers.

Also in the early twentieth century, Schumpeter sought to make an analytical break with the classical growth theorists. A clear distinction is drawn between growth and development: for Schumpeter growth is a slow and rather insignificant process, resulting from investment in additional capital financed largely by reinvestment of profits. Development is an innovatory process. It is this that provides advancing economies with their real dynamic. The key actors in development are not producer capitalists reinvesting profits, but the entrepreneurs who perceive opportunities for using existing resources in new ways and who organise and implement the exploitation of these opportunities, and the banks who create the credit that enables the entrepreneurs to finance new enterprises. In the early stages of the industrial revolution capitalist and entrepreneur were usually one and the same, but with time their functions have become separated.

Finally, Harrod and Domar have provided a model of growth in which the rate of growth of output which is warranted is given by the planned savings rate divided by the planned capital:output ratio. Since current investment plans are largely independent of current savings and consumption plans, there can be no certainty that output will actually grow at the warranted rate, for investors may be forced to adjust to unanticipated changes in demand. Such adjustments entail short-run variations in the capital:output ratio followed by adjustment of investment plans. Both Harrod and Domar were concerned that the planned savings rate 's' in Western Europe and North America was too high for the maintenance of stable growth, for actual 's' warranted a long-run growth rate in excess of that permitted by the rate of growth of the labour force. The physical impossibility of carrying out a rate of investment at full employment sufficient to match 's' would generate periodic deflationary pressures.

These were the main elements of dynamic theory that were available in the 1940s and 1950s for the early development economists to draw upon. In deciding whether, and to what extent, to draw their inspiration from them it was necessary to confront a number of controversial issues, including the following:

1. In conditions in which the industrially advanced coutries are consistently pioneering technological advance in manufacturing and agriculture, is free trade necessarily in the best interests of underdeveloped countries?
2. Is an increase in savings a necessary precondition for economic advance, or may other resource constraints (such as scarcity of entrepreneurial talent or organisational and administrative capability or foreign exchange) or market imperfections be more important?
3. If an increase in savings is needed, can this only be achieved by raising the share of capitalist profits in national income?
4. In underdeveloped countries, does an increase in savings by capitalists lead automatically to an increase in productive investment?
5. Can it be assumed that underdeveloped countries will pursue a similar path of capitalist development to the now industrially advanced ones?

How development theorists have answered these and related questions, and the extent to which they have felt able to apply pre-existing theories to the analysis of development and underdevelopment in contemporary underdeveloped countries, are issues that will be explored in the following chapters.

NOTES

1. See Hobsbawm, 1962: Chapter 1 for a description of this context.
2. Mercantilism emphasised the national advantages of a positive balance in international trade; see Barber, 1967: 16, 17, for a fuller account.
3. Smith, 1976: 486.
4. *Ibid.*: 491.
5. *Ibid.*: 507.
6. *Ibid.*: 480.
7. *Ibid.*: 480.
8. *Ibid.*: 483.
9. *Ibid.*: 194 and 473.
10. *Ibid.*: 197, 8. In Western Europe Smith observes that only in Holland has the return on capital reached so low a point that there seemed to be limited opportunities for further internal expansion. Even here, however, Holland's men of business can find ample profitable outlets in international trade and foreign loans.
11. For example, with respect to acceptance of Say's Law (see Barber, *op.cit.*: 66).
12. Barber, *op.cit.*: 70.
13. Temporarily because the rise in rents eliminates the profit advantage on intramarginal land.
14. See Ricardo, 1911: 53.
15. 'Of the features which characterise this progressive economical movement of civilised nations, that which first excites attention, through its intimate connexion with the phenomena of Production, is the perpetual, and so far as human foresight can extend, the unlimited, growth of man's power over nature' (Mill, 1852: 254, 5).
16. *Ibid.*: Book IV, Chapter IV.
17. *Ibid.*: 34, 5. Smith had not anticipated this, arguing that while growth continued real wages would remain buoyant due to the expanding demand for labour, even though following the wage increase population would also tend to expand 'as nearly as possible in the proportion which the demand for labour requires' (Smith, *op.cit.*: 183).
18. Mill, *op.cit.*: 320. Mill also observed that given these conditions a stationary state could be preferable to continuing growth.
19. As Johnson has observed, during the classical era, 'two exceptions to the case for free trade were early recognised – the terms of trade argument and the infant industry argument – (but) these were not regarded as of great practical importance. Nor did the heretics who advocated protection as a means of promoting the economic development of the relatively backward regions – notably Hamilton in the United States and List in Germany – have any significant influence on the central corpus of economic theory' (Johnson, 1964: 3).
20. Some Marxists today emphasise that fundamentally Marxism is a method of analysis and not a dogmatic set of theories: a method which seeks to uncover the essential features of social processes and which emphasises that appearance and essence may radically differ (Ken Cole, University of East Anglia: personal communication, March 1988). However, many have found in Marx's *Capital* and in his other writings what is widely accepted as a specific body of economic theory, and it is with this that what follows is concerned.

21. Marx, 1970a: 20.
22. Marx, 1970b: 333.
23. *Ibid.*: 714.
24. See Marx, 1970c: Chapter 1.
25. See Marx, 1970b: Chapter 11, pp. 212–218.
26. See Engels, reprinted in Feuer (ed.), 1959: 275.
27. See Marx, 1972: 437 and Marx, 1970a: 21.
28. See Marx, 1970b: 624–628 and Marx, 1972: 249–251.
29. Marx, 1972: 104.
30. See Marx, 1970c: Chapter XXI, esp. 493–499.
31. The rate of profit is approximately given by the formula $s/c + v$. If c rises relative to v, then s as a proportion of $c + v$ will fall unless the rate of exploitation (s/v) rises sufficiently to compensate. (See paragraph 18 above for an explanation of these symbols.) See Marx, 1972: Part III, Chapter XIII and Chapter XIV pp. 250–259.
32. See Marx, 1972: 232.
33. See e.g. Marx and Engels, 1846, reprinted in Feuer (ed.), 1959: 295–7; and Marx, 1970b: 331.
34. See e.g. Marx and Engels, 1846, reprinted in Feuer (ed.), 1959, Marx, 1970c: 20–22, and, especially, Marx, 1972: 436, 7. However, see also Feuer, *op.cit.*: 29,30.
35. 'The country that is more developed industrially only shows, to the less developed, the image of its own future', Marx, Preface to first German edition of *Das Kapital.* See also Marx, 'British Rule in India', in Marx and Engels, Selected Works Vol. I, reprinted in Feuer (ed.) 1959: 511–518.
36. See also Lenin, 1962, quoted in Warren, 1980: 5, footnote 7.
37. See, for example, the citations in Baran, 1957.
38. See Schumpeter, 1967: 65–67.
39. Schumpeter, *op.cit.*: 66.
40. *Ibid.*: 73.
41. For more recent emphasis on this factor see Rimmer, 1984.
42. See Kalecki, 1971, Keynes, 1936, and the introduction by Robinson in Kalecki, 1976.
43. Though the latter was anticipated by Schumpeter.
44. See Palma in Seers, 1981: 51 and 68, note 41. In the latter reference Palma observes that Prebisch published a study of Keynes before he made his first analytical contributions to the Economic Commission for Latin America (ECLA). On the other hand, Singer suggests that the structuralist school rejected Keynesianism due to its overemphasis on demand-side issues (see Singer in Thirlwall (ed.) 1987: 78).
45. Kaldor's solution to Harrodian instability – in 1957 Kaldor published a model of economic growth which offers an explanation of why, contrary to the predictions of the Harrod model, the growth experience of the western economies was relatively stable at close to full employment during the first post-war decade. Kaldor suggests that, contrary to Harrod's assumption, savings are not independently determined. Rather, they adjust to economic conditions through changes in the rate of profit. This flexibility, he claims, may well be sufficient to ensure sustained growth at full employment.
46. Domar's starting proposition is that net investment fulfils a twofold function. It expands employment and incomes in the short run, during the phase of physical capital creation, but it creates a potential flow of additional output for an indefinite future period (depending on the life of the capital created). If investors do not face the necessary expansion of demand to absorb new capacity, either

new equipment will lie idle, or old equipment will be scrapped early, or, if it is economic, equipment will be used to replace labour. Starting from full employment, for there to be continuing additions to productive capital while full employment of capital and labour is sustained, then $I\sigma$ (aggregate net investment multiplied by the output:capital ratio (σ) must equal $\Delta I . 1/\alpha$ (the increase in demand which is given by the increase in net investment times the multiplier, where the latter is equal to $1/\alpha$, α being the marginal propensity to save). By a simple shifting of terms the equation $I\sigma = \Delta I . 1/\alpha$ can be rewritten in the form $\Delta I/I = \alpha\sigma$. With a constant value of σ national income will grow at the same rate as investment. Thus since σ is simply the inverse of the capital:output ratio, Domar's fundamental equation is the same as Harrod's.

REFERENCES

Baran, P., *The Political Economy of Growth*, (Monthly Review Press, 1957)

Barber, W., *History of Economic Thought*, (Penguin, 1967; second Italian edition Feltrinelli, 1975).

Deane, P., *The Evolution of Economic Ideas*, (Cambridge, 1978).

Domar, E., 'Expansion and employment', *American Economic Review*, Vol. 37, March 1947

Engels, F. (1888), 'Ludwig Feuerbach and the end of classical German philosophy', reprinted in *Marx and Engels: Basic Writings on Politics and Philosophy*, ed. Feuer, L., (Fontana, 1969).

Feuer, L. (ed.), *Marx and Engels: Basic Writings on Politics and Philosophy*, (Fontana, 1969).

Harrod, R., 'An essay in dynamic theory', *Economic Journal*, (March 1939).

Hobsbawm, E., *The Age of Revolution: 1789–1848*, (Weidenfeld and Nicolson, 1962).

Johnson, E. and Johnson, H., *The Shadow of Keynes: Understanding Keynes, Cambridge and Keynesian Economics*, (Blackwell, 1978).

Johnson, H., 'Tariffs and economic development: some theoretical issues', *Journal of Development Studies*, (Vol. 1, No. 1, October 1964, pp. 3–30); reprinted in Johnson, H., *Aspects of the Theory of Tariffs*, (Allen and Unwin, 1971).

Johnson, H. G., 'The Keynesian revolution and the Monetarist counter-revolution', *American Economic Review*, (Vol. 61, Papers and Proceedings, May 1971).

Jones, H. G., *An Introduction to Modern Theories of Economic Growth*, (Nelson, 1974).

Kalecki, M., *Selected Essays on the Dynamics of the Capitalist Economy*, (Cambridge, 1971).

Kalecki, M., *Essays on Developing Economies*, (Harvester, England and Humanities Press, USA, 1976).

Keynes, J. M. (1936), *The General Theory of Employment, Interest and Money*, (Macmillan, 1973).

Lal, D., *The Poverty of Development Economics*, (Institute of Economic Affairs, London, 1983).

Lenin, V. (1917), *Imperialism, the Highest Stage of Capitalism*, (Progress Publishers, Moscow, 1975).

Lewis, W. A., 'Economic development with unlimited supplies of labour', *Manchester School*, (May 1954); reprinted in *The Economics of Underdevelopment*, ed. Agarwala, A. and Singh, S. (Oxford, 1958).

Malthus, T. (1798), *An Essay on the Principle of Population*, (Ward Lock, 1890).

Marshall, A. (1890), *Principles of Economics*, (Macmillan, eighth edition, 1920).

Marx, K. (1859), *A Contribution to the Critique of Political Economy*, (Lawrence and Wishart,1970a).

Marx, K. (1887), *Capital*, Vol I, (Lawrence and Wishart, 1970b).

Marx, K. (1893), *Capital*, Vol II, (Lawrence and Wishart, 1970c).

Marx, K. (1894), *Capital*, Vol III, (Lawrence and Wishart, 1972).

Marx, K. and Engels, F. (1846), 'The German ideology', excerpts reprinted in *Marx and Engels: Basic Writings on Politics and Philosophy*, ed. Feuer, L., (Fontana, 1969).

Mill, J. S. (1848), *Principles of Political Economy*, (third edition, Parker, 1852).

Palma, G., 'Dependency and development: a critical overview' in *Dependency Theory: A Critical Reassessment*, ed. D Seers, (Frances Pinter, 1981).

Ricardo, D. (1817), *The Principles of Political Economy and Taxation*, (Dent, 1911).

Rimmer, D., *The Economies of West Africa*, (Weidenfeld and Nicolson, 1984).

Roll, E., *A History of Economic Thought*, (Faber, third edition, 1961).

Schumpeter, J. (1911), *The Theory of Economic Development*, (Oxford, 1961).

Singer, H., 'What Keynes and Keynesianism can teach us about underdeveloped countries' in *Keynes and Economic Development*, ed. Thirlwall, A. (Macmillan, 1987).

Smith, A. (1776), *Wealth of Nations*, (Pelican Books, 1974).

Warren, B., *Imperialism: Pioneer of Capitalism* , (Verso, 1980).

Young, A., 'Increasing returns to scale and economic progress', *Economic Journal*, (Vol. XXXVIII, No. 152, December 1928).

3 · THE THEORETICAL DEBATE IN DEVELOPMENT ECONOMICS FROM THE 1940s: AN OVERVIEW

Since the mid-1970s various social scientists have reviewed the evolution of theorising about economic and social change in the Third World.[1] The approaches taken have varied in terms of purpose, coverage, the numbers of schools of thought identified, the categories used and the classification of individual theoretical contributions. It is impossible to review all these approaches here; all one can hope to do is to give some flavour of their variety.

Some analysts have adopted a partial approach, concentrating their review upon one or more analytical perspectives without attempting a general overview. These include Chenery (1975), Killick (1978), Seers (1979), Love (1980), Kitching (1982) and Chilcote and Johnson (1983). Chenery and Love both focus on the evolution of structuralism, although they each focus on different contributors to this school of thought. Killick reviews the dominant tendencies in economic thought on development in the 1950s, including some of the contributions that Chenery classifies as structuralist (but without himself using this classification), in order to demonstrate their influence on Nkrumah's policies. Seers focuses on the evolution of development economics in Western Europe and North America in the 1950s and 1960s (ignoring, for example, the development of structuralist thought in Latin America), in order to demonstrate its limited usefulness. Kitching selectively reviews the evolution of the populist content of development theory, while Chilcote and Johnson review the evolution of dependency theory (according to their categorisation of the latter).

Among reviews of the evolution of theorising on economic development by economists may be noted in particular those of Chenery, Killick and Seers (already mentioned), as well as Streeten (1981), Little (1982), Hirschman (1982) and Leeson (1983 and 1988). Meier (1984) also provides a useful (non-classificatory) review of the evolution of development economics in the early years (the 1940s and 1950s). The primary purpose of most of these surveys (though not that of Killick) is to review the current state of development theory. This has been a recurring preoccupation of development economists since the 1960s, as Seers (*op.cit.*) and Leeson (1988) both show.[2] One consequence of this is that the categorisation of theoretical contributions tends to be a subsidiary issue, and, indeed, is not always undertaken.

Of the social scientists who have undertaken more comprehensive reviews-cum-classifications of development theory, Foster-Carter (1976) categorises all social scientific development theory into two diametrically opposed paradigms – a mainstream western development paradigm and a neo-Marxist paradigm. A more common approach, however, is a three-way classification which specifies also the contribution of neo-classical theory (see e.g. Chenery, 1975; Little, 1982). Both these studies, however, substitute the category 'structuralism' for Foster-Carter's 'mainstream Western development theory'.[3]

Hirschman (1982) identifies four main schools of thought that have been applied to the study of economic development and underdevelopment – neo-Marxist, neo-classical, classical Marxist and his counterpart to Foster-Carter's western development paradigm, which he labels simply as 'development economics', noting, however, the 'far from unified' nature of this body of doctrine and policy (see Hirschman in Gersovitz *et al.*, 1982: 379).[4] Hirschman's classificatory review also takes note of a fifth category of analyses which emphasise distributional issues. (Little also discusses the emergence of these.)

Other social scientists reviewing the evolution of development studies have introduced different classifications into the discussion. Modernisation theory (which emphasises the political, sociological, and administration theory counterparts to Foster-Carter's 'mainstream western economic development theory', as well as the latter itself) is the best known and most widely used. Other classifications that have been introduced into the literature have achieved less widespread currency (see Preston, 1982, for the example of 'neo-institutionalism', a classification which he applies to the analytical work of Myrdal, *inter alia*).

These and other surveys use diverse standards of characterisation and classification. One indication of this is the variety of ways in which leading contributions to early theorising on economic development are characterised and classified. For example, Foster-Carter focuses on four propositions concerning the fact that development is a non-contentious process which involves becoming more like the West as the defining characteristics of a school of thought (Foster-Carter, 1976: 1972). Chenery, on the other hand, uses the significance assigned to distinctive features of economic structure in the theorisation of underdevelopment and development as a basis for categorisation.

In the present study, the basis upon which a range of contributions to the literature on economic development and underdevelopment have been classified is as follows. Contributions have been grouped together when they can be shown to have in common:

1. A distinctive interpretation of the essential nature of development and/or underdevelopment.
2. Important common elements in their specification of the key causal factors generating development and/or underdevelopment.

Such contributions have been further characterised as one of the dominant perspectives or paradigms in development economics when, in addition, it can be shown (as indicated in Chapter 1) that the following are true:

3. The features specified under 1 and 2 above have commanded the support of a significant group of scholars.
4. The initial articulation of these ideas can in turn be seen
   (a) to have given rise to further theoretical development;
   (b) to have guided more practical action (for example, in policy formation).

In applying this approach the author will reject the notion that all early development theory is sufficiently homogeneous to justify uniform characterisation. Rather, it will be argued that from among the early theoretical work of development economists in the 1940s and 1950s two dominant perspectives emerged: one in Western Europe and North America (the paradigm of the expanding capitalist nucleus), and one, initially at least, largely in Latin America (the structuralist paradigm). These perspectives generated two different sets of propositions and lines of reasoning concerning the nature of development, the dominant causes of underdevelopment and the route to be followed in overcoming these. True, these early theories had in common a rejection of the neo-classical paradigm as a viable basis for the analysis of the problems of underdeveloped economies. It is also true that these two dominant perspectives have certain policy conclusions in common. Indeed, with some give and take of emphasis they may be regarded as complementary (see Chapter 11). However, this does not make either the perspective or the argument identical, as will be shown in this and the following two chapters. Later on, it will also be argued that following the subsequent emergence of the neo-Marxist paradigm, development economics has given rise to the articulation of two other distinct, but related, interpretations of the development process: the Maoist and basic needs paradigms.

Of the various classificatory approaches used by previous analysts, the one which comes nearest to that used in this book is that of Hirschman. He, as we have seen, distinguishes four basic (but arguably five in total) analytical perspectives applied to the study of economic development and underdevelopment: neo-classical, Marxist, development theory of the 1940s and 1950s (out of which it is argued in the present study that two dominant perspectives emerged), neo-Marxist theory, and analyses that emphasise income distribution and basic needs (which in the present study are associated in part with two new perspectives: the Maoist and 'basic needs').

What follows is, however, again one individual's personal attempt at categorisation, and others may wish to take issue with some aspects of it. Most notably, not all development economists are agreed that there is such a thing as a 'basic needs' paradigm; nor, indeed, is the designation of a paradigm of the 'expanding capitalist nucleus' established currency among development economists. In what follows it will, therefore, be necessary to justify these categories. I will attempt to do this firstly by outlining in this chapter the core of each paradigm that is to be explored in detail later. In this way the reader should have a clear indication at the outset of the basis for the categorisation used. At the same time this chapter provides the reader who is unfamiliar with these issues with a brief account of the context and chronology of the emergence of different analytical perspectives on economic development.

The rest of this chapter is structured as follows. A survey of the origins of development economics in the 1940s and 1950s in Latin America on the one hand, and Western Europe and North America on the other, is followed by a summary of the origins and content of the structuralist paradigm and a review of the leading contributions to the early 'pre-paradigm' debate in Western Europe and North America. The role of Lewis and Rostow in the articulation of the dominant perspective that emerged from this debate – the paradigm of the expanding capitalist nucleus – is then discussed. The following sections review the subsequent emergence of the neo-Marxist, Maoist and basic needs paradigms, providing a summary of each, and provide a brief review of the neo-classical revival in development economics.

THE ORIGINS OF DEVELOPMENT ECONOMICS

The origins of development economics as we know it today can be traced to Latin America in the 1930s and 1940s, and to Western Europe – chiefly England – and North America in the fifteen year period from 1943 to 1958. These two contexts were markedly different in a number of key respects. In Latin America economists were grappling with the immediate and severe problems imposed first by the Great Depression of the 1930s and then by the further disruptions to the international economic system caused by the 1939–45 war. Individuals who had been trained in the neo-classical tradition were now confronted with empirical conditions which brought into question the continued espousal of the theory of comparative advantage and the doctrine of *laissez-faire*. Economists such as the Argentinian Raoul Prebisch were first forced into making *ad hoc* policy recommendations to cope with unfamiliar circumstances: the collapse of international trade and the consequent severe shortages of foreign exchange and manufactured imports. With the passage of time they began to develop a new body of theory that reflected their changed assessment of economic conditions in Latin America and the international economy.

Meanwhile in the 1940s and 1950s most of the economists in Western Europe and North America who turned their attention to the economically 'backward' or 'underdeveloped' regions of the world did so in response to different pressures and at a greater remove from the day-to-day problems of economic policy formation. As Seers, Preston and others have indicated, there was, after the Second World War, a growing sense of political urgency concerning the promotion of economic development in the underdeveloped regions in order to maintain international stability and to contain the expansion of communism.[5] This is confirmed in many of the writings of contemporary development economists (see e.g. Myrdal, 1957: 7 and Myint, 1954, reprinted in Agarwala and Singh, 1958: 135 and 151–2). However, the point is perhaps most graphically affirmed in Rostow's *An American Policy in Asia*:

> We as a people (the United States) have made a momentous choice. We have now clearly ruled out one conceivable approach to our international problem: namely a military attack on the Soviet Union and Communist China initiated by the United States. . . That American decision has an important consequence, it means that the American people must find other ways for protecting their interests. The alternative to total war initiated by the United States is not peace. Until a different spirit and a different policy prevail in Moscow and Peking the alternative for the United States is a mixture of military, political and economic activity. . .
>
> (Rostow, 1955: vii.)

and

> The United States must develop a more vigorous economic policy in Asia. Without such a policy our political and military efforts in Asia will continue to have weak foundations. . . Asia's economic aspirations are linked closely to the highest political and human goals of Asia's peoples: and American economic policy in Asia has, therefore, important political as well as economic meaning.
>
> (*Ibid.*: 43.)

The development economists in Britain and North America who now concerned themselves with the problems of the economically backward regions were concerned with a geographical area that embraced much of Asia and Africa as well as Latin America, and one that consequently contained a wider array of economic, social and political conditions. For instance, not all these countries were experiencing shortages of foreign exchange of the scale that contributed to the development of the structuralist perspective in Latin America. Indeed, some still had buoyant foreign balances due, *inter alia*, to the accumulation of sterling balances during World War II and the impact of the Korean War on primary commodity prices. From the outset, the British and American debate on economic development of the 1940s and 1950s concentrated upon issues of long-term strategy and basic theory. The start of the debate is usually dated to the publication in 1943 of Rosenstein-Rodan's paper proposing a strategy for the post-war economic development of South and South-eastern Europe. Rosenstein-Rodan was primarily concerned with practical rather than theoretical issues. However, the emphasis in the new literature quickly shifted towards the search for a basic theoretical perspective from which the correct strategy for economic development could be deduced.

The common tendency in this search was to look first to the existing body of neo-classical and Keynesian economic theory for inspiration and insight. Where, as was generally the case, this corpus of theory was found wanting, a number of economists each sought to specify a new theoretical perspective. The latter was intended both to throw light on the nature and causes of economic backwardness and to pinpoint the key causal factors in the process of economic development. This period was, *par excellence*, an example of 'pre-paradigm science' in which 'every individual scientist starts over again from the beginning'[6] in the search for an effective theoretical framework.

The list of early writers on economic development in Britain and North America who contributed some basic theoretical insight to the emergent discipline includes Rosenstein-Rodan, Lewis,[7] Nurkse, Rostow, Myint,[7] Myrdal, Leibenstein, Hirschman and Bauer. Rereading the major contributions to this early debate on economic backwardness, underdevelopment and development is still, today, a stimulating experience. Among the majority of these writers and those working on the theory of economic underdevelopment and development in Latin America there were important elements of common ground. Firstly, there was a widespread rejection of the neo-classical paradigm as a meaningful source of insight into either of these phenomena. Rather, most saw economic development as Schumpeter had done, as a cumulative process which falls completely outside the purview of comparative static equilibrium analysis. Almost all were to question, and most would reject, the static theory of comparative advantage as a basis for determining the appropriate pattern of imports and exports for developing countries. It was widely accepted that industrialisation was the key to economic development, and that this would not be promoted by indefinite concentration on expansion of primary exports in exchange for manufactured imports. There was also a widespread acknowledgment of the existence of both open and disguised unemployment (or underemployment) in poor economies, particularly in the agricultural sector, and a general agreement that an important aspect of economic development consisted of mobilising this labour into more productive activities. Most also took the view that achievement of a satisfactory rate of resource mobilisation for economic development would require a substantial degree of state intervention with the current operation of market forces in underdeveloped regions.[8] However, a common position on these issues still permitted considerable divergence of perspective and analysis. The following discussion first reviews the emergence of development economics in Latin America. Contrary to common convention (and the ordering of the next two chapters) this will be taken first because, as noted above,[9] the origins of the structuralist paradigm take chronological precedence (albeit slight) over the emergence of development economics in Western Europe and North America.

The discussion will, however, pass on quite quickly to review the ideas on development that evolved in Europe and the United States. Here there is a more complex story to tell, and this chapter will be used partly to give a flavour of the pre-paradigm debate in these regions. The author will then attempt to show why out of this debate a particular viewpoint was to achieve dominance, before completing the chapter with a brief summary of subsequent developments in the discipline.

THE EMERGENCE OF THE STRUCTURALIST SCHOOL IN LATIN AMERICA

The historical background to the emergence of the structuralist school of development economics in Latin America has been traced by Love (1980). Parts of the following summary are based on his work.

The emergence of economic structuralism in Latin America provides a graphic illustration of paradigm failure and replacement. The Argentinian economist Raoul Prebisch, who was the founder of the structuralist school, had, like his peers in Latin America, been educated in the neo-classical tradition. On graduation in the early 1920s he worked as a professional economist and statistician in an environment in which the application of the static theory of comparative advantage was accepted as the underlying explanation of Argentina's rapid growth over the previous six decades.

> Not only did powerful export groups espouse comparative advantage, but the Argentine Socialist Party – viewing itself as the defender of worker and consumer interests – vigorously opposed industrial protectionism in the 1920s.[10]

However, in the late 1920s, and particularly from the start of the Great Depression in 1929, there was a dramatic change in Argentina's trading conditions.

From the late 1920s, Prebisch found himself working in a context in which the Argentinian authorities were compelled to introduce a series of *ad hoc* measures to protect the balance of payments and debt repayments. Exchange controls were introduced in 1931, import controls in 1938. As world prices of primary products fell relative to manufactured goods, so Argentina's import capacity declined. However, in the 1930s, in response to the shortage of imports, there was a rapid growth of industry in Argentina (as also in Chile and Southern Brazil). These and related events were to move Prebisch to rethink the theoretical basis of policy formation in Argentina and in Latin

America in general. In 1942 Argentina's Central Bank, of which Prebisch had been made the first director in 1935, broke with the past by championing industrialisation, which was to be promoted through management of imports: the new objective was to change the composition of these from consumer to capital goods.[11]

During the 1940s Prebisch continued, both in academic and policy advisory work, to advocate industrialisation for Argentina and other Latin American countries as a means of making them less economically vulnerable. In 1948, at the University of Buenos Aires, he specifically attacked the theory of comparative advantage, adducing a number of reasons why primary exporting countries could not, in the mid-twentieth century, expect to follow a path of export-led growth. Not only did industrial countries tend to retain the fruits of technological progress in the form of higher wages (rather than passing them on in reduced prices), but the world's dominant trading nation, the United States, had a much lower import coefficient than the previously dominant Great Britain had had in the nineteenth century.[12]

1948 saw the formation of the Economic Commission for Latin America (ECLA), of which Prebisch soon became director. The ideas he had by then developed, and was still evolving, were to be central to ECLA's work. The commission drew together a band of Latin American economists, including the Brazilian Celso Furtado, who were all influenced by their knowledge of Latin America's economic experience in the 1930s and 1940s: declining primary export prices and worsening balance of payments crises, followed by war-time disruptions to international trade and continuing shortages of manufactured imports. These, and a conviction that in the long term the situation for primary exports would worsen rather than improve, led the ECLA economists to reject conventional trade theory as a basis for national economic policy formation. Convinced that the way forward lay in a transformation of domestic economic structures via the development of the industrial sector, the ECLA economists developed a new body of theory designed to explain and justify the need for such a strategy.

The new theory emphasised both the economic structure of underdeveloped economies and the nature of their exposure to the international economic system as potential constraints to growth. While growth based upon specialisation according to comparative advantage might have occurred in Latin America in the past, it could not be expected to revive on a sustained basis after the outbreak of peace and the revival of growth in the industrially advanced countries. The replacement of Britain, a very open economy relying on substantial primary imports, by the United States, with only a very small proportion of its GDP entering international trade, as the leading industrial nation, combined with other factors such as the low income elasticity of demand for primary products in the industrially advanced economies, strongly militated against such a long-term revival. Meanwhile, the industrial development of Latin America and other underdeveloped countries was deterred both by foreign competition and the small size of domestic markets. The problem was not so much lack of investible resources as of inadequate inducements to invest. In view of this, development could only be promoted by deliberate measures to block off foreign competition and to compensate for small market size. The structuralists, however, also acknowledged that the initial period of import-substituting industrialisation would put continuing pressure on the balance of payments, due to increased demand for imports of capital and intermediate goods. Preoccupation with this problem led the ECLA group to press firstly for improved conditions of trade for primary exports (something Prebisch had first done in the 1930s[13]) and secondly for improved opportunities for manufactured exports. Domestic supply rigidities were also anticipated, and this led to a new analysis of the structural causes of inflation, and of appropriate responses thereto.

During the 1950s and early 1960s the structuralist perspective attracted a number of important economists from outside Latin America who contributed to the articulation and extension of this paradigm. They included Hans Singer (whose early work on the prospects for primary exports was conducted independently of Prebisch[14]), and Dudley Seers. Myrdal also had much in common with the structuralist perspective.[15]

However, many concur that it was essentially from the ECLA context that the structuralist paradigm emerged.[16] The key elements of this paradigm can be summarised as follows:

1. There is a distinction between economic growth and economic development. Structuralist definitions of economic underdevelopment and development are not always identical but always emphasise both structural factors and technological advance. Two widely accepted definitions are those of Furtado:
   (a) an underdeveloped economy is one in which the technological level of some branches of the economy falls well below the technological level (and, hence, labour productivity) of the most advanced sector, and well below the level that could be achieved with known technologies;
   (b) economic development consists of the introduction of new combinations of production factors which increase labour productivity.

2. Essential features of economic development are a steady expansion in the number of branches using the most advanced production technologies and a change in the sectoral composition of total output. Unless the latter occurs, sustained expansion of production and productivity will not be possible (see points 4–8).

3. An expansion of output generated by an expansion of economic activity using existing production technologies represents growth but not development.

4. The existing structures of underdeveloped economies have been historically determined by the manner in which these economies have become incorporated into the international economy.
5. They have been drawn into this economy as suppliers of cheap raw materials to the industrially advanced economies, and as markets for mass-produced goods exported from the industrially advanced economies.
6. The result has been the generation of dualistic economic structures, as indentified in point 2, with the modern sector oriented to production of primary products for export.
7. Machinery and technology for the modern sector are imported, as are manufactured consumer goods.
8. As long as underdeveloped economies maintain these structures they will be incapable either of generating their own growth dynamic or of achieving economic development.
9. The economic structures of underdeveloped economies also explain the nature of certain stresses that the latter commonly experience. Of particular importance are low internal supply elasticities. For example, inflationary pressures in UDCs are often due not to easy monetary policies but to low domestic elasticity of supply in key sectors. Likewise pressure on the balance of payments can be explained in terms of low external income elasticities of demand for primary products, and internal price elasticities of supply and demand for primary and manufactured goods. It too is an inevitable consequence of attempts to promote growth given the existing structure.
10. Only government promotion of a steady process of structural transformation, focusing above all on the development of a diversified domestic industrial sector, including capital goods production, can overcome these problems.

Thus in structuralist theory the object of development is the structural transformation of underdeveloped economies in such a way as to permit a process of self-sustained economic growth more or less along the lines of today's industrially advanced countries. To achieve this it was recognised that it would be necessary to break away from reliance on foreign demand for primary exports as the engine of growth, switching instead to a supply-side dynamic to be provided by an expanding domestic industrial sector.

The policy recommendations generated by members of the structuralist school were geared to this end. To a large extent they focused on conventional policy instruments – tariff, monetary and fiscal policy in particular. (However, with time, and growing foreign exchange shortages, the pursuit of import-substituting industrialisation also came to be associated with less orthodox policy instruments, most notably investment licensing and foreign exchange licensing.) The structuralists' policy recommendations were intended for adoption by existing governments. The structuralists were, as Preston indicates, intellectuals and bureaucrats who unlike the neo-Marxists (see below) accepted a philosophy of development through capitalism. In order to make this possible, they sought to bring about long-term change in the structure of the economy through reforms in existing economic policy rather than through radical political and social change.[17]

THE EMERGENCE OF DEVELOPMENT ECONOMICS IN NORTH AMERICA AND WESTERN EUROPE

As already noted, during the 1940s and 1950s some economists working in Western Europe (mainly the United Kingdom) and in North America also turned their attention to the problems of underdevelopment. Some, as Seers has noted,[18] already had experience of working in, or teaching courses on, colonial economies. Meanwhile, the contemporary international context arguably also had a significant influence on the tenor of their work. The most notable features of this context were the successful completion in the late 1940s and early 1950s of the Marshall Plan for economic reconstruction in Europe (which generated confidence in the role of economic aid); the acquisition of political independence by a number of Asian and Arab countries, followed in the late 1950s and early 1960s by the decolonisation of much of Africa; and the emergence of the cold war between the Western and Eastern blocs. All of these events were associated with a growing political focus on the provision of economic aid to underdeveloped countries.[19]

The period that we are considering also came soon after a lengthy war in which many academics had worked closely with and for their respective governments, in support, as they often saw it, of certain strongly held ideals concerning the protection of the free world. Given these circumstances it would have been surprising if many of the economists who now turned their attention to Third World problems had not done so in order to develop a theoretical framework which in various ways was intended to inform government policy – both government policy in the Third World and Western government aid policy. It was accepted that in the long term industrialisation was desirable for underdeveloped economies. However, the dominant constraints to economic growth were widely seen as internal rather than external. Partly they lay in the indigenous institutions and attitudes, but for many the overriding constraint was seen to lie in the low rate of saving out of national income that was found to be characteristic of poor countries.

In this pre-paradigm debate economic development was generally equated with rising national per capita income. From this it was assumed that, with time, some of the benefits of growth would 'trickle down' to the mass of the population (see Streeten, 1981: 108).

The pre-paradigm debate in Western Europe and North America

The names of some of the leading contributors to the early debate on economic development have been noted on page 46. The elements of the intellectual heritage that influenced these and other contemporary analysts were various. Many, however, turned either directly or indirectly to the classical economists for inspiration. Lewis, Myint and Rostow all refer directly to classical growth theory, while Rosenstein-Rodan and Nurkse take Allyn Young's 1928 article[20] as their starting point. Some (e.g. Liebenstein and Rostow) also drew upon Schumpeter's emphasis on the key role played by entrepreneurship in economic development. Meanwhile, the most recent contribution to dynamic theory, the Harrod–Domar model, probably also exercised some influence on these analysts, although it should be pointed out that, in so far as these economists' emphasis on the role of savings and capital accumulation is taken as evidence of Harrod's and Domar's influence on them, such emphasis is also to be found in classical growth theory. Furthermore, as Hirschman and others have pointed out, in so far as the Harrod–Domar model did influence economic development theory, this was via a new interpretation and use of the model, in which the search was not for the equilibrium growth rate given *existing* savings propensities, but upon the means of *raising* the savings rate in order to warrant higher growth.[21]

As we saw earlier, one important feature which characterised the analyses of almost all these early writers on economic development was a rejection of the neo-classical paradigm. Almost all emphasised the lack of realism in a theoretical perspective which assumed that 'every disturbance provokes a reaction within the system, directed towards restoring a new state of equilibrium'.[22] Some also pointed, either explicitly or implicitly, to the failure of the static theory of comparative advantage to provide the correct basis for long-run resource allocation strategies in primary exporting economies. The rejection of the macro-economic aspects of the neo-classical paradigm was complemented by a critique of the assumptions of general equilibrium theory (in particular, perfectly competitive markets, perfect divisibility of factors and products and the absence of significant technological or pecuniary externalities) as an empirically valid basis for individual investment decisions. In other words, in the eyes of most development economists the paradigm failed to reflect a world characterised by indivisibilities, externalities and market failures and imperfections. With the notable exception of Peter Bauer, the logic of their alternative analyses was to lead the majority of early development economists in North America and Western Europe, as in Latin America, to advocate in one form or another public sector interventions designed to accelerate the pace of economic development.

The following paragraphs review the contributions to development theory of the writers named at the outset[23] in the following order:

1. Rosenstein-Rodan and Nurkse

2. Hirschman
3. Leibenstein
4. Myrdal
5. Myint
6. Bauer and Yamey
7. Lewis and Rostow

The purpose will be to give an indication of the distinctive nature of the contribution of each of these writers, and to suggest why, out of these various contributions, a particular perspective, found in the work of Lewis and Rostow, achieved dominance (in the sense that it provided the inspiration for significant further theoretical work and the authentication for policy and plan content).

Rosenstein-Rodan and Nurkse on balanced growth

The names of Rosenstein-Rodan and Nurkse are both closely linked to the concept of *balanced growth*. In the work of Nurkse[24] the concept not only provides the basis for a development strategy, but is also linked to his 'vicious circle' analysis of the causes of underdevelopment and of the constraints to development. Nurkse, indeed, provided a tightly articulated theorisation of underdevelopment and development which was widely debated but which achieved little practical influence.

Rosenstein-Rodan, in a paper published in 1943, and Nurkse, lecturing in Brazil eight years later, both drew their inspiration from Allyn Young and Adam Smith, each of whom had emphasised the importance of expanding markets as a stimulus to growth.[25]

The key points of Rosenstein-Rodan's paper are as follows:

1. The economic development of backward economic regions (he focuses on Eastern and South-eastern Europe) is necessary for international political stability.
2. The key economic characteristics of these regions are:
   (a) low income and, hence, purchasing power;
   (b) substantial unemployed and underemployed labour in the agrarian sector.
3. In order to raise income it is necessary to industrialise.
4. Industrial development strategy may be pursued either under conditions of autarky – developing self-sufficiency in all branches of industrial production, including capital and intermediate goods – or through specialisation and integration into the international economic system, according to the principle of comparative advantage. The latter is preferable to the former because it:
   (a) permits a higher level of aggregate world output;
   (b) prevents an increase of international excess capacity in certain sectors;

     (c) permits the mobilisation of international capital to fund part of the development effort with loans to be repaid from export revenues.

5. Three key factors impede spontaneous industrial investment by private enterprise in backward regions:

     (a) the small size of the domestic market;

     (b) the inability of individual firms to internalise the value of the external economies that they generate (for example, the training of labour which may leave to work for other enterprises[26]);

     (c) the inability of individual firms to anticipate the external economies which may be generated by the investment of other firms.

6. These constraints can be overcome by:

     (a) state investment in the training of the workforce;

     (b) state planning and organisation of a large-scale investment programme. The more or less simultaneous implementation of a range of investments in different branches of light industry and essential infrastructure will permit individual firms to find larger market outlets (due to the expansion of wage employment) and to benefit from external economies.[27]

7. State intervention would also be needed to help mobilise the finance for a large-scale programme of industrialisation in backward regions. If consumption standards in Southern and South-eastern Europe were not to be forced down to intolerably low levels, up to 50 per cent of the necessary funding would have to be borrowed abroad. State intervention would be necessary to guarantee these loans. This must be combined with international collaboration in programming the expansion of exports in order to permit loan repayment from export revenues without major disruption to the light industries of creditor countries.

Rosenstein-Rodan set the stage for the emergence of a body of literature on underdeveloped economies that emphasised market failure and the need for state interventionism. However, he had not entirely abandoned the neoclassical orthodoxy. Although writing about a region large in area and population and endowed with appropriate natural resources, he argued against the development of heavy industry and in favour of the development of labour-intensive light industries in over-populated areas, combined with integration into international markets. On the other hand, without analysing the reasoning behind this proposition, he saw some form of industrialisation as an absolute necessity.[28]

Eight years later Nurkse reiterated and developed Rosenstein-Rodan's argument in a set of lectures delivered at the Brazilian Institute of Economics. He restated it in such a way as to provide a carefully articulated, internally consistent statement of the causes of economic backwardness as well as a statement of the way forward. His argument was as follows:

1. Underdevelopment has two key causalities that jointly lock backward economies into a vicious circle of self-replicating poverty and stagnation. These are low per capita incomes which limit the size of the market and hence the inducement to invest, and inability to generate significant savings from low per capita incomes, so that even if the inducement to invest existed the domestic resources to finance such investment would not be available. This latter problem is exacerbated by the operation on an international scale of the Duesenberry effect – even if per capita incomes in backward regions rise due to buoyancy in primary export markets, any potentially favourable impact on savings will be annihilated by an increase in the propensity to consume as people in these regions try to catch up with the consumption standards prevalent in the industrially advanced countries.

2. To achieve a way out of this impasse requires simultaneous action on both fronts: the inducement to invest and the mobilisation of investible funds. With respect to the former, Nurkse considers and rejects a growth strategy based upon the continued expansion of primary exports, i.e. upon an external market. He rejects this due to the low international income and price elasticities of demand for primary products. Nurkse then restates points 4 and 5 from Rosenstein-Rodan's argument,[29] reconfirming the case for balanced domestic growth in consumer goods industries in order to create a balanced market, and accepting the probable need for state planning to promote this.

With respect to resource mobilisation, Nurkse also accepts Rosenstein-Rodan's assertion of the need to mobilise both domestic and foreign resources to finance the investment programme. However, his analysis of the prospects for achieving this is both more profound and less sanguine. Nurkse argues as follows:

1. Increased voluntary saving is improbable due to the Duesenberry effect noted above.

2. 'Some of the backward countries have large masses of disguised unemployment on the land, which could be mobilised for real capital formation, but not without strict curbs on any immediate rise in consumption' (Nurkse, 1952, reprinted in Agarwala and Singh, *op.cit.*: 265.) Again the demonstration effect may hamper such restraint.

3. Any increase in domestic incomes is also likely to put pressure on the balance of payments as people demand more imported consumer goods.

4. Luxury and semi-luxury import restriction is, if implemented, likely to

be only partially successful as a means of raising capital formation, for the release of foreign exchange must be matched by a corresponding increase in domestic savings. However, the potential consumers of luxury imports will not necessarily replace their thwarted consumption outlays by saving; they will look for domestic consumption outlets. The likely result is that there will be increased inflationary pressure in the domestic economy. This may generate some forced saving as profits are built up while real consumption is curtailed by availabilities, so that, as long as inflation does not get out of control, there may be some increase in net investment, but not to the full extent theoretically made possible by import control.

5. However, apart from the question of the quantity of investment, there is also that of quality. If import restrictions are not matched by restraints on consumption, and if there is sufficient effective demand, the increase in investment is likely to be channelled into relatively inessential uses, producing luxury and semi-luxury items.

6. Nurkse is also sceptical about the automatic efficacy of foreign aid in raising investment, being one of the first to emphasise the fungibility of foreign resources (*ibid.*: 270).

Nurkse's conclusion is that the onus for breaking the vicious circle of poverty in backward countries rests firmly upon their governments, with respect not only to planning a programme of balanced industrial investment but also to mobilising domestic resources, and ensuring effective use of foreign aid, through curtailing the growth of domestic consumption. The key to growth lies in the ability of these governments to match expanded investment with an effective fiscal policy. 'No solution is possible without strenuous domestic efforts, particularly in the field of public finance.'[30]

Leibenstein on the 'low level equilibrium trap'
In 1957 Harvey Leibenstein published another explanation of economic backwardness and a specification of the route to growth which had at least one important element in common with the strategy of balanced growth.

Leibenstein explains economic backwardness in terms of a 'low level equilibrium trap': at low levels of income forces operate to restore increased *per capita* incomes to their original level. Of these forces the most important are population growth – already high, but accelerated by any increase in mass living standards – and a high marginal propensity to consume stimulated by the Duesenberry effect already emphasised by Nurkse. In contrast, at higher levels of economic development advanced economies are more accurately seen as 'disequilibrium systems' in which change is cumulative, while development itself is an 'explosive disequilibrium path.'[31] The problem then, is presented as one of breaking out of the trap into cumulative growth. Any relatively small-scale effort designed to generate gradual change will be inadequate; any potential increase in savings will be absorbed in increased consumption, and any initial increase in per capita incomes will soon be offset by an induced acceleration in population growth.

For Leibenstein the only solution lies in a *critical minimum effort* in which the scale of increased investment enables a country to achieve, and sustain, a growth rate which exceeds the maximum feasible rate of population growth by enough to pemit the following to occur:

1. Rising consumption per capita.
2. Maintenance of the growing capital stock.
3. Generation of sufficient net savings to sustain further growth.

Leibenstein acknowledges that the effort will have to be substantial, since the maximum feasible rate of population growth may be as high as 4 per cent per year. On the other hand, an effort on this scale should make it possible to reap the benefits of external economies and industry interdependence, and to achieve 'balanced growth' (where the balance referred to relates chiefly to inter-industry demand).[32] Attainment of the critical minimum effort will depend heavily on the development of entrepreneurship, knowledge and skills.[33] Governments, Leibenstein indicates, can help to foster the growth of these factors. Meanwhile the supply of savings *per se*, although important, is not seen as the dominant constraint to growth. The problem lies at least as much in achieving more productive use of the existing savings potential, currently used up in luxury consumption and unproductive investments such as land purchase.

Unlike Nurkse, Leibenstein's analysis leaves the international trade aspects of economic development out of the discussion; what he offers must, therefore, be regarded as a 'partial' theory of development. By implication, however, it is reasonable to assume that Leibenstein sees the central causes of backwardness and the main key to growth as lying within the underdeveloped economy and not in the international sector.

The concepts of balanced growth and of the critical minimum effort both received widespread discussion in the 1950s, and by the 1960s the writings of Nurkse and Leibenstein featured widely on reading lists for courses in development economics. It would seem inevitable that both had some influence in the applied field of policy formation. The growing interest in the 1950s and 1960s in the use of input-output analysis as a planning tool was linked to a preoccupation with the need for balance in national investment programmes. Meanwhile, there has been a continuing preoccupation amongst development economists and others with the interrelationship between economic development and demographic change. Yet neither Nurkse's thesis nor Leibenstein's came to be accepted as the basis of a dominant paradigm of development. Nurkse's, as we shall see, was to be hotly debated at the conceptual level.[34] However, almost certainly of equal significance in the failure of both theses to achieve dominance was their emphasis upon paths to development which seemed particularly difficult to achieve. In both cases there was, as Furtado noted in his critique of Nurkse,[35] a presumption that the main impetus for a substantial growth programme must be generated internally, through the interaction of government and domestic entrepreneurs. Not merely that, but the scale of the effort to mobilise resources for productive investment would, as compared with past experience in backward economies, have to be massive, as would the investment programme itself, for only in that case could the diseconomies of small scale be overcome, risks of market failure reduced, and external economies fully exploited. Only then, too, could output growth surpass that of population and generate sustained increases in per capita income. To many economists, particularly those working in the Third World, what Nurkse and Leibenstein proposed must have seemed, quite simply, unrealistic.

Myrdal's thesis of cumulative causation
In the mid-fifties Myrdal presented another perspective on the nature and causes of underdevelopment in his theory of cumulative causation. Focusing on the link between low average incomes in the underdeveloped countries and the pattern of change elsewhere in the world economy, his argument states essentially that a small group of countries, having achieved major advances in science, technology and industrial production, have become locked into a path of cumulative development, while the majority of countries, which have not achieved these breakthroughs, are condemned to stagnation or, worse, declining per capita incomes. Factors making for growing international inequality and continuing Third World poverty include continuing scientific and technical progress in the advanced countries, the presence of larger markets in these countries, the tendency of finance capital to flow into areas where cost structures and market prospects look most promising and the relative income elasticities of demand in the industrially advanced countries for manufactured and primary products. Meanwhile in poor countries low levels of per capita output and savings, high rates of population growth, low levels of skills, the poor health of the work force, a production structure locked into the export of primary products facing poor world market prospects, and the import of cheap manufactures which undercut local artisan production, all contrive to perpetuate and exacerbate existing poverty. Within these countries, low government revenues prohibit major outlays on social and economic infrastructure, and what limited infrastructural resources and modern productive capital there are tend to be concentrated in the regions with most economic potential, mainly export enclaves. Thus national poverty is associated with rising intra- as well as international inequality. For poor countries to break out of this impasse can only be achieved by government planning and deliberate interference with market forces. The static theory of comparative advantage fails to provide an adequate guide to resource allocation. Industrial development must be promoted, and this can only be achieved by protecting infant

manufacturing industries from foreign competition. Only then can they overcome the problems posed by the small size of the domestic market and be adequately compensated for the external benefits that they generate.

Myrdal's analysis had much in common with the work of the Latin American structuralist school. This was quite quickly recognised, and as such his perspective on underdevelopment came to be regarded as complementary to other structuralist analyses and, thus, part of the corpus of structuralist literature.

Myint on the nature of economic backwardness

Another widely respected early writer on economic development was Hla Myint. In no single publication did Myint proffer a potential paradigm of underdevelopment and/or development. Yet he did offer, in an article published in 1954, a distinctive analysis of the nature of economic backwardness, couched in terms of backward peoples rather than backward nations, in which can be found an anticipation of later concerns with poverty reduction and meeting basic needs.

In Myint's view economic backwardness is a state of being characterised by an objective and a subjective component. The former is reflected in low productivity and stagnation, the latter in a 'sense of economic discontent and maladjustment' generated by awareness of the higher living standards attained in industrially advanced economies. Myint specifies a number of causes of economic backwardness, based upon the typical economic circumstances of backward people as unskilled workers and peasant producers, borrowers of capital, and consumers. His thesis is that as underdeveloped regions have been 'opened up' to international markets the pattern of trade and development that has ensued has consolidated rather than transformed the condition of backward peoples – they have 'specialised' in unskilled work as wage labourers or peasant producers. As the latter they face monopsonistic buyers of their produce, while as consumers they face the monopolistic markets of the big import companies and of middlemen merchants and moneylenders. A combination of unequal market forces, social institutions and prejudice act to prevent backward peoples from improving their economic status, and these forces are compounded by their lack of business experience.

In principle, suggests Myint, the way forward seems to lie in the development of countervailing powers to counteract the existing unequal distribution of market power. The development of trade unions, state marketing boards and peasant co-operatives are all potential sources of such countervailing power. But here too he strikes a note of pessimism. In reality these latter institutions require a high degree of businesslike behaviour, and such advances can be fostered only slowly. Furthermore, even where marketing boards and co-operatives mobilise additional resources, the problem of finding investment outlets for them remains. Meanwhile, the scope for use of other forms of countervailing power such as economic protection or development of trade unions is also limited by the potentially adverse effects these may have in terms of reduced efficiency and increased costs of production.[36]

In Myint's analysis, as in Nurkse's, there is a noticeable tone of pessimism concerning the prospects for development, seen in this case as raising the incomes of backward peoples.

Hirschman's strategy of unbalanced growth

In 1958 Hirshman published a critique of early development theories which included a major attack on the balanced growth theories of Rosenstein-Rodan and Nurkse. Hirschman argued that previous attempts to identify dominant causes of underdevelopment in terms of the lack of a key factor, be it savings, entrepreneurship, or skilled labour, had all been disproved; each of these factors had been shown by experience to be latent in underdeveloped economies. What was lacking was a 'binding agent', the organisational capability to call forth and combine these latent resources in order to generate growth. Hirshman argued that where organisational and managerial skills are in scarce supply the pursuit of balanced growth would overstretch these resources. Consequently, he proposed a strategy of unbalanced growth, in which planners and policy-makers would not attempt to anticipate supply and demand imbalances, but would be guided by major resource bottlenecks as revealed in the market. Such a strategy would emphasise 'induced investment' in both the public and private sectors. However, Hirschman too identified an interventionist role for government in guiding resource allocation. To maximise the rate of development, investment should be encouraged in branches of production with substantial backward and/or forward linkages. His analysis can be interpreted as providing a justification for backward-linked import substitution (starting with consumer goods production).

Hirschman also advocated the use of large-scale capital-intensive techniques of production which, he claimed, tend to minimise demands on organisational and managerial resources. He also favoured foreign capital for its ability to pick successful priority sectors and regions, its innovatory capacity, and its foreign market contacts which can be used to ease temporary input bottlenecks.[37]

Agriculture received little attention in Hirschman's analysis. Primary production in general has, in Hirschman's view, virtually no backward linkages (strangely he ignores its demand for means of production). Meanwhile, the forward linkages from agriculture to other branches of production he also sees as minimal, since most agricultural output in underdeveloped countries is either consumed or exported. Again Hirschman plays down the scope for forward linkages into the expansion of agricultural processing.[38]

The ECLA economists did not regard Hirschman as a member of the structuralist school. His analysis can, however, be regarded as providing an *ex post facto* theoretical justification for the particular pattern of import substituting industrialisation that was pursued in Latin America in the 1950s. Indeed, his analysis was based upon a year's experience of working in Colombia.

Bauer and Yamey

In 1957 Peter Bauer and Basil Yamey published a reaction in the neo-classical tradition to the dominant interventionist trend amongst development economists. However, Bauer and Yamey go beyond the conventional confines of the neo-classical paradigm in their frequent references to traditional institutions and cultural values in underdeveloped economies. Their central theme concerns the positive role of expanding market opportunities in the generation of economic growth. They accept that in certain cases traditional institutions may impede the efficient operation of market forces (for example the determination of the reserve price of labour in the traditional sector at a level nearer to average per capita income than to the marginal product of labour,[39] and the operation of the extended family system). However, they argue that in general small-scale producers in the Third World are highly market-responsive, and that relative prices guide their productive effort.[40] Governments of underdeveloped countries, rather than trying to mobilise large quantities of capital for public development expenditure, should concentrate upon removing the numerous impediments to private saving and investment. 'These include the imperfect maintenance of law and order, political instability, unsettled monetary conditions, lack of continuity in economic life, the extended family system with its drain on resources and its stifling of personal initiative, and certain systems of land tenure which inhibit savings and investment' (*ibid.*: 132). The role of governments is not to interfere with the operation of market forces, but to concentrate upon making markets operate more efficiently and upon ensuring widely dispersed dissemination of new technical knowledge to private producers.[41]

However, in the 1950s the preponderance of opinion among development economists remained interventionist. In Western Europe and the United States a version of the view that capital accumulation was the key to economic development, and that the state has a role to play in promoting this, came to dominate both theorising on development and the formation of economic policy. However, this version did not take the form initially articulated by Rosenstein-Rodan and Nurkse, but instead gave greater emphasis to autonomous capital accumulation in the private sector as one of two potential routes to economic development. It is to the emergence of this perspective, as reflected in the largely complementary contributions of Lewis and Rostow, that we now turn.

THE LEWIS MODEL, ROSTOW'S 'STAGES OF GROWTH' AND THE EMERGENCE OF THE PARADIGM OF THE EXPANDING CAPITALIST NUCLEUS

Lewis' 1954 article on 'Economic development with unlimited supplies of labour' and Rostow's work on the stages of growth (subsequently heavily criticised for the rigidity of his interpretation of the five stages) at first inspection may seem very different in focus and character – the one almost pure theory, the other much more historical. Indeed, in some classifications of early development theory Lewis has been classed as a structuralist (see e.g. Chenery, 1975) and Rostow as a modernisation theorist (see e.g. Toye, 1987). Yet more careful inspection reveals a common theme in Lewis' seminal article on the one hand, and Rostow's (1956) work on the take-off into self-sustained growth on the other. Our concern in what follows is primarily with the most enduring part of Rostow's theoretical contribution, his theorisation of the take-off.

The basis for Chenery's classification of Lewis' work on economic development as structuralist lies in the latter's emphasis on the dualistic structure of underdeveloped economies. These Lewis represents as having a large subsistence sector dominated by family farming and a small emerging capitalist sector using wage labour. Starting from this proposition Lewis develops a theory of the relationship between the two sectors, in which lies much of the originality and significance of his analysis. However, it is typical of early attempts to theorise the causes of underdevelopment and development, including those by neo-classical theorists such as Bauer and Yamey, to begin with a statement of the relevant distinguishing characteristics of less developed countries. These invariably include the characteristics just specified. Using this criterion probably all early work on development could be classified as 'structuralist'. Certainly one could make out a case that Rostow's preoccupation with the role of different productive sectors in the 'take-off' justifies the label. What is equally important, however, is the theorisation that is derived partly from such interpretations of empirical reality, in combination with other premises reflecting the values, judgements and beliefs of the theorist.

Common elements in the perspective articulated by Lewis in his 1954 article and by Rostow in various writings on the take-off into self-sustained growth include the following:

1. Economic growth, measured by rising per capita income, is the focal defining characteristic of economic development.
2. More broadly interpreted, economic development entails the transformation of a traditional, stagnant, subsistence-oriented economy into a dynamic, capitalist economy based on wage-labour, capable of self-sustained growth and of providing, in the long term, rising real wages.
3. It is possible to specify the common – and dominant – characteristics of

this transformation process for all countries, both those now relatively developed and those less developed, provided that their starting point is a condition of abundant supplies of labour in the traditional sector (see Lewis, 1954, and Rostow, 1956, reprinted in Agarwala and Singh, *op.cit.*: 157–9).

4. A key determinant of the rate of growth is the rate of capital formation, which is in turn governed by the share of savings in national income.

5. The capitalist/entrepreneurial class plays a crucial role in capital accumulation, for its members have a higher propensity to save and invest out of their profit income than any other class.

6. An essential element in the *initiation* of economic growth is therefore the emergence of a class variously described as entrepreneurial (Rostow) or capitalist (Lewis) operating either in the private or the public sector.

7. In order to *maximise the subsequent rate of growth* it is necessary to concentrate as large a share as possible of national income in the hands of those with a high propensity to save, i.e. the capitalist class. The aim should be to steadily increase this share over time.

From these propositions more specific recommendations follow with respect to wages policy, monetary policy, fiscal policy and the choice of production technology, all designed to enhance the rate of profit and the command over scarce resources of the capitalist class, and, hence, the rate of productive accumulation.

Within this framework Rostow also explores both the cultural and institutional preconditions for development, and the role of different productive sectors in contributing to the take-off. Lewis on the other hand focuses, as we have seen, on various aspects of the interaction between the capitalist and pre-capitalist sectors.

The main attractions of this perspective may be said to have derived from the relative simplicity of its fundamental elements, its potential fruitfulness at the theoretical level (see Chapter 4), its relative optimism, and the fact that it pinpointed a constraint to growth about which there was both widespread, though not universal, consensus and a feeling that, with aid, it could be overcome. Finally, the fact that it was politically acceptable, both in Western industrially advanced countries and in many of those countries in which it was to be applied, also helps to account for its widespread influence during the late 1950s and the early 1960s.

THE SUBSEQUENT EVOLUTION OF DEVELOPMENT ECONOMICS

In the late 1950s and early 1960s development economics witnessed the coexistence of the structuralist paradigm and the more optimistic paradigm of the expanding capitalist nucleus as the dominant perspectives that governed theoretical work in the discipline. However, by the mid-1960s there were growing indications of dissatisfaction with both perspectives and by the late 1960s they were being widely challenged. Some critics argued that after a decade and more of emphasis on capital accumulation and import substitution, a period which in many countries had indeed seen high growth of GDP, the lot of the masses in the Third World had not improved and in some cases had worsened. Moreover, in some countries growth itself was also apparently slowing down. Meanwhile other critics argued that attempts to maximise the rate of modern sector capital accumulation and, more particularly, to promote import substitution, had been associated with widespread inefficiency in resource allocation.

The critics of the early development orthodoxies came both from the radical left and from the tradition of neo-classical economics. The former will be reviewed first, and then the neo-classical critique on pages 69–71.

The neo-Marxist paradigm

In the 1950s Paul Baran, working in the United States, had, more or less alone among leading development economists of the time, explored in depth the relevance of Marxist principles to the analysis of the contemporary problem of underdevelopment. Baran found Marxist theory a fruitful source of insights into underdevelopment, but he also found it wanting in certain respects. He argued that Marx had not had sufficient information to develop a comprehensive theory of the nature of underdevelopment. More specifically, he claimed that Marx had been over-optimistic concerning the prospects for capitalist development in the Third World. In developing an alternative view of the impact of political and economic imperialism on backward economies, Baran drew his inspiration from the work of Lenin and his contemporaries. He also introduced a conceptual innovation into his analysis, by focusing upon the class modes of appropriation and use of the 'actual economic surplus' in underdeveloped economies, where the latter is defined as the difference between actual output and actual consumption (Baran, 1962: Chapter 2).

In the late 1960s Baran's approach to the analysis of underdevelopment gained a wide following. This was partly due to the work of Andre Gunder Frank. Frank went from the University of Chicago to work in Latin America in the early 1960s. He writes that he went there thinking of the problems of development 'in terms of largely domestic problems of capital scarcity, feudal and traditional institutions which impede savings and investment, and many of the other universally known supposed obstacles to the economic development of supposedly traditional societies' (Frank, 1969: xviii). Frank, however, rapidly became converted to Baran's perspective which he applied, with some modification, to the analysis first of particular Latin American economies and then, generalising from these case-studies, to Latin America as a whole.

For Baran, underdevelopment is a state characterised by low per capita incomes. For Frank, however, taking up a theme actually introduced by Baran, it is a process: the process of continuing extraction of surplus from the underdeveloped countries, and its transference to the centres of world capitalism. The manner in which this process occurs within individual countries (chiefly through monopsonistic trade) leads to the perpetuation of mass immiseration.

For both Baran and Frank the cause of the perpetuation of underdevelopment lies in the failure of the dominant classes in underdeveloped countries to use the surplus for productive accumulation within the domestic economy. Instead the surplus that is extracted from peasants and wage labour is either exported or used to finance luxury consumption, land purchase and urban property speculation. Both concur that these propositions apply as much to merchant capitalists and to any capitalist with investments in production as to that traditionally prodigal class, the landlords. For capitalist activity in underdeveloped countries, whether foreign or domestically owned, is typically monopolistic and, hence, conservative and non-dynamic. Underdeveloped economies have bypassed the phase of *competitive* capitalism due to the mode of their incorporation into the international economy. Their monopoly capitalists are content to appropriate existing monopoly profits and have no interest in promoting a competitive, dynamic capitalist sector. Meanwhile the classes that control the use of the surplus also hold political power, and they use this power to maintain the status quo. In these circumstances, the only possible way forward is through a social and political revolution that will replace the existing alliance of the domestic *comprador* bourgeoisie and foreign capitalists with a socialist regime committed to social and economic development.

An important element of Frank's version of the neo-Marxist paradigm, for which he was later criticised both by more orthodox Marxists and fellow neo-Marxists, was his emphasis upon surplus appropriation through trade. Frank implicitly equated capitalism with relations of exchange rather than interpreting it as a system of production. He argued that monopolistic merchant capitalism had penetrated the remotest reaches of all underdeveloped economies via a series of trading networks in which small-scale merchants in rural areas were linked to larger monopolistic suppliers, and monopsonistic buyers, and so on up the chain to large-scale import-export activities dominated by foreign interests. He used this thesis as the basis of his widely-contested claim that all branches of underdeveloped economies have been incorporated into the world capitalist system.

In the late 1960s Emmanuel contributed to the analytical content of the neo-Marxist paradigm through his elaboration of the theory of unequal exchange. This provided a more sophisticated account of surplus extraction through trade (and was subsequently espoused by Frank).

The neo-Marxist paradigm can be summarised as follows:

1. The prospects for the development of the capitalist mode of production in any one country are largely determined by its position in the international economy.
2. This position is in turn historically determined.
3. Present-day underdeveloped countries cannot expect to pass through the same phases of economic development as the now industrially advanced capitalist economies because the international conditions are different.
4. The industrially advanced countries at various stages of their development have been able to use today's underdeveloped economies as sources of cheap raw material, markets for their goods, and outlets for surplus capital.
5. These opportunities are not open to contemporary underdeveloped economies. Instead the very nature of foreign capitalist investment in the Third World has locked these countries into the production of primary products for export based on cheap labour drawn from the traditional sector. The manufactured goods supplied in exchange for these exports have destroyed indigenous industries and represent a strong disincentive to the local development of manufacturing production. In these countries production is characterised by export of primary products and by the existence of a small, protected, monopolistic modern industrial sector dominated by foreign capital and using imported technology. Meanwhile the mass of the population remain impoverished. Indeed, in some cases the appropriation of land for plantations and mines, the destruction of indigenous industry and the intervention of middlemen and moneylenders between small-scale primary producers and their markets have led to increasing immiseration.
6. Given their sources of income, the dominant classes – landlords, the commercial bourgeoisie, owners of monopoly capital, and foreign capitalists – have limited interest in the development of producer capitalism in the periphery. Instead, they channel most of the surplus abroad.
7. Meanwhile trade between advanced capitalist economies and underdeveloped economies is characterised by unequal exchange, i.e. the difference in returns to labour embodied in the products traded exceeds the difference in labour productivity. In this way too surplus is extracted from the periphery.
8. Only following a socialist revolution can these economies embark on a path of full development, through productive and equitable use of the surplus.

Parts of the neo-Marxist analysis of the position of underdeveloped economies in the international system reveal similarities with the structuralist analysis of the same phenomenon, yet the two analyses are certainly not identical. The neo-Marxist paradigm employs a class analysis to determine the causes of continuing underdevelopment, while the concept of the 'economic surplus' also plays a central role, although the interpretation given to this concept is no longer that used by Marx.[42] In the structuralist paradigm existing economic structures are the immediate cause of underdevelopment, but in the neo-Marxist paradigm the existing pattern of class control over the disposition of the surplus is the immediate cause.

A fundamental difference between the two perspectives also emerges when it comes to the conclusions which they generate. Most members of the structuralist school have aimed to play an active part in influencing policy design in underdeveloped countries, trying to achieve policy reforms within individual countries and within the international economic system. As has been shown, from the 1940s to the 1960s they emphasised import substitution as the means to structural change and economic development. Neo-Marxists conclude that the path to development within the international capitalist system is blocked for underdeveloped countries. If economic development is to occur, the masses must replace the existing ruling class alliances in the countries of the periphery, take control of the economic surplus and move immediately to a socialist development path, withdrawing from the international capitalist system. As Little (1982: 219) notes, this conclusion is also in stark contrast to Marx's conclusion that capitalism (and its ultimate collapse) is almost certainly a necessary and inevitable stage on the road to socialism.[43]

Dependency theories

Neo-Marxist theory has been subject to criticism both from other Marxists and from non-Marxists. Throughout the 1970s these critics were able to mobilise a growing quantity of evidence to question the empirical validity of the neo-Marxist paradigm. That is to say, they were able to point to a growing number of countries in the Third World which had experienced very respectable rates of capital accumulation over quite prolonged periods of time.[44] There remained none the less considerable disquiet amongst neo-Marxists concerning the nature of the economic changes taking place in the countries of the periphery. Yet, confronted with the evidence of high growth rates in some of these countries, they were forced to concede that some form of capitalist accumulation, associated with expanding industrial production, was taking place.

Frank and Amin, both influential neo-Marxists, responded to this criticism partly by emphasising a concept already present, although not strongly highlighted, in some of the earlier work written from a neo-Marxist perspective – the concept of dependence. The argument now given prominence was that while industrial growth had indeed occurred in some countries of the periphery, this growth had particular undesirable features that distinguished it from economic growth in industrially advanced countries. Specifically, such growth was not generated by an autonomous indigenous capitalist class within these economies and, indeed, the latter remained incapable of generating their own internal growth dynamic. Rather, the underdeveloped economies remained dependent on the world metropolitan economies for access to markets, finance and, above all, technology. As a result, and as a result also of the continuing class alliance between the *comprador* bourgeoisie of the periphery and the metropolitan bourgeoisie, the latter continue to determine the pattern of change in the periphery. The conclusion is still that the only route to full autonomous development is via socialist revolution (see e.g. Frank, 1978).

However, neo-Marxists were not alone in focusing on international dependency in the 1970s. From the late 1960s there emerged from several different schools of thought a cluster of theoretical analyses, all of which focused upon the extent and significance of the international dependence of Third World economies. One of these groups of analyses was undertaken by analysts from the structuralist school. These reflect a strong sense of disillusion with the consequences of import-substituting industrialisation. They were written at a time when not only had most Latin American countries exhausted the easy opportunities for import-substituting industrialisation, but there was also growing disenchantment with the dominance of this process by multinational corporations.

Both the neo-Marxist and the structuralist dependency theorists attempt to provide a basic framework from which the analysis of dependence, and its implications for development and underdevelopment, can proceed. The neo-Marxists do this largely by incorporating the concept of dependent industrial development into their evolving analytical perspective. In the 1970s the latter, while still using many of the tools and concepts developed by the neo-Marxists in the 1960s, was focused upon explaining the evolution and *modus operandi* of the capitalist system as a whole, rather than just the causes of underdevelopment in the periphery. The structuralists, meanwhile, sought to achieve the same end by identifying a primary case of economic dependence (the cultural dependence of the élite in the case of Furtado, 1973; multinational corporations in Sunkel, 1973), and by then tracing the manner in which, through a series of causal linkages, economic dependence is created (see Chapter 7).

Meanwhile, however, during the 1970s a body of literature also developed based on the thesis that not only is dependent development possible and, in some countries, occurring, but that this may also lead to the breaking of existing dependency relations. This is the theme of Cardoso and Faletto, 1979. Warren (1973 and 1980) develops a similar theme, arguing that changes have been taking place in the international economic and political system that are conducive both to industrialisation in at least parts of the periphery and to a shift in the balance of international (inter-) dependence.

Thus, while from the late 1960s dependence became a focus of study, no single perspective on its significance emerged. (Cf. Palma, 1978, revised and reprinted in Seers, 1981, who argues this same point at length.) Nor, indeed, did any one of the perspectives from which dependency was studied both during the 1970s and subsequently generate a major new analytical framework for the interpretation of the causalities of development and underdevelopment, however defined. Yet none the less, as will be shown in Chapter 7, the focus on the concept of dependency did serve to draw attention to a number of factors which can constrain the degree of autonomy faced by less developed countries in the choice of development strategy.

The revival of the neo-classical paradigm[4][5]

In the latter part of the 1960s, neo-classical theorists initiated a major critique of the policy recommendations of the structuralist school. This was the 'rightist' counterpart to the neo-Marxist attack on received development theories. But whereas the neo-Marxists were preoccupied chiefly with the class distribution of control over, and use of, the surplus, the neo-classical theorists were preoccupied with efficiency in resource allocation and its implications for growth.

The main focus of the neo-classical critique was the programme of import-substituting industrialisation that had been followed by most politically independent underdeveloped countries. By the mid-1960s it was clear that a number of countries were experiencing a slowing down in their rates of industrial growth, and of GDP as a whole, as the easy opportunities for import substitution were exhausted. Simultaneously a number of problems were emerging which suggested that any intensification of existing policies could be counterproductive – merely exacerbating the tendency for the pace of growth and structural change to decline. Most notable of these problems, which were now becoming serious constraints upon further advance, were a worsening balance of payments combined with rising shortfalls in domestic food production (which contributed to the foreign exchange shortages), domestic inflation and an unwillingness on the part of industrial firms in the larger underdeveloped economies to support backward-linked import substitution by switching their purchases of intermediate and capital goods from overseas suppliers to domestic producers.

The dominant theme of neo-classical critiques of import-substituting industrialisation was that policy-makers should have paid greater attention to promoting a structure of prices which gave producers a true indication of the relative opportunity cost of resources, rather than using a mixture of selective import controls together with underpricing of both foreign exchange and bank credit to encourage industrial investment.[46] There would then have been far less short-run inefficiency, exports might have expanded and the pace of growth might have been sustained.

In the face of growing concern about income distribution it was also claimed that prices which more accurately reflected the relative scarcity of labour and capital would help to expand employment opportunities and, hence, the incomes of the poor.

From the late 1960s the neo-classical critique was complemented at the micro-economic level by a growing volume of literature on cost-benefit analysis, designed to contribute to greater efficiency in investment decisions. This literature acknowledged market failure in a number of key areas (for instance the failure of the supply price of labour from the traditional sector to reflect its true social opportunity cost), and emphasised the need for adjustment for both market failure and government-induced market distortion through the correct estimation of shadow prices.[47] In other words, the underlying thesis was that neo-classical principles could, and should, be used to govern resource allocation even where the market did not conform to the perfectly competitive characteristics assumed in neo-classical general equilibrium models.[48]

In the late 1970s the pace of revival of the neo-classical paradigm in development theory received a temporary set-back as attention was diverted to proposals for meeting basic needs (although neo-classical theorists were among the critics of these proposals). However, in the 1980s the neo-classical revival gathered renewed vigour. 1981 saw the publication by the World Bank of *Accelerated Development in Sub-Saharan Africa*, a widely circulated and influential report that emphasised the importance of correct pricing policies and reduced government intervention in economic activities as two of the main keys to a revival in African growth rates. The neo-classical revival was reinforced in the early 1980s by the increase in applications from developing countries to the International Monetary Fund for assistance with stabilisation and structural adjustment programmes. The terms on which the Fund provides assistance, which emphasise not only control of the money supply but removal of price distortions (including that of foreign exchange) and the freeing of markets from public sector interventionism, are underpinned by the neo-classical paradigm.[49]

The foregoing paragraphs already indicate a particular difficulty that arises in analysing the neo-classical contribution to the development debate: many of the contributions focus on particular issues, such as the optimal forms of adjustment for domestic price distortions, investment appraisal or stabilisation policy. It is rare for a neo-classical theorist to begin a contribution to the development debate from what, from the perspective of this book, might be regarded as a statement of first principles – for example, with a definition of development. On the one hand, the first principles of neo-classical theory are taken as given (i.e. already known) and, on the other, many neo-classical welfare economists regard it as the task of governments, not economists, to set development objectives. They claim that what they can offer is guidance on the most efficient means of reaching these. None the less it is widely held that there are identifiable values and beliefs, including certain presumptions about key economic objectives, that underlie the various neo-classical contributions to the development debate. Chapter 10 will seek to identify these before turning to the specific contributions in the areas just noted.

Now, however, further contributions to the development debate in the 1970s will be considered. These, unlike the neo-classical approach, did give particular and explicit emphasis to the interpretation of development.

THE REDEFINITION OF DEVELOPMENT

In the late 1960s and early 1970s, neo-Marxist class-based analyses of the causes of the perpetuation of mass poverty in the Third World had a widespread appeal, particularly among young social scientists. However, they were not the only ones to be preoccupied by the problem of continuing widespread poverty. The fact that the fruits of development over the preceding decade had been unevenly distributed was widely acknowledged. Among some economists it was accepted that an increase in inequality was inevitable in the early stages of economic growth, to be followed later by a tendency towards greater equality when wages are bid up after surplus labour has been absorbed.[50] Others, however, were dissatisfied with this argument, while at the same time they were unwilling to accept the political conclusion of the neo-Marxists. Their unwillingness to accept the inevitability of growing inequality in the early stages of growth stemmed from a variety of factors both humanitarian and political – concern to contain mass discontent and pre-empt political violence, and misgivings concerning the length of time for which poor countries might expect to experience growth combined with growing inequality and continuing mass poverty. Some also questioned the inevitability of a trade-off between growth and equity.

Discussion of these issues was pursued in various fora including both academic institutions and certain branches of the United Nations, most notably the International Labour Office (ILO). Out of this debate there emerged during the early and mid-1970s a number of key publications which reflected the evolution of thinking amongst this group of economists. Three of these publications were widely noted. Seers 1972 argued that development should be reinterpreted to take account of trends not only in growth but in poverty, income distribution and employment. The 1972 ILO Kenya report identified the 'informal sector' (consisting of very small-scale labour intensive enterprises) as an important potential source both of output growth, and of employment and productivity gains for the working poor. None the less, the report accepted that a transfer of resources from the rich in order to promote small-scale productive investment by the poor would entail a trade-off between growth and equity; the authors made the conventional assumption that the marginal savings rate of the rich and middle income groups (partly enforced through taxation) is high, while the poor save little.[51] Two years later a team drawn from the World Bank and the Institute of Development Studies (IDS) at Sussex published *Redistribution with Growth* (Chenery *et al.*, 1974). This collection of papers was clearly intended to provide the analytical foundations for a new approach to development analysis and planning. Seers' definition of development was endorsed, and a more sophisticated version of the quantitative model of redistribution with growth contained in the Kenya report was presented. This again assumed different savings rates for rich and poor and, consequently, also endorsed the conclusion of a trade-off between the rate of growth of GDP and greater equity. The authors of *Redistribution with Growth* also explore in depth the measurement and policy implications of the new definition of development – what sorts of uses of redistributed resources would minimise the growth/equity trade-off which they regard as inevitable.

Lefeber on redistribution *for* growth

In 1974 there also appeared in print a paper which reached a smaller audience than those already cited, but which arguably merited a readership at least as wide. This was Lefeber's 'On the paradigm for economic development'. Lefeber's more radical paper argued the logic for a new perception of the development process. His case rests not so much on equity as on the need to sustain the growth process itself. In the structuralist tradition, Lefeber emphasises the demand constraint to growth and reaffirms that this must be overcome internally. However, writing at a time when in many underdeveloped countries the phase of rapid industrial growth based on import substitution was drawing to a halt,[52] he argues that if the demand needed to support growth and industrialisation is to be generated internally, this can only be achieved by first raising output and incomes in that sector which still contains the majority of the Third World's population – agriculture.[53] Yet there is also a demand constraint to the expansion of agricultural output. The upper income groups have a low income elasticity of demand for food, while the poor cannot afford to pay for it. Hence the generation of a sufficient volume of effective demand depends on the redistribution of income towards those in the rural sector who have a high marginal propensity to consume food, as well as other locally produced goods – the rural poor.[54] Furthermore, if growth is to be sustained, not only should the existing agricultural demand constraint be overcome, but the foundations must be laid for the steady expansion of demand. In future industry must serve agriculture, providing it with the improved inputs and equipment needed to generate further increases in income and demand.

Lefeber argued that in overpopulated underdeveloped countries the most effective means of combining income redistribution with output expansion (rather than simply generating a one-off increase in consumption demand) would be through the redistribution of land rights and the creation of a communal framework of rural production along Chinese lines. With India in particular in mind, Lefeber reasons that the prohibitively high budgetary costs of large-scale public works projects, however productive, combined with distributional problems pertaining to who would benefit from public works in irrigation and land drainage where land is privately owned, both militate in favour of communal land ownership and communal labour mobilisation. In reaching this conclusion Lefeber reflected a growing interest in the Chinese experience amongst development economists at this time. This was heightened by the growth in concern that in most Third World countries industrialisation had over the 1950s and 1960s proved highly inegalitarian and that industrial growth was in any case slowing down due both to lack of foreign exchange and inadequate domestic demand.

THE THEORISATION OF THE CHINESE DEVELOPMENT EXPERIENCE, 1949–1976: 'THE MAOIST PARADIGM'

We have just seen that during the 1970s a growing interest developed in the West in the Chinese experience of growth and development after the revolution in 1949. The fact that the Chinese appeared to have succeeded in combining growth and structural change with improvements in mass welfare made the Chinese development experience of particular interest. (There were of course also other political and economic reasons for the growth of interest in China, in particular the decision of the Chinese authorities in the early 1970s that China should play a greater role in the international arena.[55])

It is widely agreed, and was already acknowledged by China scholars in the 1970s, that the policies pursued in China from 1949–1976 were not consistent. Partly for this reason, and partly for the standard reason associated with all social theorising – that one cannot in theory reproduce the whole of reality, but only what are perceived to be certain key elements of it – the theorisation of a dominant development perspective that prevailed in China during this period inevitably entails a degree of simplification and selectivity. Many sinologists at this time were, as we have seen, impressed by China's development performance, and their theorisation of the dominant perspective reflects this favourable impression. More recent, and less sympathetic, critiques of policy and performance in the Maoist era have, as we shall see, tended to interpret this performance in a different light.

Meanwhile, the question arises, why in this present study should one review a particular interpretation of development policy in a particular country and a particular period. There are at least four objections to doing so: that the philosophy, policies and development experience concerned are country-specific; that this 'package' is not replicable elsewhere; that one might equally well study other country and/or leader specific approaches to development, such as Castroism; and that the development perspective concerned has insufficient economic theoretical content to justify its inclusion in the present study.

Against these points, however, there are a number of countervailing arguments. In so far as one can accurately specify a dominant perspective that guided policy formation in China at this time, it is one that directly affected the lives of over one quarter of the population of the Third World. The approach followed in this period achieved some notable successes, starting from a very poor resource base in terms of cultivable land and physical capital. Elements of the policy innovations introduced in China *have* proved replicable elsewhere, even though the approach followed in its entirety is not duplicatable. What is often referred to as the 'Maoist perspective' is not totally devoid of economic theoretical content, and that content includes some significant innovations as compared to other earlier contributions to economic development theory. This perspective presents an integrated view of social, political, ideological and economic change, and this arguably adds to its interest value given that other intellectual approaches to economic development have been criticised for giving insufficient attention to these issues. Lastly, elements of what is often referred to as the 'Maoist perpective', as this was theorised in the 1970s, and of Chinese 1949–76 development experience influenced some of the subsequent attempts to theorise a more generally applicable 'basic needs first' approach to development.

The interpretation of the Maoist view of the nature of socio-economic development and of how this can be achieved will be reviewed in greater detail in Chapter 8. However, it can be summarised as follows:

1. The ultimate aim of economic development is to achieve material abundance with income differentials abolished and all productive property socially owned and operated.
2. To achieve progress towards this goal it is necessary to simultaneously build up the economy's productive capacity and to socialise the production process by moving towards social ownership of the means of production and social control of production decisions and distribution of the product.
3. In the development of productive capacity the build-up of modern heavy industry plays a central role.[56]
4. However, expansion of different branches of production (heavy industry, light industry, agriculture) as well as the emphasis given to different scales of plant, using different technologies, and to the rural-urban distribution of these, are all perceived to be interlinked. It is necessary to search for that set of relative emphases (varying over time) in resource mobilisation and allocation which will maximise the overall

rate of capital accumulation while providing for a sufficient increase in mass welfare to maintain support for socialist transformation.

5. The expansion of small-scale heavy and light industry in rural areas can serve both to increase the rate of surplus mobilisation for state investment in heavy industry and to increase mass welfare. It raises the surplus through
   (a) mobilisation of slack resources for productive use;
   (b) the short gestation and capital cost recovery periods for investment in small-scale industry, after which a part of the value of the increased output can be mobilised by the state.

   Expansion of small- and medium-scale rural industry can increase mass welfare through its direct and indirect contributions to expanding employment and labour productivity (indirect via the production of producer goods such as farm implements), and through expansion of the supply of basic consumption goods. Such industries also contribute to human capital formation through the development of technical skills.

6. In the rural sector seasonally slack labour can and should also be mobilised for labour-intensive capital formation.

7. Concerning economic equity and economic incentives:
   (a) economic and political equality between regions should be promoted by
       (i) promoting regional self-sufficiency in heavy and light industry and in basic food-stuffs;
       (ii) giving greater power in decision-taking to the regions;
   (b) income differences between persons should be minimised as fast as possible, but not faster than the masses are prepared to accept. As a part of this process reliance on material incentives should be steadily reduced;
   (c) professionals should work among the masses, learn from them about their needs and use their skills towards helping to overcome concrete difficulties.

During the 1970s the Chinese authorities released a growing volume of data on development performance. Among the data on China's development performance that received emphasis in the West were not only those for the growth of GDP and modern industry, but those for food-grain production per capita and for the development of small- and medium-scale rural industries which provided extra employment and income to the rural population while producing both agricultural inputs and basic consumer goods.[57]

BASIC NEEDS APPROACHES TO DEVELOPMENT

The same preoccupation with growing economic inequality within Third World countries that contributed to Western interest in the Chinese experience resulted also in the articulation in the late 1970s and early 1980s of basic needs oriented approaches to the formulation of development targets and policy. These emerged from a growing concern, manifest in the literature from the mid-1970s, that policies of redistribution with growth might not be sufficient to guarantee an increase in welfare for the poorest of the 800 million or so people estimated to be living in absolute poverty, mostly in developing countries.[58] There was a preoccupation, *inter alia*, that redistributive policies would be focused chiefly on the least badly-off of the poor – those whose incomes could most easily be raised above the poverty line (see e.g. Singer, 1979). During the mid-1970s a growing body of evidence on the extent of mass poverty in much of the Third World became available. The impact of such evidence in the West was probably increased by the reports of widespread human and livestock deaths from famine during the 1973–4 Sahel drought.

In 1976 the ILO attempted to increase the national and international emphasis given to poverty alleviation. In his report to the 1976 World Employment Conference the ILO Director-General proposed that all countries should give priority to the meeting of the basic needs of all members of their populations by the year 2000, such needs being defined to include the minimal consumption requirements needed for a physically healthy population, certain minimal standards of access to public services and amenities, access by the poor to employment opportunities which would enable them to achieve a target minimum income, and the right to participate in decisions that affect the lives and livelihood of the people. The proposal that all governments should work to ensure that these needs be universally met by the year 2000 was endorsed unanimously by the delegates of all the member states of the ILO. The conference also endorsed the outlines of a Programme of Action both for national governments and the ILO itself to promote attainment of the target.

As will be shown in Chapter 9, the early proposals for meeting basic needs encountered a wide range of criticisms. These included criticisms of the feasibility of the objective, of its implications for growth and structural change, of the motives of many of the national governments that endorsed the proposal, and of the nature of the economic analysis used to support it, *inter alia*. These early criticisms prompted further work, partly by the staff and associates of the World Employment Programme, designed to examine in greater depth the resource implications of, and the case for, acceptance of this priority. In the subsequent literature there emerged certain differences of emphasis and interpretation. Some analysts, including several associated with the World Bank, concentrated on arguing the case for, and assessing the resource costs of, improved public service provision chiefly in education and health care, justifying this as investment in human capital. Others took a broader and more radical view of what was entailed in a 'basic needs first' strategy, arguing that the latter incorporates, but goes beyond, improved public service provision. Emphasising the need also to raise directly the incomes of the working poor, these analysts explored the nature of, and the case for, a comprehensive 'basic needs first' strategy. In justifying this they argued that not only was there no need for a growth:equity trade-off, but that a 'basic needs first' approach to development could provide the basis for faster and more self-sustained growth. It is from these contributions to the debate that it can be argued that a 'basic needs paradigm' has emerged. Following Lefeber (1974), a central element of the theoretical core of this paradigm is that the expansion of a homogeneous mass market is likely to promote faster long-term growth and structural change than is the concentration of expanding demand in the upper income bracket, for the latter has a much higher direct and indirect import content than the former. The paradigm has much in common with Lefeber's earlier proposal (although this is not widely cited, and may not have been seen by all the later contributors to the debate). This perspective is also clearly influenced by Western interpretations of the 'Maoist paradigm' and Chinese development strategy. However, it is argued by proponents of the 'basic needs first paradigm' that growth combined with absolute poverty elimination can be achieved also in market economy underdeveloped countries, Taiwan and South Korea being cited as examples.

Summary of the basic needs paradigm

The main elements of the basic needs paradigm can be summarised as follows:

1. Economic development includes not merely economic growth but steady, measurable progress towards absolute poverty elimination and a sustained expansion in the employment opportunities and incomes of the poor.
2. A 'basic needs first' development strategy can lay more effective foundations for sustained growth than any other strategy.
3. This is primarily because of its impact on the structure of domestic demand and the associated inducement to invest.
4. Among the range of consequences that flow from the restructuring of domestic demand that is entailed in a basic needs first strategy are an easing of the two dominant constraints encountered by traditional strategies of import-substituting industrialisation – the domestic demand constraint and the balance of payments constraint.
5. A redistribution of resources towards the poor would also both increase the productive mobilisation of at present untapped small-scale savings potential, and provide opportunities to tap and develop the technical and innovatory skills of the labour force.
6. In addition to the foregoing, in agriculture an expansion of small-scale labour-intensive farming could lead to greater efficiency of land use,

reduced use of imported machinery, and reduced food imports (and/or increased agricultural exports).

7. Compared with development strategies based on unequal income distribution, this pattern of development is likely to promote more effectively the development of capital and intermediate goods production within developing countries. Some of this would be achieved by small- to medium-scale relatively labour-intensive methods. However, where large-scale capital-intensive investments remain essential, foreign exchange savings in other branches would increase the supply of this resource to finance essential imports.

8. Such a strategy can be expected to help to promote trade between developing countries as more goods appropriate to their needs are produced by them.

9. Meanwhile, the rate of expansion of essential services can also be accelerated by greater and more imaginative use of low-cost, often labour-intensive, methods of capital construction and service provision.

In contrast to the paradigm of the expanding capitalist nucleus, this paradigm emphasises the high marginal propensity to save of the *petite bourgeoisie*, the small-scale producers who often work in their own enterprises and tend to use labour-intensive production methods. Meanwhile, while there are significant structuralist elements in the analytical methodology embodied in this paradigm, this interpretation of development and of its key causalities differs markedly from classical structuralism.

The main policy recommendations that follow from the basic needs paradigm concern the following:

1. Removal of the legal, institutional and financial impediments which discriminate against the expansion of small-scale and labour-intensive production.

2. Use of a package of policy instruments to promote small farm production (land reform, agricultural research, extension, credit, marketing).

3. Commitment of more resources to research on the development of small-scale, labour-intensive production technologies in all sectors in which these are likely to be efficient.

4. Expansion, and revision of the technologies and methods, of public service provision, in order to reach the poor more effectively.

While the paradigm of the expanding capitalist nucleus is a paradigm of capital concentration, the basic needs paradigm is a paradigm of capital dispersal.

The debate on meeting basic needs initiated in the mid-1970s has served to reinforce concern to raise the welfare of the poor in the Third World. However, with the revival of the influence of the neo-classical paradigm in the 1980s, and with major policy changes in China, both the Maoist paradigm and the basic needs paradigm have declined in influence and appeal, for various reasons. In the case of the former, these range from criticism of Maoism for generating inefficiencies in resource use to its advocacy of 'utopian socialism'. In the case of the basic needs paradigm, criticisms range from the perceived costs in reduced growth of a comprehensive basic needs strategy to, probably the most telling criticism of all, its political non-viability in most developing countries. Currently it is advocacy of a more modest approach to meeting basic needs – public service provision justified as investment in human capital – that predominates. The arguments for this are presented, as we shall see in Chapter 9, in a manner apparently intended to be compatible with the neo-classical perspective. Meanwhile, in the mid- and late 1980s, substantial criticism of the policy recommendations of the neo-classical school continue to stem from the structuralists in particular, some of whom have modified their interpretation of development to incorporate a concern with meeting basic needs.

CONCLUSION

At the time of writing, the second half of the 1980s, the sub-discipline of development economics still lacks a generally received paradigm. Since the mid-1970s there has been a minor spate of retrospective writing, reviewing both trends in development theory and the current state of the discipline, as a result of which there has been some increase in readiness to acknowledge the contribution made by different analytical perspectives.[59] Certainly, however, none of these has achieved unequivocal dominance. Nor, as Hirschman observes, has a new synthesis yet emerged.

Instead, while the debates of the 1970s continue, two new themes have come increasingly to the fore, which leave the theoretical debate wide open. First, some economists have revived the early emphasis of writers such as Leibenstein and Myint on the importance of non-economic factors in the development process.[60] Secondly, analysts of all ideological persuasions are increasingly agreed that that basic construct sought by theorists from the 1940s to the 1960s, the 'typical underdeveloped country', simply does not exist. Increasingly it is being emphasised that the circumstances – economic, political and social – of each underdeveloped economy vary, and that the appropriate path of economic and political development cannot be determined a priori, but only in the context of these specific conditions. At most one can seek to theorise in terms of groups of countries with similar conditions[61] and key characteristics.

While harking back to some of the early writings of the 1950s in his emphasis on the relevance of non-economic variables (sociological, political, cultural, moral) to the economic development process, Bruton (1985) sees the key to the way forward as lying in certain *processes* which each economy must undertake within the constraints and opportunities presented by its own specific conditions. The processes he emphasises – search, learning and choice – are more abstract and open-ended than previous specifications of the key to development.

However, such theorisation, and the search for development options emphasised by Bruno, are unlikely to be undertaken *de novo*. Whether consciously or unconsciously, they are likely to be informed by elements of one or more of the analytical perspectives that have already been applied in development economics. Given these facts, the present study has two purposes: firstly, to analyse the essential elements of the main perspectives that have, and do, dominate the economic development debate, and, secondly, to establish the bases of the main areas of incompatibility between them, as well as any potentially complementary elements. For these different approaches are not invariably exclusive. In some cases they are, but in others they deal with a distinct, or partially overlapping, range of issues and may be seen as containing potentially complementary elements. That this is so arises partly due to the diversity of interpretations of development that the different approaches employ, and partly due to their focus on different key causalities.

This is not to say that incorporation of elements of one perspective into another would not alter the latter, for clearly it would; but sometimes such incorporation is logically possible and may serve, in the minds of some, to enrich a particular perspective. Such incorporation may entail a modification of the interpretation given to development itself, but this is not necessarily so. The issues of incompatibility and complementarity are explored in Chapter 11, after a more detailed analysis of the individual perspectives and of the main criticisms to which they have given rise.

Finally, a word of warning: one should not necessarily try to classify all important elements of the debate on development under one or other of a limited number of paradigm headings. Apart from anything else, unduly extreme deference to classification can lead to a most unfruitful intellectual rigidity. The merit of classification is simply that it can help to clarify what otherwise seems at times a confused mass of contradictions (and sometimes unanticipated agreement) between analyses which all purport to be concerned with closely-related issues. Such clarification, to be successful, must spell out the underlying values and assumptions and the internal logic of each of the main lines of reasoning. This will be attempted in more detail in later chapters.

NOTES

1. This term was coined in 1952 by the demographer and economic historian Alfred Sauvy on the model of the Abbé Siéyè's revolutionary *Tiers Etat* of 1789 (see Love, 1980: 56).

2. A further range of recent publications have this objective but do not attempt an historical overview; see e.g. Lewis, 1984.
3. Thus their classification is: structuralist, neo-Marxist and neo-classical.
4. See also Streeten, 1981: 101.
5. Preston, 1982: 41 *et seq.* and Seers, 1979: 708.
6. See Masterman in Lakatos and Musgrave, 1970: 74; see also Kuhn, 1970: 13 and Chapter 1 above.
7. Although Lewis and Myint came from the West Indies and Burma respectively, both these economists were based at this time in Britain.
8. Two notable sceptics in this regard were Peter Bauer and Basil Yamey.
9. See p. 44 above.
10. Love, *op. cit.*: 48.
11. See Love, *op.cit.*: 51.
12. *Ibid.*: 55. See also Prebisch, 1962.
13. *Ibid.*: 50,1.
14. *Ibid.*: 58. See also Singer, 1950.
15. The analytical contribution of Myrdal is discussed briefly below: see pp. 58–9.
16. For an alternative account of the origins of structuralism which gives less weight to the ECLA contribution see Chenery *op.cit.*
17. See Preston, 1982: 145, 6.
18. Seers, *op.cit.*
19. See e.g. Rosenstein-Rodan, 1943, Hansen, 1945, and Rostow, *op.cit.*; also Little and Clifford, 1965: Chapter 1, and Preston, 1982: Chapter 4.
20. See Chapter 2, pp. 12–13.
21. See Hirchman, 1958: Chapter 2. See also Myint, 1954: 157 and Rostow, 1953: 88–96.
22. Myrdal, 1957: 9.
23. See p. 46.
24. See Nurkse, 1952 (reprinted in Agarwala and Singh, 1958) for a succinct statement of the essence of Nurkse's thesis. Nurkse, 1953, provides a more elaborate exposition; it also includes a statement of Nurkse's views on the scope for labour-intensive capital formation in underdeveloped countries. (A useful idea of the scope and focus of early work in development economics can be obtained from the classic set of readings collated by Agarwala and Singh. The readings include examples of work which reflect various schools of thought, but particularly well represented is the work of non-Marxist economists working in the United States and Western Europe.)
25. See Chapter 2, pp. 10–13.
26. The case in which a firm benefits from the labour market created by the establishment of other firms is probably the most widely cited example of an industrial external economy; cf. Scitovsky, 1954, reprinted in Agarwala and Singh, *op.cit.*: 299.
27. Rosenstein-Rodan, reprinted in Agarwala and Singh, *op.cit.*: 249.
28. Implicitly, Rosenstein-Rodan seems to have assumed that any expansion of primary production in Eastern and South-eastern Europe would occur chiefly through labour productivity gains. Industrialisation was necessary to absorb underemployed labour.
29. See pp. 53–4 above.
30. The quotations in this section are all from Nurkse's 1952 article. His ideas are developed at greater length in a book published one year later. Nurkse notes that two economies, Japan and Soviet Russia, minimised the international operation of the Duesenberry effect through radical isolation of their economies during the early phases of industrialisation.

31. Leibenstein, 1957: 15–17.
32. See Leibenstein, *op.cit.*: 96 and 106.
33. *Ibid.*: 111.
34. See the section on unbalanced growth, pp. 60–61.
35. See Furtado, 1954, reprinted in Agarwala and Singh, *op.cit.*: 309 *et seq.*
36. Myint notes the potentially contradictory role of trade unions as expanders of effective demand on the one hand, but as a source of increased costs on the other.
37. See Hirschman, *op.cit.*: 206, 7.
38. *Ibid.*: 109, 110 and 112.
39. Bauer and Yamey, 1957: 77.
40. *Ibid.*: 91–101.
41. See, for example, *ibid.*: 153 and 156. The contribution of Bauer and Yamey to development theory is discussed further in Chapter 10.
42. In Marx's own work the rate of surplus value is given by the ratio of surplus labour to necessary labour used in production. Baran in fact introduced two broader interpretations of economic surplus into his analysis of underdevelopment and these have been widely adopted by other neo-Marxists. The most commonly used interpretation is that which, as noted above, defines the actual economic surplus as the difference between the total domestic output of an economy and the actual consumption of its residents; the second defines the potential surplus as the difference between total output and essential consumption.
43. See Palma in Seers, 1981: 23–27 and 30–31 for a review of Marx's writing on this with specific reference to backward regions.
44. See e.g. Warren, 1973 and 1980; see also Chapter 6, pp. 190–1.
45. A summary of this paradigm is provided in Chapter 2, pp. 31–4.
46. See e.g. Little, Scitovsky and Scott, 1970 and McKinnon, 1973.
47. See e.g. Little and Mirrlees, 1974 and Little, 1982: 25.
48. However, shadow pricing as a basis for public sector investment decisions remains controversial. See Rudra, 1972 and Chapter 10 below.
49. See Khan and Knight, 1981.
50. See Kuznets, 1955 and 1963, Oshima, 1962 and Paukert, 1973, for the main studies that provided the basis for this belief.
51. In the report's quantitative model the poor save nothing. ILO, 1972: 369.
52. Cf. the quotation from Palma on p. 208 below.
53. Lefeber in Mitra (ed.) 1974: 166 and 174.
54. *Ibid.*: 168–170.
55. President Nixon visited China in 1972, the first United States President to do so. During the 1970s China both substantially expanded her foreign trade and embarked upon a number of joint investment ventures with foreign companies.
56. Heavy industries are those which produce capital and intermediate goods. Their main components are mining, cement production, power production, steel and machinery and petro-chemicals.
57. See e.g. Paine, 1976, Singh, 1979 and Magdoff, 1975.
58. Estimates of the numbers living in absolute poverty varied. This is the figure given by MacNamara, 1973.
59. See in particular Hirschman, 1982; also Killick, 1978: Chapter 2, and Little, 1982.
60. See e.g. Seers, 1979 and Bruton, 1985.
61. See e.g. Cardoso and Faletto, 1979 and Bruton, *op.cit.*

REFERENCES

Baran, P., *The Political Economy of Growth*, (Monthly Review Press, 1957; reprinted with new Foreword, 1962).

Bauer, P. and Yamey, B., *The Economics of Underdeveloped Countries*, (Cambridge, 1957).

Bruton, H., 'The search for a development economics', *World Development*, (Vol. 13, No. 10/11, October/November 1985).

Cardoso, F. and Faletto, E., *Dependency and Development in Latin America*, (University of California, 1979; first published in Spanish in 1971).

Chenery, H., 'The structuralist approach to development policy', *American Economic Review*, (Papers and Proceedings, May 1975).

Chenery, H. *et al.*, *Redistribution with Growth*, (Oxford, 1974).

Chilcote, R. and Johnson, D. *Theories of Development*, (Sage Publications, 1983).

Duesenberry, J., *Income, Saving and the Theory of Consumer Behaviour*, (Harvard, 1949).

Emmanuel, A., *Unequal Exchange*, (New Left Books, 1972; first published as *L'Echange Inégal*, François Maspero, 1969).

Foster-Carter, A., 'From Rostow to Gunder Frank: conflicting paradigms in the analysis of underdevelopment', *World Development*, (Vol. 4, No. 3, March 1976).

Frank, A. G., *Capitalism and Underdevelopment in Latin America: Historical Studies of Chile and Brazil*, (Monthly Review Press, 1967; revised edition, 1969).

Frank, A. G., *Dependent Accumulation and Underdevelopment*, (Macmillan, 1978).

Furtado, C., 'Capital formation and economic development', *International Economic Papers*, No. 4, (1954); reprinted in *The Economics of Underdevelopment*, eds. Agarwala, A. and Singh, S., (Oxford, 1958).

Furtado, C., *Development and Underdevelopment*, (University of California, 1964; translated from *Desenvolvimento y Subdesenvolvimento*, Editora Fundo de Cultura, Rio de Janeiro, 1961).

Furtado, C., 'Underdevelopment and dependence: the fundamental connections', Seminar Paper, (Centre of Latin American Studies, Cambridge University, November 1973).

Hansen, A. H., *America's Role in the World Economy*, (Allen and Unwin, 1945).

Hirschman, A., *The Strategy of Economic Development*, (Yale, 1958).

Hirschman, A., 'The rise and decline of development economics' in Hirschman, A., *Essays in Trespassing: Economics to Politics and Beyond*, (Cambridge, 1981); also in *The Theory and Experience of Economic Development*, eds. Gersovitz, M. *et al.*, (Allen and Unwin, 1982).

IDS (Sussex) Bulletin, *Sub-Saharan Africa: Getting the Facts Straight*, Vol. 16 No. 3, (July 1985).

International Labour Office, *Employment, Incomes and Equality: A Strategy for Increasing Productive Employment in Kenya*, (ILO, Geneva, 1972).

International Labour Office, *Employment, Growth and Basic Needs: A One-World Problem*, (ILO Geneva, 1976; second edition 1978).

Khan, M. and Knight, M., 'Stabilisation programs in developing countries: a formal framework', *IMF Staff Papers*, (1981).

Killick,T., *Development Economics in Action*, (Heinemann, 1978).

Kitching, G., *Development and Underdevelopment in Historical Perspective: Populism, Nationalism and Industrialisation*, (Methuen, 1982).

Kuhn, T., *The Structure of Scientific Revolutions*, (2nd edition, University of Chicago, 1970).

Kuznets, S., 'Economic growth and inequality', *American Economic Review* (March 1955).

Kuznets, S., 'Quantitative aspects of the economic growth of nations: VIII distribution of income by size', *Economic Development and Cultural Change*, (January 1963, Part II).

Leeson, P., *Development Economics and its Companions*, Manchester Discussion Papers in Development Studies, Discussion Paper No. 8304, (Manchester University International Development Centre, 1983).

Leeson, P., 'Development economics and its companions' in *Perspectives on Development*, eds., Leeson, P. and Minlogue, M., (Manchester University Press, 1988).

Lefeber, L., 'On the paradigm for economic development', in *Economic Theory and Planning*, ed. Mitra, A., (Oxford, 1974).

Leibenstein, H., *Economic Backwardness and Economic Growth*, (Wiley, 1957).

Lewis, W. A., 'Economic development with unlimited supplies of labour', *Manchester School*, (May 1954); reprinted in *The Economics of Underdevelopment*, eds. Agarwala, A. and Singh, S., (Oxford, 1963).

Lewis, W. A., 'The state of development theory', *American Economic Review*, (Vol. 74, No. 1, March 1984).

Little, I., *Economic Development: Theory, Policy and International Relations*, (Basic Books, 1982).

Little, I. and Clifford, J., *International Aid*, (Allen and Unwin, 1965).

Little, I. and Mirrlees, J., *Project Appraisal and Planning for Developing Countries*, (Heinemann, 1974).

Little, I., Scitovsky, T. and Scott, M., *Industry and Trade in Some Developing Countries*, (Oxford, 1970).

Love, J., 'Raoul Prebisch and the origins of the doctrine of unequal exchange', *Latin American Research Review*, (1980).

McKinnon, R., *Money and Capital in Economic Development*, (Brookings, 1973).

MacNamara, R., 'Address to the Board of Governors', Nairobi, Kenya, September 4, 1973, (World Bank reprint).

Magdoff, H., 'China contrasts with USSR', *Monthly Review*, (1975).

Masterman, M., 'The nature of a paradigm', in *Criticism and the Growth of Knowledge*, eds. Lakatos, I. and Musgrave, A., (Cambridge, 1970).

Meier, G., 'The formative period', in *Pioneers in Development*, eds. Meier, G. and Seers, D., (Oxford, 1984).

Myint, H., 'An interpretation of economic backwardness', *Oxford Economic Papers*, June 1954; reprinted in *The Economics of Underdevelopment*, eds. Agarwala, A. and Singh, S., (Oxford, 1958).

Myrdal, G., *Economic Theory and Underdeveloped Countries*, (Duckworth, 1957).

Nurkse, R., 'Some international aspects of the problem of economic development', *American Economic Review*, (May 1952); reprinted in *The Economics of Underdevelopment*, eds. Agarwala, A. and Singh, S., (Oxford, 1958).

Nurkse, R., *Problems of Capital Formation in Underdeveloped Countries*, (Blackwell, 1953).

Oshima, H., 'The international comparison of size distribution of family incomes, with special reference to Asia', *Review of Economics and Statistics*, (November 1962).

Paine, S., 'Development with growth: a quarter century of socialist transformation in China', *Economic and Political Weekly*, (Vol. XI, Special Number, Nos. 31, 32 and 33, August 1976).

Palma, G., 'Dependency: a formal theory of underdevelopment or a methodology for the analysis of concrete situations of underdevelopment?', *World Development*, (Vol. 6, 7/8 1978); revised version 'Dependency and development: a critical overview' in *Dependency Theory: A Critical Reassessment*, ed. Seers, D., (Frances Pinter, 1981).

Paukert, F., 'Income distribution at different levels of development: a survey of evidence', *International Labour Review*, (1973).

Prebisch, R., 'The economic development of Latin America and its principal problems', *Economic Bulletin of Latin America*, (Vol. VII, No. 1, February 1962; first published 1949).

Preston, P., *Theories of Development* (Routledge and Kegan Paul, 1982).

Rosenstein-Rodan, P., 'Problems of industrialisation of Eastern and South-eastern Europe', *Economic Journal*, (June–September 1943); reprinted in *The Economics of Underdevelopment*, eds. Agarwala, A. and Singh, S. (Oxford, 1958).

Rostow, W., *The Process of Economic Growth*, (Norton, New York, 1952 and Clarendon Press, Oxford, 1953).

Rostow, W., *An American Policy in Asia*, (Technology Press of MIT, 1955).

Rostow, W., 'The take-off into self-sustained growth', *The Economic Journal*, (March 1956); reprinted in *The Economics of Underdevelopment*, eds. Agarwala, A. and Singh, S. (Oxford, 1958).

Rudra, A., 'The use of shadow prices in project evaluation: a critique', *Indian Economic Review*, (Vol. 82, 1972).

Scitovsky, T., 'Two concepts of external economies', *Journal of Political Economy*, April 1954; reprinted in *The Economics of Underdevelopment*, eds. Agarwala, A. and Singh, S., (Oxford, 1958).

Seers, D., 'What are we trying to measure?' *Journal of Development Studies*, (Vol. 8, No. 3, April 1972); reprinted in *Measuring Development*, ed. Baster, N., (Frank Cass, 1972).

Seers, D., 'The birth, life and death of development economics', *Development and Change*, 10, (1979).

Seers, D., 'Development options: the strengths and weaknesses of dependency theories in explaining a government's room to manoeuvre', IDS Sussex Discussion Paper 165, (September 1981).

Singer, H., 'The distribution of gains between investing and borrowing countries', *American Economic Review*, (papers and proceedings, Vol. 40, No. 2, May 1950).

Singer, H., 'Thirty years of changing thought on development problems', in Hanumantha Rao, C. and Joshi, P. (eds.), *Reflections on Economic Development and Social Change*, (Allied Publishers, 1979).

Singh, A., 'The "basic needs" approach to development vs the new international economic order', *World Development*, (Vol. 7, No. 6, June 1979).

Streeten, P., 'Development ideas in historical perspective', in *Development Perspectives*, (Macmillan, 1981); reprinted in *Pioneers in Development*, eds. Meier, G. and Seers, D., (Oxford, 1984).

Sunkel, O., 'Transnational capitalism and national disintegration in Latin America', in *Social and Economic Studies*, (1973).

Toye, J., *Dilemmas of Development*, (Basil Blackwell, 1987).

Warren, B., 'Imperialism and capitalist industrialisation', *New Left Review*, (No. 81, September/October 1973).

Warren, B., *Imperialism: Pioneer of Capitalism*, (Verso, 1980).

World Bank, *Accelerated Development in Sub-Saharan Africa: An Agenda for Action*, (World Bank, 1981).

4 · THE PARADIGM OF THE EXPANDING CAPITALIST NUCLEUS

As the last chapter showed, the early work of the Western European and North American development economists was characterised by a common preoccupation with raising the rate of capital accumulation in underdeveloped economies. Around this common theme a number of early writers built more complex theories of the causes of underdevelopment and of the means by which capital accumulation might be raised. These were each characterised by their central concepts: the big push, balanced growth, unbalanced growth, the low-level equilibrium trap, cumulative causation, and so on. All these theories were widely debated. However, one particular perspective on the causes of low capital accumulation and the route forward came to predominate both in terms of the influence exerted on applied work and of the impetus it gave to future theoretical work.

This perspective has much in common with what is now often represented as the economic component of modernisation theory.[1] However, the present author has chosen to denote it differently, as the paradigm of the expanding capitalist nucleus. This has been done for several reasons. Firstly, the intention is to emphasise that we are concerned with more than a body of theory; what is involved is also a set of values and beliefs about the nature of economic development, its fundamental desirability and its feasibility. Secondly, it is also intended to emphasise the essential focus of this perspective, which underpins both the various theoretical developments and the applied work to which it has given rise.

In elaborating the core of this perspective the author will seek to show why both Lewis' seminal article on economic development with unlimited supplies of labour and Rostow's work on the take-off into self-sustained growth should be seen as two key and complementary instances of its articulation – even though while Rostow is conventionally classified as a modernisation theorist, Lewis, as was shown in Chapter 3, is sometimes classed as an early structuralist.

The complementarity of the seminal articles of Lewis (1954) and Rostow (1956) derives from the fact that while both emphasise the key role of increased savings and investment rates in generating economic growth, and perceive that a change in the class distribution of control over resources is necessary in order to achieve this, Lewis' relatively abstract analysis provides the paradigm with its theoretical core, while Rostow's adds both an historical and an institutional dimension.

THE ESSENTIAL ELEMENTS OF THE PARADIGM OF THE EXPANDING CAPITALIST NUCLEUS

The core of the paradigm of the expanding capitalist nucleus was summarised in Chapter 3, pp. 62–3. This section will review in greater detail its early articulation in the work of Lewis and Rostow, its policy implications, the further theoretical developments to which it has given rise and some of the main criticisms levied against it.

W. A. LEWIS ON 'ECONOMIC DEVELOPMENT WITH UNLIMITED SUPPLIES OF LABOUR' [2]

Lewis' purpose

In his 1954 article Arthur Lewis states his purpose to be an investigation of the use that can be made of the classical analytical framework in solving problems of economic growth in contemporary poor, labour-abundant economies. He gives as his reason for returning to classical economic theory the inappropriateness of both neo-classical and Keynesian theory for the analysis of the problems posed by such economies. He regards neo-classical theory as inappropriate firstly because it assumes full employment of all resources, and secondly because it is not concerned with problems of long-run growth (the latter being taken for granted). Keynesian theory he regards as inappropriate because in the short run it assumes an unlimited supply not only of labour, but also of land and capital, while in the long run growth is constrained not by a shortage of savings, but by a superfluity thereof. The classical economists, on the other hand, were preoccupied with economies having unlimited supplies of labour at subsistence wages.

> They then enquired how production grows through time. They found the answer in capital accumulation, which they explained in terms of their analysis of the distribution of income.
>
> (Lewis, 1954: 400.)

Lewis sets out to see to what extent this interpretation of the classical framework can solve present-day problems of distribution, accumulation and growth in poor, labour-abundant economies, first in a closed economy and then, albeit more briefly, in an open economy.

It should be noted at the outset that in his ensuing analysis Lewis is predominantly concerned with the causes of, and constraints on, economic growth. Economic growth and development are equated.[3] At two stages in his analysis Lewis makes, as will be seen, a brief reference to the impact of growth on contemporary mass welfare. However, his persistent theme is that high growth now accelerates the transition to higher mass incomes in the future.

The structure of an underdeveloped economy with unlimited supplies of labour

Lewis take as his starting point an economy, typical of many in the Third World, which has unlimited supplies of labour at a subsistence wage. This labour is to be found in various branches of the economy – chiefly in traditional agriculture, but also in the urban sector. Here people eke out a living in casual employment or as surplus retainers employed by both private individuals and businesses – in the latter case usually as office messengers – both for reasons of social prestige and because the social ethic in overpopulated countries requires this. In addition, the many women who remain outside the labour market due to lack of employment opportunities and the additional numbers arising from population growth contribute to this excess labour supply.

Such labour-surplus economies can be analytically divided into two sectors: the capitalist sector and the subsistence sector. The former is very small, the latter large. 'The capitalist sector is that part of the economy which uses reproducible capital, and pays capitalists for the use thereof' (Lewis, *op.cit.*, reprinted in Agarwala and Singh, 1963: 407). The capitalists hire wage labour. Capitalist production occurs in mines, plantations and in industry; it is not spacially concentrated in one location, but is geographically fragmented. The subsistence sector in contrast does not use reproducible capital, and output per head is consequently much lower. It is also based upon family labour rather than hired labour.

Hirschman has observed that Lewis' focus on rural underemployment as the principle economic characteristic of underdevelopment lies at the heart of his contribution to development theory:

> he managed – almost miraculously – to squeeze out of the simple proposition about underemployment a full set of 'laws of motion' for the typical under-developed country, as well as a wide range of recommendations for domestic and international economic policy.[4]

In fact, in the Lewis model there are also other key features of such economies. These concern their class structure and the related savings propensities. However, the next section will examine this simple proposition from which Lewis indeed derived a number of distinctive features concerning the *modus operandi* of underdeveloped economies.

Labour is available to the capitalist sector at a wage that is determined by earnings in the subsistence sector. Since individuals in this sector generally work in household enterprises, and/or pool their earnings with other household members, their effective income reflects the *average*, rather than the *marginal*, income of household members. It is thus *average* per capita income (which Lewis tends to equate with average labour productivity[5]) that is the material opportunity cost to a labourer of moving from the subsistence to the capitalist sector. The wage paid by the capitalist sector is set at the level of this opportunity cost plus a margin which is just sufficient to induce workers to move into wage employment.

In one of the two asides on mass incomes and welfare noted above, Lewis, when discussing the determination of the capitalist wage, observes:

> the fact that the wage level in the capitalist sector depends upon earnings in the subsistence sector is sometimes of immense political importance, since its effect is that capitalists have a direct interest in holding down the productivity of the subsistence worker's income.
>
> (*Ibid.*: 410.)

By way of illustration, he notes that the imperial record in Africa is one of impoverishing the subsistence economy, by taking away land, or demanding forced labour, or imposing taxes to force people to work in the capitalist sector.

Lewis links his observations on the availability of abundant labour at a subsistence wage to his analysis of growth in the following manner.

The causes of, and constraints to, growth

Lewis' central problem is to identify the causes of, and constraints to, growth. The fundamental constraint to growth in output is, for Lewis, the lack of accumulation of productive capital, and the overriding constraint to capital accumulation is, in his view, as in that of the classical economists, the rate of savings.

> The central problem in the theory of economic development is to understand the process by which a community which was previously saving and investing 4 or 5 per cent of the national income, or less, converts itself into an economy where voluntary saving is running at about 12 or 15 per cent of national income or more. This is the central problem because the central fact of economic development is rapid capital accumulation (including knowledge and skills with capital).
>
> (Lewis in Agarwala and Singh, *op.cit.*: 416.)

Lewis rejects the possibility that this increase in savings could occur simply because the population as a whole become more thrifty. This is not plausible, firstly because 90 per cent of the population in poor countries with surplus labour never manages to save a significant proportion of its income, and secondly because in underdeveloped countries a substantial proportion of the rich are landowners. These have a high propensity to consume out of rental income and even when rents are saved they are usually used unproductively (to buy existing assets rather than to create new ones). This leaves the other, minority, component of the richest 10 per cent – the capitalists.

Lewis assumes, in the classical tradition, that capitalists' profits are saved and invested (*ibid.*: 417). The question then becomes what are the circumstances in which the share of profits in national income increases, because in these circumstances the share of savings will also increase. Lewis constructs a model of a closed economy which is intended to throw light on the nature of this process.

Where a capitalist nucleus exists, however small, and where there is an unlimited supply of cheap labour, then the capitalists will reinvest at least part of their profits, so expanding the capital stock. More labour is then drawn into the capitalist sector. With each round, as the surplus is reinvested, total profit increases. With wages in the capitalist sector remaining at subsistence level, the share of profits in national income rises as the capitalist sector expands. As the share of profits rises, the share of savings and investment in national income rises too, thereby increasing the rate of economic growth.

This is the process that Lewis illustrates, as shown in Figure 4.1.

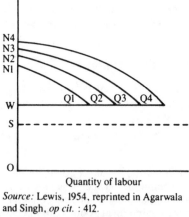

Quantity of labour

Source: Lewis, 1954, reprinted in Agarwala and Singh, *op cit.* : 412.

Figure 4.1   The Expansion of the Capitalist Sector in the Lewis Model

In Figure 4.1, *OS* is average subsistence earnings, *OW* the capitalist wage, and *NQ* the schedule of the marginal productivity of labour.

WN_1Q_1 represents the surplus in the initial stage. Since some of this is reinvested, the amount of fixed capital increases. Hence the schedule of the marginal productivity of labour is now raised throughout, to the level of N_2Q_2.

Both the surplus and capitalist employment are now larger. Further reinvestment raises the schedule of the marginal productivity of labour to N_3Q_3. And the process continues so long as there is surplus labour.

(*Ibid.*: 413.)

Lewis observes that this model enables us to face squarely the problem which confronts backward countries. They do not save so little because they are poor, but because their capitalist sector is so small. Lewis adds

remembering that 'capitalist' here does not mean private capitalist, but would apply equally to state capitalist. . . (The state capitalist can accumulate capital even faster than the private capitalist, since he can use for the purpose not only the profits of the capitalist sector, but also what he can force in tax out of the subsistence sector.)

(*Ibid.*: 419.)

On the possible origins of either private or state capitalists Lewis has little to say except that they are often imported, while, if they do emerge internally, this

is probably bound up with the emergence of new opportunities, especially something that widens the market, associated with some new technique which greatly increases the productivity of labour if labour and capital are used together.

(*Ibid.*: 420.)[6]

Lewis continues with the following sanguine comments:

Once a capitalist sector has emerged it is only a matter of time before it becomes sizeable. If very little technical progress is occurring, the surplus will grow only slowly. But if for one reason or another the opportunities for using capital productively increase rapidly, the surplus will also grow rapidly, and the capitalist class with it.

(*Ibid.*)

Aids and constraints to the expansion of the capitalist nucleus

Having set up his model of the expanding capitalist nucleus, Lewis considers certain factors that may aid or impede its expansion. This in turn permits him to derive a number of policy conclusions from his analysis.

The role of deficit financing in promoting growth

Lewis shows that in certain circumstances expansion of the money supply and an associated price inflation can accelerate the rate of growth in a country with surplus labour. This can occur when credit is created in favour of private capitalists or when it is used to finance government capital formation, provided that the projects financed generate increased output fairly quickly.[7] An important point about a 'one-off' expansion of the money supply to finance increased capital formation is that the inflation of monetary demand and prices will be liquidated as new goods begin to flow into the market. Furthermore in labour-surplus economies output expansion financed by monetary expansion need not entail withdrawing land and capital from other uses (as assumed in the neo-classical model) since there is significant scope for infrastructural capital creation using labour intensive methods (e.g. roads, viaducts, irrigation networks).

Lewis, however, also notes three factors that may constrain the effectiveness of monetary expansion as a growth promoter. Firstly, if prices rise too fast or for too long, investors may lose confidence and turn to various forms of unproductive investment such as speculation in commodities and land purchase. Secondly, the smaller the capitalist class, the greater the likelihood that much of the expanded money supply will find its way into the pockets of other groups (such as merchants, who speculate in commodities, the middle classes 'who buy big American cars with it or go on trips to Europe' or peasants who 'ought to use it to improve their farms, but would probably use it only to pay off debt or to buy more land'). (Lewis, *op.cit.*: 429.) Thirdly, in an open economy expansion of monetary demand would put pressure on the balance of payments. Only if the balance of circumstances is favourable, and the authorities can contain the pressure on the foreign balance while ensuring that the monetary expansion leads to a significant increase in investment, should monetary expansion be used as a means of accelerating growth.

Lewis also notes that it is the natural tendency of governments to try to control price inflation and to do so by fixing industrial prices. However, in an inflationary context governments should not control industrial prices, since it is the industrial capitalist class which saves most. Industrial price controls reduce profits, and, therefore, savings and investment, while perpetuating inflationary pressures.

The subsistence sector as a source of restraints upon growth

So far Lewis has shown that sustained economic growth is possible so long as there is an initial capitalist nucleus and an abundant supply of labour at subsistence wages. In these circumstances the capitalist surplus will be a rising proportion of the national income. However, this cannot go on for ever. The process will slow down and finally come to a halt when the capitalist sector has absorbed all the surplus labour. At this point wages will inevitably rise, eating into profits and reducing the incentive to invest.

The process may, however, also be brought to a premature halt if wages rise prematurely. This may happen for one of four reasons:

1. If the rate of labour absorption in the capitalist sector exceeds the rate of population growth in the subsistence sector. In this case the number of people in the subsistence sector will begin to fall, and even though subsistence output at first remains constant,[8] their average product will rise and so will the supply price of labour.
2. If the capitalist sector buys goods (e.g. food) from the subsistence sector and if the supply of marketed output from this sector is price inelastic,

then as the capitalist sector grows the terms of trade may turn against it. This will force the capitalists to devote a larger proportion of the value of their output to the payment of wages in order to sustain the real subsistence value of the wage.

3. Subsistence producers may imitate certain of the improved production methods introduced by the capitalists (adopting new seeds or crop varieties, for example), thereby raising their average productivity and so also the supply price of labour.

4. Industrial workers may seek to emulate the living standards of their employers, and so bid for higher wages.

Of these four possibilities, 2 and 3 arise because the capitalist sector obtains goods as well as labour from the subsistence sector. Lewis observes that if the capitalist sector pursues a self-contained development path in terms of material supplies, drawing only labour from the subsistence sector, they will not occur. In reality, however, the capitalist sector does usually obtain food and raw materials from the subsistence sector.

The possibility that the subsistence sector may constrain capitalist growth raises the question of how capitalists and governments should manage the relationship between the two sectors with a view to maximising economic growth.

As peasant per capita output and/or income per unit sold rises, capitalist growth will be maximised if the state extracts from the peasants most of the increase in income (through taxes and other levies) and if it then uses these revenues to promote capital accumulation. 'By contrast a state which is ruled by peasants may be happy and prosperous, but it is not likely to show such a rapid accumulation of capital.' (Lewis, *op.cit.*: 434).

Meanwhile, the growth of trade unions should also be restrained. Ultimately, however, labour supplies in the subsistence sector will dwindle, and capitalists competing for labour will then bid up the wage.

The opening of the economy

Lewis observes that when the labour surplus disappears,

> our model of the closed economy no longer holds.

In the final section of his analysis the model is opened up into one in which labour is scarce but other labour-abundant economies exist. While the reasoning of the *coda* is perfectly acceptable if it is read as a self-contained analysis, it does not link altogether satisfactorily with the preceding analysis.

The economy that now takes centre stage is a developed, labour-scarce one, perhaps entering into relations with other underdeveloped countries. The capitalists in such an economy may export capital to labour-abundant economies. On the other hand, technical progress combined with the co-existence of skilled labour, external economies and a capitalist rather than pre-capitalist culture in the advanced country, may serve to sustain the rate of profit in the latter and make continued reinvestment of capital in the advanced economy more attractive than capital export. Lewis observes that in fact capital exports flow in both directions, both to and from under-developed economies. Quite how the reader is supposed to relate this point to Lewis' prior elaboration of a model of capitalist development in a closed economy is not spelt out. The implication is that capital exports from some underdeveloped countries might slow down the process of capitalist growth in these countries if not offset by equal or greater capital imports. However, this point is not explicitly stated, and there is no discussion of it.

The opening up of the model also permits Lewis to examine the impact on underdeveloped economies of trade with more developed ones. Firstly he is able to explain why when productivity rises in capitalist plantations and mines producing for export in poor countries this is not followed by a wage increase. Wages remain determined by the supply price of labour and all the benefits of the productivity increase are passed on to consumers in rich countries in the form of lower prices (*ibid.*: 442, 3). Here Lewis anticipates an argument later to be emphasised by the neo-Marxists, particularly Arghiri Emmanuel (1972). However,

> this is not to say that the tropical countries gain nothing from having foreign capital invested in commercial production for export. They gain an additional source of employment, and of taxation
>
> (*Ibid.*)

Lewis shows too that because labour in the subsistence sector is paid its average and not its marginal product,[9] the application of the law of comparative costs is usually distorted in underdeveloped countries. Given diminishing returns to labour in the subsistence sector, the wage paid by the capitalists exceeds labour's true social opportunity cost. Lewis suggests that governments might provide tariff protection to capitalists in such economies as a means of compensating them for this cost distortion.

In a lengthy analysis, Lewis offers what is predominantly a rather optimistic account of the steady expansion of the capitalist sector, an expansion which he equates with economic development. However, he also shows that the working population cannot expect an immediate rise in living standards if capitalist growth is to be maximised. Meanwhile, capital export may slow down capitalist growth (although in principle at least there may be some scope for policy control of such outflows.[10]) Finally, capitalist accumulation may also be slowed down by the distorted operation of the law of comparative advantage (due to the mode of determination of subsistence incomes) unless the government introduces compensatory measures.

The main policy conclusions that follow from this analysis are that, in order to maximise the pace of economic development, governments should take the following measures:

1. Use tax policy to contain premature increases in subsistence incomes.
2. Restrain the premature development of trade union wage bargaining power.
3. Judiciously expand the money supply to help finance capital formation.
4. Refrain from attempting to control any ensuing price inflation by fixing industrial prices.
5. Protect the domestic capitalist sector from foreign competition in order to compensate for the distorted operation of the law of comparative advantage.
6. It is also implied, but not explicitly stated, that capital exports should be discouraged.

ROSTOW ON THE STAGES OF GROWTH

Both Lewis and Rostow had published works on economic development before their key publications appeared. In Lewis' case his article on the industrialisation of Puerto Rico (published in 1949) and his contribution to the 1951 United Nations report on industrialisation in underdeveloped countries both provide interesting insights into the development of his ideas.[11] In Rostow's case we find the first exposition of the ideas that recur in Rostow 1956 and 1960 in the *Process of Economic Growth* (1952). It is also in this earlier book that Rostow makes explicit the influence on his work of earlier dynamic theorists, Schumpeter and the classical economists.[12] Here too Rostow criticises the application of the Harrod–Domar model to underdeveloped countries.

While the Harrod growth formula neatly pinpoints two key variables in the growth process, it does not provide a satisfactory theory of growth, because it does not permit one to establish what really determines the rate of investment, nor does it adequately indicate what determines the value of the capital:output ratio. These issues, argues Rostow, cannot be adequately understood without taking into consideration a number of characteristics of a country's population that are as much sociological as economic (the so-called 'propensities') and the various factors that influence investment yields.

In reality, the factors determining the investment rate include both prospective returns – which Rostow argues are strongly influenced by the availability of technical innovation and the pace of its adoption, and the propensities of potential investors including readiness to take risks. The capital:output ratio meanwhile varies *inter alia* both with changes in technology and the efficiency with which the existing stock is used.[13] (It is noteworthy that Lewis too did not acknowledge a debt to Harrod and Domar, even though later commentators have claimed to detect their influence on his work, but chose instead to emphasise his theoretical debt to the classical economists.[14])

It should, however, be emphasised that Rostow's criticism of the Harrod–Domar model is of its inadequacy as a *theory* of growth. Such criticism is not incompatible with the adoption and use of the Harrod–Domar growth formula for purposes of calculating target rates of savings and investment in economic planning, or for estimating foreign aid requirements. Used in this way, as a technical device, the formula did in fact become part of the methodology of the paradigm of the expanding capitalist nucleus.

Rostow's purpose

It has already been shown in Chapter 3 that Rostow's perception of the purpose of the United States' promotion of economic development in the Third World was governed by a strongly anti-communist stance.[15] His theoretical work in development economics was governed by the same ideological perspective. However, in a context in which other Western development economists, who also accepted the desirability of developing countries remaining non-communist, applied their skills to theorising the causes of and constraints to economic growth with a view to identifying the role of aid therein, Rostow set himself a more ambitious task. He aimed to provide

> an alternative to Karl Marx's theory of modern history.
>
> (Rostow, 1960: 2.)

Rostow's ambitious claim, made for his 1960 book, certainly served to draw increased attention to it. However, his thesis that all countries pass through the same sequence of five economic stages, from stagnant subsistence economy to the age of high mass consumption, with each transitional stage being of similar duration in all countries, was soon discredited by appeal to historical evidence. Today Rostow's attempt to generate a grand theory of economic history is no more accepted than is the mechanistic interpretation of Marxism which suggests that Marx held that all economies pass sequentially through an identical series of modes of production.

However, part of Rostow's theoretical contribution proved more enduring. This concerns his theorisation of the 'take-off' into self-sustained growth, and it is with this that we are concerned here. This is also the focus of his 1956 article, to which we shall chiefly refer.

Rostow's theorisation of 'the take-off'

In many respects the best way to demonstrate how Rostow complements Lewis is to let him speak for himself. The following set of extracts have been selected with this end in view. They demonstrate in particular the following.

For Rostow, like Lewis, a crucial factor which serves to lift an economy out of low income stagnation on to a sustained growth path is a significant increase in the share of savings and investment in national income. For this to occur a new class of entrepreneurs/businessmen must emerge. For the rest, Rostow attempts to give a rather precise time perspective to this process, to establish the nature of the main social, political and institutional changes which form an integral part of it and to flesh out on the supply side the structural nature of the process of economic change that is associated with the initiation of sustained growth.

Rostow (1960) identifies five 'stages of growth': the traditional society, the establishment of the preconditions for take-off, the take-off. the drive to maturity and the age of high mass consumption. Of these, it is the middle three which are central to his analysis, and upon which Rostow's earlier work (1956) concentrates.

Rostow asserts that take-offs have occurred in two types of societies, those already settled and those newly settled. The former constitute the more general case.

Prior to the take-off the preconditions for growth are established in already settled societies over what is likely to be a long time period (up to a century or more).

> We start with a reasonably stable and traditional society containing an economy mainly agricultural, using more or less unchanging production methods, saving and investing productively little more than is required to meet depreciation. Usually from outside the society, but sometimes out of its own dynamics, comes the idea that economic progress is possible: and this idea spreads within the established *élite* or, more usually, in some disadvantaged group whose lack of status does not prevent the exercise of some economic initiative. More often than not the economic motives for seeking economic progress converge with some non-economic motive, such as the desire for increased social power and prestige, national pride, political ambition and so on. Education, for some at least, broadens and changes to suit the needs of modern activity.
> (Rostow: 1956, reprinted in Agarwala and Singh, 1958: 157, 8.)

In this period 'new enterprising men come forward, willing to take risks in pursuit of profit, notably in commerce.' Markets widen. 'Basic capital is expanded notably in transport and communications, often to bring to market raw materials in which other nations have an economic interest'. Financial institutions develop to support this increased activity, and 'here and there, modern manufacturing enterprise appears, usually in substitution for imports.' During the pre-take-off phase 'the rate of productive investment may rise to up to 5 per cent of national income'[16] (Rostow, *op.cit.*: 158).

This phase is followed by the take-off into self-sustained growth:

> during which the rate of investment increases in such a way that real output per caput rises and this initial increase carries with it radical changes in production technique and the disposition of income flows which perpetuate the new scale of investment and perpetuate thereby the rising trend in per caput output. . .[17]
> The take-off requires, therefore, a society prepared to respond actively to new possibilities for productive enterprise, and it is likely to require political, social

and institutional changes which will both perpetuate an initial increase in the scale of investment and result in the regular acceptance and absorption of innovations.

(Ibid.: 154–155.)

The beginning of take-off can usually be traced to a particular sharp stimulus. The stimulus may take the form of a political revolution . . . [or] a techno-logical (including transport) innovation . . . [or] a newly favourable internat-ional environment, such as the opening of British and French markets to Swedish timber in the 1860s . . . but it may also come as a challenge posed by an unfavourable shift in the international environment, such as a sharp fall in terms of trade (or a war-time blockade of foreign trade) requiring the rapid development of manufactured import substitutes.

What is essential here, however, is not the form of stimulus but the fact that the prior development of the society and its economy result in a positive sustained and self-reinforcing response to it.

(Ibid.: 160.)

Rostow observes that while national income aggregates reveal little of the essential underlying changes,

it is nevertheless useful to regard as a necessary but not sufficient condition for the take-off the fact that the proportion of net investment to national income rises from (say) 5 per cent to over 10 per cent, definitely outstripping the likely population pressure . . . and yielding a distinct rise in real output per capita.

(Ibid: 161: 2.)

This proposition is very similar to that quoted from Lewis on p. 89 above.

It is implicit in Rostow's analysis that, although some premature take-offs fail because the country has still not completed the preconditions phase, modern economic history consists basically of a linear progression from a traditional to a mature economy. Once a country is brought into contact with the world capitalist system, changes in social values and economic institu-tions begin to occur. At a certain point, when appropriate investment opportunities and the impetus to exploit them have also developed, this will lead to a successful take-off into economic growth.

The concept of the 'leading sector'

In an attempt to disaggregate the nature of the growth process, Rostow analysed the interrelationship between the growth performance of different sectors, introducing the concept of the primary, or leading, sector, which plays a key role both during the take-off and subsequently. Thus, the sectors of an economy may be grouped into three categories:

(a) *Primary growth sectors*, where possibilities for innovation or for the ex-ploitation of newly-profitable or hitherto unexplored resources yield a high growth rate and set in motion expansionary forces elsewhere in the eco-nomy.

(b) *Supplementary growth sectors*, where a rapid advance occurs in direct response to – or as a requirement of – an advance in the primary growth sectors, e.g. coal, iron and engineering in relation to railroads. . .

(c) *Derived growth sectors*, where advance occurs in some fairly steady relation to the growth of total real income, population, industrial production or some other overall, modestly increasing parameter. Food output in relation to population, housing in relation to family formation are classic derived relations of this order. . .

At any period of time it appears to be true even in a mature and growing economy that forward momentum is maintained as the result of rapid expansion in a limited number of primary sectors, whose expansion has significant external economy and other secondary effects. From this perspective the behaviour of sectors during the take-off is merely a special version of the growth process in general, or, put another way, growth proceeds by repeating endlessly, in different patterns, with different leading sectors, the experience of the take-off. Like the take-off, long-term growth requires that the society not only generate vast quantities of capital for depreciation and maintenance, for housing and for a balanced complement of utilities and other overheads, but also a sequence of highly productive primary sectors, growing rapidly, based on new production functions. Only thus has the aggregate marginal capital-output ratio been kept low.

(*Ibid.*: 180, 1.)

To achieve satisfactory growth in balance with rising demand in the derived growth sectors requires the diffusion of technical innovations in these sectors too. Thus Rostow (1960) notes that revolutionary changes in agricultural technology are also essential for successful take-off, 'for modernisation of a society increases radically its bill for agricultural products.'[18]

Examples of leading sectors in the take-off include the textile industry in Britain, railway development in the United States, Germany and France, the timber industry in Sweden and armaments production for rapid militarisation in Russia.

Although Rostow's stages theory specifies a very long pre-take-off phase in which the preconditions for growth are established (up to 100 years or more), his analysis did not generate as hostile or gloomy a reaction from the general body of development practitioners as might have been expected. This is probably because the theory offers no certain means of identifying what stage a country has reached in the growth process, other than retrospectively. It was therefore possible for planners and others to assess that a country was ready, or nearly ready, for the take-off even if this contained an element of wishful thinking. Furthermore it was also possible to argue that the preconditions phase could be accelerated through active government intervention.

A note on the classification of Rostow's work

Rostow presented his theory of the stages of growth as something which had general validity for all countries. Hirschman (1981) has suggested that for this reason his analysis belongs to the category of 'mono-economics', along with neo-classical economics and Marxist theory: the characteristic feature of all types of mono-economics being a claimed universality of relevance and applicability. This observation is valid, but it is also an illustration of how opposites can be classed together on the basis of a single characteristic. While Hirschman uses this characteristic to distinguish Rostow's work from development economics (the latter, according to Hirschman, being regionally-specific in its original analytical intent[19]), Rostow in fact developed his model specifically in order to throw light upon the contemporary condition and future prospects of the underdeveloped countries of the mid-twentieth century. In particular, he set out to shift the balance of growth theory from a focus on economies that are already set on a path of long-run expansion to a broader focus which incorporated the economics of the preconditions and of the take-off – especially the latter.[20]

Rostow's analysis of these two phases reveals that his argument and that of Lewis share a common core, and are complementary in other respects. While Lewis focuses on the interaction of (declining) rural underemployment and increasing capitalist accumulation, Rostow takes increasing investment, the emergence of a leading, high-growth sector and political, social and institutional change as the three foci of his analysis of the take-off. Where Lewis refers to the key role played by the emerging capitalist class, Rostow, taking his inspiration from Schumpeter, refers to an entrepreneurial class. However, it is clear from the tone of Rostow's analysis that this entrepreneurial class consists largely of the capitalist-entrepreneurs that Schumpeter observes were to be found in Britain and elsewhere in the nineteenth century, rather than the distinct category of entrepreneurs of a mature industrial society.[21]

So far, then, the work of Lewis (1954) provides the theorisation of a process of expanding capitalist accumulation which over time absorbs the labour force of the traditional sector. Meanwhile in Rostow's work, leaving aside its more ambitious claims, there is an attempt to give some sort of time perspective to the initiation of capitalist expansion and the take-off into self-sustained growth, together with an attempt to pinpoint more succinctly than Lewis (1955) the political, social and institutional changes that are likely to be associated with the take-off. Rostow also offers an empirical analysis of the likely leading sectors in this process.

Lewis and Rostow thus, in distinct but complementary ways, gave theoretical articulation to a prevalent emphasis in the debate on economic development in Western Europe and North America – an emphasis upon the role of capital accumulation in economic development. In both cases their theorisation of development was suggestive of a process which, once started, offered the prospect of cumulative growth. Governments have a role to play in promoting and sustaining this process, and in Rostow's theorisation they also have a role to play in creating the conditions for its initiation. This perspective meshed well with dominant preoccupations in the West at this time *vis-à-vis* the less developed countries.

The main elements of further theoretical development and debate to which this perspective gave rise also mesh with these preoccupations. Thus Ranis and Fei (1961) seek to integrate the main elements of Lewis' and Rostow's theoretical contributions in an attempt to give this analytical framework greater rigour and to explore further the role of the agricultural sector in the take-off. In addition, the application of this perspective to the theoretical debate on investment criteria and choice of techniques, and its application both to the theoretical analysis of the role of foreign aid in promoting development and to the practical calculation of the extent of foreign aid requirements, each reflect a concern to inform the provision of both technical assistance and financial aid to developing countries. These contributions are briefly reviewed in the following paragraphs.

THEORETICAL EXTENSIONS OF THE PARADIGM OF THE EXPANDING CAPITALIST NUCLEUS

Ranis and Fei on the transition to self-sustaining growth

Ranis and Fei, building upon the earlier analytical work of Lewis, seek both to give greater rigour to Rostow's concept of the take-off, and to explore more fully the role of traditional agriculture therein.

Taking the former point first, Ranis and Fei (1961) subdivide the process of absorption of surplus labour as analysed by Lewis into two phases. Phase one is the absorption by the capitalist sector of redundant labour with a zero social opportunity cost, and phase two the absorption of the disguised unemployed, where the latter are defined as those members of the labour force whose marginal physical product is positive but worth less than the institutional wage. These two phases are equated with the take-off stage as defined by Rostow. With the completion of the transfer of the disguised unemployed, wages in agriculture and industry will rise, being determined by competitive market forces and reflecting the true opportunity cost of labour. 'This landmark may be defined as the end of the take-off process' (Ranis and Fei, 1961: 537).

Having set their conceptual framework, Ranis and Fei employ this chiefly in order to explore the role of rising agricultural productivity in speeding up the completion of the take-off.[22] Provided that the institutional wage remains unchanged until the take-off any rise in agricultural productivity in the preceding transition period will have two consequences. It will increase the potential agricultural surplus that can be mobilised for capital accumulation, and it will shorten the period of completion of the take-off (*ibid.*: 540–542). Thus the transition period can be speeded up by the allocation to agriculture of a part of the investible surplus, and the design of policy instruments to mobilise that part of the surplus generated by agriculture so that its use can be geared to investment in either agriculture or industry. As Ranis and Fei observe, their emphasis on the importance of allocating part of the investible surplus to agriculture during the transition period constitutes a particular interpretation of the concept of balanced growth.

Ranis and Fei also use their model to emphasise two further points. Firstly, the higher the proportion of a country's labour force that is initially redundant (i.e. has zero marginal productivity in traditional agriculture), the higher the proportion of the labour force that must be transferred to new industries if the economy is to achieve self-sustaining growth. In countries that are by definition resource-poor, achieving this transfer will require a considerable effort of resource mobilisation. Furthermore, 'this already difficult task is further complicated by the fact that these countries are usually subject to severe population pressure.' (*Ibid.*: 549.)

With population figures rising, the longer the transition period, the larger are the absolute numbers that must be transferred into industry before the take-off can occur. Thus there is a trade-off between the share of national income that is invested each year and both the length of the transition period and the certainty of completing it. The shorter the targeted transition period, the higher investment activity must be. As Ranis and Fei observe, this part of their analysis

> may be interpreted in terms of a critical minimum effort thesis.

Thus they integrate Leibenstein's preoccupation with the development retarding effects of population growth[23] into the analytical content of the paradigm of the expanding capitalist nucleus.

Investment criteria, technical choice and savings mobilisation

Rostow and Lewis offer little guidance on the issues of which type of production techniques should be encouraged in the capitalist sector, and which sectors should be assigned priority in investment programmes. Lewis (1949) had recommended investment in relatively labour-intensive branches of manufacturing in Puerto Rico. Lewis (1955) suggests that in labour-abundant economies, agriculture and cottage industries should use labour-intensive methods; mechanisation of these branches would simply create unemployment. However, Lewis' most influential publication makes no reference to choice of technique beyond the suggestion that there is scope for output-raising labour-intensive infrastructural investment and the observation that the faster the rate of technical progress, the faster growth will take place. Meanwhile Rostow's discussion of specific leading sectors is couched in terms of historical experience, rather than of any deductive logic. It was left to other economists to explore the implications of inadequate rates of saving and capital accumulation for choice of technique. In the socialist literature on economic planning various economists have explored the question of sectoral priorities as well. We shall review that debate in the Appendix to this chapter.

Since the 1940s and 1950s a substantial body of literature on these issues has developed. The contributions have been written from various perspectives. Some fit logically within the paradigm of the expanding capitalist nucleus,[24] and are discussed in what follows. However, it will be helpful to begin with the earlier contributions to the debate.

From early on an important theme that occupied development economists concerned with economic planning was the choice of investment criteria. Two early contributors to this debate – Polak (1943) and Buchanan (1945) – recommended the capital turnover criterion for use in capital scarce economies. If capital is scarce, then the important thing is to maximise its productivity. By implication this indicated the use of labour-intensive techniques. However, Kahn (1951) argued, *inter alia*, that the Polak–Buchanan criterion assumed a zero opportunity cost for all other productive factors. Since this was not necessarily true, even for labour in labour-surplus economies (since there may be training, transport and housing costs involved in mobilising this labour), Kahn argued instead for the social marginal productivity criterion in which all factors are measured at their social opportunity cost, and in which also the evaluators take into account the full contribution of a proposed investment to national product, and not merely that part 'which may accrue to the private investor.'[25] These principles were subsequently developed in the literature on cost-benefit analysis techniques for developing countries.[26]

In 1955 Galenson and Leibenstein entered the debate, as did Maurice Dobb.[27] The dominant theme of their contributions, to be found also in A.K. Sen (1960), is a preoccupation with the inadequacy of the savings rate in underdeveloped countries, where savings and investment are seen as closely interrelated, and as key determinants of the growth rate of national income. The correct choice of investment projects, they argue, entails the choice of those projects which will contribute most to raising the rate of savings and investment. Although there are differences between the analyses of Galenson and Leibenstein on the one hand and Sen and Dobb on the other, they also have the following important elements in common:

1. In line with Lewis and Rostow, their central assumption is that the capitalist class[28] have the highest propensity to save in underdeveloped countries. In order to raise the overall savings rate it is therefore necessary to raise the capitalists' share of national income as fast as possible.

2. The correct choice of production techniques in underdeveloped countries can help to do this. Although labour is cheap in these countries, labour-intensive techniques should generally be avoided in the capitalist sector because techniques with a high ratio of labour to capital will

generate a high ratio of wages to profits. Capital-intensive techniques will tend to do the opposite. The saving and reinvestment rate from new projects is therefore likely to be greatest where relatively capital-intensive methods are chosen.

Galenson and Leibenstein (1955) propose that the investment criterion to apply in underdeveloped economies is the *marginal per capita reinvestment quotient*. This quotient is a function of seven variables which reduce to two basic ones: the amount of profit generated per employee and the rate of population growth (Galenson and Leibenstein, 1955: 352). As a rule of thumb, the marginal per capita reinvestment quotient is likely to be maximised where the capital:labour ratio is highest.

Galenson and Leibenstein suggest that there is a case for allowing modern sector wages to rise above the basic supply price of labour in order to achieve the following:

1. Encourage the choice of capital-intensive techniques with high labour productivity.
2. Improve the quality of the workforce (due both to improved living standards and to working with advanced equipment).
3. Bring down the fertility rate, also as a result of rising living standards (*ibid.*: 365).

Galenson and Leibenstein thus seek to show that the logic of Lewis' central preoccupation with growth maximisation goes against any earlier predilection that the latter may have had for the use of labour-intensive production technology. They also suggest that there may be a case for not restraining wages as rigidly as Lewis had originally proposed.

Galenson and Leibenstein also note briefly that their investment criterion may have implications for the sectoral allocation of investment: 'our criterion of maximising the capital:labour ratio tends to favour those (heavy) industries which are essential to the development of modern industry', because capital:labour ratios are generally higher in these branches than in light industry.

Meanwhile, Maurice Dobb had also, slightly earlier, made the same central point:

> The choice between more or less capital intensive forms of production has nothing to do with existing factor-proportions. . . It depends, not on the existing ratio of available labour to capital (treated as a stock), but on precisely the same considerations as those which determine the choice between a high and a low rate of investment.
>
> (Dobb, 1955: 149.)

Sen (1960) also reconfirms this point for a closed economy. It applies whether the hard assumption is adopted that all profits are saved and wages consumed (as it was by Galenson and Leibenstein and by Dobb) or the softer assumption that the marginal propensities to save out of profits and wages are both positive and both less than one, but the former exceeds the latter. Sen, however, also explores the significance of foreign exchange scarcity and the need to import capital goods. These will tend to lower optimal capital intensity to some extent.[29]

The savings constraint and foreign aid analysis

Chapter 3 showed that preoccupation with inadequate rates of capital accumulation was a common characteristic of early theorising about underdevelopment amongst the majority of development economists in North America and Western Europe. The differences between them lay in the perception of the dominant causalties within which this preoccupation was located. It is therefore not surprising to find that in 1951 the United Nations report on Measures for the Economic Development of Underdeveloped Countries used a simple interpretation of the savings constraint in its pioneer projection of foreign aid requirements: 'external capital requirements [for 1950–1960] were the difference between total capital requirements and domestic savings.'[30]

While the emphasis of the Lewis model on the savings constraint could be taken to support simple savings gap models for foreign aid, the complementary work of Rostow identified a further role for aid.

Earlier in this chapter we noted Rostow's emphasis on the importance of both institutional change and of change in the propensities (values and beliefs) of traditional societies as part of the preconditions for a successful take-off into self-sustaining growth, along with an increase in the savings rate.[31] These ideas came to exert a significant influence on foreign aid analysis, especially from the mid-1950s to the mid-1960s. They came to be discussed under the general heading of a country's 'absorptive capacity', i.e. the ability to absorb effectively an increase in investment made possible by financial aid.

In 1955 Rostow himself urged that foreign capital and technical assistance should be made available only where they could be effectively used.[32] In 1957 Millikan and Rostow pioneered an attempt to estimate foreign aid requirements by taking into account both absorptive capacity and the savings-investment gap,[33] and in 1961 Rosenstein-Rodan also used this approach in an attempt to project the foreign aid requirements of over 100 underdeveloped countries.

Rosenstein-Rodan suggested three indices that could be used to estimate absorptive capacity. These are as follows:

1. The rate by which a country 'has succeeded in increasing her volume of investment during the past five or more years. If a rate of increase of investment could be realised in the past, then a slightly higher rate made possible by technical assistance can plausibly be projected for the future.'[34]

2. An estimate of the extent to which a country has succeeded in raising the deviation between the marginal and average propensity to save over the past five years, and of tax performance.
3. A judgement on a country's overall administrative and developmental organisation.

His article applies these principles in a projection of the actual aid requirements of underdeveloped countries for the period 1960–1976.[35]

Chenery and Strout (1966) take up and extend this approach in their 1966 paper. They identify three sequential roles which aid must fulfil as countries first establish the preconditions for the take-off into self-sustained growth, and then move into the take-off itself. During the preconditions stage aid is needed first to develop skills, build institutions and so on. During this period the financial aid that should flow to a country is determined by its absorptive capacity. Chenery and Strout employ the first of the three methods proposed by Rosenstein-Rodan for estimating this. Next, during the first part of the take-off stage itself, foreign aid will be needed to plug a savings gap. For elimination of this gap the two parameters whose marginal values are crucial are the marginal propensity to save and the incremental capital:output ratio. If the marginal propensity to save exceeds the average, the latter will steadily rise over time, while if the incremental capital:output ratio is below average, the latter will fall with time, so making possible a faster rate of growth of output for any given savings rate. Provided the marginal propensity to save is high enough, and/or the incremental capital:output ratio is sufficiently low, it will ultimately become possible to sustain the desired rate of growth from domestic savings without recourse to external finance. However, into the latter part of the take-off Chenery and Strout introduce a new dominant growth constraint which is more closely associated with the structuralist perspective – shortage of foreign exchange. This third constraint will be discussed in the next chapter.[36]

APPLICATIONS TO DEVELOPMENT PLANNING

Some of the ideas embodied in the paradigm of the expanding capitalist nucleus also found expression in a number of early development plans. They did so most notably in plans for countries where foreign exchange shortages, which receive little attention in this analytical perspective, were not perceived to be a potentially overriding constraint on economic expansion. India's *First Five Year Plan* (Government of India, 1953) is one such example. This plan was published in 1953, before either of the two seminal articles by Lewis and Rostow reviewed in this chapter. However, as has been noted already in Chapter 1, new paradigm statements do not appear in a vacuum, but in response to problems that scientists or social scientists have already been worrying about. The introductory chapter of India's *First Five Year Plan* clearly reflects some of the preoccupations of the pre-paradigm development debate. Entitled 'The Problems of Development', the chapter reflects *inter alia* a number of the central ideas discussed by Rostow in his 1950–51 lectures in America and in Cambridge, United Kingdom, on which Rostow (1952) is based. Like Rostow, the plan's authors review the past growth experience of more advanced economies as a source of insight into the contemporary growth process of a less developed country.

The planners conclude that India's rate of capital accumulation must be raised from about 5 per cent of national income to 20 per cent. The two main factors that will determine the scale of investment are the savings rate and the volume of unutilised human and material resources which can be used for direct investment,[37] with the former being the more important. On savings, they observe that:

> Social customs and habits, the distribution of incomes, the rates at which incomes of different classes go up and the efficiency of banking and other institutions for mobilising savings – all these – play a part in determining the rates of savings attained.

With an acknowledgement of the influence of Harrod–Domar, the plan's growth projections are based on the target rate of investment and the projected capital:output ratio. The planners also emphasise the need to take a long-term view in planning India's economic transformation. While the development of a modern industrial sector is taken as a major objective, they advocate emphasis on agriculture, including irrigation and power, in the first plan period. This is justified on the basis of the need to expand the output of food and raw materials for industry and also by reference to the early experience of modern economic growth in Britain and Japan.

The Kenyan Development plan 1966–1970 was also written largely in the vein of the paradigm of the expanding capitalist nucleus.[38] The savings constraint is seen as dominant, followed by skill shortages. Productive investment is to be encouraged in all branches of the economy where it can be shown to be profitable. However, with respect to choice of techniques, the planners favoured labour-intensive projects so as to make the limited capital available provide maximum employment opportunities.[39]

CRITICISMS OF THE PARADIGM OF THE EXPANDING CAPITALIST NUCLEUS

The ideas reviewed in this chapter have been subjected to wide-ranging criticism, from various analytical perspectives, and at various analytical levels. These range from a questioning of some of the underlying assumptions to points of empirical accuracy or technical detail.[40] Here we are concerned with those criticisms which, if valid, must seriously call into question the value of this perspective as a basis for the analysis of problems of development and for policy prescription.

Inadequate domestic demand

The emphasis on an overriding savings constraint to development ignores the possibility that investment is constrained not by lack of savings but by lack of demand. Thus, for example, the first and major part of the Lewis model is based upon the assumption of a closed economy. Nowhere in this section does Lewis consider the possibility that inadequate demand may deter capitalist investment and slow down the rate of growth. With mass incomes held constant, much of the inducement to invest must come from within the capitalist sector itself (although there will also be some undercutting of artisan production). Yet the ability of the capitalist sector to sustain this inducement will be a function of the size both of the economy as a whole and the sector itself. These issues are not raised in the Lewis model. It appears that the capitalists are assumed to have so high a motivation to engage in capital accumulation that they will do so whatever the return on investment. Later too, when Lewis drops the assumption of a closed economy, and when he briefly notes the possibility of capital export from an underdeveloped economy, the assumption is that this will be induced not by inadequate domestic demand but by more favourable cost structures in industrially advanced countries.

Likewise, the Ranis and Fei model, Galenson and Leibenstein and savings-gap aid models also ignore this potential constraint. While Rostow does give some attention to the inducement to invest, he too does not treat this as an overriding constraint. Yet the omission is potentially serious, for if the overriding constraint *is* lack of inducement to invest, pursuit of many of the policies advocated by proponents of this perspective can exacerbate the problem. For example, use of capital-intensive techniques limits domestic market expansion in three ways:

1. By constraining the growth of domestic demand.
2. By concentrating income increases in the hands of upper income groups with a high marginal propensity to consume imported goods.
3. By making it virtually inevitable in most countries that capital goods will have to be imported, so reducing backward linkages.

The foreign exchange constraint

While this perspective ignores the possibility of a domestic demand constraint to capitalist accumulation, it also ignores the possibility of a foreign exchange constraint. Neither the Lewis model nor Galenson and Leibenstein in their analysis of choice of techniques discuss the possible implications of a decision by capitalists to use imported capital equipment. Likewise Rostow does not confront the implications of the fact that technical innovation in most underdeveloped countries is based heavily on imported technology. Not only may this put pressure on foreign exchange availability, but, equally important, the use of imported technology effectively eliminates the internal backward linkages that Rostow considers so important. Yet the low income elasticity of demand for many primary products in the industrially advanced countries and increasing self-sufficiency in industrially advanced countries in primary products or their synthetic substitutes, combined with a growing technological gap between the technical and innovatory capacities of industrially advanced countries and underdeveloped economies, make it seem likely to many that today's developing countries can expect to encounter serious balance of payments difficulties, exacerbated by their own high income and low price elasticities of demand for imports.

These first two points, emphasised by the structuralist school, are discussed further in the next chapter.

The importance of market imperfections

The structuralist criticisms that we have just reviewed implicitly accept the need to raise capital accumulation in order to generate growth. However, neo-classical critics of the perspective reviewed in this chapter question the focus on capital accumulation as the basic causal factor in economic growth. In their view the overriding constraint on increased output in developing countries is inefficiency in the use of existing resources – inefficiency generated jointly by market imperfections endogenous to traditional societies and by government interventions in resource allocation. In this context the single-minded pursuit of capital accumulation can simply lead to a growing stock of 'white elephants' – underutilised new capital stock, poorly matched to the needs of the economy – without necessarily generating a significant expansion of output. The overriding need is to remove market distortions, whether government-induced or otherwise.

The implications for equity

A further criticism that can be levelled against this perspective (as Lewis acknowledges) concerns its equity implications. Mass incomes must stagnate in order to maximise growth. Virtually all the increase in income generated by the expansion of production is to be concentrated in the hands of the owners of capital for an indefinite time period (that is to say, until all surplus labour is absorbed).

The use of capital-intensive techniques of production will in itself serve to postpone this absorption date, unless offset by the effect of any increased savings and investment so generated. Furthermore, the labour- as well as capital-saving nature of technological innovation in the industrially advanced countries means that, as underdeveloped countries import both replacement equipment and new capital stock, the increasingly labour-saving characteristics of these will tend to further reduce the rate of growth of modern sector employment. Technical advance may prevent indefinitely the full absorption of surplus labour into the modern sector, particularly when its impact on demand is also taken into account.

The impact of capital-intensive technology on the surplus per worker
Meanwhile, the assumption that capital-intensive techniques will lead to a higher rate of surplus per worker is not necessarily valid. This will depend upon the impact on unit costs of such factors as the level of capacity utilisation, the standard of maintenance and operation of machinery, the time (itself a cost) and payments involved in obtaining spare parts and servicing, etc. (see Meier, 1976: 423).

The impact of capital-intensive technology on the quality of
the labour force
Galenson and Leibenstein claim that the use of capital intensive technology will not only raise the savings rate in underdeveloped countries, but will raise the quality of the labour force. However, it is not clear that the effect of capital-intensive production methods will be to promote the development of those qualities which are most urgently needed. That is to say, automated and highly-specialised production methods, in which most members of the work-force each concentrate on a single routine task, do not serve to develop basic technical skills, nor the workers' latent technical innovatory capability.[41] Nor do they provide opportunities for the development of small-scale entrepreneurship.

Inaccurate representation of savings, and productive investment,
propensities
It is also open to question whether the assumptions made by the exponents of the paradigm of the expanding capitalist nucleus concerning savings and investment propensities are correct in certain key respects.

For example, in the Lewis model five classes are identified: the peasants, wage-earners, middle-classes, landowners and capitalists. According to Lewis' assumptions the peasants save little if at all. If their incomes rise any savings that occur are not used to expand production but to pay off money-lenders or buy land. The wage-earners' savings are minimal; the middle-classes also save little. The landlords engage in prodigal consumption. Only the capitalists have a high propensity to save and to use these savings to finance the expansion of productive capital. In the Lewis model the only problem is that the capitalists may export some of their savings rather than investing them productively within the underdeveloped economy. Rostow also makes similar assumptions concerning relative savings propensities, as do the theorists of choice of techniques who argue for greater capital intensity.

These assumptions may be questioned on two grounds: firstly, that they are over-optimistic concerning the nature of the savings and investment propensities of the capitalist class; secondly, they either ignore or underestimate the savings potential of another class. These two issues will be considered in the order stated.

Lewis has relatively little to say about the origins of the capitalist class. One contribution of Rostow in this respect is to note, following the classical economists, that the capitalist class in the industrially advanced countries usually emerged first in commercial activities. Both Lewis and Rostow also note that modern sector investment in underdeveloped economies is quite often financed by foreign capital.[42] Both these observations have a potential significance that the authors do not explore. Firstly, various factors may discourage or prevent members of the merchant capitalist class in underdeveloped countries from moving into investment in production. These include foreign competition, political insecurity and a preference for commodity speculation and trade, as well as inadequate demand. Secondly, while foreign capitalists may invest in these countries, they will not necessarily reinvest their profits there.

In practice, unproductive but relatively secure investments in agricultural land, commodity speculation, urban real estate and capital export, can each reduce significantly the rate at which capitalists' savings are transformed into productive investments in underdeveloped countries.

Meanwhile, whereas the proponents of the paradigm of the expanding capitalist nucleus may have exaggerated the capitalists' marginal propensities to productive investment within developing countries, they may have underestimated the savings and investment propensities of certain other groups. These are the operators of small-scale enterprises, often family-based. They may be peasant farmers, artisans, or the operators of small-scale businesses, often catering to low-income mass demand, but sometimes also supplying the modern sector with inputs and services. In Marxists terms they are the *petite bourgeoisie*. In recent years various economists have suggested that the savings and investment propensities of these groups have been underestimated, partly due to a distortion of investment opportunities in underdeveloped economies in favour of large-scale capital[43] and partly due to the relatively inconspicuous, and seemingly insignificant, nature of their individual investments. Furthermore, it is the sort of policies that are advocated by, *inter alia*, the proponents of the paradigm of the expanding capitalist nucleus that help to create the aforementioned distortion – the protection of modern industry, development of financial institutions to serve the capitalist sector, and so on.

CONCLUSION

This section will conclude the review of the paradigm of the expanding capitalist nucleus as applied to mixed economies. It has been shown to emphasise one overriding, supply-side constraint to growth – the rate of capital accumulation, which in turn is determined by the supply of savings. Although Rostow, in his contribution to this perspective, also gives some attention to the inducement to invest in his discussion of leading sectors, in general this is not treated as a potentially overriding constraint. Meanwhile the possible existence of external (international) constraints to national economic development is also ignored. Rather, the constraints are seen as predominantly internal to the traditional society, lying in its class structure and the related savings propensities, its culture and its institutions. Finally, the paradigm of the expanding capitalist nucleus equates economic growth with economic development. The maximisation of growth in poor countries is the desideratum. The long-term benefits of increased per capita output will outweigh the short-term costs in terms of equity. The main criticisms of this paradigm suggest that it is too simplistic (key variables are omitted) and consequently over-optimistic. In at least one case, a crucial variable (relative savings propensities) may also have been mis-specified.

APPENDIX

The socialist version of the paradigm of the expanding capitalist nucleus

During the 1920s debate in the Soviet Union on economic strategy and policy there emerged a dominant perspective which in many ways parallels that reviewed in the core of this chapter. It is reviewed separately here because of the distinctive characteristics of the context in which it emerged and the implications thereof. The focus was on economic development in a centrally-planned economy rather than in market economies, and the theorists who articulated this perspective were concerned with the development of the economy of which they were nationals and residents. However, the difference of context renders the parallels in the two perspectives doubly interesting.

It is Preobrazensky who is generally credited with being the leading originator of this perception of the nature and mechanisms of economic development under socialism. A key objective is to maximise the rate of growth of national output. Meanwhile the two sectors of the market economy version of the paradigm of the expanding capitalist nucleus – the traditional subsistence-oriented sector and the wage-labour based profit-oriented sector – are replaced by two others. These are the private sector and the state sector. According to Preobrazensky it was essential to the success of socialist development that the state, or socialist sector, take responsibility for a steadily-increasing share of national production. This was necessary not only to ensure the socialist transformation of the economy, but to maximise the rate of growth of output, for the state could fix the savings rate from its expanding modern sector profits (at 100 per cent) and it could also determine the pattern of investment to be financed by these savings.

In the early years of the transition to socialism, the economy would also need the support of private producers. However, their relative and absolute importance should steadily diminish. The success of the revolution required as rapid as possible a reduction in the power of those reactionary elements whose influence derived from continuing control over productive resources, while, as just noted, the state sector could be expected to generate a faster growth of, and more efficient pattern of, investment.

Preobrazensky, like Feldman, who gave a more precise mathematical statement of the same argument (see below), favoured assigning priority to investment in heavy industry – capital and intermediate goods. This would not only provide means for the production of armaments to protect the revolution, but in purely economic terms it would provide the basis for maximising long-run output growth. While the population might have to tighten their belts in the short-run, forgoing any immediate rise in per capita consumption while the basic industrial structure was created[44], in the long run both annual levels, and the rate of growth, of output of all types would be higher than under any alternative growth path.

Preobrazensky also explored the policy implications of seeking to maximise the rate of expansion of the state sector,[45] proposing a number of measures to accelerate mobilisation of both financial and real resources for state accumulation. These policy instruments (taxation, interest rate policy, the terms of trade between sectors, public utility pricing) are, with the possible exception of the last,[46] familiar also to Western development economists. Thus Preobrazensky advocated the following approach:

1. The state should tax the private sector (cf. Lewis on the traditional sector).
2. The banks should charge higher interest rates to private borrowers than to state industry.
3. The state should replace private intermediaries in trade, and should set the terms of trade between the private and the state sector so as to permit extraction from the former of part of its surplus product.
4. The state should charge higher rates to private users of the railways.

The analogies with the paradigm reviewed in this chapter are clearcut – indeed, it was the type of strategy outlined here that Lewis, Rostow and others had in mind when they stated that development could be maximised by concentrating an increased share of national income in the hands of either private or state capitalists.

Meanwhile Feldman's statement of the case for concentrating investment in capital goods production is also of interest, for it provides a theoretical extension of the paradigm of the expanding capitalist nucleus (albeit one without an automatic application in market economies due to the problems of market size and the inducement to invest). Feldman's model is summarised by Domar in Nove and Nuti (1972). Here we seek simply to indicate its essence.

Consider an economy which each year has 1 million units of surplus to reinvest. The capital output ratio we initially assume to be constant across all industries at 4:1 except for raw materials; these for simplicity are assumed to be produced by labour-intensive methods. While capital is scarce, labour is in abundant supply at the prevailing wage. All investment has less than one year's gestation, and machines have an infinite life. The economy is centrally planned and the authorities have the choice of investing in one or both of two sectors: 'Category 1 produces all capital goods for both [sectors], while all consumer goods, including the corresponding raw materials, are produced in Category 2'.[47]

Table 4.1 summarises the implications of investing in consumer goods production for an eight-year period. Investible resources are used entirely to purchase abroad the machines to produce finished consumer goods. As Table 4.1 shows, both the capital stock and the output of consumer goods rise in arithmetic progression (i.e. by the same absolute amount each year),

Table 4.1 Model 1: The consequences for consumer goods output of concentrating annual investment in category 2 (consumer goods production)

Year	Value of annual investment (millions of units of account)	Cumulative value of capital stock created (millions of units of account)	Output of consumer goods (millions of units of account)
1	1	1	0.25
2	1	2	0.5
3	1	3	0.75
4	1	4	1.00
5	1	5	1.25
6	1	6	1.5
7	1	7	1.75
8	1	8	2.00

the additional output of consumer goods reaching a total value of two million by year 8.

Table 4.2, in contrast, explores the consequences of concentrating annual investment in the capital goods sector. Each year all investment is used to finance the import of machines to make the equipment to produce consumer goods. Since raw materials are produced by labour-intensive methods, and labour is in abundant supply, as soon as the equipment for consumer goods manufacture is produced it can be installed and put to work. We see from Table 4.2 that initially consumer goods production rises more slowly in absolute terms than in Model 1, but the pace of growth is faster because the annual capacity to supply equipment to the consumer goods sector is steadily expanding. By year 8 the level of output of consumer goods equals that of Model 1. It will take several more years to produce the extra output needed to compensate consumers for the lower welfare levels experienced in the preceding years under this strategy, but beyond that breakeven point society will become increasingly better off.

Although Feldman concentrates on a two-sector model, it is possible, using the same approach, to divide category 1 into two branches, one producing machines to make the equipment for consumer goods production, and one producing the basic equipment (including other machines) needed to make machines for the capital goods sector. Under the given assumptions, and concentrating investment on expanding the capacity to make machines for the capital goods sector, it will take a little longer (two more years) to equal the Model 1 level of consumer goods output, but the same conclusions apply *a fortiori*. In the longer term, society will be better off as a result of concentrating investment on expanding its own capacity to produce the machines that can in turn produce the equipment for consumer goods

Table 4.2   Model 2: The consequences for consumer goods output of concentrating annual investment in category 1 (capital goods production)

Year	Value of annual investment in category 1	Cumulative value of capital stock in category 1	Cumulative annual output of category 1	Value of capital stock in category 2	Output of consumer goods
1	1	1	0.25	0.25	0.06
2	1	2	0.5	0.75	0.19
3	1	3	0.75	1.5	0.38
4	1	4	1.00	2.5	0.63
5	1	5	1.25	3.75	0.94
6	1	6	1.5	5.25	1.31
7	1	7	1.75	7.00	1.75
8	1	8	2.00	9.00	2.25

production. In other words, the 'deeper' the investment, the faster the rate of growth of output of consumer goods.

If we drop the assumptions that there is no need to replace machinery and that a constant capital:output ratio is maintained (assuming instead that this is higher in Category 1) this will lengthen the period before breakeven, but it will not necessarily change the conclusion. This will only happen if the difference in the capital:output ratios in the two sectors is sufficiently wide.[48] Likewise if the problem of labour scarcity emerges, it may be necessary to allocate some investment to increase the productivity of the remaining labour in other sectors (e.g. raw materials production). This too will lengthen the breakeven period, but will not necessarily affect the model's conclusion. (This would depend on the severity of the labour shortage and the speed with which the shortage emerges.[49])

The preparation of India's second five year plan was strongly influenced by the analytical approach developed by Feldman (see Mahalanobis, 1963).

NOTES

1. See e.g. Toye, 1987: 11 for a brief summary of the latter.
2. Lewis in *Manchester School*, May 1954, reprinted in Agarwala and Singh (eds.), 1963: pp. 400–449.
3. Thus implicitly assuming that the household has no dependants.
4. Hirschman in Gersovitz *et al.*, 1982: 376, 7.
5. Only correct in a community with no dependants.
6. In his earlier (1949) paper on the industrialisation of Puerto Rico Lewis had attached great emphasis to the importance of attracting foreign (United States) capital into the country.

7. To finance school building by creating credit is asking for trouble. On the other hand, there are a lot of agricultural programmes (water supplies, fertilizers, seed farms, extension) where quick and substantial results may be expected from modest expenditure.

    (Lewis, 1954; reprinted in Agarwala and Singh, *op.cit.*: 430)

8. Because the marginal product of labour is still zero.
9. Because in households in the traditional sector income is shared between members.
10. Lewis himself does not note this.
11. In Lewis, 1949, there is an emphasis on the potential importance of market size as a constraint to growth which is dropped in Lewis, 1954. Other ideas, however, including the potential contribution to growth of imported capitalists and concerning the role of government policy, recur.
12. See Rostow, 1953: especially Chapter 4. (Rostow, 1952, was published in the United Kingdom in 1953; all references are to the UK edition.)
13. See Rostow, 1953: 88–96. For another discussion of the dangers of excessive reliance on the Harrod–Domar model for purposes of analysing growth in developing countries, see Hirschman, 1958: 29–33.
14. The readiness to assume that such an influence was exerted may derive from the fact that Joan Robinson had earlier proposed that Harrod's growth theory should be applied to capital-poor underdeveloped countries (Preston, 1982: 63).
15. See p. 45 above
16. Rostow is ambivalent on the role of population growth at this time. It will put pressure on the food supply and the institutional structure of agriculture,

    creating thereby an economic depressant or stimulant (or both in turn) depending on society's response.

    (*Ibid.*: 158)

17. Later Rostow observes that:

    'The notion of economic development occurring as the result of income shifts from those who will spend (hoard or lend) less productively (to those who will spend (or lend) more productively) is one of the oldest and most fundamental notions in economics. It is basic to the *Wealth of Nations*, and it is applied by W. Arthur Lewis in his recent elaboration of the classical model.'

    (*Ibid.*: 175)

18. Rostow, 1960:8.
19. However, see Hirschman in Gersovitz *et al.*, 1982: 379 for an example of the relevance of structuralist theory to the industrially advanced countries.
20. See Rostow in Agarwala and Singh, *op.cit.*: 164.
21. See Chapter 2, pp. 24–5 for an explanation of this distinction.
22. Ranis and Fei, like many others, reinterpret the Lewis two-sector model in terms of traditional agriculture and modern capitalist industry.
23. See Chapter 3, pp. 56–8.
24. Others are based on the neo-classical paradigm.
25. Kahn, 1951: 39.
26. See Chapter 10 below.
27. Dobb in fact first published on the capital intensity of investment in French a year earlier. However, he was working largely outside the mainstream of western

development economics in Europe and the United States. Dobb's intellectual interests were primarily with socialist economic theory.

28. i.e., either private capitalists or the state (see p. 91).
29. The notion that labour-abundant economies should use capital-intensive techniques was controversial from the outset. Some of the criticisms it has generated are noted later in this chapter (see pp. 109–10).
30. Mikesell, 1968: 77.
31. Key attitudes are those towards family size, productive accumulation, sources of social status and the ability of man to control his physical environment. These issues are also taken up in Lewis (1955). However, this lengthy and rather loosely-structured book was to be far less influential than Lewis (1954).
32. Rostow, 1955: 48.
33. See Mikesell, *op. cit.*: 78.
34. Rosenstein-Rodan, 1961: 108.
35. For a critique of the empirical assumptions made by Rosenstein-Rodan in conducting this analysis, see Belassa, 1964.
36. See p. 144 below.
37. Government of India, 1953: 17. This last point might seem to suggest the influence of Nurkse (see Chapter 3, p. 55). The planners, however, go on to note that lack of technical skills or shortages of specific commodities and services are likely to impose severe restraints on the mobilisation of unutilised human and material resources (*ibid.*).
38. See Government of Kenya, 1966: 235–237.
39. See Government of Kenya, 1966: 35–50. In this discussion of the constraints to growth less than one full page is devoted to the balance of payments.
40. On the latter, see, for example, Weeks, 1971 and Fishlow, 1965, reprinted in Meier (ed.), 1984: 94 *et seq.*
41. This point will be further discussed in Chapters 8 and 9.
42. Something strongly advocated in Lewis, 1949.
43. See, e.g., McKinnon, 1974, Lipton, 1976, Adams, 1980, Streeten, 1981: 109. These points are discussed more fully in Chapters 9 and 10.
44. See Preobrazensky, 1922: 35.
45. See Preobrazensky, 1926.
46. Although differential railway charges to large and small farmers were used in Kenya to promote the development of settler and plantation agriculture (see Leys, 1974).
47. Domar, in Nove and Nuti, *op.cit.*: 151.
48. On this point see Domar in *Nove and Nuti, op.cit*: 161, and Appendix.
49. These issues are also explored in Dobb (1960) with similar results.

REFERENCES

Adams, D., 'Recent performance of rural financial markets' in *Borrowers and Lenders: Rural Financial Markets and Institutions in Developing Countries*, ed. J. Howell, (Overseas Development Institute, 1980).

Belassa, S., 'The capital needs of the developing countries', *Kyklos*, (Vol. 17, No. 2, 1964).

Buchanan, N., *International Investment and Domestic Welfare*, (Holt, 1945).

Chenery, H. and Strout, A., 'Foreign assistance and economic development', *American Economic Review*, (Vol. LVI, No. 4, Part 1, September 1966).

Dobb, M., 'A note on the so-called degree of capital-intensity of investment in underdeveloped countries', *Economie Appliquée*, (No. 3, Paris 1954); reprinted in Dobb, M., *On Economic Theory and Socialism*, Routledge and Kegan Paul, 1955.

Domar, E., *Essays in the Economic Theory of Growth*, (Oxford, 1957); excerpts reprinted in *Socialist Economics*, eds. Nove, A. and Nuti, D., (Penguin, 1972).

Fishlow, A., 'Empty economic stages?', *Economic Journal*, (Vol. 75, No. 297, March 1965); reprinted in *Leading Issues in Economic Development*, ed. G. Meier, fourth edition, (Oxford, 1984).

Emmanuel, A., *Unequal Exchange*, (New Left Books, 1972; first published as *L'Echange Inégal*, François Maspero, 1969).

Galenson, W. and Leibenstein, H., 'Investment criteria, productivity and economic development', *Quarterly Journal of Economics*, (August 1955).

Government of Kenya, *Development Plan 1966-1970*, (Government Printer, 1966).

Government of India, *First Five Year Plan*, (Government Printer, 1953).

Hirschman, A., *The Strategy of Economic Development*, (Yale, 1958).

Hirschman, A., 'The rise and decline of development economics' in Hirschman, A., *Essays in Trespassing: Economics to Politics and Beyond*, (Cambridge, 1981); also in *The Theory and Experience of Economic Development*, eds. M. Gersovitz *et al.*, (Allen and Unwin, 1982).

Kahn, A., 'Investment criteria in development programs', *Quarterly Journal of Economics*, (Vol. LXV, 1951).

Lewis, W.A., 'The industrialisation of Puerto Rico', *Caribbean Economic Review*, (December 1949).

Lewis, W.A., 'Economic development with unlimited supplies of labour', *Manchester School*, May 1954; reprinted in *The Economics of Underdevelopment*, eds. Agarwala, A. and Singh, S., (Oxford University Press, 1958).

Lewis, W.A., *The Theory of Economic Growth*, (Allen and Unwin, 1955).

Leys, C., *Underdevelopment in Kenya*, (Heinemann, 1975).

Lipton, M., 'Agricultural finance and rural credit in poor countries', *World Development*, (Vol. 4, No. 7, 1976).

Mahalanobis, P., *The Approach of Operations Research to Planning in India*, (Asia Publishing House, 1963).

McKinnon, R., *Money and Capital in Economic Development*, (Brookings, 1973).

Meier, G., 'The rationale of capital allocation – note', in *Leading Issues in Economic Development*, ed. Meier, G., third edition, (Oxford 1976).

Mikesell, R. *The Economics of Foreign Aid*, (Weidenfeld and Nicolson, 1968).

Polak, J., 'Balance of payments problems of countries reconstructing with the help of foreign loans', *Quarterly Journal of Economics*, (February, 1943); reprinted in *Readings in the Theory of International Trade*, eds. Ellis, H. and Metzler, L., (American Economic Association, 1949).

Preobrazensky, E. (1922), *From NEP to Socialism: A Glance into the Future of Russia and Europe*, (New Park Publications, 1973).

Preobrazensky, E. (1926), *The New Economics*, trans. Brian Pearce, (Clarendon Press, Oxford, 1965); excerpts reprinted in *Socialist Economics*, eds. Nove, A. and Nuti, D., (Penguin 1972).

Preston, P., *Theories of Development*, (Routledge and Kegan Paul, 1982).

Ranis, G. and Fei, G., 'A theory of economic development', *American Economic Review*, (Vol. L1, No. 4, September, 1961).

Rosenstein-Rodan, P., 'International aid for underdeveloped countries', *Review of Economics and Statistics*, (Vol. XL111, No. 2, May 1961).

Rostow, W., *The Process of Economic Growth*, (Norton, New York, 1952 and Clarendon Press, Oxford, 1953; revised edition, 1962).

Rostow, W., *An American Policy in Asia*, (Technology Press of MIT, 1955).

Rostow, W., 'The take-off into self-sustained growth', *Economic Journal*, 1956; reprinted in *The Economics of Underdevelopment*, eds. Agarwala, A. and Singh, S., (Oxford, 1958).

Rostow, W., *The Stages of Economic Growth: A Non-Communist Manifesto*, (Cambridge, 1960).

Sen, A. K., *Choice of Techniques*, (Oxford, 1960).

Streeten, P., *Development Perspectives*, (Macmillan, 1981).

Toye, J., *Dilemmas of Development*, (Basil Blackwell, Oxford, 1987).

United Nations, Dept. of Economic Affairs, *Measures for the Economic Development of Underdeveloped Countries*, (United Nations, New York, 1951).

Weeks, J., 'The political economy of labour transfer', *Science and Society*, (1971).

5 · THE STRUCTURALIST PARADIGM

The paradigm of the expanding capitalist nucleus assigns the central role in economic development to increased savings and capital accumulation. It gives little scope to the notion that slow growth rates may be due not to lack of savings but to a lack of inducement to invest. It ignores too the possibility of a growth constraint due to a lack of foreign exchange, meaning that necessary capital goods cannot be imported. In contrast, these constraints are central to the structuralist paradigm.

The key elements of the structuralist paradigm were summarised in Chapter 3 (pp. 49–50). This perspective was developed first to throw light on the causes of underdevelopment and development in Latin America. The main tenets of the classical structuralist analysis of underdevelopment, as articulated between 1949 and the mid-1960s, are as follows:

1. An undeveloped economy is characterised not only by a low per capita income but by certain important structural features. The latter refer primarily to:
   (a) the sectoral composition of output, employment and the capital stock;
   (b) economic institutions, including agrarian systems;
   (c) the joint effect of the foregoing on elasticities of supply and demand.
2. Key structural features of underdeveloped economies are:
   (a) the juxtaposition of a traditional largely agricultural sector using a technology with low levels of productivity and a modern sector using much more advanced technology (these parallel the capitalist and traditional sectors of the expanding capitalist nucleus paradigm);
   (b) the modern sector is usually established by foreign capital engaged in primary production for export;
   (c) the modern sector is characterised by a high degree of openness (i.e.

a large proportion of its output is exported and a large proportion of its requirements both for capital equipment and the manufactured consumption goods is imported);

(d) underdeveloped economies themselves are not able to design and manufacture the capital goods required by the modern sector;

(e) the numbers employed in the modern sector are typically a small proportion of the total population;

(f) the indigenous agricultural sector in underdeveloped countries is usually characterised by forms of land tenure which constrain the expansion of output;

(g) underdeveloped economies are characterised by domestic supply rigidities in key branches of the economy, and by high income and low price elasticities of import demand in the modern sector. These elasticities of supply and demand mean that underdeveloped economies do not respond effectively to conventional monetary measures of control;

(h) these economies are usually characterised by high rates of population growth.

3. The first seven of the above characteristics inhibit the generation of an internal growth dynamic. Meanwhile low elasticities of supply and demand also create inherent tendencies towards inflation and balance of payments crises.

4. Economic development consists not only of raising per capita incomes but also in structural transformation, i.e. the transformation of the economic structures of underdeveloped economies so that they acquire the internal capacity to initiate and sustain economic growth.

5. The main constraints to economic development are the same structural features as those outlined above. Policy recommendations centre on finding ways in which governments can intervene to help private producers change these structural characteristics via the promotion of import substitution in individual underdeveloped countries and the establishment of common markets among underdeveloped countries, as a means to develop their industrial sectors and to diversify the structure of domestic production into a pattern which is capable of sustaining economic growth. Land reform is also advocated, but does not receive priority attention.

6. Main policy instruments are tariffs and quotas, foreign exchange rationing, low formal sector interest rates and tax concessions to industrial investors. Foreign investment is welcomed as a potential purveyor of finance and technology.

7. Underdeveloped countries cannot be expected to replicate the development paths of the now industrially advanced countries due to the nature of their position in the international economy. (In this too the structuralist perspective differs from the paradigm of the expanding capitalist nucleus.)

8. However, industrially advanced countries can assist the development of the periphery by opening their markets to its exports and by providing financial aid to ease foreign exchange shortages.

The focus in this chapter is on the ideas of the structuralist school as they emerged from the late 1940s to the mid-1960s (classical structuralism). We are not concerned here with modifications of the structuralist school of thought which emerged after the mid-1960s, when some structuralists contributed to aspects of dependency theory[1]; nor are we directly concerned with the subsequent application of the structuralist perspective to the analysis of inflation and unemployment in industrially advanced countries.

The founding father of the structuralist school was Raoul Prebisch. It was he who gave early articulation first to the new policy responses, and then to their theoretical justification, that were imposed upon Latin America by the harsh international environment of the early 1930s and 1940s. However, what is arguably the most sophisticated theorisation of the structuralist position did not come from Prebisch, who continued to be concerned primarily with practical policy issues, but from Prebisch's colleague, Celso Furtado, in a book first published in 1961. In this chapter we shall therefore begin with a review of Furtado's work before returning to that of Prebisch, and to certain other structuralists – including Singer and Seers – who also contributed to the articulation of the paradigm.

FURTADO ON THE CONTRASTING GROWTH DYNAMIC OF INDUSTRIAL AND UNDERDEVELOPED COUNTRIES

Both Celso Furtado and Oswaldo Sunkel, another leading member of the structuralist school, acknowledge the influence on their work of Marxist theory and methodology.[2] Indeed, any reader of Furtado's theory of underdevelopment on the one hand, and Baran's (1957) on the other, cannot fail to be struck by certain similarities. Not only do both adopt a historical approach, but in certain important respects their interpretation of history is the same. Both conclude that the central features of economic underdevelopment have been caused by the impact of the developed countries on their underdeveloped counterparts. Underdevelopment is not a phase through which every growing economy passes, but a specific historical condition. None the less, there are important differences both in methodology and in findings, as this chapter and the next will show.

The development dynamic of the industrially advanced countries

Furtado draws a distinction between *growth* and *development*, the latter consisting not just in rising output, but in the steady incorporation of the labour force into lines of production in which the most advanced technologies are applied, and potential labour productivity is maximised.[3] Central to Furtado's analysis is the contrast he draws between the development path pursued in the past by the industrially advanced countries of the mid-twentieth century, and the paths possible for present-day underdeveloped countries. The economic development of the industrially advanced countries over the past two centuries has been based on a continuing technological revolution in domestic production, first in consumer and later in capital goods: development, in other words, was initiated and sustained by an internal supply-side dynamic. In contrast, in the underdeveloped countries what development has occurred has been generated externally, on the demand side. This difference is crucial in explaining differences in development performance and development potential.

Furtado outlines the key features of development at the centre as follows. Towards the end of the eighteenth century, the first consequence of the introduction of improved technology in consumer goods production was to make it possible to lower the price of these goods. This had two consequences: it led to increased demand for the output of producers using the new technology, leading in turn to an expansion in supply. Secondly, artisan production was undercut, thereby creating a surplus supply of labour. Those who invested in improved technology experienced healthy profits and as a result expanded production further. This led to increased demand for the capital goods that were required in the new branches of consumer goods production. At first these capital goods were produced using essentially artisan methods of production. Thus there was not only increased employment in the new forms of consumer goods production, but also, and more particularly, given the labour intensive methods used, in the capital goods sector. Meanwhile, output was expanded not only for the domestic market, but for foreign markets as well. As a result, by the 1870s, the point was being reached, first in Britain and then elsewhere, at which the supply of cheap labour was exhausted. At this time there was a risk that the process of economic growth would come to a halt. As the labour supply became inelastic, wages began to rise and to squeeze profits in the modern consumer goods sector. This in turn began to lower the rate of investment in consumer goods production, thereby lowering demand for the output of the capital goods where profits were already also being squeezed by higher wage costs. Any substantial cut-back in production in this latter sector would mean growing unemployment, consequent decline in consumer demand, and a further decline in consumer goods production, with stabilisation finally occurring at a lower level of output and employment. The rate of output growth would subsequently be limited by the rate of growth of the labour force.

However, the outcome just described did not occur because of a crucial adjustment made in the capital goods sector. Towards the end of the nineteenth century a continuing process of technological innovation in capital goods production was initiated. This served to release labour, contain the upward pressure on wages, and restore the rate of profit in both branches.

Meanwhile, 'the advent of an industrial nucleus in eighteenth century Europe disrupted the world economy of the time and eventually conditioned later economic development in almost every region in the world'.[4] The disruptive effects of industrial development operated in three directions: on the traditional artisan economies of Western Europe, on those regions where there was still unoccupied land with characteristics similar to Europe itself (America, Australia, Canada), and 'already inhabited regions, some of which were densely populated, whose old economic systems were of various, but invariably pre-capitalistic types'.[5] In the latter case the contacts made were of various types too. In some cases they were confined to opening up lines of trade, while in others there prevailed from the start a desire to develop the production of raw materials for export. However, both where the contacts were confined to trade and where they included direct investment in raw material production by companies from the industrially advanced countries, the result of these links was the same. They led to the creation of hybrid structures in the backward economies, 'part tending to behave as a capitalist system, part perpetuating the features of the previously existing system. The phenomenon of underdevelopment today is precisely a matter of this type of dualistic economy'. (*Ibid.*)

The growth dynamic of the underdeveloped economies

The question then arises why there was not a smooth expansion of the modern capitalist enclave (as propounded by the expanding capitalist nucleus theorists). According to Furtado, the extent of the expansion of the modern enclave depends on two key factors:

1. The relative importance of the income to which it gives rise.
2. The extent to which this income remains within the underdeveloped (national) economy.

The latter depends very much on the inducement to invest in that economy, so the question becomes what determines this inducement. Initially – as already outlined – the inducement was production for export (external demand). However, Furtado, like all members of the structuralist school, took the view that external demand could not be relied upon to sustain growth indefinitely.[6] The central issue is therefore whether export production can in turn generate an internal impetus to further growth, i.e. could it generate sufficient internal demand to induce a process of sustained investment to supply an expanding *domestic* market?

The scale of demand generated in the export-oriented capitalist nucleus depends on the following factors:

1. The amount of labour the modern nucleus employs.
2. The average real wage.
3. The amount of tax paid by enterprises in the modern sector (which determines the possible scale of public sector expenditure).
4. The demand for locally-manufactured producer goods which is generated by this sector.
5. The extent to which profits and salaries are spent within the developing economy.

The quantity of labour employed in the nucleus will depend on the scale of production and the technology used. The wage paid in the modern sector will be determined by the supply price of labour from the traditional sector. Similarly to Lewis, Furtado held that this will be given by the average subsistence standard in the traditional economy. Therefore wage rates are initially likely to be low. Turning to tax revenues, Furtado did not think that these would be important and hence they could not be expected to create a basis for substantial public sector expansion of demand. Frequently tax exemptions are offered to attract foreign capital into underdeveloped countries. Fourthly, as long as the scale of modern sector production is insufficient to induce local investment in capital goods production, the latter will be imported. This is invariably the case in the early stages of expansion of the nucleus. Retention of profits and salaries to purchase locally-produced luxury consumption goods will be determined by whether the goods demanded are produced locally to an internationally-competitive standard. In the early stages of development there is an insufficient volume of demand to induce investment in local production of these goods and such demand is met by imports.

Since the wage rate is initially low, tax revenues are low and local production of capital and luxury consumption goods cannot compete with imports, the extent to which profits are retained and invested within the local economy will depend on the rate of growth of external demand and the scale of employment in the modern sector. If we assume export demand to be constant, then the inducement to invest locally will be determined entirely by the proportion of labour that has already been absorbed into the modern sector. For if a large proportion of the population has been absorbed, this would create a more favourable population:resource ratio in the traditional sector, thereby increasing both per capita incomes in this sector and the modern sector wage which they determine. Such an increase in basic incomes would expand the demand for mass consumption goods and could thereby create the necessary inducement to invest.

For Furtado much hinges on the extent to which labour is drawn into the modern sector. However, he is pessimistic about the likelihood of this occurring on a large scale in most countries, and gives a figure of 5 per cent as typical of the proportion of labour that is usually absorbed into export production.[7] We thus come to the crux of the problem and to a crucial difference between this paradigm and that of the expanding capitalist nucleus. The latter assumed that there would be reinvestment of profits within the host economy. The structuralists suggest the contrary – an outflow of profits from the host economy. This is central because the dynamism of a capitalist system depends greatly on how profits are disposed of.

However, Furtado admits that there are a few exceptions to the rule, where the size of the modern sector labour force may become large enough to justify some investment in diversifying production in the modern sector into the manufacture of consumption goods for the local market. He illustrates this point with the case of Brazil. Since the nineteenth century the export nucleus in Brazil has been based primarily on coffee production. A sufficiently large number of people have been drawn into this sector to generate a substantial volume of consumer demand. However, even where a large volume of effective consumer demand is generated by the export nucleus, this will not automatically lead to local investment to meet it, for under normal conditions local enterprises using inexperienced labour will have to compete with the existing flow of manufactured imports from the industrially advanced countries. It requires some disruption to the normal flow of these imports (for example a decline in export prices and a consequent reduction in the capacity to import) to induce local investment in this branch.[8]

Furtado foresaw that in a country as large as Brazil the scale of activity in the modern sector might expand to the point where there is sufficient demand to induce investment not only in consumer goods production but also in that of intermediate and capital goods. However, the causes which could lead an underdeveloped economy along this path remain distinct from those experienced by the industrially advanced countries. The main dynamic continues to rest with external demand; firstly, as the underlying stimulus to expanded production, employment and domestic demand; secondly, as the purveyor of foreign exchange to finance the purchase of investment goods. Industrialisation generates a succession of new import demands for capital goods, spare parts and replacements that are needed for domestic production of the previous imports, not only in the consumer goods sector but in the capital goods sector itself.

Even in countries like Brazil Furtado saw no evidence of the generation of indigenous technology to substitute for imported equipment, designs and know-how.

> The greatest concern of the local industrialist is to provide an article similar to the one imported and, consequently, to adopt production methods that make it possible to compete with the foreign producer.
>
> (Furtado, *op.cit.*: 139.)

This implied a continuing demand for foreign exchange to finance the necessary imports.

Use of imported technology also has other implications. Since the imported technology is capital-intensive, it results in low rates of surplus labour absorption, which implies a perpetuation of the dualistic nature of these economies. In underdeveloped economies, 'technology assumes the character of an independent variable.'[9] It becomes one of three variables, the others being the rate of modern sector capital formation and the national rate of population growth, which determine whether the modern sector's share of total employment expands over time, i.e. whether growth is combined with development.

In the context of export demand-led growth, the size of the export sector thus determines the depth of industrial development. The majority of underdeveloped countries have much smaller export sectors than Brazil. Given the limited size of the domestic market, industrial development to supply home demand has been confined to a limited range of consumer and intermediate goods. Furtado concludes that in the absence of appropriate policy intervention, industrial development is likely to remain blocked, and economic dualism, which characterises underdeveloped economies, will be perpetuated. To break out of this impasse, economic strategy must emphasise the formation of common markets to enlarge market size and the deliberate promotion of import substitution by the public sector in those products that show particularly high income elasticities of demand.

In the final section of his analysis, Furtado explores the policy issues that so preoccupied the structuralist economists – the persistent tendencies in the Latin American economies towards domestic inflation and balance of payments crises. Before turning to these issues, however, this discussion returns briefly to another aspect of industrial development strategy, that of sectoral sequence, and to the views on this expressed not only by Furtado, but by other structuralist economists.

THE SEQUENCE OF INDUSTRIAL DEVELOPMENT IN THE PERIPHERY

There was a consensus amongst the leading structuralist economists that the rational sequence for industrial development ran from light industry (consumer non-durables and then consumer durables) through to intermediate goods and, lastly, basic capital goods. This was the reverse of the sequence which the socialist economists – Preobrazhensky, Feldman and Dobb – had argued would maximise the long-run rate of growth. The main reason for this difference of view lies in the structuralists' preoccupation with the impact of market size upon the inducement to invest, a factor that does not have the same significance in a centrally planned economy. To Furtado and Prebisch, however, it seemed self-evident that this was how industrialisation would proceed. Indeed, they could already point to the experience of industrialisation in the more advanced regions of Latin America, such as Southern Brazil, in support of their contention (see e.g. Furtado, *op.cit.*: 135–138).

Hirschman, however, provided a more elaborate theoretical justification for this sequence.[10] Although the Latin American structuralists did not consider that the body of Hirschman's theoretical work in the 1950s was fully consistent with structuralist thinking, this particular element of his work appears to mesh so neatly with structuralist views on import substitution that it is summarised here.

As Chapter 3 showed, Hirschman argued that a crucial scarce 'resource' in the underdeveloped economies is a 'binding agent' which will call forth the resources that are available and promote their use in ways that will most effectively contribute to economic growth. In contexts in which experience and knowledge of efficient growth paths are lacking, and in which difficult decisions have to be taken, some of which conflict with traditional norms and/or with current ideas concerning the nature of development itself, there is a need for 'pressures' and 'inducement mechanisms' that will elicit and mobilise the largest possible amounts of resources for development while minimising the need for difficult development decisions. 'We must call forth as much decision-making ability as possible by maximising induced and routinised decision-making.'[11]

Hirschman argued that the inducements to invest in the industrial sector could be maximised if economies followed an investment path in which each stage of investment generated, through backward and forward linkages to other branches of the economy, cumulative inducements to invest in these branches also.[12] He emphasised the need to use the market as the main inducement mechanism, an approach which indicated a strategy of backward-linked industrialisation, starting with import-substitution in consumer goods production, i.e. goods for which a known market exists, given by the existing scale of imports.[13] Hirschman foresaw that with time the development of these branches could generate sufficient demand for intermediate and capital goods to induce investment in local production of these also.[14] Meanwhile, the development of manufacturing production could also be expected to put increased pressure on existing supplies both of agricultural output (food and raw materials) and on the existing infrastructure of transport facilities, power supplies, communications, etc. It would thus induce expansion in agricultural production, while bottlenecks and shortages in the use of infrastructure would provide the necessary information to guide public sector investment into the areas where it too would be most effective in promoting growth. These are, of course, the ideas that underlie Hirschman's advocacy of 'unbalanced growth' and his rejection of the opposing 'balanced growth' strategy advocated by Nurkse. For Hirschman it was quite unrealistic to assume that such a strategy could be effectively organised and implemented.

THE TERMS OF TRADE AND BALANCE OF PAYMENTS DISEQUILIBRIA AS POTENTIAL CONSTRAINTS ON DEVELOPMENT

The structuralists, as we have already seen, laid great stress on the position of underdeveloped economies in the international economic system. They considered external factors to be at least as important as internal factors in determining the growth prospects of peripheral, underdeveloped economies and in influencing both their long-term development strategies and short-run economic policies. Structural analyses focused on two important aspects of the external economic relations of peripheral countries – the long-run trend in the terms of trade and the causes of balance of payments disequilibria (the latter are also closely linked to domestic disequilibria in supply and demand in key sectors).

The strategic implications of trends in the international terms of trade

In 1949 Prebisch prepared for the Economic Commission for Latin America (ECLA), which had been founded the year before, a paper entitled 'The Economic Development of Latin America and its Principal Problems'. This was dubbed by Hirschman the 'ECLA Manifesto'.[15] It concentrates largely upon an analysis of the international economic context, and the strategic and policy implications thereof for the Latin American economies. Early in the paper Prebisch uses the results of a recent study of long-run trends in the international terms of trade to attack the theory of comparative advantage, to urge that development strategy and policy in Latin America should no longer be based on conclusions derived from this theory, and to propose an alternative strategy.

Prebisch, like Furtado and other ECLA economists, stresses the central role of rising labour productivity in economic development. Only this can provide the basis for a steady increase in mass living standards. His attack on the theory of comparative advantage is linked to the empirical observation that, contrary to the theory's prediction, the benefits of technological advance in primary exporting and manufacturing economies are not equitably distributed between the two trading partners. The data upon which Prebisch's argument is founded are summarised in Table 5.1, which indicates an adverse long-run trend in the terms of trade for primary commodities from the mid-1870s to the mid-1930s.

Major advances in productivity have occurred in the main manufacturing nations since the late nineteenth century. According to the theory of comparative advantage, this should have been reflected in a decline in the price of their exports, and a consequent improvement in the terms of trade of primary exporters. Yet this has not occurred. It has not done so, argues Prebisch, due to the downward rigidity of wages and prices in the manufacturing nations.

Table 5.1   Ratio of prices of primary commodities to those of manufactured goods

Average import and export prices, according to data of the British Board of Trade
(1876–80 = 100)

Periods	Amount of finished products obtainable for a given quantity of primary commodities
1876–80	100
1881–85	102.4
1886–90	96.3
1891–95	90.1
1896–1900	87.1
1901–05	84.6
1906–10	85.8
1911–13	85.8
— —	—
1921–25	67.3
1926–30	73.3
1931–35	62.0
1936–38	64.1
— —	—
1946–47	68.7

Source: 'Post war price relations in trade between underdeveloped and industrialised countries',
document E/CN.1/Sub. 3/W.5, 23 February 1949, reproduced in Prebisch, 1962: 4.[16]

Instead, these productivity gains have been fully absorbed within the industrially advanced economies in the form of higher real wages and profits. Consequently the terms of trade of primary exporting countries, which should have improved, have not.

Furthermore, while the manufacturing nations have retained the benefits of their own productivity gains, the extent of the movement in the terms of trade suggests that they have also absorbed part of the productivity gains of primary exports (which *were* passed on through a decline in relative prices, as the theory of comparative advantage would predict).[17] Thus the conclusion of the theory of comparative advantage that where two countries have different internal relative productivities in the production of two goods, both can gain if they enter into international trade (and even in the unlikely case that all the gains are absorbed by one country, the other will not lose) no longer applies in the real world.

The cause of the centre's ability not only to retain its own productivity gains but also to appropriate part of those of the periphery derives, in Prebisch's view, largely from different responses to recession in the two regions. Specifically, it derives from trade union success in the centre in claiming wage increases in the upswing of the trade cycle while ensuring wage rigidity in the downswing.

> When profits have to be reduced during the downswing, the part that had been absorbed by wage increases loses its fluidity, at the centre, by means of the well-known resistance to a lowering of wages. The pressure then moves to the periphery. . . The less that income can contract at the centre, the more it has to do so at the periphery.

> The characteristic lack of organisation among the workers employed in primary production prevents them from obtaining wage increases comparable to those of the industrial countries and from maintaining the increases to the same extent. The reduction of income – whether profits or wages – is therefore less difficult at the periphery.'
>
> (*Ibid.*: 6.)

Although the prices of primary products rise rapidly in the upswing of a trade cycle, this is more than offset in the downswing, hence the long-run downward trend in the terms of trade for primary producers.

This is another explanation of a phenomenon, the failure of the periphery to retain the benefits of its own productivity increases in traded goods, that was also noted by Lewis.[18] However, while Lewis emphasises the unlimited supply of low-cost labour as the key causal factor leading to the loss of surplus, Prebisch emphasises the lack of effective unionisation of wage labour in primary production in the periphery. It would seem that here it is Lewis that offers the more profound explanation, since the lack of effective unionisation is itself surely due to the excess supply of labour that Lewis emphasises.

From his analysis of the causes of the long-run trend in the terms of trade of primary exporters, Prebisch concludes that the economies of the periphery have no option but to industrialise and produce their own manufactured goods. They will then be able to reap the benefits of their own productivity gains both in primary production and in manufacturing.

Prebisch (1949) also adduces a second reason for promoting industrial development in the periphery. In the nineteenth century the leading industrial economy, Great Britain, pursued a policy of free trade in a context in which a substantial proportion of the gross domestic product of this expanding economy was traded for imports of raw materials. When the United States took over as the leading industrial economy a notable change occurred, for its import coefficient is much lower than that of Great Britain. Already only 5 per cent in 1929, it fell further during the following recession and stood at 3 per cent in 1948. This low import coefficient reflects the United States' high degree of self-sufficiency in many raw materials and does not augur well for the primary export growth prospects of the underdeveloped economies.

In his later work, Prebisch incorporated into his argument concerning the poor prospects for primary export expansion a separate point first made by Singer (1950). Singer argued that a further reason both for the downward long-term trend in the terms of trade for primary products, and for expecting only relatively low growth of future primary export volume (with slower real revenue growth), lay in the different income elasticities of demand for primary and industrial goods, these being generally low for the former and high for the latter. Another reason, noted by Nurkse (1952), was the development in the industrially advanced countries of synthetic substitutes for primary products.[19] Prebisch (1964) emphasises both these factors and, in addition, the further depressing effects on demand for primary exports from the periphery of growing protectionism in European agriculture and increased efficiency in the industrial economies in the use of raw materials, leading to less input per unit of output.[20]

Prebisch, however, had already stated his central conclusion in 1949:

> Before the great depression development in Latin-American countries was stimulated from abroad by the constant increase in exports. There is no reason to suppose, at least at present, that this will again occur, except under very exceptional circumstances. These countries no longer have an alternative. . . Industrialisation has become the most important means of expansion.
>
> (Prebisch, 1962: 3.)

This conclusion immediately became a key element in the structuralist perspective, although the methodology and hence the validity of the empirical terms of trade analysis on which it is partly based have been criticised (see pp. 146–8 below).

While predictions concerning the likely long-run trend in the terms of trade are given little explicit attention in Furtado's historical analysis of the growth dynamic in the centre and the periphery, they complement and reinforce his argument. The periphery must begin to control this dynamic by deliberately introducing measures to reduce dependence on foreign demand as the engine of growth.

The rising import coefficient in the periphery

However, the same external factors that made industrialisation necessary combined with existing conditions in underdeveloped economies to create a situation in which the path to industrialisation would be neither automatic nor smooth. While poor prospects for expanding primary export earnings underlie the case for industrialisation, they also represent a major constraint to its attainment. For, as we have seen in our review of Furtado, and as Prebisch and other structuralists also emphasise, the expansion of the modern sector is itself heavily import-dependent. Increased self-sufficiency in the long term requires, as a precondition, increased imports and, hence, increased access to foreign exchange.

In the early stages of development of the periphery, the very openness of the economy is likely to prevent the emergence of excess demand for foreign exchange. Where the modern enclave is confined to primary export production, the domestic multiplier will be negligible, and any increase in demand for imports that stems from an increase in export incomes is highly unlikely to exceed the value of the income increase. However, as the modern sector develops and diversifies, so the value of the domestic multiplier rises, and accelerator effects also begin to operate. Any initial stimulus to demand, whether external or internal, will be augmented by the domestic interaction of the multiplier and the accelerator. Due to the import content of both recurrent production and investment in the modern sector, this multiple expansion in income and demand will inevitably increase the demand for imports.[21]

As the modern sector becomes increasingly diversified and the composition of investment changes towards increased emphasis on producer goods production, so the upward movement in the marginal propensity to import is accelerated for a second reason – the higher import content of investment in the producer goods sector as compared with the consumer goods sector.

> Brazil's experience in the recent past indicates that, for an import coefficient of about 10 per cent in the economy as a whole, participation of imports in the value of net investments amounts to about a third, which leads to a coefficient more than three times as high as the average. Furthermore if we single out from among investments those actually creating productive capacity, then the need for exchange cover rises to about two thirds.
>
> (Furtado, *op.cit.*: 151.)

Thus, the low income elasticities of demand at the centre for the periphery's primary exports combine with high income and low price elasticity of demand for imports in the periphery to render the latter increasingly susceptible to balance of payments crises as it attempts to develop.

The impact of international trade cycles on development in the periphery

Peripheral economies must also confront the inherently cyclical nature of capitalist growth and the tendency, already noted, of the industrially advanced countries to export their cycles. While the vulnerability of primary export earnings to the trade cycle constitutes part of the argument for industrialisation, it also represents a further impediment to its smooth attainment. Whereas in the past dramatic falls in export earnings (in the 1930s and early 1940s) led to accelerated industrialisation in parts of the periphery, the likelihood of this effect being repeated in the future declines as the import content of modern sector investment rises.[22] Rather, these periods are likely to witness overutilisation of existing capacity in an attempt to meet existing demand, while foreign exchange earnings in the early phase of the upswing will be used largely for capital maintenance and replacement.[23] In the international recession, capital accumulation in the periphery will tend to be concentrated in activities with a relatively low import content, such as the building industry.[24] The periphery cannot rely on a steady flow of foreign exchange earnings to finance its industrialisation programme.

Policy response to balance of payments disequilibria

While structuralist analyses represent balance of payments disequilibrium as an inevitable feature of economic development, they equally emphasise the importance of finding means to reduce the pressure on the foreign balance so that development can continue. A distinctive feature of the structuralist school of thought is the rejection of neo-classical, monetarist solutions to the problem of imbalance, as well as to that of domestic inflation. Already in 1949 Prebisch questioned whether balance of payments problems in the periphery could be solved simply by applying 'sound rules of monetary behaviour'. Sound rules for these countries, he observed, are still in the making.[25] With time the structuralist theoretical position on these issues came to be more clearly articulated. Furtado (1964) provides a clearly stated summary of the perceived weaknesses in the monetarist approach.

According to the monetarist view, both pressure on the balance of payments and domestic price inflation are symptoms of the same problem: excess demand generated by an unduly rapid expansion of the money supply. The solutions lie in domestic deflation, and in devaluation of the currency in order to both reduce the demand for foreign exchange and increase foreign currency earnings. According to structuralist analyses, recommendation of these solutions derives from an incorrect diagnosis of the problem, based on the assumption that all economies function in a similar manner. Adoption of monetarist solutions to these pressures in the periphery would amount to throwing out the baby (development) with the bath-water (monetary disequilibria). The impact of devaluation will be considered first.

Devaluation may adversely affect development for three reasons. Firstly, its impact on the balance of payments may be negative rather than positive due to low price elasticities of demand for imports and exports. If the sum of these two elasticities is less than unity then a country's balance of trade will be worse following a devaluation than preceding it. Particularly in the intermediate and late stages of underdevelopment, when most imports consist of essential capital and intermediate goods, the price elasticity of demand for imports is likely to be low. Hence only if export demand is price elastic will there be an overall gain from devaluation. If foreign exchange outlays are unlikely to fall significantly, then foreign exchange earnings must rise. Yet in practice the latter is unlikely to occur, partly because the exporting country's competitors may cut their prices rather than lose their market share, while aggregate demand in the advanced countries for primary imports is also unlikely to be highly price sensitive.[26]

Secondly, devaluation may have a further negative impact on the foreign balance where primary export production is under foreign ownership. If, due to either external demand conditions, capacity limitations or other reasons, it is impossible to expand exports, at least in the short term, the sole immediate consequence of devaluation on the export side will be to raise the domestic price of the export. All the value of the price increase will accrue to the firm's owners as increased profit and will probably then be remitted abroad, thus increasing foreign exchange outflows.

Thirdly, devaluation will raise the domestic price of imports. The immediate effect will be felt most severely in those branches of the economy with the highest capital intensity. Since in the intermediate and late stages of under-development the import coefficient is higher in investment than consumption, it is here that the effects will be most severe. With an increase in the relative cost of investment there will be a decline in the real value of savings.[27]

For these reasons the monetarist response to balance of payments dis-equilibrium was rejected by structuralist economists, while alternative responses which would not impede development were proposed. However, before considering these alternatives, the next section considers structuralist analyses of inflation in underdeveloped economies.

THE CAUSES OF DOMESTIC PRICE INFLATION IN THE PERIPHERY

In the late 1940s the Latin American economies were experiencing moderate to rapid domestic price inflation as well as balance of payments problems. Prebisch (1949) discusses the impact of inflation on the balance of payments, income distribution, saving, and the pace of development. The continuing preoccupation with inflation is well illustrated by Sunkel (1960), Seers (1962), Furtado (*op.cit.*) and Felix (1964). These later analyses gave greater emphasis to the causes of inflation than did Prebisch, culminating in the formal statement of causality contained in the Seers model.

Prebisch (1949) sees the causes of inflation as lying jointly in the inter-national operation of the Duesenberry effect in the sphere of public expenditure.[28] and in the belief that 'inflation is an unavoidable means of forced capitalisation where voluntary saving is evidently insufficient'.[29] With respect to the consequences of monetary expansion, a moderate credit expansion may contribute to expanded employment and output. Here Pre-bisch seems to anticipate the argument in Lewis (1954).[30]

Prebisch concludes that monetary expansion is more likely to raise prices than employment in the first instance, resulting in a redistribution of income towards the recipients of profit.

> The rise in prices, by creating exceptional profits, places in the hands of a comparatively small group great opportunities for savings.

Again Prebisch apparently foreshadows Lewis. However, the analyses are not identical. Firstly, Prebisch does not accept that profits are automatically converted into investment. Rather, he concludes on the basis of evidence from Brazil that only some 50 per cent of profits are so used.[31] Secondly, those who consume out of profits have a high propensity to import. How-ever, the nub of the matter lies in the fact that, while monetary expansion *may* increase savings, it cannot increase the supply of foreign exchange needed to finance the import of capital and intermediate goods. Meanwhile it is likely to reduce voluntary saving among other income groups while increasing income inequality. Prebisch, writing in 1949, focused only on the conventionally-accepted cause of inflation – monetary expansion. However, his analysis already emphasised a key characteristic of the structuralist school – preoccupation with the foreign balance.[32]

It is, however, in the later work of the structuralist school that the distinctive structuralist analyses of inflation emerge. These focus on the structural causes of inflation, and their implications for policy. Just as international and domestic demand elasticities render underdeveloped economies inherently susceptible to balance of payments crises, so domestic supply inelasticities in key sectors – agriculture, due largely to tenurial conditions, infrastructure, certain branches of industry, and also shortages of skilled labour and entrepreneurial skills – render underdeveloped economies inherently susceptible to cost-inflation during the transformation process.[33] Such pressures on costs are also exacerbated by diseconomies of small-scale production in newly created industries. Inflation 'is not an autonomous phenomenon, but an overt expression of structural maladjustments which follow in the wake of the growth process in some phases of underdevelopment.' (Furtado, *op.cit.*: 168.) 'With short-run supply elasticities typically quite low, rises in some prices are bound to be substantial.' (Hirschman, *op.cit.*: 158.) Inevitably price rises which are due to supply shortages, while initially located in specific sectors, tend to be transmitted throughout the economy. For example, food shortages lead to money wage increases and so to price increases in the modern sector (see Seers, 1962; Felix, 1964: 379).[34] Where new industries are protected monopolies, the likelihood of cost increases being fully passed on in price increases is high, and 'once price rises get under way, there will be familiar cumulative tendencies as each class attempts to protect itself from the rise in prices.' (Seers, 1962: 180.)[35] Meanwhile any attempt to cope with balance of payments disequilibria, however caused, through devaluation will add to domestic inflationary pressures.

As Seers observes,

> It is true that some expansion of the supply of money is a necessary condition for this process to go very far (though one must expect some elasticity in the velocity of circulation). A restrictive monetary policy would, however, only permit the necessary rate of growth to be combined with price stability if the price rises due to the influences mentioned above were offset by price falls in other sectors. Since the upward pressures are strong, and cover wide areas of the economy (through rising prices of imports, skilled labour, etc.), and unskilled wage-earners and existing firms are assumed to have some defensive strength, this is very unlikely.
>
> (Seers, 1962: 180,1.)

While these later structuralist analyses concur that inflationary pressures are inevitable during phases of growth combined with structural transformation, they also concur that if inflation gets out of hand its impact on development becomes negative; 'long-term productive investment becomes discouraged in favour of more speculative uses of capital, such as hoarding inventories, buying foreign exchange, and building apartments and shops for the higher income groups' (Seers, *op.cit.*: 180). Thus it is essential to seek ways of containing the upward pressure on prices within tolerable bounds, but without lowering the rate of growth and structural change. Foreign credit has an important role to play in helping to contain inflationary pressure. Domestic governments also have a role to play in guiding investments into key areas and in the implementation of institutional reforms, particularly agrarian reform, in order to improve domestic supply elasticities.   Structuralist theories of inflation, while not universally accepted, have had an enduring and widening influence in the field of policy debate. Indeed, the ideas first developed in Latin America have come to be applied also to the analysis of inflation in the industrially advanced countries by economists who were dissatisfied with alternative, monetarist, analyses.[36]

THE DOMESTIC POLICY RECOMMENDATIONS OF THE STRUCTURALIST SCHOOL

Many of the policy recommendations that stem from structuralist analyses of underdevelopment relate in one way or another to the international context. The tenor of the policy debate, with its preoccupations with the balance of payments constraint, the small size of the domestic market and domestic supply inelasticities, is noticeably different from that to be found in those analyses which perceive inadequate domestic savings to be the dominant constraint to growth. Understandably, since the preoccupations and the logic of the two perspectives differ, the policy recommendations are also often different, although there are notable exceptions.

Wages

We have seen how the Lewis model, given its assumptions, demonstrates that if growth is to be maximised there must be no increase in wages until the labour surplus has been absorbed from the subsistence sector (although Galenson and Leibenstein questioned this, see p. 104 above). The leading structuralist economists revealed no equivalent preoccupation. Indeed, some revealed a preference for a degree of wage increase.

Some of the reasons for this lack of preoccupation with the potentially adverse effect of premature wage increases are to be found in Prebisch (1949). Three of his observations are particularly worth noting:

> It does not appear essential to restrict the individual consumption of the bulk of the population, which, on the whole, is too low, in order to accumulate the

capital required for industrialisation and for the technical improvement of agriculture.[37]

If productivity in agriculture can be increased by technical progress and if, at the same time, real wages can be raised by industrialisation and adequate social legislation, the disequilibrium between incomes at the centre and the periphery can gradually be corrected.[38]

A general increase in wages resulting from greater productivity in industry gradually spreads to other activities, which are thereby obliged to use more capital, per capita, in order to achieve the increase in productivity without which they would be unable to pay higher wages.[39]

The structuralist economists never lost sight of the fact that economic development is fundamentally concerned with raising the productivity of labour and with reaping the benefits of increased productivity through increased incomes. Apart from equity reasons, Prebisch suggests a consistency between some real wage increase in the modern sector and economic development for the following reasons:

1. This helps to expand the domestic market.
2. Some general increase in wages may act as a stimulus to raising labour productivity in technologically backward branches of productive activity.[40]
3. Real wage increases are a crucial means of retaining the benefits of rising productivity within an open economy.[41]

Felix (1964) also argues that where Latin American economies have been forced to implement a decline in real wages as part of a deflationary package this has been developmentally counterproductive. Through its impact on the structure of domestic demand, the reduction of real wages tended to divert investment in the industrial sector excessively and indiscriminately to consumer and capital goods that are technologically sophisticated and import-intensive. In contrast, the less sophisticated and more labour-intensive consumer goods industries are generally industries whose demand depends more heavily on wage income.[42] These, argues Felix, are also precisely the industries which in the early stages of industrialisation offer the best prospects for export development.

Fiscal policy

Taxation

The reference in Prebisch (1949) to the role of taxation in the promotion of development also reveals a difference in emphasis to that in Lewis (1954). In the structuralist theoretical literature we do not find a preoccupation with restraining premature increases in the supply price of labour through taxation of peasant incomes. Rather, the ECLA economists emphasised the need to use taxation to restrain luxury consumption with its high import content, and to encourage investment.

> The State has the means of stimulating the investment of a large portion of profits and inflationary incomes through progressive taxation of the part spent and consumed, while lowering the tax or granting exemption on the part invested.
>
> (Prebisch, 1962: 15.)

Thus, the emphasis is upon guiding resource use through differential rates of taxation, both direct and indirect.

Public expenditure

There is an implicit assumption in the structuralist theoretical literature that the bulk of productive capital accumulation will be undertaken in the private sector. The role of government is to guide and facilitate the correct pattern of investment *inter alia* through infrastructure creation.[43] Prebisch (1949) expressed a concern that too fast an increase in public outlays on nonproductive services could detract from capital accumulation and contribute to inflationary pressures. Latin Americans should not aspire to achieve prematurely the same standard of public services as in the United States.

Monetary policy and inflation

This was to some extent discussed above (pp. 136–8). Some inflation is inevitable during the development process due to inelasticities of supply in key sectors of the domestic economy. Consequent upward pressures on costs are likely to be increased by the need to operate new industrial plant at below its optimum scale and possibly also by the need for periodic devaluations of the domestic currency. Purely monetarist policy measures to counteract cost-inflation can only succeed in stabilising prices if they slow down the pace of investment and structural change that induced the upward pressure on costs in the first place. Stringent control of the money supply suppresses inflation by slowing the pace of development and, hence, the growth of demand for the output of key sectors, but it does not eliminate the underlying problem. This can only be achieved by development itself. 'The essence of a fundamental stabilisation policy is a long-term development programme to achieve the structural changes which are needed.' (Seers, *op.cit.*: 192.) Governments have an important role to play in guiding investments to key sectors and in the promotion of relevant institutional reforms (for example, in land tenure) which will encourage expansion of production. Foreign borrowing can help to ease inflationary pressures during the process of structural change.[44] The establishment of common markets between underdeveloped economies in the same region can enable investors in the periphery to reap the same economies of scale as their competitors in industrially advanced countries.

Balance of payments management

In the structuralist view, as in the monetarist, the causes of domestic price inflation and balance of payments disequilibria are closely linked, but of course they differ in the two theoretical perspectives. According to the former, long-run structural change should lead to a permanent decline in the import coefficient and hence to elimination of excess pressure on the foreign balance. In the short- to medium-term, various measures can help to reduce the inevitable pressures on foreign currency supplies. Some require action in the periphery, but others necessitate action by industrially advanced countries and/or international institutions. In the periphery, governments can take the following action:

1. Cut non-essential imports (through the use of tariffs, quotas and foreign exchange controls).[45]
2. Expand primary exports and, as industrial development proceeds, manufactured exports.[46]
3. Guide investment into key import-substituting sectors:

> investments in the sector substituting imports must grow at a rate higher than that of investment in the sectors which have already been producing for the domestic market for some time. The risk involved in such investments is greater, however, and experience in the newer sectors is smaller or even non-existent.
>
> (Furtado, 1964: 170.)

Thus essential infant industries must be identified and promoted by the public sector.
4. Pursue policies to counteract international trade cycles through stringent import control – including that of deferrable capital goods imports – during the downswing.
5. Form common markets in the periphery to increase the range of viable import-substituting investment.

Meanwhile, industrially advanced countries and international institutions can reduce balance of payments pressures in the periphery through the following measures:

1. Pursuit of countercyclical policy and maintenance of full employment.[47]
2. Reduction of protectionism in the industrially advanced countries for both agriculture (especially in Europe) and manufacturing production.[48]
3. Direct foreign investment in the periphery.[49]
4. Increased lending to the periphery.[50]
5. Establishment of compensatory finance schemes to assist primary exporting economies to meet their foreign payments obligations during the downswing of the trade cycle.[51]

6. Provision of a temporary system of preferences for manufactured exports from developing countries[52] (as a means of helping infant industries in the periphery which need access to wider markets in order to become cost competitive).

Choice of techniques

During the fifteen year period 1949–1964 which saw the articulation of the 'classical' structuralist paradigm, choice of techniques was not perceived as a central issue by structuralist theoreticians. Despite some indication of misgiving in the early work of Furtado, it appears to have been broadly accepted that import substitution entailed import replication, and, hence, adoption of identical technologies to those employed in different branches of industry in the industrially advanced countries.[53] In 1955 Eckhaus argued in the *American Economic Review* that choice of technique is in reality often limited:

> In large sectors of an economy there are only a few alternative processes that can be utilised.
> (Eckhaus, 1955, reprinted in Agarwala and Singh, *op.cit.*: 354.)

This view is either explicitly or implicitly accepted in most structuralist analyses; see e.g. Furtado, 1964: 142.

Sectoral priorities

It is a central tenet of structuralist theory that industrialisation should receive priority. However, it should be supported by the expansion of agricultural output for the domestic market and also, whenever possible, of primary exports.[54] Within industry, the most efficient sequence of development determined by market size runs from import substitution in consumer goods production to intermediate goods production and lastly to capital goods.

The structuralists had relatively little to say about agricultural development. However, they noted agriculture's potential contributions to development as a source of foreign exchange and urban food supplies, and the inefficiency and inequity of the *latifundista-minifundista* tenurial system that predominated in the Latin American region. They also emphasised the contribution to domestic price inflation made by a sluggish agricultural sector. Sunkel and Felix both emphasise the need for agricultural expansion as one of the means of reducing domestic price inflation, but have little to say about how this is to be achieved beyond noting the potential contribution of institutional reform.[55]

Common markets

Common markets and free trade areas formed between clusters of neighbouring underdeveloped economies can, through the enlargement of market size, make a major contribution to the range of viable industrial investment within the region.

Foreign investment

Foreign investment is to be welcomed – and actively encouraged, through tax concessions, etc. – as a source of foreign finance and technology. However, such investment should, like investment by national companies, be guided into the branches of production in which it is most needed (Prebisch, 1962: 3, 16).

Prices as a guide to resource allocation

Given the existing structure of production in the periphery, the market price mechanism alone cannot bring about a socially acceptable rate of growth and structural change. Public sector intervention to change relative prices (through taxation, tariffs and multiple exchange rates) and to control access to scarce resources (finance capital, foreign exchange) is needed in order to guide investment into priority branches of production, including new, relatively high-risk spheres of import substitution (Prebisch, 1962; Furtado, 1964: 169–171; Felix, 1964). The need for such policy interventions is a key element in the structuralist logic. It is based on the explicit argument that market forces will not induce a pattern of resource allocation in underdeveloped countries that can promote long-run development, and on the assumption that policy-guided interference with market forces can do better.

THE ROLE OF FOREIGN AID IN THE STRUCTURALIST PARADIGM

For the ECLA economists, preoccupied with frequent, though fluctuating, shortages of foreign exchange in the national economies of Latin America, the primary role of foreign aid was to help relieve balance of payments pressures (and associated pressures on domestic prices).[56]

During the 1950s and early 1960s both ECLA and GATT used foreign exchange gap models to project the foreign aid requirements of underdeveloped economies. Essentially, the procedure employed was based upon the following:

1. Projected rates of growth of GDP for developed and for underdeveloped countries.
2. Assumed income elasticities of demand on the part of developed countries for Third World exports.
3. Assumed stability in sources of supply of primary exports.

4. Assumptions concerning trends in import needs in the underdeveloped economies.

During the 1950s and early 1960s projections of foreign aid requirements generally used either the investment-savings gap approach (sometimes linked to an estimate of absorptive capacity)[57] or the foreign exchange gap approach. However, between 1962 and 1966 several papers were published, each written essentially in the structuralist tradition, which suggested that any one country may be subject, at different times, to either of these overriding constraints. This idea was put forward by Chenery and Bruno (1962), Manne (1963), McKinnon (1964) and Chenery and Strout (1966).[58]

We have already considered Chenery and Strout's treatment of absorptive capacity and the savings gap in Chapter 4.[59] In their model, the foreign exchange constraint is the third of three overriding constraints to growth which emerge sequentially in underdeveloped countries. It emerges once a country, having overcome the skill constraint, and having increased domestic savings propensities, endeavours to sustain rapid growth in the face of a need for structural change. The constraint emerges due to

> a country's inability to change its productive structure to meet the changing patterns of internal and external demand. Although this problem is not likely to be serious in a slowly developing economy, rapid growth requires a large increase in the supplies of machinery and equipment, raw materials, and other manufactured goods that are typically imported in a poor country. The more rapid the rate of growth, the larger the reallocation of labour and capital away from traditional patterns that will be needed to prevent bottle-necks developing. If this reallocation is not sufficiently rapid, shortages of imported goods will provide a limit to further growth quite apart from the investment limitation.
>
> (Chenery and Strout, 1966 : 682.)

In these circumstances foreign aid can help to finance essential imports. Meanwhile for elimination of the foreign exchange gap the two crucial parameters are the rate of growth of exports and the marginal propensity to import. The former must rise, and/or the latter fall, if the gap is to be eliminated.

APPLICATIONS TO DEVELOPMENT PLANNING

The contribution of the ECLA structuralist school to development planning in Latin America is reviewed in Furtado (1976).[60] ECLA's perspective both contributed to the formation of the Latin American Free Trade Area (LAFTA) and exerted some influence on national development planning in the region. ECLA's frequently reiterated concern with the small size of domestic markets had no immediate practical outcome but it 'helped to create the psychological climate that led to the formation of a free trade area in 1960.' (Furtado, 1976: 233.)

Furtado also claims that the application of the structuralist perspective to national planning resulted in:

> an entirely new approach in the evolution of ideas on economic planning, since it differed not only from socialist planning – an outcome of the determination to change the overall economic structure and the need to coordinate investment decisions in a system involving greatly diminished consumer freedom – but also from planning in Western Europe, for which the starting point was the concern to coordinate sectoral programmes or to achieve conditions of full employment for labour.
>
> (Furtado, 1976: 244.)

In contrast, ECLA's ideas on planning sprang from a concern to regulate the import-substitution process:

> The methodology worked out by ECLA and later widely adopted in [Latin America] is based on a diagnosis of the national economy in question and on a set of macro-economic projections established essentially on the basis of hypotheses concerning the evolution of the capital-output ratio and the income elasticities of demand for final products. . . On the basis of the capital-output data and the analysis of inter-industrial relationships, a system of projections can be worked out that makes it possible to forecast the structural inadequacy of the capacity to import, the rate of private domestic savings or of fiscal revenue in terms of various hypotheses as to the probable growth of the domestic product, the increase in the demand for exports and probable trends in relative export prices, as well as in terms of the estimated income elasticities of demand for the major items of consumption. In other words the technique involves a prospective analysis that makes it possible to define the conditions of internal and external balance, given certain development targets.
>
> (Furtado, 1976: 244, 5.)

ECLA's influence on national development planning in Latin America has been quite widespread. Furtado reports that 'the Target Programme carried out in Brazil in the second half of the 1950s was directly inspired by this type of diagnosis'. However, he also observes that the authorities, while successful in promoting industrialisation, were unable to avoid aggravation of inflationary pressures and a sizeable external debt. Elsewhere in Latin America it appears from Furtado's diagnosis that the same constraints which lie at the heart of the structuralist analysis of underdevelopment made really effective planning essentially unattainable – although he notes considerable advances in planning public sector investment, in external resource mobilisation, and in the orientation of private investment. Key outstanding problems were: '(a) short-term fluctuations in the external sector and the difficulties encountered in increasing the capacity to import, (b) the rigidity of the agricultural sector and (c) the inadequacy of the public sector's mobilisation of resources.'[61]

The strategy of backward linked import-substituting industrialisation has of course not been confined to Latin America. We have already seen that there was a significant element of *ex post facto* theorisation in the evolution of structuralist theory, and there were other parts of the Third World apart from Brazil, Chile and Argentina where this process of industrialisation got under way as a pragmatic response to objective conditions rather than the application to development planning and policy of the structuralist theoretical perspective, for example Taiwan and South Korea in the 1950s. However, among the later-comers to development planning and industrialisation, for example in Africa, there is clear evidence of the influence of structuralist thought on economic planning in the 1960s. This applies, for example, to Ghana's *Seven Year Plan* for 1963/4–1969/70, for which Seers and Hirschman, as well as Arthur Lewis, were expatriate advisors.[62] Likewise Uganda's *Second Five Year Plan, 1966–1971* reflects the structuralist approach,[63] as does the Tanganyika *Five Year Plan* for 1964–1969.[64]

Meanwhile the structuralist perspective has also had a major influence on policy negotiations at the international level, most notably through the policy stance taken by the United Nations Conference on Trade and Development of which Prebisch became the first Secretary-General.[65]

CRITICISMS OF THE STRUCTURALIST PARADIGM

Although many development economists, not only in Latin America, have found it fruitful to apply a structuralist perspective in their analytical work, criticisms have also been levelled against various aspects of the structuralist paradigm. These fall into four categories. Some question the methodological and conceptual foundations of the empirical terms of trade analyses that partly underpin the case for industrialisation; some query the conceptual and/or logical validity of structuralist theory; some focus on the consequences of government promotion of import substitution for efficiency and consumer welfare, and some focus on errors of omission.

The methodological foundations of structuralist analyses of historical trends in the terms of trade

The structuralist case for industrialisation in the periphery rests partly on an analysis of historical trends in the terms of trade and partly on predictions concerning likely future trends. Methodological and conceptual criticisms of the former do not, therefore, suffice to undercut the case. None the less, as what was the future in 1949 becomes the past, it has become possible to use similar analyses to test the predictions that were then being made. The importance of selecting the correct methodology remains, therefore, an important issue, although exactly how important is controversial. Among the methodological errors noted are the following:

1. Sensitivity of the estimates to the base and terminal years chosen.
2. Data inaccuracy, including:

    (a) failure to take into account the impact of quality changes and product innovation upon the value of manufactured exports;

    (b) failure to take account of declining transport costs for the import price of *both* primary and manufactured exports (Prebisch's study did so only for primary exports);

    (c) equation of primary exports with underdeveloped country, and manufactured exports with developed country, exports.

3. Conceptual error: i.e. use of trends in the commodity terms of trade alone in order to determine whether a country has gained from trade.

Data accuracy

The original United Nations study upon which the arguments in Prebisch (1949) are based has been faulted both for the use of imprecise proxy data and for misleading data aggregation. With respect to the former, the study actually analysed trends in the United Kingdom's terms of trade, the United Kingdom being, in the period covered, primarily an exporter of manufactured products and an importer of primary products. From these data the trend for underdeveloped, primary exporters was then inferred. In his review of the weaknesses of the methodology used, Meier lists the following:

> The import price index conceals heterogeneous price movements within and among the broad categories of foodstuffs, raw materials, and minerals; no allowance is made for changes in the quality of exports and imports;[66] there is inadequate consideration of new commodities; and the recorded terms of trade are not corrected for the substantial decline in transportation costs. The introduction of new products and qualitative improvements have been greater in manufactured than in primary products, and a large proportion of the fall in British prices of primary products can be attributed to the great decline in inward freight rates. The simple use of the 'inverse' of the United Kingdom's terms of trade to indicate the terms of trade of primary producing countries involves therefore a systematic bias which makes changes appear more unfavourable to the primary exporting countries than they actually were.
>
> (Meier, 1984: 504–5.)

Conceptual error

Meier continues:

> Even if it were true that the less developed countries experienced a secular deterioration in their commodity terms of trade, the question would still remain whether this constituted a significant obstacle to their development. The answer depends on what caused the deterioration and whether the country's factoral terms of trade and income terms also deteriorated. If the deterioration in the commodity terms is due to increased productivity in the export sector, the single factoral terms of trade (commodity terms corrected for changes in productivity in producing exports) can improve at the same time. As long as productivity in its export industries is increasing more rapidly than export prices are falling, the country's real income can rise despite the deterioration in the commodity terms of trade: when its factoral terms improve, the country benefits from the ability to obtain a greater quantity of imports per unit of

factors embodied in exports. Also possible is an improvement in the country's income terms of trade (commodity terms multiplied by quantity of exports) at the same time as its commodity terms deteriorate. The country's capacity to import is then greater, and this will ease the development effort. When due weight is given to the increase in productivity in export production and the rise in export volume, it would appear that the single-factoral terms and income terms of trade actually improved for many poor countries, notwithstanding any possible deterioration in their commodity terms of trade.

(Meier, 1984: 505.)[67]

These conceptual criticisms do not, however, confront Prebisch's argument that industrially advanced countries fail to pass on their own productivity gains in lower prices, although it can be claimed that this argument is partly met by the prior observation that quality increases which do not show up in the terms of trade indices have been greater for manufactured goods.

Selection of the base year
A further criticism levelled against both the original United Nations study and subsequent studies conducted by ECLA of trends in the terms of trade during the 1950s concerns the selection of the base year. For example, when 1950 is selected as the base year it is hardly surprising that the subsequent trend is downwards since this was a year of very high primary product prices associated with the outbreak of the Korean War. Likewise, when the mid-1870s are selected as the base, the long-term trend in the commodity terms of trade for primary products again appears to be downwards until the mid-1930s. Conversely, however, when 1900 is taken as the base year, a number of analysts have found no clear trend.

In reply to these criticisms, however, it can be argued that it is not so much what is happening to the terms of trade that is important, as what is happening to export demand. If demand is growing slowly then *irrespective of what is actually happening to the measured terms of trade* this means that foreign demand cannot be relied upon to act as a major inducement to growth. Adverse shifts in the terms of trade will tend to induce some changes in the allocation of factors in the exporting country away from the affected sector. This will tend to offset to some extent the initial impact of the adverse movement in the terms of trade. But it will not alter the fundamental trend in demand.

The validity of the concept of a foreign exchange constraint to growth

Doubts have also been raised concerning the conceptual validity of the notion of a foreign exchange constraint to growth and development. According to this line of criticism, most, if not all, apparent foreign exchange constraints actually boil down to a savings constraint: if populations in the Third World consumed less of domestic output and exported more, they would have more foreign exchange.

According to Joshi (1970) for a true foreign exchange constraint to exist, it must be impossible to transform additional domestic production into additional foreign exchange – the price elasticity of reciprocal demand for existing exports must be unity or less. It must also be impossible to increase foreign exchange earnings by introducing new exports, or to raise foreign exchange availability for growth-promoting imports by reducing other imports. Joshi also points out that even if existing imports are of producer goods, it may be possible to economise on foreign exchange by using these more efficiently.

Joshi concludes that while the existence of a pure *ex ante* foreign exchange constraint is in principle possible, its empirical likelihood has been exaggerated. Two-gap models such as those of McKinnon and Chenery have contributed to this exaggeration through their assumption of fixed import coefficients and capital:output ratios and of a given maximum feasible rate of growth of exports that is not amenable to policy influence.

Inflation, monetary policy and the balance of payments

Structuralist theories of inflation and balance of payments crises also remain controversial. Monetarist critics continue to argue that prices cannot rise without a prior expansion of the money supply, and balance of payments crises reflect domestic excess demand and an overvalued domestic currency. In the face of inflation and balance of payments pressures, devaluation provides an incentive to expand exports and contract imports while domestic deflation (restraint on the money supply) reduces excess demand for both domestically-produced goods and imports, and hence the inefficiencies (speculation, hoarding) that excess demand often generates.

A substantial number of empirical studies have been undertaken in an attempt to test the explanatory power of these alternative theories. However, recent studies have generated conflicting results.[68]

Interest rate policy has received little attention in structuralist theory. However, another aspect of monetary policy widely associated with the structuralist approach to development planning (but also linked to the paradigm of the expanding capitalist nucleus) is that of keeping real interest rates low in the modern sector in order to encourage new investment. Shaw and McKinnon have both argued that this policy has repressed the much-needed development of financial institutions in the periphery. It has had the following results:

1. Reduced savings mobilisation.
2. Encouraged inefficient, low return uses of investible resources in the modern sector.
3. Deprived potentially efficient small-scale investors from access to essential credit, partly by curtailing the risk premium available to lenders.[69]

This interest rate structure has also been criticised for encouraging excessive capital intensity in production.

The economic efficiency and political viability of common markets as a means of enlarging market size in the periphery

The welfare costs and benefits of common markets

During the 1950s a substantial body of literature was published devoted to customs-union theory. The theoretical debate was of a general nature and the contributors did not necessarily make explicit reference to Third World countries. The debate culminated in the publication of a seminal article by Lipsey in 1960. The implications of Lipsey's theoretical conclusions for Third World countries are clear-cut, indicating that the welfare costs of custom unions are likely to outweigh the benefits. However, in reaching this conclusion Lipsey employs the technique of comparative statistics, itself open to criticism.

Structuralists emphasise increased industrial diversification as the main potential benefit of common market creation in the periphery. However, given the variation in levels of industrial and infrastructural development that so frequently characterises neighbouring countries, new investment is unlikely to be evenly distributed: it will concentrate in the most favourable location. For countries that experience little or no increase in investment, the potential benefits of common market entry are confined to any reduction in the cost of commodities to domestic users due to rationalisation and economies of scale in the use of existing capacity. Meanwhile the costs of entry take the following forms:

1. Loss of customs revenue on goods previously imported from outside the union.
2. Any increase in the price that has to be paid by local users for products previously imported from outside the region but now manufactured elsewhere in the region behind a common external tariff.
3. Any reduction in the quality of these goods.

Unless the new industries generate a significant demand for products that can be supplied by the industrial laggards in the common market, the costs to the latter of trade diversion will exceed any gains from trade creation.

Meanwhile, an analysis based on the neo-classical technique of comparative statics can also demonstrate that, within countries containing regional growth poles there may be welfare losses following the creation of a customs union if the main consequence is the establishment of new industries behind a common external tariff whose output costs more, and is of lower quality, than previous imports. This is simply a special case of the standard neo-classical criticism of import substitution (see pp. 152–3).

With respect to the welfare costs and benefits of customs unions Lipsey (1960) reached two general conclusions:

> *given a country's volume of international trade*, a customs union is more likely to raise welfare the higher is the proportion of trade with the country's union

partner and the lower the proportion with the outside world. . . A customs union is more likely to raise welfare the lower is the total volume of foreign trade, for the lower is foreign trade, the lower must be purchases from the outside world relative to domestic commodities.

(*Lipsey op.cit.*: 508–9.)

Lipsey did not explicitly apply his conclusions to underdeveloped economies, choosing to concentrate his empirical analysis upon the European common market. However, the implications for Third World countries are clearly pessimistic.

The structuralist counter-argument has been that in this, as in other areas of analysis, the tools of comparative statics lead one to ignore the potential long-term dynamic implications of a policy initiative. In this case, if an acceptable sharing of the benefits of customs unions can be arranged, the benefits would be the further development of regional industrial self-sufficiency, reduced dependence on primary exports to the industrially advanced countries as the 'engine of growth', enhanced creation of domestic skills and infrastructure and, with time, hopefully a diffusion of industry throughout the region either through planned location of investment and/or due to the impetus of the diseconomies that must ultimately result from further concentrations of investment around a particular growth pole (traffic congestion, delays in the service sector, pollution, the rising cost of industrial sites, etc.).[70] With time too, the promotion of import substitution in this and other ways can lead to a beneficial change in the comparative advantage of countries in the periphery.

The political viability of common markets in the periphery

Doubts have also been raised concerning the political viability of common markets among underdeveloped countries. Here the implied criticism of structuralist proposals for common market formation is one of omission – of failure to consider the political constraints.

Doubts were voiced during the 1960s with respect to the likelihood of assent between national governments concerning the following:

1. The distribution of new investment.
2. Proposals to reallocate productive activity in order to increase efficiency.

It was argued, for example, that no country would wish to reduce its existing degree of self-sufficiency in food production, even if the national staple could be produced at lower per unit cost in the agricultural sector of a fellow common market member. With respect to 1 it was argued that in underdeveloped countries, even more than elsewhere, the preferred location, on grounds of profitability, for new industrial investment will usually be the market's most advanced industrial centre(s). Here a new plant can reap external economies due to proximity to skilled labour, regional head offices of banking, insurance and legal services, a large urban market and a transport network providing access both to imports and more distant market outlets. This tendency, if uncontrolled, is likely to arouse resentment from other common market members. Indeed, it was precisely this concern that led Tanzania to withdraw from the East African common market after watching the growing concentration of industrial investment in Nairobi and Mombasa (both in Kenya). While arrangements that compensate for these tendencies can be designed, they too require political acceptance from all member countries. Furthermore, the solution that is likely to be preferred by the less industrially advanced members – the regional planning and distribution of industrial investment – will lower the profitability of investment and in some cases, if enforced, may deter potential investors.

An alternative form of compensation for the concentration of regional industrial investment is fiscal. This was also tried in East Africa, but the level of tax revenue transfer between countries when set against the perceived costs of the lack of industrial investment did not satisfy Tanzania (see Hazlewood, 1975).[71]

The efficiency costs of import substitution

Together with the structuralist theory of inflation and balance of payments crisis, the other aspect of the structuralist paradigm that has provoked the most widespread debate and criticism concerns import substitution. In this case criticism has focused upon the efficiency and welfare impact of the policy instruments used, especially when conjoined with an apparent political inability to remove infant industry protection.

With respect to the choice of policy instruments, those that have been widely used, and also widely criticised, are tax remission on capital investment, cheap credit, overvalued exchange-rates (to keep down the cost of capital imports), foreign exchange and investment licensing, selective tariffs and import quotas. These, it is claimed, have distorted relative prices and thereby have also distorted the choice of techniques in production, the inter-sectoral allocation of resources and the pattern of investment within industry. Meanwhile, administrative intervention in resource allocation has led to corruption (which has pushed up production costs), and to inefficiency and delay in the allocation of resources. The two most important forms of distortion in sectoral resource allocation that are cited are the following:

1. The discouragement of agricultural investment due to both the artificial raising of the rate of profit in industry, and the shift in the terms of trade against agriculture that has stemmed from the production of high cost import-substitutes in industry.
2. The discouragement of exports – primary and manufactured – due to the overvaluation of the exchange rate.

This critique was spearheaded in the late 1960s by the OECD-sponsored study of industrial development policy and performance in seven Third World countries conducted under the leadership of Little, Scitovsky and Scott. These economists, and others who argue in the same vein, also claim that the distorted relative price of capital and labour generates an inequitable growth path from which many members of the labour force are excluded. The use of capital-intensive techniques has also restricted the growth of the domestic market, while discouragement of exports and undue reliance on imported capital and intermediate goods has resulted in severe foreign exchange shortages. Thus, this growth path is not only inefficient and inequitable but short-lived, since it creates or accentuates precisely those two constraints that preoccupied the structuralists in the first place.

This neo-classical critique is linked to a series of alternative policy recommendations: underdeveloped countries should reduce government intervention in resource allocation and leave this to the market, confining any intervention to the correction of existing market distortions rather than the creation of new ones. Unduly prolonged protection of infant industries should be eliminated, and tariff structures (typically high on consumer goods and zero on capital goods) should be rationalised. Existing industries should be forced to greater efficiency by requiring them to face foreign competition. Meanwhile, exchange rates should be restored to equilibrium levels, thereby providing a much needed boost to exports.

So far as these criticisms refer to *outcomes* of import substitution, the great majority of development economists would agree with them whatever the paradigm within which they view and analyse underdevelopment. However, they would not all agree with the diagnosis of causality which lays the blame for these problems so heavily on government interference with relative prices, nor would they all accept the policy conclusion that the solution lies simply in the removal of price distortions, establishment of free market prices and exposure of overly-protected industrial sectors to the invigorating winds of international competition.[72] These issues are further discussed in chapters 9 and 10.

The contribution of transnational capitalism to the perpetuation of underdevelopment

We have already indicated that neo-classical theorists were not the only ones who were preoccupied with the outcome of import-substituting industrialisation. Structuralist economists themselves were, from the second half of the 1960s, increasingly preoccupied with such unanticipated phenomena as the slowing down of growth, worsening balance of payments crises, stagnation of the domestic market and the perpetuation of dualism. They, however, developed a different diagnosis of the causes. This diagnosis continued to focus, in the classical structuralist tradition, on the interaction of features of domestic socio-economic structure with the international context within which development was pursued. However, the emphases in these new analyses – well illustrated in Furtado (1973) and Sunkel (1973) – were new. They focused on such issues as the impact on the economies of the periphery of international cultural dependence and of transnational capitalism. Indeed, from this body of work emerged one of the three branches of dependency theory which are discussed in Chapter 7.

Here it is sufficient to note the argument of Sunkel and others that the rapid expansion of transnational capitalism from the mid-1950s transformed the nature and impact of foreign investment in the periphery. Peripheral economies, trying to industrialise, had to rely increasingly on 'external support for know-how, technology, administrative capacity, equipment, financing, etc.' (Sunkel, 1973). These were accepted largely from organisations which had not previously been involved to any significant degree in manufacturing in the periphery. In the outcome, it was argued, the transnationals provided those resources which they offered, particularly technology, in a manner which enabled them to control the pattern and pace of industrial development in the periphery. The transnationals determined, on the basis of their global policy, whether a new industry in a particular peripheral economy might break into the export market. By their deliberate use of capital-intensive technology in the periphery (partly in order to minimise industrial relations problems) they contributed to the perpetuation of import dependency for producer goods, to domestic dualism and to stagnation of the domestic market. By the use of persuasive advertising and by the demonstration effect of the consumption behaviour of expatriate managers and skilled personnel, they encouraged the consumption of capital and import-intensive consumer durables among the middle- and higher-income groups, thus exacerbating social tensions. By failing to train local personnel in technical supervisory and managerial skills, the transnationals perpetuated their influence.

The policy logic of this line of analysis, sometimes made explicit, and sometimes, as in Sunkel's pessimistic 1973 analysis, left implicit, is that only if peripheral economies can develop the necessary stock of skilled national manpower, if national governments can enforce control over élite consumption patterns and if they can improve the bargains that they strike with transnational corporations, can they regain control of industrial development. Neither Sunkel (1973) nor Furtado (1973) conclusively answers the question of whether existing élites can be expected to adopt these and related measures in the interest of national development.

The neo-Marxist critique of structuralism

The neo-Marxist critique of classical structuralist theory has elements in common with the dependency-oriented auto-critique of some of the structuralists themselves. None the less it remains distinctive both in the analytical concepts employed and in the logic of the argument. Furthermore, while the structuralist auto-critique was influenced by, and overlaps with, elements of neo-Marxism, by the time that this auto-critique was being generated the neo-Marxists themselves had moved towards a more ambitious framework of analysis: the global development of the capitalist system. Within this framework, however, they continued to argue that full capitalist development of the periphery is impossible due to the nature of the economic interests of those classes who hold political and economic power. Structuralist policies can therefore never represent more than superficial reformism. These points are elaborated in the next chapter, which is devoted to the neo-Marxist paradigm, and in the discussion of dependency theories in Chapter 7.

CONCLUSION

By the mid-1960s, signs of apparent stagnation and hard evidence of growing inequality were combined with widespread evidence of the role of transnational corporations in industrial investment in the Third World. Proponents of the structuralist school of thought were faced with a barrage of criticism – for interfering with the market mechanism on the one hand and for failing to analyse the class logic of the economic situation on the other – and were compelled to reappraise their position. This period marked the end of the heyday of the structuralist school in Latin America, but, as subsequent events have shown, it did not mark the end of structuralism as an intellectual approach to the analysis of macro-economic problems. The paradigm continues to generate new theoretical and methodological literature.[73]

Structuralist theory continues to influence the thought of many – though certainly not all – development economists and policy makers. It has *inter alia* continued to underpin the negotiating position of UNCTAD. Meanwhile, the growing acceptance of the view that small to medium-sized underdeveloped countries need to move, after a preliminary phase of import substitution, into the export of light manufactures, before they can hope to develop large enough markets for capital and intermediate goods to justify much local production of these, represents a shift in emphasis but not a total abandonment of structuralist industrialisation strategy. In the field of inflation analysis too, structuralist theory continues, as we have seen, to prove fruitful, even if not to the conviction of all economists.

However, structuralist economists themselves have been compelled by circumstances to make two major adjustments to their thinking – to take account of the phenomenon of foreign private investment and its impact, and to take account of the problems of worsening inequality and growing absolute poverty in the Third World. In the former case a dominant response was, in the 1970s, to contribute to the evolution of a form of dependency theory; in the latter case the response at the theoretical level, particularly among the Latin American structuralists, was arguably initially weaker. Rather, there emerged a pragmatic preoccupation with choice of technique and a renewed sense of urgency about land reform. However, in the 1970s a growing number of structuralist economists were drawn to accept Seer's redefinition of development and the ILO's redefinition of the employment problem in the Third World, and became engaged, first in the debate concerning the nature and role of the informal sector, and, secondly in the debate concerning basic needs oriented development strategies. These issues are discussed further in Chapter 9.

NOTES

1. These are discussed in Chapter 7.
2. See Furtado, 1964: 11–35.
3. See Furtado, *op.cit.*: 141, and Chapter 3, p. 49.
4. Furtado, *op.cit.*: 127.
5. *Ibid.*: 129.
6. See Chapter 3, p. 50.
7. Furtado, *op.cit.*: 130.
8. Furtado argues that where real wages are supply-determined, variations in export revenues are absorbed predominantly by profit fluctuations. Although the quantity of labour employed might also fluctuate in these conditions, Furtado asserts that this usually varied relatively little (Furtado, *op.cit.*: 132, 3).
9. Furtado, *op.cit.*: 142.
10. Hirschman wrote *The Strategy of Economic Development* immediately after working in Colombia.
11. Hirschman, 1958: 28.
12. Backward linkages are linkages to actual or potential suppliers of inputs and equipment to the expanding branch of activity; forward linkages are those that result from expansion of supplies by the investing branch to other branches in the sphere of manufacturing production.
13. 'Industrialisation can of course start only with industries that deliver to final demand, since *ex hypothesi*, no market exists as yet for intermediate goods', (Hirschman, 1958: 111). See also *ibid.*: Chapter 7.
14. All the structuralists assumed that to some extent the expansion of local manufacturing of consumer goods production would feed on itself as the expanding wage labour force increased their demand for these goods.
15. See Love, 1980: 57.
16. Prebisch, 1949, was first published in English in 1962. All references are to this English language version.
17. See Prebisch, 1962: 4.
18. See Chapter 4, p. 94.
19. See Nurkse in Agarwala and Singh, *op.cit.*: 261.
20. Prebisch, 1964: 11–13.
21. See Furtado, *op.cit.*: 147.

22. Furtado, *op.cit.*: 137.
23. Prebisch, 1962 : 19, 20.
24. Furtado, *op.cit.*: 138.
25. Prebisch, 1962: 2.

26. 'If . . . Chile were to reduce by 10 per cent the supply price of copper (in foreign currency), there would obviously be a need for increasing exports by more than 11 per cent merely to maintain exchange availabilities. Since Chilean exports of copper amount to some 400,000 tons, the increase would have to be more than 44,000 tons, a figure hard to achieve without harming other exporting countries', (Furtado, *op.cit.*: 164).

27. See Furtado, *op.cit.*: 167.
28. See p. 55 above for an explanation of the Duesenberry effect.
29. Prebisch, 1962: 14.
30. Reprinted in Agarwala and Singh, *op.cit.* pp. 420–431, and see pp. 91–2 above.

31. 'In 1946 the large corporations reinvested 30 to 40 per cent of their profits and distributed the rest among shareholders . . . of which one fourth . . . represented various forms of saving', (Prebisch, *op.cit.*: 15).

32. Lewis, in his 1954 article, devoted twelve pages to the relationship between inflation and savings. The implications for the balance of payments are contained in three sentences placed in parentheses.

33. This is the central argument in Sunkel, 1960, Seers, 1962 and Felix, 1964.

34. 'Since the income elasticity of demand for food in poor countries is likely to be quite high – on the order of 0.5–0.6 – a slow rate of growth of food production per capita (in Chile the rate has been negative over the past 25 years) limits the non-inflationary increase in aggregate output per capita to perhaps twice the rate of growth of food output per capita' (Felix in Baer and Kerstenetzky, eds., 1964: 379).

35. Kalecki, who also contributed to the structuralist theory of inflation, when lecturing in Mexico in 1953, also stressed that agricultural supply rigidity could, in the face of rising demand, cause a fall in real wages and a wage-price spiral. See Kalecki, 1976 and also the comment on this in Arndt, 1985.

36. See Canavese, 1982, for a comparative analysis of the Latin American and the European branches of the structuralist school of inflation theory.

37. Prebisch, *op.cit.*: 3.
38. *Ibid.*
39. *Loc. cit.*: 17.
40. Cf. the argument of Galenson and Liebenstein, summarised in Chapter 4, p. 104.
41. See discussion on pp. 140–1 above.
42. Felix in Baer and Kerstenetzky (eds.), *op.cit.*: 39.
43. Hirschman, however, notes that it may also be necessary for governments to intervene to pioneer investment in key industrial sectors.
44. Guidance of investment is strongly emphasised in Prebisch, 1949, and Furtado, 1964, and the potential contribution of foreign borrowing by both Prebisch and Seers.
45. See Prebisch, 1962.
46. See Prebisch, 1962: 17, Furtado, *op.cit.* and Prebisch, 1964.
47. See Prebisch, 1962.
48. See Prebisch, 1964.
49. See Prebisch, 1962.

50. *Ibid.*, and Seers, 1962.
51. Prebisch, 1962 and 1964: 79–83.
52. See Prebisch, 1964: 65 *et seq.*
53. Furtado expressed his misgiving concerning imported capital-intensive techno-
    logy in a paper written in 1952 as a critique of Nurkse's proposed balanced
    growth strategy:

    'The aim of economic development must be to increase the physical produc-
    tivity of labour. In an underdeveloped economy the introduction of auto-
    matic boot-making machinery will not mean an improvement in the physical
    productivity of labour for the community as a whole if the workmen who
    previously produced boots are left without any work. Moreover, the entre-
    preneur who introduces this kind of machinery will suffer too, since it will
    have to stay idle five days in the week. But the entrepreneur who introduces
    improvements in the tools used for the production of boots by hand, thereby
    making possible an increase in productivity, will turn out more boots with
    the same number of man-hours without a disproportionate increase in other
    cost.'

    (Furtado, 1954, reprinted in Agarwala and Singh, *op.cit.*: 313.)

54. See Prebisch, 1964 and Sunkel, *op.cit.*: 127; also Furtado, 1976, Chapter 22,
    p. 248 and Chapter 23.
55. See Sunkel, *op.cit.*: 110, 112–115 and 127.
56. See Prebisch, 1962.
57. See Chapter 4, pp. 105–6.
58. Chenery and Strout and McKinnon are both summarised in Mikesell, 1968.
59. See p. 106 above.
60. The first edition of the study was published in 1970.
61. *Ibid.*: 248.
62. See Government of Ghana, 1964: 14, 15.
63. See Clark, 1965. Clark was one of the expatriate advisors to the Ugandan
    planning team. In the plan itself see, for example, pp. 4, 5 and 20.
64. See Government of Tanganyika and Zanzibar, 1964, pp. 8 and 11.
65. The ideas which have underlain UNCTAD's approach to international negoti-
    ations are set out in Prebisch's report as Secretary-General to the first conference
    in Geneva in 1964. See Prebisch, 1964.
66. A point acknowledged in Prebisch, 1949.
67. These conceptual criticisms were raised in Viner, 1953, and made also in Baldwin,
    1955, and Haberler, 1957. There is now a substantial literature on the topic. A
    useful list of further references may be found in Meier, *op.cit.* The point that
    productivity gains in export production may more than offset the impact of
    declining unit prices has been made by a number of neo-classical economists
    including Haberler, 1957 and Bauer, 1971 in support of the view that it is the
    factoral and not the commodity terms of trade that are the relevant concept for
    the analysis of gains from trade. However, on this there seems to be some
    disagreement among the neo-classicals. Lal, in a critique of Emmanuel (see pp.
    180–3), apparently takes a dissenting view (Lal, 1983: 42).
68. Saini, 1982, rejects the monetarist explanation of inflation for six Asian countries,
    arguing that the model erroneously excludes various internal and external cost
    pressures. See also Bogdanowicz-Bindert, 1983, Ffrench-Davis, 1983, and Corbo
    and De Melo, 1985, for three varying interpretations of the Latin American
    experience.

69. The McKinnon and Shaw thesis is discussed further in Chapter 10.
70. See Andic, Andic and Dosser, 1971. See also the collection of readings in Robson, 1972, for discussion of the application of comparative static customs union theory to developing countries.
71. More recently, the political and economic implications of attempts to establish common markets in the periphery have been subjected to a class analysis by Vaitsos, 1978. Vaitsos concludes that if *potential* benefits from integration are to be realised, they are most likely to be achieved if regional cooperation takes the form of agreement on the joint pursuit of specific objectives and tasks together with an explicit statement of which economic and political actors are likely to benefit. Attempts to create common markets and free trade areas have suffered from political naivety about the automacity of subsequent progress.
72. None the less, in the late 1960s and early 1970s the neo-classical analytical perspective adopted by the Little, Scitovsky, Scott analysis found widespread support. 'The work on effective protection by Johnson, Corden and Belassa . . . research by the Brookings Institution and the World Bank, and the doctrines of the Chicago School that influenced many Latin American policy makers reflected a recoil against inefficient protectionism and inward-looking planning' (Streeten, 1981: 107).
73. See e.g. Chaudhuri, 1984, and Taylor, 1983.

REFERENCES

Andic, F., Andic, S. and Dosser, D., *A Theory of Economic Integration in Developing Countries*, (Allen and Unwin, 1971).
Arndt, H., 'The origins of structuralism', *World Development*, (Vol. 13, No. 2, 1985).
Baldwin, R., 'Secular movements in the terms of trade', *American Economic Review*, (Papers and Proceedings, May 1955).
Baran, P., *The Political Economy of Growth*, (Monthly Review Press, 1957; Penguin, 1973).
Bauer, P., *Dissent on Development*, (Weidenfeld and Nicolson, 1971).
Bogdanowicz-Bindert, C., 'Portugal, Turkey and Peru: three successful stabilisation programmes under the auspices of the IMF', *World Development*, (Vol. 11, No. 1, January 1983).
Canavese, A., 'The structuralist explanation in the theory of inflation', *World Development*, (Vol. 10, No. 7, 1982).
Chaudhuri, P., 'Structural problems and development policy', paper presented to conference on agriculture and economy, (Agricultural Bank of Greece, Athens, 1984).
Chenery, H. and Bruno, M., 'Development alternatives in an open economy: the case of Israel', *Economic Journal*, (March 1962).
Chenery, H. and Strout, A., 'Foreign assistance and economic development', *American Economic Review*, (Vol. LVI, No. 4, Part 1, September 1966).
Clark, P., *Development Planning in East Africa*, (East Africa Publishing House, 1965).
Corbo, V. and De Melo, J., 'Overview and summary', *World Development*, (Vol. 13 No. 8, August 1985). (Special Issue on 'liberalisation with stabilisation in the southern cone of Latin America'.)
Eckhaus, R., 'The factor proportions problem in underdeveloped countries', *The American Economic Review*, (September 1955); reprinted in *The Economics of Underdevelopment*, eds. Agarwala, A. and Singh, S., (Oxford, 1958).

Felix, D., 'Monetarists, structuralists and import-substituting industrialisation: a critical appraisal' in *Inflation and Growth in Latin America*, eds. Baer, W. and Kerstenetzky, I., (Yale, 1964).

Ffrench-Davis, R., 'The monetarist experience in Chile: a critical survey', *World Development*, (Vol. 11, No. 11, November 1983).

Furtado, C., 'Capital formation and economic development', *International Economic Papers* (No. 4, 1954); reprinted in *The Economics of Underdevelopment*, eds. Agarwala, A. and Singh, S., (Oxford, 1958).

Furtado, C., *Development and Underdevelopment*, (University of California, 1964); translated from *Desenvolvimento e subdesenvolvimento*, (Editora Fundo de Cultura, Rio de Janeiro, 1961).

Furtado, C., *Economic Development of Latin America*, (Cambridge, 1970; second edition, 1976).

Furtado, C., 'Underdevelopment and dependence: the fundamental connections', Seminar Paper, (Centre of Latin American Studies, Cambridge University, November 1973).

Government of Ghana, Office of the Planning Commission, *Seven Year Plan for National Reconstruction and Development: 1963/64–1969/70*, (Government Printer, Accra).

Government of Tanganyika and Zanzibar, *Five-year Plan for Economic and Social Development: 1964–1969*, Volume I, (Government Printer, Dar-es-Salaam).

Government of Uganda, *Work for Progress: Uganda's Second Five Year Plan, 1966–1971*, (Government Printer, Kampala, 1966).

Haberler, G., 'Critical observations on some current notions in the theory of economic development', *L'Industria*, (No. 2, 1957); reprinted in *Leading Issues in Economic Development*, ed. Meier, G., second edition, (Oxford, 1970).

Hazlewood, A., *Economic Integration: The East African Experience*, (Heinemann, 1975).

Hirschman, A., *The Strategy of Economic Development*, (Yale, 1958).

Joshi, V., 'Saving and foreign exchange constraints', in *Unfashionable Economics*, ed. Streeten, P., (Weidenfeld and Nicolson, 1970).

Kalecki, M., 'The problem of financing economic development', in *Essays on Developing Economies*, (Harvester, Sussex, and Humanities Press, New Jersey, 1976).

Lal, D., *The Poverty of 'Development Economics'*, Hobart Paperback 16, (Institute of Economic Affairs, 1983).

Lewis, W. A., 'Economic development with unlimited supplies of labour', *Manchester School*, (May 1954); reprinted in *The Economics of Underdevelopment*, eds. Agarwala, A. and Singh, S., (Oxford, 1958).

Lipsey, R., 'The theory of customs unions: a general survey', *Economic Journal*, (September 1960).

Little, I., Scitovsky, T. and Scott, M., *Industry and Trade in Some Developing Countries*, (Oxford, 1970).

Love, J., 'Raoul Prebisch and the origins of the doctrine of unequal exchange', *Latin American Research Review*, (1980).

McKinnon, R., 'Foreign exchange constraints in economic development and efficient aid allocation', *Economic Journal*, (Vol. 74, June 1964).

McKinnon, R., *Money and Capital in Economic Development*, (Brookings, 1973).

Manne, A., 'Key sectors of the Mexican economy, 1960–1970', in *Studies in Process Analysis*, eds. Manne, A. and Markowitz, H., (Wiley, 1963).

Meier, G., 'Conditions of export-led development: note' in *Leading Issues in Economic Development*, ed. Meier, G., fourth edition, (Oxford, 1984).

Mikesell, R., *The Economics of Foreign Aid*, (Weidenfeld and Nicholson, 1968).

Nurkse, R., 'Some international aspects of the problem of economic development', *American Economic Review*, (May 1952); reprinted in *The Economics of Under-development*, eds. Agarwala, A. and Singh, S., (Oxford, 1958).

Prebisch, R., 'The economic development of Latin America and its principal problems', *Economic Bulletin for Latin America*, (Vol. VII, No. 1, February 1962; first published in 1949).

Prebisch, R., *Towards a New Trade Strategy for Development*, Report by the Secretary-General of the United Nations Conference on Trade and Development, (United Nations, New York, 1964).

Robson, P. (ed.), *International Economic Integration*, (Penguin, 1972).

Saini, K., 'The monetarist explanation of inflation: the experience of six Asian countries', *World Development*, (Vol. 10, No. 10, October 1982).

Seers, D., 'A theory of inflation and growth in underdeveloped countries', *Oxford Economic Papers*, (1962, pp. 173–195).

Shaw, E., *Financial Deepening in Economic Development*, (Oxford, 1973).

Singer, H., 'The distribution of gains between investing and borrowing countries', *American Economic Review*, (Papers and Proceedings, Vol. 40, No. 2, May 1950).

Streeten, P., *Development Perspectives*, (Macmillan, 1981).

Sunkel, O., 'Inflation in Chile: an unorthodox approach', *International Economic Papers*, (Vol. 10, 1960).

Sunkel, O., 'Transnational capitalism and national disintegration in Latin America', *Social and Economic Studies*, (1973).

Taylor, L., *Structuralist Macroeconomics: Applicable Models for the Third World*, (Basic Books, 1983).

United Nations, Dept of Economic Affairs, *Relative Prices of Exports and Imports of Underdeveloped Countries*, (United Nations, New York, 1949).

Vaitsos, C., 'Crisis in regional co-operation among developing countries: a survey', *World Development*, (Vol. 6, No. 6, June 1978).

Viner, J., *International Trade and Economic Development*, (Oxford, 1953).

6· THE NEO-MARXIST PARADIGM

The neo-Marxist paradigm derives from an attempt to develop and adapt traditional Marxist theory to the analysis of underdeveloped economies. The paradigm gained widespread influence in the late 1960s, providing an ideological and analytical framework for radical critiques of contemporary development theories and praxis. Drawing their inspiration from the ideas of Marx and Lenin, and influenced also by other early Marxists, particularly Rosa Luxemburg, the neo-Marxists set out to investigate a problem that Marx himself had touched on only briefly – the process of economic change in the economies of Asia, Africa and Latin America.

With respect to the Third World, the primary concern of the neo-Marxists is with what is happening to national output and to its distribution, and why. Particularly in the 1950s and 1960s there was little concern on the part of leading neo-Marxists to explore the essential nature of the mode(s) of production that prevail within the periphery. Instead the emphasis was on the economic and political relations between the centre and periphery of the world economy, and the impact of these in the periphery. In investigating these issues the neo-Marxists use a terminology for the key concepts in their analytical framework that appears to derive from Marxism. However, we shall see that the interpretation they give to certain central concepts differs from that given to the same concepts by Marx.

All the neo-Marxists are explicitly politically engaged writers. Their purpose is to expose the exploitative nature of the world capitalist system in order to mobilise support for revolutionary change.[1] None the less, these same individuals have submitted their work to academic debate and clearly expect it to be judged also on its analytical content – on its ability to expose the causes of underdevelopment. It is from that perspective that it is discussed here.

The purpose of this chapter is to review the way in which, from the 1950s to the early 1970s, leading neo-Marxists have articulated and analysed their perception of the process of underdevelopment, starting with the work of Paul Baran, the founder of the neo-Marxist school. We shall then turn to three other leading neo-Marxists – Frank, Emmanuel and Amin – two of whom (Frank and Amin) drew part of the impetus for their analytical work from their detailed knowledge of patterns of economic change in those continents (Latin America and Africa) which Baran largely ignored.

Chapter 3 showed how the neo-Marxist paradigm leads unequivocally to the conclusion that radical political change is necessary in underdeveloped economies before these can begin to develop fully. However, any discussion of the subsequent development path is in most leading neo-Marxist analyses (with the exception of Baran's) exceedingly brief. Less space is therefore given to this issue in this chapter, which has a different structure from the previous two. The main emphasis in the latter part of the chapter will be upon the theoretical debate, largely within a Marxist framework, to which the neo-Marxist interpretation of underdevelopment has given rise.

SUMMARY OF THE NEO-MARXIST PARADIGM

The main elements of the neo-Marxist analytical framework can be summarised as follows:

1. Economic underdevelopment is a process whose dominant feature is the persistent outflow of economic surplus generated in the periphery to the advanced capitalist economies. The surplus is defined as the difference between either actual or potential output and either actual or essential consumption (see p. 166).
2. Economically underdeveloped countries are, as a result, characterised by low average per capita incomes and by slow rates of accumulation.
3. Economic development consists, by implication, in national reinvestment of the surplus and the consequent expansion of national output, the latter being equitably distributed.
4. The prospects for economic development through capitalism in any one country are determined by its position in the international economy.
5. Two central elements in the neo-Marxist analytical method are the adoption of a historical perspective, and a focus on the class distribution of control over the surplus in underdeveloped countries.
6. In the past the now industrially advanced capitalist economies drew the countries of the periphery into a system of unequal exchange relations through which economic surplus was extracted from the periphery.
7. These unequal exchange relations, initially often imposed by force, persist to this day, and it is largely they which block capitalist development in the periphery.

8. International exchange with the centre has destroyed pre-capitalist artisan production in the periphery and has largely removed the incentive for indigenous capitalist industrial development there.

9. Competition from the manufactured exports of the centre continues to undercut the incentive for industrial development in the periphery.

10. The industrial development which has occurred consists predominantly of a limited range of industrial monopolies owned by nationals and/or foreign capitalists (who repatriate profits to the centre).

11. The dominant classes in the periphery (landlords, the commercial bourgeoisie, owners of monopoly capital, and foreign capitalists) given their sources of income have no interest in the sustained development of producer capitalism there.

12. Thus contemporary underdeveloped economies cannot pass through the same phases of economic development as the new industrially advanced capitalist economies because the international conditions have changed irrevocably. The phase of national competitive capitalist development, when capitalism is at its most dynamic, has been undercut in the periphery by foreign competition.

13. Full economic development can only occur after radical political change.

PAUL BARAN'S ANALYSIS OF THE CAUSES OF UNDERDEVELOPMENT

Background

The first, and subsequently highly influential, articulation of the neo-Marxist perspective on underdevelopment is contained in Baran (1957).

Baran moved to the United States in 1939, having already pursued academic study at the Plakhanov Institute of Economics in Moscow, and obtained an MA from Harvard two years later. He considered himself both a socialist and a Marxist[2], although subsequently some Marxist critics of his work have questioned the latter.

In the post-war era Baran considered three international issues of over-riding importance: 'the vicissitudes of monopoly capitalism during its current period of decline and fall, the outlook for the nascent socialist societies in Europe and Asia' and the circumstances of the underdeveloped economies.[3] With respect to the latter, the relevant chapters of Baran (1957) are a passionate attack on a capitalist system apparently able to provide decent conditions of life to only a small fraction of the world's population.

Baran's analysis of underdevelopment

Baran (1957) was preceded by an article published in 1952 which offered a foretaste of the underlying analytical perspective that Baran was later to employ. This reflects the influence on his ideas not just of Marxism but of the early development debate in Western Europe and North America.[4]

The central section of Baran (1952)[5] presents a largely familiar analysis of the constraints to economic growth in backward economies, having much in common with the early analyses of Nurkse, Myint, Scitovsky and others.[6] Growth is constrained both by low savings and the lack of inducement to invest. The latter stems primarily from low domestic demand and the non-existence of the external economies and physical infrastructure which serve to reduce production costs in industrially advanced economies. Meanwhile, savings are low not only due to the poverty of the masses but to high standards of luxury consumption among landed and urban élites. Generation of growth requires an effective programme of state intervention – both of progressive taxation and public sector investment – to break out of the impasse.

The originality of this article lies in a class-based analysis of the constraints to implementing such a programme, located within a review of the impact of Western capitalism upon the periphery. Baran first analyses by class the determinants of the disposition of the surplus, before turning to examine the nature and motivation of the class alliances that typically hold state power. He is led by this analysis to the conclusion, reached later by other neo-Marxists as well, that the prospects for development in the periphery based upon an indigenous capitalist bourgeoisie are essentially non-existent. The following paragraphs summarise Baran's analysis in more detail. They are based on the fuller analysis in Baran (1957).

Baran starts from the proposition that in order to understand the changing interrelationships of the world economy, and their impact on the periphery, it is necessary to comprehend first the internal mechanisms, the driving force, and the pattern of evolution of capitalism itself. It then becomes possible to establish how capitalism has generated underdevelopment.

Central to Baran's analysis of underdevelopment are four key concepts, those of monopoly capitalism, imperialism, class and economic surplus. Baran adopts Marx's interpretation of the nature of capitalism[7] and monopoly capitalism. Following Lenin, he perceives imperialism as a political and military manifestation of the search for economic surplus – specifically, in the late nineteenth and early twentieth century the manifestation of this search by monopoly capitalism. Baran defines class in the classical Marxist sense, as a social category representing a group of individuals all of whom have, *inter alia*, the same relationship to the means of production and the same rights over the output of labour. However, his use of this concept is more narrowly focused than in classical Marxism, being concentrated on its significance for the distribution of the surplus, rather than on social relations in the production process.[8] Meanwhile, in relation to the fourth and last of these concepts, Baran is innovatory. He introduces into his analysis two new interpretations of the concept of economic surplus: the actual and the potential surplus. The former represents 'the difference between society's *actual* current output and its *actual* current consumption'.[9] The latter represents 'the difference between the output that *could* be produced in a given natural and technological environment with the help of employable productive resources, and what might be regarded as essential for consumption'.[10] Baran uses the concept of the potential surplus in order to expose what he perceives as the waste and irrationality of monopoly capitalism with its heavy outlays on, *inter alia*, packaging and advertising on the one hand, and militarism on the other. In his analysis of underdevelopment in the periphery, however, it is the concept of the actual surplus, and the modes of its disposition, that hold centre stage.

One criticism levelled against Baran is that although he claims to be writing in the Marxist tradition, his use of the concept of the 'economic surplus' is very different from Marx's. It was stated in Chapter 2 that Marx defined the surplus in terms of the surplus product of labour, and that under capitalism this surplus product becomes surplus value. That is to say, it becomes the additional value that is extracted from wage labour by employing it for a longer period per day than is needed to generate a value of output equivalent to the constant capital (c) used up in production, plus the wage (v).[11] This definition of the surplus (s) permits Marx to introduce a second concept, the rate of surplus value, which is equal to the rate of exploitation of labour. Baran has been accused of 'fudging' the concept of the economic surplus, and of turning it into something that is much less clear-cut and has no clear relationship with the rate of exploitation. However, for better or for worse Baran's interpretation of the economic surplus has been widely used by neo-Marxist and other radical economists.[12]

The origins of underdevelopment

In *The Political Economy of Growth* (1957) Baran divides his analysis of underdevelopment into two sections: an historical account of the origins of underdevelopment, and an analysis of the 'morphology' of contemporary underdevelopment.

In Baran's view the origins of underdevelopment can be traced to the era of Western imperialism in the seventeenth and eighteenth centuries – a period when European merchant capitalists successfully sought to accumulate wealth through plunder and enforced trade with more densely-populated regions of the non-European world. Marx appears to have believed that the growing contacts first with merchant, and then with producer, capitalism would lead to the capitalist development of the periphery. 'The country that is more developed industrially only shows to the less developed the image of its own future' (Marx, *Capital*: Vol. 1, pp. 8, 9).[13] However, Baran sets out to demonstrate why capitalist development in the periphery cannot be realistically anticipated, and why, instead, the new relationships that evolved between centre and periphery effectively blocked the development of the latter.

Marx had observed that in order to build, capitalism also destroys. Stagnant, traditional social formations must be eliminated and replaced by the institutional conditions and social relations appropriate to the development of a dynamic capitalist economy. This destruction of traditional formations, Baran readily concedes occurred, as, in part, did their replacement by wage-labour based production. This was also accompanied by changes in legal and property relations needed for an expanding market economy and by the establishment of

> administrative institutions required for their enforcement. Western capitalism also forced the diversion of some of the periphery's economic surplus to the building of railroads, harbours and highways, providing thereby, facilities needed for profitable investment of capital.
>
> (Baran, 1973: 275).

This is, however, only one side of the ledger. For these changes have been made to serve the interests of imperialist monopoly capitalism. Profits are not necessarily reinvested in the periphery, but, more often, are repatriated; and no efforts are made to promote the development of indigenous capitalism – rather, the opposite.

For Baran, the economically backward countries have the worst of two worlds, feudal and capitalist. The exploitative elements of feudalism remain, compounded now by those of (chiefly foreign) capitalism;[14] but the progressive forces of capitalism are blocked. It is these points that Baran explores in greater depth in his analysis of the morphology of contemporary backwardness, to which this discussion now turns.

The morphology of backwardness
As noted above, Baran's perception of the objective conditions in underdeveloped countries, and of the appropriate path for economic development, accords in many respects with that of most of his non-Marxist contemporaries. Thus, he starts from the propositions that these economies are predominantly rural, that the marginal productivity of labour in agriculture is close to zero, and that industrialisation is essential in order to absorb the excess population in agriculture. Industrialisation in turn presupposes substantial and sustained new capital formation. In many economies development is seemingly constrained by the small size of the domestic market, combined with competition from cheaper and/or higher quality imports, the absence of external economies in the form of essential infrastructure and low tax revenues which make it difficult to finance a programme of public investment in infrastructure. Yet, observes Baran, it can be argued that

today's industrially advanced countries began their agricultural and industrial revolutions from what were in many respects similar initial conditions. If so, then why not also today's backward economies? For while the surplus is low in absolute terms, the surplus that is potentially available for accumulation accounts for a significant share of total output. The consumption standards of the mass of the population are contained to the barest minimum, leaving a substantial proportion of GDP potentially available for accumulation that could overcome and transform these initial disadvantages. The problems are that the actual surplus falls well below the potential, and that the actual surplus is used in ways that contribute little to the accumulation of productive capital by either the state or the private sector.

In underdeveloped economies the surplus potentially available for capital formation takes the form of land rent, interest on credit, and profits from trade and production based on wage-labour. The main classes that appropriate these surpluses are fourfold – domestic landowners, indigenous merchants and monopoly capitalists, and foreign capitalists.

In most underdeveloped economies, much of the surplus is generated in agriculture, where production is organised in two forms, subsistence peasant agriculture and commercial plantations. Since a large proportion of peasant smallholdings are rented, the behaviour of the landlord class in the disposition of its revenues is crucial to the pace of development. Meanwhile, surplus is also extracted from the peasantry by moneylenders, merchants, and, to a smaller extent, the state in the form of tax revenues, leaving the peasants themselves unable to engage in significant accumulation.

The feudal landowning class deploys much of the potential surplus for luxury consumption. In so far as this class seeks ways of raising its revenues it seeks fast and safe returns through moneylending to the peasantry and purchase of more land and urban real estate. Meanwhile, the merchant class, like the landowners, is discouraged from moving into agricultural producer capitalism by the relatively risky and long-term nature of such investment. Instead, it uses its revenues both for reinvestment in trade and commodity speculation and in a similar manner to the landowners.

Of the remaining two classes that dispose of significant surpluses, both derive their revenues from capitalist production. Here, according to Lewis, is the core of profits from which expanding capitalist accumulation can take place. However, Baran, like the structuralists, lays emphasis on the failure of the capitalist nucleus to generate a development dynamic. In his view this is not due to the inadequacy of the scale of the capitalist nucleus, but to the motivations of the capitalists themselves. In this context it may be helpful to consider foreign capital first.

In the periphery, foreign capital is invested first in primary resource extraction – in mining and plantation agriculture. Writing in the early 1950s before the main era of foreign investment in import substitution, it is on these enterprises that Baran concentrates. These enterprises, he argues, are usually highly profitable. They have often been started with very low capital investment, the natural resources being secured either through forcible expropriation or through payment of nominal prices to local rulers. Yet they do not represent a viable starting point for capitalist development in the periphery for the following reasons:

1. Initial investment outlays have their expansionary (multiplier) effect in the countries at the centre rather than in the periphery; equipment is imported, while local expenditures are low. Meanwhile the salaries of expatriate skilled and managerial staff are largely remitted to the centre, to pay for luxury imports and as savings.

2. Investments in infrastructure are planned and located to serve the interests of foreign enterprise and not the development of the productive capacity of the economy as a whole. Furthermore, private investment in transport infrastructure designed to facilitate movement of primary exports likewise serves to facilitate movement of merchandise *imports*. It promotes the development of mercantile capitalism rather than producer capitalism.

3. Reinvestment of profits is determined by conditions in the world market and the overall interests of the foreign enterprise. In the aggregate, only a fraction of foreign enterprise profits in the periphery are reinvested there.

4. Soils are often overworked and exhausted, and reserves of exhaustible mineral resources are steadily depleted.

5. While a fraction of profits are paid in tax to local governments, the significance of these payments for local development depends upon the manner in which they are used by the state (see below, this page).

If foreign producer capital cannot be relied upon to develop the economies of the periphery, what of the small group of local monopoly capitalists who have invested in production for the domestic market?

[Their] monopolistic status would be swept away by the rise of industrial capitalism. Concerned with preventing the emergence of competitors in their markets, they look with favour upon absorption of capital in the sphere of circulation, and have nothing to fear from export-oriented enterprise. They too are stalwart defenders of the established order.

(Baran 1973: 337, 8.)

Members of the small middle class, who might perhaps be expected to challenge these monopolists, in fact save and invest little as they strive to emulate the consumption standards of those whose ranks they aspire to join. They are further discouraged by the structure of the state and of the interests that it promotes.

Since the state is the only other entity that can actively intervene to promote economic development in the periphery, a crucial question concerns the nature of the class interests that dominate state policy. Baran classifies the relevant governments in the 1950s under three headings – colonial, *comprador* (the majority of post-colonial governments) and a few with 'what might be called a "New Deal" orientation – principally India, Indonesia and Burma'. Both the former groups clearly promote the interests of foreign capital. However, Baran concludes that the third category is destined also to become committed to maintenance of the status quo.

The roots of this problem lie in the nature of the class alliances which struggled for independence from colonial rule. Even where independence movements in the periphery have had a significant populist component of workers, peasants and urban *petite bourgeoisie*, led by intellectuals seeking a better future for their country, they have usually represented an alliance of all the main local interests. They have generally included representatives of some, or all, of the dominant local classes whose interests have just been reviewed.[15]

After independence such heterogeneous alliances, their common goal achieved, become increasingly fragile. Attempts to fulfil the objectives of increased growth and economic diversification based on indigenous enterprise, combined with increased equity, are thwarted. Fulfilment of these objectives depends on the effective mobilisation of the surplus[16] and on redistribution of land rights from rentier landlords to the actual producers, but both are resisted by important sections of the ruling alliance, supported by foreign capital. The latter has an interest in blocking local development so that it can keep unskilled labour costs at subsistence level. Meanwhile local merchant and monopoly capitalists have no interest in the development of industrial competition which could undercut existing lines of import trade and sources of monopoly profit. The landlord class is likewise concerned to protect its interests. All these elements therefore combine to convince the middle classes of the folly of any populist move to expropriate foreign capital or to implement land reform. These would represent a threat to the general sanctity of private property. Thus is cowed any incipient radicalism of the middle classes.

As the disillusion of the masses increases, the resources of the state are used, not to promote national economic development, but to protect and maintain the status quo. As long as governments in the periphery steadfastly pursue this objective they can also count on the support of metropolitan governments, military if necessary, in times of political crisis.

With the collapse of plans for genuine development, capitalism in these, as in other economies in the periphery, remains predominantly mercantile. What little investment in industry occurs is largely foreign investment which

consists in the main of assembly plants or factories producing consumer goods to satisfy the demand increases resulting from government spending. Being chiefly investment in kind [using imported equipment and materials], it expands but little the host country's internal market, and does not lead to the emergence of basic industries indispensable to rapid and lasting economic growth.

(Baran, *op.cit.*: 360.)

Any increase in foreign investment also increases the hold of foreign capital and metropolitan governments over the economies and governments of the periphery. Imperialism has taken new forms in the post-colonial era, but remains as vigorous as ever.

Baran concludes that any prospects for the emergence of an indigenous, dynamic, competitive capitalist class in the periphery have been eliminated by the past history and contemporary economic conditions in these economies. Capitalism has no more to offer the underdeveloped world: 'the capitalist system, once a mighty engine of economic development, has turned into no less a formidable hurdle to human advancement'. (*Ibid*: 402.) Instead 'the establishment of a socialist planned economy is an essential, indeed indispensable, condition for the attainment of economic and social progress'.

The 'steep ascent': post-revolutionary development strategy
Baran devoted the final chapters of *The Political Economy of Growth* to a review of the essential elements of a socialist development strategy. He proposes a predominantly Stalinist/Feldmanite path of economic development, based upon immediate compulsory collectivisation of agriculture and rapid expansion of capital accumulation in state-owned industry, initially in capital goods production. This part of his analysis is not original and has not provided the basis for further work by the neo-Marxist school. Rather, the latter has concentrated on the elaboration and extension of the analysis of the causes of underdevelopment in the periphery.

THE CONTRIBUTION OF ANDRÉ GUNDER FRANK TO THE NEO-MARXIST THEORISATION OF UNDERDEVELOPMENT

Background

At the level of theoretical innovation, A. G. Frank's contribution to neo-Marxist theory has been less than that of Baran's and also more controversial, but at the level of dissemination and popularisation of that theory it has probably been greater. In the 1950s the general climate of opinion amongst development economists was unreceptive to Baran's analysis of the causes of underdevelopment and to his conclusion that the only route to development was via socialist revolution.

However, by the mid-1960s the climate of opinion had begun to change. In the United States, the Berkeley Free Speech Movement, initiated on the Berkeley campus of the University of California in the late 1950s, heralded the end of the political repression of the McCarthy era, and the emergence of a new generation of social scientists some of whom were to break away from the conventional orthodoxies. Conventional social science in the United States became, during the 1960s, increasingly quantitative and 'positive'. Applied to economic development, this approach reached its apogee in the work of Kuznets and Chenery on the patterns of economic growth. While the approach generated some interesting empirical results (amongst them Kuznets' conclusion that as per capita income rises inequality in income distribution first rises and then later declines[17]), for mainstream development economics this period was not nearly as rich in fundamental theoretical innovation as the 1950s had been. During the 1960s the major theoretical development in the discipline, which arose from the mid-1960s onwards, was the rapid diffusion and application of neo-Marxist ideas amongst a burgeoning group of radical young social scientists.

A. G. Frank played a crucial role in attracting part of the new generation of development economists to the neo-Marxist perspective. Frank had trained as an economist in the United States in a context which was, as he says, dominated by the liberal maxim 'according to which only political neutrality permits scientific objectivity'.[18] After going to Latin America in 1962, he came to condemn this maxim as one

> widely used to defend social irresponsibility, pseudo-scientific scientism, and political reaction. . . I had to learn from those who have been persecuted . . . in the name of liberty and liberalism. I had to learn that *social* science must be *political* science.
>
> (Frank, 1969, xviii.)

Frank does not refer in the autobiographical section of the preface to his first and most influential book – *Capitalism and Underdevelopment in Latin America* – (from which the above quotations are taken) to the work of Thomas Kuhn, which he may well not have read, although he had probably heard it discussed. *Capitalism and Underdevelopment in Latin America* is, however, as the preface makes clear, an archetypal example of a paradigm switch. Frank tells us that before he went to Latin America he had read, but not understood, Paul Baran. When he went there, three phenomena appear to have particularly impressed him: the unevenness of economic development in the region, the pervasiveness of extreme poverty, both in the countryside and in the shanty towns, and the success of the Cuban revolution in achieving both political change and an increase in mass welfare.

In an attempt to understand the causes of the first two of these phenomena, Frank turned to Latin American writers and he reread Baran. In the latter he found the perspective that he was looking for: one that could provide him with an explanation of the causes of uneven development and continuing mass poverty in Latin America. However, in applying Baran's neo-Marxism to the analysis of underdevelopment in Latin America, Frank also gave this perspective his own imprint. He did so partly by shifting the relative emphasis given to different elements in Baran's theoretical framework, and partly by extending this; but in certain respects, for example concerning the continuing existence of elements of feudalism in the periphery, he differed with Baran.

Frank's interpretation of the 'development of underdevelopment'

A major theme in Frank's work, argued for example in his essay on 'Capitalist development of underdevelopment in Chile' (in Frank, 1969), is that while the relations between the centre and periphery of the world capitalist system may appear superficially to change over time, fundamentally they have not done so since the countries of the periphery were first brought into contact with world capitalism. In this seminal essay Frank specifies three features of capitalism which in his view jointly constitute the dominant causes of underdevelopment. These are as follows:

1. The expropriation of surplus from the many and its appropriation by the few.
2. The polarisation of the capitalist system into metropolitan centres and peripheral satellites.
3. The continuity of the fundamental structure of the capitalist system, which ensures the perpetuation of 1 and 2 , even while more superficial elements of this system are constantly changing.

At first glance it might appear that the first two of these propositions represent a restatement of elements of Baran's perspective, while the third represents a simple extension of this. However, it is in his elaboration of these relationships that Frank's distinctive theoretical contribution emerges.

Surplus extraction through trade

We have seen how Baran applies a class analysis in order to establish the pattern of appropriation and use of the economic surplus in underdeveloped countries. In Frank's analysis there is one overriding method of surplus extraction which has permitted in the past, and continues to permit today, the expropriation of surplus from the masses and its appropriation by the capitalist class: this is surplus extraction through trade. While other methods of surplus extraction co-exist, it is this that predominates.

Frank argues that in the past, in the sixteenth century, Latin America was drawn into the world capitalist system as a result of the development of expansionist trading empires based in Western Europe. The colonisation of the sub-continent by Spain and Portugal was designed to establish control by these countries over its natural resources, and to ensure a flow of mineral wealth and other products back to the colonising countries. The whole population of the sub-continent was rapidly caught up in networks of exchange whose ultimate purpose was to transmit surplus to Europe.

Since capitalism is implicitly defined by Frank in terms of exchange relations and not relations of production, his observation that merchant capital penetrated even the remotest corners of the periphery leads him to conclude, in contrast with Baran,[19] that capitalism itself permeated the whole of the periphery. Feudalism, Frank asserts, has not existed in Latin America since the first penetration of the continent by metropolitan merchant capital. Large estates were established in Latin America specifically to produce for the market. Their owners then used all means possible to maximise the surplus expropriated and appropriated from the actual producers. The subsequent evolution of feudal-type institutions of land tenancy, including payment of labour dues, was simply a response by surplus-maximising *hacienda* owners to commercial pressures and opportunities – rising demand for land for tenancy on the one hand, and rising demand for labour by the estate owners themselves.[20] Apparently *subsistence-oriented* feudal structures have only subsequently emerged, following a collapse in market opportunities, while they have generally disappeared again following a market revival.[21]

Frank thus rejects dualist theories of development and underdevelopment. While the latter characterise underdeveloped countries as possessing two sharply distinguished sectors – one modern, dynamic, integrated into the world economy, and the other traditional, stagnant, often feudal, supplying labour but little else to the former – Frank argues that individual underdeveloped countries are internally integrated through the permeation of merchant capital. Indeed, the world capitalist economy is a single integrated whole.

Metropolis – satellite polarisation
Frank argues that within the world capitalist system only those metropolitan centres which are not subjected to the expropriation of part of their surpluses can develop fully. All regions that are subjected to such expropriation are destined to *under*develop, the latter being a process and not a state.

Frank perceives the world capitalist system as a hierarchy or pyramidal structure with, at the base, the rural regions of the periphery. These satellite regions are linked, through trade, to small centres of surplus accumulation, their local 'metropolises'. These in turn are satellites of, and subject to, the trading and other surplus extraction activities of larger 'metropolises' (regional towns) which are in turn linked, as satellites, to the main sub-metropolises in the different national economies of the periphery, usually the capital city and/or the main port. These centres are in turn subjected to surplus extraction and appropriation by the world centres of capitalism.

Frank not only asserts that merchant capital has reached out to the very base of the pyramid, but also argues that these exchange relations are all *monopolistic*.[22] At every level surplus extraction is maximised by monopolistic traders who buy cheap and sell dear, although in the latter case always with the possibility of lowering the price of manufactured imports should it be necessary to undercut local producers.

Frank argues that those historical periods in which parts of the periphery have achieved a certain degree of development have been precisely those in which for one reason or another the ties with the relevent metropolis have been loosened, as in this century during the recession of the 1930s and both World Wars. These periods, as earlier ones in which either war or economic recession in the metropolitan centres have disrupted links with the periphery, have been characterised by development and diversification in the latter, with the temporary burgeoning of manufacturing to produce import substitutes. However, the revival of international trade has always led to the undercutting of the fledgling manufacturing industries of the peripheral economies. These have then reverted to their traditional role as exporters of cheap natural resources to the metropolitan centres of international capitalism. Opposition to this reversion in the periphery is overridden by foreign capital, operating, since political independence, in alliance with a domestic *comprador* bourgeoisie whose own economic interests are predominantly commercial.

Continuity in change
The observation that over time the satellite–metropolis relationship has remained a persistent feature of the world capitalist system leads Frank to the specification of the third major feature of this system – continuity in change. Even though the status of the original world metropolitan centres to which Latin America was linked was later transformed, and even though Latin American countries achieved independence from colonial rule, the satellite–metropolis relationship, and the linked processes of surplus expropriation and appropriation through trade, have continued. Thus, when Portugal and Spain became satellites of Britain, British commercial interests established dominance over Latin America. Acquisition of political independence in Latin America was associated with some attempt to promote increased economic independence and development. However, such efforts, being undertaken without a deliberate withdrawal from the international capitalist system, failed in the face of the greater strength of foreign merchant capital. Thus attempts in Chile in the nineteenth century to build up a national merchant fleet and indigenous industry were both undercut in a matter of decades. The merchant marine was bought out by foreign capital, while attempts to develop industry were undercut by the free trade measures that were imposed by the British 'metropolis'. Newly-independent Latin American economies in the nineteenth century were forced back into the mould of underdevelopment characterised by a trade regime geared to primary exports to the metropolis and manufactured imports from it.[23]

Throughout his analysis of the causes of underdevelopment Frank emphasises not only their operation and impact at the national level, but also their internal impact upon socio-economic structures and conditions within the underdeveloped economy – both the impact upon the structure of production, and the contemporary impact upon the functional, regional and personal distribution of income and upon the absolute living standards of the masses. He produces figures to show that since 1940 personal inequality has been rising and mass living standards falling.[24]

Frank's conclusion is, inevitably, similar to Baran's. While Baran concludes that a class alliance dominated by landlords, merchants and monopoly capitalists, with a strong *comprador* element, cannot be expected to promote national economic development, Frank also concludes that the predominantly merchant capitalist *comprador* bourgeoisie that dominates the periphery must be replaced if genuine and equitable economic development is to occur.

Frank's analysis of underdevelopment quickly achieved a wide influence. In Latin America he found a ready audience among the growing number of radical social scientists, who were dissatisfied with their countries' development performance and increasingly concerned by the growing evidence of poverty and immiseration amongst the masses (brought home to urban dwellers by the rapid growth of shanty towns). In North America too, Frank found a sympathetic audience, particularly amoung the new generation of students many of whom were alienated from their own political, social and economic environment by their country's involvement in the Vietnam War, and by what they perceived as the uncaring materialism and individualism of the 'American way of life'. Concerned already by what they perceived as American imperialism in Asia, and concerned to create new, more egalitarian, political, economic and social structures at home, they were a receptive audience to Frank's analysis of the contemporary impact of capitalism in Latin America. Frank's work also quickly became influential in Europe, where the radical movements of the late 1960s also provided a receptive audience.

Yet Frank was not without his critics, who included members of the radical left as well as more 'orthodox' social scientists. Later in this chapter there will be a review of the fundamental criticisms that have been levelled against neo-Marxist theory as a whole. Here, however, the emphasis is on the criticisms that have been levelled specifically against those elements of this perspective that were introduced by Frank.

Criticisms of Frank's contribution to neo-Marxism

Frank has been accused of imprecision, inaccuracy and incompleteness by some of his fellow radicals. Four criticisms are particularly relevant to the present discussion:

1. Frank has misunderstood the defining characteristics of a mode of production in general, and of the capitalist and feudal modes in particular (Laclau, 1972).
2. He has consequently misspecified the nature of the mode(s) of production in the periphery (Laclau, *op.cit.*; Brenner, 1977).
3. He fails to provide any form of class analysis of the socio-economic structures in the periphery (Brenner, *op.cit.*).
4. As a result of 1–3 he fails to provide a convincing analysis of the causes of underdevelopment in the periphery.

Modes of production
Laclau has shown that for Frank the defining characteristics of the capitalist mode of production are production *for the market*, which is motivated by the desire to maximise profit where this profit is realised for the benefit of someone other than the direct producer. In contrast, the feudal mode of production is characterised by the self-sufficiency of the feudal estate and the absence of production for the market.

Laclau contrasts these two interpretations with more orthodox Marxist definitions of capitalism and feudalism based in turn upon a more orthodox Marxist definition of a mode of production in general. The latter is not geared to the presence or absence of *exchange* relations. Rather, it is the relations of *production* that are one of the defining characteristics of any particular mode of production, where the latter refers to 'an integrated complex of social productive forces and relations linked to a determinate type of ownership of the means of production'.[25]

A correct definition of feudalism, Laclau argues, does not emphasise the absence of exchange relations. Indeed this is not a characteristic of feudalism at all. Market exchange, some of it over long distances, occurred regularly under the feudal and slave modes of production as under capitalism. Rather, the distinctive features of the feudal mode are as follows:

1. The economic surplus is produced by a labour force subject to extra-economic compulsion.
2. The economic surplus is privately appropriated by someone other than the direct producer.
3. Property in the means of production remains in the hands of the direct producer (Laclau, *op.cit.*: 33).

In contrast, under capitalism neither 1 nor 3 apply. Under capitalism 'ownership of the means of production is severed from ownership of labour power'. It is this that permits the emergence of wage-labour, i.e. of a labour force subject to economic compulsion. Exchange relations exist under capitalism, but they are not a characteristic that is particular to this mode.

Modes of production in the periphery

Laclau, Brenner and others have sought to show that once the definitional emphasis is shifted back from exchange relations to production relations, abundant empirical evidence can be adduced to refute Frank's assertion that since the conquest period the socio-economic complexes of Latin America have all been capitalist. After the conquest, feudal and slave production relations were both employed in expansion of production for the market.

Laclau argues that with the expansion of world market opportunities feudal production relations were often intensified, that this process continued until the late nineteenth century and that 'semi-feudal conditions are still widely characteristic of the Latin American countryside'. Feudal production relations did not prohibit expansion of production for the market in Latin America (and nor had they done so in Europe).

Frank's critics on the left do not necessarily refute his main obser-vation – that underdevelopment in the periphery is the necessary counterpart of development at the centre. Rather, it is his explanation of this phenom-enon that is the focus of criticism. Thus, Laclau continues his critique by arguing that the causality of underdevelopment lies in the relations of production (correctly specified) and not the relations of exchange.

At the centre, a rise in the organic composition of capital is inevitable under capitalism as capitalists strive simultaneously to expand output and to maintain a reserve army of labour.[26]

> But unless a rise in the organic composition of capital is linked to a more than proportional increase in the rate of surplus value, it will necessarily produce a decline in the rate of profit.[27]

Laclau suggests that a key role of the periphery in sustaining the world capitalist system has lain in the past in the use by the metropolitan capitalist class of investments in the periphery to help sustain the average rate of profit, although he also notes the need for further data on this point.

> Let us take the example of plantations or haciendas. In these the organic composition of capital is low. . . the labour force is in general subjected to the forms of extra-economic coercion characteristic of the feudal or slave modes of production; finally, to the extent that free labour exists, it is generally super-abundant and therefore cheap. If it could then be proved that investment in these sectors has played an important role in determining the rate of profit, it would follow that the expansion of industrial capitalism in the metropolitan countries necessarily depended on the maintenance of pre-capitalist modes of production in the peripheral areas.
>
> (Laclau, 1972: 36, 7.)

Laclau also suggests that Frank's rejection of dualism is based on the wrong premises:

> to affirm the feudal character of relations of production in the agrarian sector does not necessarily involve maintaining a dualistic thesis.

His counter-suggestion is that the influence of capitalism has penetrated throughout the economies of the periphery, but in a manner which in agriculture often uses, rather than replaces, pre-capitalist production relations.

The absence of a class analysis applied to the periphery

Brenner's criticism of Frank for failing to apply any class analysis to the periphery complements Laclau's emphasis upon the significance of the use of cheap labour there to sustain the average rate of profit. Brenner argues that the same pre-capitalist production relations that combine use of cheap labour with a low organic composition of capital have inevitably curtailed the inducement to invest in the periphery, for the demand for both mass consumption goods and capital goods is severely restrained, while the exploiting classes gladly meet their luxury consumption requirements through imports.

However, writing in the latter half of the 1970s, Brenner concludes that even if there were an expansion of capitalist production relations in the periphery, this would not necessarily result in an expanding mass market for wage goods, nor in rising welfare for the masses. For with contracting profit opportunities in the advanced industrial countries, the *raison d'être* of investment in the periphery would be low wages and a politically repressed labour force.

Frank's critics have a two-fold concern: with the quality of his analysis and with his conclusions. With respect to the latter, Laclau himself is less conclusive than Frank. The logic of Frank's analysis is that capitalism must be replaced in the periphery if development is to occur. Having exposed the prior argument as fallacious, but having demonstrated that underdevelopment in the periphery is none the less inextricably linked to the development of the centre, albeit for different reasons, Laclau reserves his judgement on the prospects for the future. It follows from his analysis that if it is pre-capitalist production relations that are serving to hold back the development of the periphery, then the possibility re-emerges, in principle at least, that their replacement by the capitalist mode of production might open up new opportunities for progress. Laclau implies that in practice the likelihood of capitalist development occurring in Latin America probably varies between countries, but he deliberately does not explore this issue.[28]

Brenner, meanwhile, takes a different tack. Like Frank, although following a different logic, he concludes that the system should be changed. However, he is concerned by the implication of Frank's analysis that the countries of the periphery should withdraw into autarky, detaching themselves from the world economy. This withdrawal could have negative consequences for the development of the productivity of labour, itself the essence of economic development. Brenner's writing reflects the view that the only viable route to economic progress in the periphery, given the existing level of development of the productive forces at the centre, is through international co-operation between working-class socialist movements at the centre and the periphery.

Frank remained a prolific writer on underdevelopment throughout the 1960s and 1970s. In his later work he has maintained his emphasis on the significance of surplus extraction through trade, and has increasingly emphasised the concepts of dependency and unequal exchange (the latter as interpreted and analysed by Arghiri Emmanuel). Frank's later work on dependency is discussed in Chapter 7, while Emmanuel's interpretation of unequal exchange is discussed in the next section of this chapter.

EMMANUEL AND THE THEORY OF UNEQUAL EXCHANGE

The theory of unequal exchange

In 1969, two years after the publication of Frank's *Capitalism and Unequal Development in Latin America* the French economist Arghiri Emmanuel published his main contribution to the neo-Marxist debate: *Unequal Exchange: A Study of the Imperialism of Trade.* As the title suggests, Emmanuel, like Frank, argues that the root causes of underdevelopment lie in the exchange relations between centre and periphery. However, while Frank specifies monopoly control over trade as the means by which surplus is extracted, Emmanuel focuses on a different mechanism of surplus extraction. This is based on the divergence of labour costs (as reflected in the money wage) between the centre and the periphery. In focusing on the money wage he uses a different interpretation of the value of labour from Marx.

Emmanuel starts his analysis from a proposition that is common to the neo-Marxists – that the development of capitalist imperialism imposed a particular set of trade relationships on the periphery. Like Frank too, Emmanuel argues that this trade relationship, once it had been imposed upon the periphery, has led to the perpetuation of underdevelopment.

In his explanation of this process Emmanuel sets out to demonstrate what he regards as a major exception to the conclusion of the Ricardian theory of comparative advantage, i.e. that where there are two countries producing two identical goods, one having a comparative advantage in the production of one, and one in that of the other,[29] both may gain if they enter into trade, and certainly neither will lose. Emmanuel's thesis is that under certain conditions countries may indeed become net losers when they engage in international trade. It has been seen in Chapter 5 that the structuralists too rejected the law of comparative advantage. However, Emmanuel distances himself from the 'Prebisch–Singer thesis', with its emphasis on the different income-elasticities of demand for primary and manufactured goods (Singer, 1950; Prebisch, 1949 and 1964), claiming that his analysis is differently, and more securely, founded.

In expounding the theory of comparative advantage Ricardo emphasised that in any two countries the relative productivity of labour in producing any two commodities is likely to differ. (This may be for a variety of reasons ranging from climate through quality of raw materials to the skills and aptitudes of labour itself.) In each country there will therefore be a different relative price for the two commodities determined by the two sets of relative labour costs. When the two countries enter into international trade, each specialising in the product in which it is relatively more efficient (as measured by the output of the alternative product that is foregone for each unit produced) then they will exchange goods at relative prices that lie within a range that is limited by the two sets of domestic price relatives. Ricardo's analysis is presented entirely in real terms; the nominal prices of exchange are incidental.

In Emmanuel's model of unequal exchange the emphasis shifts. The causal role in the distribution of gains from trade is now assigned to monetary variables, although behind these operate real economic forces.

Emmanuel assumes a world in which capital is internationally mobile but labour is not. With capital being mobile, the rate of profit is assumed to be equalised in all countries.[30] Thirdly, Emmanuel assumes that to a large degree the products exported from the periphery cannot also be exported from the centre, and vice versa. Under these conditions, he argues, the ratio in which products are exchanged is determined not by the forces of supply and demand – not, that is, by competition between centre and periphery in international markets – but by the domestic costs of production in the two contexts.

While capital costs are assumed uniform in the two regions, wage costs are not. Thus, 'prices depend on wages'.[31] The rate at which goods are exchanged between the centre and the periphery depends primarily not on the amount of labour embodied in their production, but on the relative unit cost of labour. Underlying this relative money cost is of course the relative value of the real wage in the centre and the periphery. The higher standard of living enjoyed by labour at the centre is directly reflected in the price of the centre's exports relative to that of exports from the periphery.

Emmanuel emphasises that his theory of unequal exchange is totally distinct from the arguments put forward by Nurkse and the structuralist school to explain the adverse trend in the barter terms of trade for under-developed countries. Although others have pointed to a similarity between Prebisch's (1949) analysis of the terms of trade and Emmanuel's later theoretical work, the latter is at pains to distance himself from Prebisch, arguing that for Prebisch, like Nurkse and Singer, the crucial explanatory factor in price determination is, ultimately, the income elasticity of demand for manufactured products as compared with that for primary products. Even in Prebisch (1949), argues Emmanuel, wages have a causal effect on prices only in developed countries and only during recessions.[32] Of non-Marxist economists who have written on the trade issue, Emmanuel singles out W. A. Lewis as the one whose views correspond most closely to his own.[33]

Emmanuel acknowledges that there are some products that are exported by both centre and periphery. In this case, the periphery's lower wage costs impose a competitive upper limit on price, and the centre's ability to compete, given its higher unit labour costs, is entirely due to differential productivity. However, he argues that in most cases the exports from the two regions are distinct and in these cases the centre's prices are not forced down by lower cost competition from the periphery.

Emmanuel reinforces his dissociation from the Nurkse/structuralist view by taking the examples of timber, exported chiefly by industrially advanced countries (Sweden, Norway, Canada, Australia), and petroleum, exported from parts of the periphery. Both are primary products. However, the income elasticity of demand is substantially higher for petroleum than for timber. Petroleum also 'benefits' from the absence of synthetic substitutes of which there are many for timber. Between 1913 and 1962 world production and consumption of petroleum rose from 50 to 1215 million tons while timber consumption per capita fell in Europe and America. Yet despite its extraordinary market superiority, the price index and terms of trade for petroleum both fell, while those for timber rose. The petroleum price index fell from '100 in 1913 to index 42 in 1952 and index 27 in 1962, while that of timber rose from index 100 in 1913 to index 559 in 1952' (Emmanuel, *op.cit.*: 173). Emmanuel notes too the different price trend of timber exports from the periphery – this moved downwards over the same period.

Like Lewis, Emmanuel concludes that as long as wages remain at subsistence level in the periphery, productivity gains there will simply be passed on to the centre in the form of lower prices, thus leading to an outflow of potential surplus from the periphery. For, when such productivity gains occur, the profit rate will rise and output will be expanded – leading to a decline in unit price – until the rate of profit has again been equalised internationally.

Unequal exchange is likely to lead to cumulative growth in per capita income inequality between the centre and the periphery for three main reasons. Firstly, in the centre, trade union success in bargaining for wage increases puts sustained pressure on capitalists to counteract the ensuing fall in the rate of surplus value and, hence, profit, by seeking new means of raising labour productivity – for Emmanuel wage increases cause productivity gains and not the reverse. Secondly, wage increases expand the domestic market, thereby inducing further investment in high wage areas. Thirdly, in circumstances where roughly the same proportion of GDP is taken in tax in the centre and the periphery, and is used by the state to finance social expenditure on health, education, infrastructure and law and order, the absolute expenditure per capita on this 'social wage' is higher at the centre. Although orthodox Marxist theory would class these outlays as unproductive, they do in fact, argues Emmanuel, have a cumulative effect on economic growth.

Unequal exchange has political as well as economic implications. It casts a wedge between the interests of the working classes at the centre and in the periphery. At the centre there has emerged a 'labour aristocracy', in possession of a standard of living that is much higher than the average for the world's proletariat. This labour aristocracy, realising its privileged position will fight (literally) to protect it. This is reflected in the emergence of strong nationalist sentiments among the labour aristocracy, who have become committed defenders of imperialist and neo-imperialist interests: 'a *de facto* united front of the workers and capitalists of the well-to-do countries, directed against the poor nations, co-exists with an internal trade union struggle over sharing the loot'.[34] Far from forming a united front with workers in the periphery, the division of interest between the two branches of the working class is firmly entrenched. The commonality of interest of the capitalist class in the centre and the periphery is far greater than that of the working class.

The implication of Emmanuel's analysis is ultimately the same as that of Baran's and Frank's. The periphery will continue to lose surplus value as long as it remains part of the international capitalist system. The promotion of economic autarky is the only way to retain the surplus and promote economic development. It is better to reinvest surplus value in the comparatively inefficient domestic production of manufactured goods than to lose the surplus permanently through unequal exchange. To achieve this, however, requires a radical change in the class distribution of power in the periphery.

Criticisms of the theory of unequal exchange

Emmanuel's model of unequal exchange has been criticised on various counts. These include the following:

1. The treatment of wages as the 'independent variable' with no adequate explanation of how they in turn are determined. (Bettelheim, 1972.)
2. A failure likewise to provide an adequate explanation of why particular countries are high-wage, developed economies while others are low-wage and underdeveloped. (Bettelheim, 1972; Barratt-Brown, 1974.)
3. A failure to explain the causes of the different structures of production in developed and underdeveloped countries. (Brewer, 1980.)
4. A failure of the theory to stand up to empirical testing. (Barratt-Brown, 1974.)

Criticisms 1–3 also provide the basis of the further criticism that Emmanuel has claimed too much for his theory. While he has identified an important phenomenon, he has not, as he himself claims,[35] provided the fundamental explanation of underdevelopment.

Barratt-Brown has adduced time series data which suggest that there have been significant periods during the last century in which the terms of trade have moved in favour of underdeveloped countries, while in the first half of the nineteenth century the terms of trade also moved against Britain, then the leading economy at the centre.[36] These data certainly call into question Emmanuel's claim that his theory has had general empirical validity at least since the nineteenth century. Indeed, Barratt-Brown suggests that it is only the trends in the terms of trade in the 1930s and again from 1950 to 1969 that are fully consistent with Emmanuel's thesis.

Meanwhile, at the theoretical level, Bettelheim has levelled against Emmanuel a critique analogous to that levelled against Frank by Laclau. He takes Emmanuel to task for trying to locate the fundamental cause of underdevelopment in the relations of exchange, rather than in the relations of production and their interrelationship with the level of development of the forces of production. Bettelheim argues that this latter approach would have permitted Emmanuel to explain both relative wages in the centre and periphery and why some countries have achieved developed status while the majority have not (see Bettelheim in Emmanuel, 1972: Appendix 1, pp. 288–290).

Brewer level against Emmanuel's analysis a criticism which, as we shall see, he also raises against Amin (Brewer, 1980 : 227 and 248). This is that neither provides a satisfactory explanation of the contemporary structure of world production.

> The objection is very simple: why should the high-wage, high-price products go on being produced in the high-wage countries? Given free mobility of capital between countries, why should any investment go to the high-wage countries at all? For some products the answer is clear: oil will be extracted from Alaska, the North Sea and so on because it is a natural resource which must be extracted where it is found. But the advanced countries specialise mainly in the products which are least tied to the location of natural resources: manufactured goods, and especially high-technology products whose raw material content is very small in relation to their total cost.
>
> (Brewer, 1980: 227.)

We shall return to this point when reviewing Brewer's observations on Amin's analysis of underdevelopment.

SAMIR AMIN ON UNDERDEVELOPMENT IN THE PERIPHERY

When Amin published *Accumulation on a World Scale* in 1970[37] he drew upon not only the theoretical work of Marx and the early Marxist writers on imperialism (Lenin, Luxemburg, etc.) but also on the analytical work of the new school of neo-Marxists, in particular Baran and Emmanuel, and, to a lesser extent, Frank, while incorporating also his own analytical contribution. As Amin himself states, and as Brewer has noted in his exegesis of Amin's work, this is largely a work of critical synthesis.[38] (It has also played a major role in expanding the teaching and use of neo-Marxist theory throughout Africa.) Amin presents his purpose as:

> to analyse that single process which is at once a process of development at the centre and a process of underdevelopment (or rather, using André Gunder Frank's expression, 'development of underdevelopment') in the periphery.[39]

In common with other neo-Marxist theorists, Amin takes the view that Marx had little empirical information concerning the periphery, that he was wrongly sanguine concerning the impact of colonial capitalism upon development in the periphery, and that development of capitalism at the centre has in reality been based partly upon the blocking of development in the periphery. Amin rejects Frank's definition of capitalism in terms of exchange relations, and, hence, the thesis that the capitalist mode of production pervades the periphery, while none the less accepting that metropolitan capitalism dominates the latter. This enables Amin to analyse the significance of the actual pre-capitalist formations that are still to be found in the periphery. In this respect his analytical work is closer to that of Baran, and aims to meet some of the criticisms of Frank that we reviewed above. While the specific experiences of economic change have varied among different countries in the periphery, Amin regards the following propositions as generally valid – they constitute a general theory of underdevelopment which underlies the great variety of specific types.[40]

1. The key to an understanding of the causes and process of underdevelopment lies in an analysis of the social formations in the centre and the periphery, and of the relations between these. This analysis must adopt an historical perspective, for the nature of these formations, and of their interrelationship, has changed over time.
2. In the contemporary periphery there are three key structural 'symptoms' of underdevelopment which must be understood or explained:
   (a) unevenness of productivity between sectors;
   (b) disarticulation of the national economic system;
   (c) domination from outside.
   These are not characteristics of purely traditional economies but of ones that have been drawn into the international economy in a particular manner.
3. The social formations that have these characteristics are not purely capitalist. Rather, the capitalist mode of production dominates the high productivity branches of the economy while traditional and peasant social formations contain the branches of low productivity. Capitalism has, however, penetrated and used these formations (through trade and

the extraction of cheap labour) and continues to dominate and use them.

4. In the contemporary centres of world capitalism the social formations consist in virtually pure forms of the capitalist mode of production, now developed to the level of monopoly capitalism.

5. The monopoly capital of the centre dominates the modern sectors of underdeveloped economies and blocks their development. It does so in two ways:

    (a) domination of investments in these sectors, controlling their composition and extracting surplus in the form of repatriated profit;
    (b) through a new form of primitive accumulation – surplus extraction and appropriation through trade based on unequal exchange.

6. Neither of these forms of domination was possible before the emergence of monopoly capitalism at the centre in the late nineteenth century. With the emergence of monopoly capitalism, concentrations of capital at the centre became large enough to permit private resource mobilisation to finance investment in the periphery. Simultaneously, the transition to monopoly capitalism was associated with a decline in price competition at the centre which enabled individual firms to carry real wage increases by passing these on in higher prices, thereby introducing the era of surplus extraction through unequal exchange.

7. While the current domination of the periphery by the centre takes these two forms, it did not always do so in the past. The periods of close interaction between centre and periphery can be divided into three epochs:

    (a) primitive accumulation by the centre based upon forced, uncompensated extraction of resources. This epoch, which was also the age of mercantile capitalism, ran from the sixteenth century to the Industrial Revolution;

    (b) Between the Industrial Revolution and the complete conquest of the world (in 1880–1900), a century elapsed that was in the nature of a pause. . . The trade that continued during this period seems to have been equal, products being exchanged at their value . . . the rewards of labour at the centre were very low, tending to be kept down to subsistence level.

    (Amin, 1974: 87;)

    (c) this was followed by the epoch of monopoly capitalism which still continues.

These three epochs or phases have generated a series of changes in the structure of production and the allocation of labour in the periphery that have consistently impeded the transition to a process of sustained capitalist development (a process which Brewer later describes as 'unequal specialisation').[41]

The outward-oriented commercialisation of Phases I and II undercut both artisan producers in the periphery and the scope for indigenous capitalist development of industry. Displaced artisans were forced back into agriculture, where they increased the person:land ratio in the small farm sector and lowered the rural wage. However, while the lowering of the wage reduced the size of the domestic market for consumer goods, it need not have impeded development. In the nineteenth century the industrially advanced countries developed on the basis of a low-wage economy, exploiting cheap labour to expand production of producer goods; industry provided its own market (Amin, *op.cit.*: 156). The crucial question is why the recipients of surplus in the periphery did not respond to the incentive offered by lower wages in a similar manner.

Amin answers this question as follows. In Phase II the move to local capitalist investment in industry was blocked because the productivity gains already achieved in manufacturing production at the centre enabled the latter to undercut any indigenous attempts to develop manufacturing in the periphery. Meanwhile

> the immediate effect of the ruin of the craftsmen is to aggravate the agrarian crisis. The mass movement back to the land implies real economic retrogression. It has not helped to make agriculture more commercial. On the contrary it [and the consequent rising pressure on the land] has compelled the peasants to devote a larger proportion of their efforts to production for their own consumption, and so to sell less on the market.
>
> (Amin, *op.cit.*: 157.)

In those cases where local capital was invested, the low wage-level influenced the choice of technique, favouring intensive use of men rather than machines.

Phase III, the era of monopoly capitalism at the centre, is characterised also by exports of capital to the periphery. However, due both to continuing competition in manufacturing from the centre, with its high productivity of labour, and to the small size of the domestic market, this capital is invested first and foremost in export production – in mineral extraction and tropical agriculture. Later this is followed by some investment in industry, but such investment is overwhelmingly in light, labour-intensive branches of manufacturing as opposed to capital goods production. Investment by foreign capital not only distorts the pattern of industrial development in the periphery, it also stunts it by discouraging investment on the part of potential indigenous capitalists – a phenomenon that is reinforced by the continuing adverse impact on indigenous accumulation of trade between the centre and the periphery. The joint impact of these two forms of competition from the centre (investment and trade) leads to distortion towards export activities, tertiary activities and light industry, and also, to a lesser degree, light techniques.[42]

Not only has this limited advance been distorted, but it has been highly disjointed. It has been marked by 'brief bursts of very vigorous growth, shifting from country to country, followed by long periods of stagnation'. (Amin, *op.cit.*: 166.)

Amin's interpretation of the development of underdevelopment thus emphasises that underdevelopment is reflected both in the outflow of surplus through trade and in a distorted and stunted process of industrial growth in the periphery. More than Baran, Frank or Emmanuel, he emphasises that in the first half of the twentieth century significant capitalist industrialisation occurred in the periphery: the problem was not its absence but its nature – a problem which in turn is created by the dominance exercised over the periphery by the centres of the world capitalist system.

Various criticisms have been levelled against Amin's analytical approach as manifested both in the study reviewed here and in other work. They fall into four categories:

1. Criticism of his dialectical method.
2. Criticism of his interpretation of history.
3. Criticism of specific elements of his personal contribution to neo-Marxist theory.
4. Criticism of elements of his theoretical framework that form part of the common core of the neo-Marxist paradigm.

With respect to 1, Smith (1982) takes Amin to task for using a mixture of assertion and abuse to state his case and undercut criticism. With respect to 2, Smith also criticises Amin for drawing implicitly, if not explicitly, a false comparison between the experience of growth in the centre and the periphery, implying that the former was a smooth, continuous process when in fact this was not so. With respect to 3, Brewer (1980) argues that Amin's analysis of uneven specialisation between centre and periphery is incomplete. It does not explain why in the current era of multinational capitalism there is not a widespread movement of industrial production from the centre to the low-wage periphery. Yet the absence of such movement is central to Amin's perspective. Brewer suggests that in the early twentieth century Amin could have explained this absence by the presence of significant external economies, including a skilled labour force, at the centre.

> In the present stage of development, however, there are very large wage differentials, and multinational firms have great experience of transferring technology, so that it is much harder to see why a productivity gap should persist. Without it, Amin's main arguments would collapse.
>
> (Brewer, 1980: 249.)

Those criticisms of Amin that apply to the neo-Marxist school in general are discussed on pages 189–92.

FURTHER DEVELOPMENT OF THE NEO-MARXIST PARADIGM

The 1970s witnessed further development in the work of the neo-Marxist school, along lines already presaged in Amin (1970). The emphasis in the work of leading neo-Marxists – Frank, Amin and also Wallerstein – was on the analysis of the functioning of the world capitalist system *as a whole*, of which the periphery is an integral part. This work continues to emphasise the inevitability of the underdevelopment of the periphery. As a subsidiary element in their later work both Frank and Amin take up the concept of dependency and examine the nature and significance of dependent relations between the centre and the periphery. Their contribution to the 1970s dependency debate is examined in the next chapter.

CRITICISMS OF THE OVERALL INTELLECTUAL FRAMEWORK OF NEO-MARXISM

Neo-Marxism has aroused criticism both from non-Marxist economists and from those who regard themselves as more orthodox Marxists. It is indeed from within Marxism that the most detailed attack on neo-Marxism has been mounted. Right-wing economists such as Lal do not devote time and space to detailed criticism, but reassert their belief in the greater effectiveness of capitalism (over socialism) in raising growth, alleviating poverty and promoting civil liberties including – in their view – in the Third World (see e.g. Lal, 1983: 45). According to this view, the notion of 'delinking' from the international capitalist system is ludicrous. It would generate economic inefficiency and stagnation while, it is claimed, socialist regimes are also notorious for the suppression of civil liberties.

Non-Marxist but more radical economists have also written little in systematic criticism of the neo-Marxists. In their own work some have either implicitly or explicitly acknowledged a positive contribution of neo-Marxism in the development debate, through drawing attention to the significance of class interests in the disposition of the surplus – a theme which some have taken up. However, neo-Marxism is either implicitly or explicitly criticised by some of these economists, among others, for espousing an overly rigid and homogeneous interpretation of patterns of class dominance in the periphery.

The following considers a further body of criticism that has been generated largely from within the Marxist perspective, most notably by Bill Warren.

Warren and the 'Orthodox Marxist' critique of neo-Marxist theory

In 1973 Bill Warren published a major critique of the neo-Marxist school. It was not intended primarily as a critique of any particular theorist but as a fundamental questioning of the neo-Marxist consensus that

> the prospects of independent industrialisation in such [underdeveloped] countries are nil or negligible (unless they take a socialist option); and that the characteristics of backwardness, underdevelopment and dependence which prevent such development are the necessary results of imperialist domination.

Warren set out to argue, on the contrary, that

empirical observations suggest that the prospects for successful capitalist economic development (implying industrialisation) of a significant number of major underdeveloped countries are quite good; that substantial progress in capitalist industrialisation has already been achieved; that the period since the Second World War has been marked by a major upsurge in capitalist social relations and productive forces (especially industrialisation) in the Third World; that in so far as there are obstacles to this development, they originate not in current imperialist-Third World relationships, but almost entirely from the internal contradictions of the Third World itself; that the imperialist countries' policies and their overall impact on the Third World actually favour its industrialisation; and that the ties of dependence binding the Third World to the imperialist countries have been, and are being, markedly loosened, with the consequence that the distribution of power within the capitalist world is becoming less uneven.

(Warren 1973: 3, 4.)

Warren (1973) does not in fact give much space to the internal contradictions of Third World countries, but he treats the other points at some length, both in the 1973 article and in a book published posthumously in 1980, adducing considerable empirical evidence in support of his argument.

Warren's aim is not to demonstrate that imperialism has already ceased to exist as a system of inequality, domination and exploitation, but that the system is changing. One of the major weaknesses of neo-Marxist theory is that it takes a static view of the world. It does not allow for the possibility that significant changes may occur either within individual underdeveloped economies or in the relations between countries of the centre and the periphery.[43]

An important feature of Warren's critique is his interpretation of development. This differs from that of the neo-Marxist school in that Warren is concerned specifically and solely with the existence of capitalist development in the periphery, i.e. with the continuing and expanding reproduction of capital. He does not also take into account issues of equity.[44] His gauge of capitalist development in the periphery is the rate of development of the industrial sector, which in his empirical data he restricts to the rate of development of manufacturing production.

Warren argues that the empirical data show that manufacturing output in the 1950s and 1960s actually grew faster in the Third World than in the industrially advanced countries despite abnormally fast growth, by historical standards, in the latter. He presents 1951–1969 average annual manufacturing growth rate figures for 22 underdeveloped countries, all of which exceed the average for the advanced countries for the same period. These figures, Warren argues, demonstrate the ability of underdeveloped countries to sustain high growth rates over longish periods (not just short spurts, as suggested by Amin) and, what is more, 'in a period when neither war nor world depression have acted to "cut off" the Third World from the advanced capitalist countries' (Warren, 1973: 6). Meanwhile the share of manufacturing in the aggregate GDP of Third World countries has also risen, and by 1973 was already over half that in developed ones. Warren acknowledges that the growth rates of manufacturing output per capita of underdeveloped countries lag behind those of industrially advanced countries, due to high population growth in the former, but argues that per capita rates give a misleading impression of the underlying dynamic.

> Clearly, from the point of view of living standards, per capita growth rates are the most relevant criterion. However, from the perspectives of the distribution of world industrial power and the growth of the market (which are more relevant to the problem at hand) total, rather than per capita, growth rates are the central issue.
>
> (Warren, *op.cit.*: 7.)

Two factors have favoured capitalist development in the Third World in the post-war period which have been either ignored, under-emphasised or misinterpreted by the neo-Marxists: the termination of the colonial era and the emergence of a new phase of imperialist rivalries. Political independence has

> *permitted* industrial advance by breaking the monopoly of colonialist power and creating the conditions in which Third World countries can utilise inter-imperialist and East-West rivalries. Independence has been a *direct cause* (not just a permissive condition) of industrial advance in that it has stimulated popular pressures for a higher living standard where these have been a major internal influence sustaining industrialisation policies.
>
> (Warren, *op.cit.*: 11.)

Political independence provides Third World countries with increased bargaining power, which they can use individually or collectively in the international arena. They can play off capitalist states and multinational firms against each other and play upon East–West rivalries. They can also increase bargaining power through collective action such as that of OPEC or of the Andean Pact countries which have established common policies towards foreign firms.

Meanwhile growing competition between a rising number of multinational firms seeking investment outlets in a finite world is also likely to enable Third World countries to negotiate steadily improving terms with the multinationals. Such firms have already shown themselves willing to invest in manufacturing in the periphery, including heavy industries, capital-intensive industries and export-oriented industries.

The fact that imperialist countries collaborate with rulers and exploiting classes in Third World countries to suppress anti-capitalist movements can also aid capitalist development, as in South Korea. However, Warren acknowledges that such support may backfire, leading to the shoring-up of corrupt and inefficient regimes.

Warren also attacks the notion that even if some industrial development has occurred in the Third World, this has only led to a new form of dependence, i.e. that independent industrial development is impossible. His comments on this issue are summarised in Chapter 7, p. 216.

Lastly, Warren attacks the neo-Marxist notions that full, sustained, capitalist development cannot be initiated in the Third World without the prior emergence of a vigorous national bourgeoisie, and that this is prevented by the forces of imperialism. He argues that the analytical emphasis should be shifted from specification of the social forces *leading* to industrialisation to those *compelling* it:

> Once emphasis is placed on the many forces compelling industrialisation, however, then we need no longer associate industrialisation with any particular ruling class. . . Significant capitalist industrialisation may be initiated and directed by a variety of ruling classes and combinations of such classes or their representatives, ranging from semi-feudal ruling groups (northern Nigeria) and including large landowners (Ethiopia, Brazil, Thailand), to bureaucratic-military elites, petty-bourgeoisies and professional and state functionaries (especially in Africa and the Middle East). These 'industrialisers' may themselves become industrial bourgeoisies or may be displaced by the industrial Frankensteins they have erected or they may become fused with them. . . This partly explains the importance of the state in most underdeveloped countries where it often assumes the role of a bourgeois ruling class prior to the substantial development of that class.
>
> (Warren, *op.cit.*: 43, 4.)

The neo-Marxist response to Warren's critique

Warren's contribution to the debate on the prospects for capitalist development in the Third World has had a widespread influence.[45] Inevitably, however, it has also provoked a critical response from the neo-Marxist school. The main criticisms levelled against Warren's analysis are as follows:

1. It is highly empirical and has no coherent overall theoretical framework (McMichael, Petras and Rhodes, 1974).
2. Warren is not justified in ignoring the performance of the agriculture sector in the Third World.

> If one accepts that capitalism is a system representing the highest form of commodity production, then it is not sufficient to isolate the manufacturing sector as one aspect of capitalist development, as Warren does. Such a model requires attention to the crucial importance of the transformation of the rural social economy as a precondition of development of the internal market necessary for the realisation of the highest development of the commodity form.
>
> (McMichael *et al.*, *op.cit.*: 86.)

3. Warren's empirical data on industrial development in the Third World are highly selective (McMichael *et al.*, *op.cit.*).
4. Warren is unjustified in his decision to focus on trends in aggregate output rather than output per capita, for 'the only conceivable purpose

of development is to improve men's material well-being.' (Emmanuel 1974: 64.)

5. Warren's approach leads him to ignore the fact that labour productivity has been advancing much faster in the developed countries' agricultural and manufacturing sectors than it has in the Third World's manufacturing sector (Emmanuel, *op.cit.*: 66, 7). The difference in productivity levels was 1:6 in 1900; it had widened to 1:13.2 by 1970. 'Here it is indeed hard to discern the significant and continuing reduction of inequality that Warren observes.' (Emmanuel *op.cit.*: 71.)

6. These widening productivity differentials are associated with relatively rapid market growth in the industrially advanced countries that reduces the need for foreign capital to flow to the Third World (Emmanuel, *op.cit.*: 75, 77).

If Warren were still alive he would probably respond in part to these and other related criticisms with the comment that they mostly miss his central point: that whatever international cross-section comparisons may show at a particular point in time, the trends in the world economy are essentially as he has described them. With respect to criticisms 5 and 6 he would probably say that it is aggregate output that determines the size of the market and not output per capita, and that continuing industrial development in the periphery is laying the grounds for faster productivity gains in the future.

The diversity of developing economies

Meanwhile a school of thought has also been gathering strength since the late 1970s to the effect that it is unrealistic to expect to reach significant conclusions concerning the prospects for, and constraints to, capitalist development in all the countries of the periphery, which are equally valid for all of them. (Indeed, Warren (1973) did not seek to do this.) This view was espoused by Cardoso and Faletto (1971), and gained wider influence following the republication of this book in English in 1979. It is discussed further in Chapter 7.

SUMMARY AND CONCLUSION

In summary, among the leading contributions to the neo-Marxist paradigm of the 1950s and 1960s there were a number of common elements. Of these, the most significant include a common reference to Marx's political economy as their analytical starting point and the following propositions:

1. Marx failed to predict accurately the impact of capitalism upon the economies of the periphery.

2. Lenin's theoretical work on imperialism extends Marxism in such a way as to incorporate relations between centre and periphery into the main body of Marxist political economy.

3. The interaction of the peripheral economies with those of the centre has been dominated by the latter both in trade and investment in production. The result is a steady outflow of the surplus from the periphery to the centre.

4. The same interaction has blocked the emergence of indigenous competitive capitalism in the periphery.

5. The élite in the periphery continue to derive a large part of their incomes from non-productive activity (chiefly trade and land rent). The impact of metropolitan monopoly capital on the periphery has substantially increased the trading opportunities of indigenous merchant capital.

6. The incomes of the élite in the periphery are used chiefly for luxury consumption and non-productive investment, or are invested in the metropolitan economies.

7. Any limited indigenous investment in capitalist production in the periphery has been from the outset monopolistic in nature.

8. Metropolitan monopoly capital and metropolitan governments seek to maintain the status quo through shoring up *comprador* regimes in the periphery.

9. Only a socialist revolution can create the conditions for the full development of the periphery.

The most far-reaching contribution of the neo-Marxist school has been the attention it has drawn to the significance of the class distribution of control over the 'surplus' (as defined by Baran) in peripheral economies, and, likewise, to the class distribution of political power. However, many consider that one of the main failings of the school is its emphasis on the unchanging nature of the distribution of economic and political power in underdeveloped economies, and its consequent failure to give adequate recognition to the scope for development therein. This last point represents a theme that recurs in the following chapter.

NOTES

1. See Preston, 1987, on this point.
2. Baran, 1973: Foreword. All references in this chapter are to the 1973 edition of Baran, 1957.
3. *Ibid.*
4. See Chapter 3, pp. 52–63.
5. Reprinted in Agarwala and Singh, *op.cit.*: 75–92.
6. See Chapter 3, pp. 54–6 and 59–60.

7. Chapter 2, pp. 18–22.
8. Ken Cole drew the author's attention to this and to a range of other divergences between Marxism and neo-Marxism.
9. Baran, 1973: 132.
10. *Ibid.*: 133. Baran also introduces the concept of the planned economic surplus, but notes that

     'this is only relevant to comprehensive planning under socialism.'

     (*Ibid*: 155.)

11. See pp. 21–2.
12. Although Emmanuel in his analysis of unequal exchange claims to stick to Marx's original definition. See Emmanuel, 1972: 53 *et seq.*
13. This was written by Marx in the Preface to the first German edition of *Capital.*
14. See Baran, 1952, reprinted in Agarwala and Singh, *op.cit.*: 76; also Baran, 1973: 276.

15. 'In some countries even essentially reactionary segments of the feudal aristocracy joined the nationalist camp, interested primarily in deflecting popular energies from the struggle for social change into a fight against foreign subjugation.'

     (Baran, 1973: 366.)

16. Baran refers here to the 'potential surplus', but it appears from the sense of the argument that it is mobilisation of the 'actual surplus' that is the immediate issue (Baran, 1973: 225).
17. See Kuznets, 1966.

18. 'I was an intellectual schizophrenic: I kept my political opinions and my intellectual or professional work apart, accepting scientific theories more or less as they were handed to me and forming my political opinions largely in response to feeling and isolated facts.'

     (Frank, 1969: xviii; all references are to the second (1969) edition of Frank, 1967.)

19. See Baran, *op.cit.*: 195.
20. Frank, *op.cit.*: 35, 48–51 and 234–6.
21. *Ibid.*: 148 and, for an empirical example, 153–4.
22. See Frank, *op.cit.*: 17–20.
23. See Frank, *op.cit.*: 67 *et seq.*
24. *Ibid.*: 108, 9.
25. Laclau's definition is based upon Lange, 1962. For a more elaborate explanation of this concept see also Hindess and Hirst, 1975: 9–12. See also Chapter 3, p. 19 above.
26. The organic composition of capital refers to the ratio of the value of capital consumed in the production process (including raw materials, depreciation of equipment) to the value of labour.
27. Laclau, *op.cit.*: 36.
28. See Laclau, *op.cit.*: 34, 37.
29. I.e., given each country's own factor productivities, one country incurs a lower domestic opportunity cost in producing Good A, and the other country in Good B.
30. In the theory of comparative advantage both factors are assumed to be internationally immobile (although as Emmanuel notes it would make no fundamental difference to the system which the theory models if one were to assume that labour is mobile, provided that it is paid everywhere the same subsistence wage).

31. Emmanuel, 1972: 172 (all references here are to the second (1972) edition of Emmanuel, 1969).
32. Emmanuel, *op.cit.*: 84, 5, and see Chapter 5, pp. 131–2 above.
33. See Chapter 4, pp. 94 above.
34. Emmanuel, *op.cit.*: 180.
35. Emmanuel, *op.cit.*: 265.
36. Barratt-Brown, *op.cit.*: 248.
37. The first English language edition appeared in 1974.
38. Amin, 1974: 2; Brewer, 1980: 233.
39. Amin, *op.cit.*: 20 and 168. Amin, 1976, which gives more emphasis to the concept of dependency, is discussed in Chapter 7.
40. Amin, *op.cit.*: 168.
41. Brewer, *op.cit.*: 241–250.
42. Amin, *op.cit.*: 170.
43. This point has subsequently been emphasised in other critiques of elements of neo-Marxist theory (see e.g. Kay, 1975, on unequal exchange).
44. 'Successful capitalist development is . . . that development which provides the appropriate economic, social and political conditions for the continuing reproduction of capital, as a social system representing the highest form of commodity production . . . The problem as posed in these terms differs from that posed by many authorities who analyse instead the *adequacy* of "development" (sometimes capitalist development) as a process satisfying the needs of the masses (or "the problems of the nation").

(Warren, *op.cit.*: 4.)

45. See e.g. Swainson, 1980; Schiffer, 1981; and Sender and Smith, 1986.

REFERENCES

Amin, S., *Accumulation on a World Scale*, (Monthly Review Press, 1974); translation of *L'Accumulation à l'Echelle Mondiale*, (Editions Anthropos, Paris, 1970).

Baran, P., 'On the political economy of backwardness', *Manchester School*, (January 1952); reprinted in *The Economics of Underdevelopment*, eds. Agarwala, A. and Singh, S., (Oxford, 1958).

Baran, P., *The Political Economy of Growth*, (Monthly Review Press, 1957; Penguin, 1973).

Barratt-Brown, M., *The Economics of Imperialism*, (Penguin, 1974).

Bettelheim, C., 'Theoretical comments', Appendix I in Emmanuel, A., *Unequal Exchange*, (New Left Books, 1972).

Brenner, R., 'On Sweezy, Frank and Wallerstein', *New Left Review*, (104, July–August 1977).

Brewer, A., *Marxist Theories of Imperialism: A Critical Survey*, (Routledge and Kegan Paul, 1980).

Cardoso, F. and Faletto, E., *Dependency and Development in Latin America*, (University of California, 1979; first published 1971).

Chenery, H. and Syrquin, M., *Patterns of Development: 1950–1970*, (Oxford, 1975).

Emmanuel, A., *Unequal Exchange*, (New Left Books, 1972; first published as *L'Echange Inégal*, François Maspero, 1969).

Emmanuel, A., 'Myths of development versus myths of underdevelopment', *New Left Review*, (85, May–June 1974).

Frank, A. G., *Capitalism and Underdevelopment in Latin America: Historical Studies of Chile and Brazil*, (Monthly Review Press, 1967, revised edition 1969).

Hindess, B. and Hirst, P., *Pre-Capitalist Modes of Production*, (Routledge and Kegan Paul, 1975).

Kay, G., *Development and Underdevelopment: A Marxist Analysis*, (Macmillan, 1975).

Kuznets, S., *Modern Economic Growth*, (Yale, 1966).

Laclau, E., 'Feudalism and capitalism in Latin America', *New Left Review*, (67, May–June 1971).

Lal, D., *The Poverty of 'Development Economics'*, Hobart Paper 16, (Institute of Economic Affairs, 1983).

Lange, O., *Economia Politica*, (Editori Riuniti, Rome, 1962).

McMichael, P., Petras, J. and Rhodes, R., 'Imperialism and the contradictions of development', *New Left Review*, (85, May–June 1974).

Marx, K., *Capital*, Volume I, (Lawrence and Wishart, 1970; text of the English edition of 1870).

Prebisch, R., 'The economic development of Latin America and its principal problems,' *Economic Bulletin for Latin America*, (Vol. VII, No. 1, February 1962; first published in Spanish (mimeo) May 1949).

Prebisch, R., *Towards a New Trade Strategy for Development*, Report by the Secretary General of the United Nations Conference on Trade and Development, (United Nations, New York, 1964).

Preston, P., *Rethinking Development*, (Routledge and Kegan Paul, 1987).

Schiffer, J., 'The changing post-war pattern of development: the accumulated wisdom of Samir Amin', *World Development*, (Vol. 9, No. 6, 1981).

Sender, J. and Smith, S., *The Development of Capitalism in Africa*, (Methuen, 1986).

Singer, H., 'The distribution of gains between investing and borrowing countries', *American Economic Review*, (Papers and Proceedings, Vol. 40, No. 2, May 1950).

Smith, S., 'Class analysis versus world systems: critique of Samir Amin's typology of underdevelopment', *Journal of Contemporary Asia*, (Vol. 12, No. 1, 1982).

Swainson, N., *The Development of Corporate Capitalism in Kenya, 1918–1977*, (Heinemann, 1980).

Wallerstein, I., *The Capitalist World Economy*, (Cambridge, 1979).

Warren, B., 'Imperialism and capitalist industrialisation', *New Left Review*, (81, September/October 1973).

Warren, B., *Imperialism: Pioneer of Capitalism*, (Verso, 1980).

7· DEPENDENCY ANALYSES: THE SEEDS OF A NEW PARADIGM?

THE ORIGINS OF DEPENDENCY ANALYSES

Dependency analysis emerged as an influential branch of development economics in the late 1960s. To paraphrase Jose Villamil, it was at this time that dependency entered the vocabulary of development economics.[1] The significance of this occurrence has been variously interpreted. Some analysts have since reviewed dependency theories as if the latter represented a well-integrated, and dominant, school of thought, referring also to the existence of a dependency paradigm (e.g. Roxborough, 1979; Browett, 1985). Others, however (e.g. Palma in Seers, 1981a), have taken issue with this interpretation due to the diversity of theoretical perspectives from which dependency analyses have been approached.

In this chapter we review the main perspectives from which the study of dependency has been approached, and the main interpretations given to, and significance attached to, this concept, with a view to establishing, *inter alia*, the extent to which dependency approaches have generated new theoretical insights into development and underdevelopment, and the extent of common ground between these.

This discussion will be primarily concerned with the economic aspects of dependency. However, it is a common characteristic of dependency studies that dependency relations are seen to extend beyond the economic sphere – they are cultural and political also. Furthermore, these different aspects of dependency are perceived as intertwined. It is therefore not surprising to find that they have been analysed not only by economists but by other social scientists – sociologists and political scientists – as well.

Most of the early work on dependency was carried out in Latin America. However, in the 1970s dependency analyses were more widely applied – both to much of the rest of the Third World and to the countries of the European periphery. This work culminated in a spate of publications on dependency in the late 1970s and early 1980s. In all cases the focus has been on a range of unequal and dependent relationships which are seen to exist between the countries of the periphery and the advanced capitalist economies. These dependent relations are held to constrain, either partially or totally according to the perspective of the analyst, development in the periphery.

THE CLASSIFICATION OF DEPENDENCY ANALYSES

Dependency analyses have been variously categorised, and have also been dated back to various points in time, in several cases earlier than the date specified by Villamil. For example, Frank (1977) identifies two branches of dependency theory:

1. The early work of the ECLA structuralists.
2. A new branch introduced by Frank himself in *Capitalism and Underdevelopment in Latin America*, 1967 (discussed in the previous chapter) and developed to its analytical limits in Frank's *Lumpenbourgeoisie: Lumpendevelopment*, first published in Spanish in 1970, and in English in 1972.

Frank's dating of dependency theory seems to reflect the view that, whether or not the concept was explicitly emphasised at the time, this coincides with the two major attempts, structuralist and neo-Marxist, that were made in the 1950s and 1960s to theorise the causes of underdevelopment emphasising external factors.

However, Frank's classification ignores important differences between the work of the early ('classical') structuralist school, and the subsequent, explicitly dependency-focused, development in the thinking of some of its members, especially Sunkel and Furtado (see Chapter 5, p. 154). It also fails to pinpoint another important category of contributions to dependency analysis as epitomised by the work of Cardoso and Faletto. In addition, it both exaggerates the explicit emphasis on dependency in Frank (1967) and fails to take account of later work on dependency stemming from the neo-Marxist tradition.

Palma (1979) meets two of these objections, identifying three categories of dependency studies: those in the Latin American neo-Marxist tradition begun by Frank, the *later thinking* of some members of the ECLA school, and studies reflecting the third perspective just referred to which is epitomised in the work of Cardoso and Faletto. Palma, however, still retains Frank's dating of neo-Marxist dependency analysis.

In this chapter two elements of Palma's classification are adopted. However, a later dating is adopted for neo-Marxist dependency analysis, on the grounds that it was not until 1969/70 that the concept explicitly became a focal one in neo-Marxist theory. It is to this branch of dependency analysis that the discussion turns first.

NEO-MARXIST DEPENDENCY ANALYSES

The first leading contribution to dependency theory written from a neo-Marxist perspective is Dos Santos (1969). It was also the contribution that made the most ambitious claims for dependency theory. Other leading neo-Marxists, such as Frank and Amin, were much more lukewarm in their adoption of 'dependency' as a focal concept in their analytical framework.

Dos Santos sees dependency theory as the 'periphery-focused' counterpart to the theory of imperialism. 'By understanding dependence and conceptualising and studying its mechanisms and its historical force one both expands and re-formulates the theory of imperialism' (Dos Santos, 1969, reprinted in Bernstein, 1973:73). Frank, on the other hand, while he used the concept in the title of a book published in 1978, goes half-way to disavowing the concept in his introduction to an earlier book – noting that its use appears to be a contemporary fashion, but that its interpretation is often imprecise (see Frank, 1972: 8). Amin, in *Unequal Development* (first published in French in 1973) ostensibly devotes a chapter to dependence, but in practice gives little space to the concept, continuing to emphasise the earlier neo-Marxist notion of the 'development of underdevelopment' (see Chapter 6, p. 183), while also introducing his own linked, but arguably more precise notion of 'extraverted' accumulation.[2]

Neo-Marxist definitions of dependency

The most widely quoted neo-Marxist definition of dependency is that of Dos Santos. This is to be found, with a slight variation in wording, in both Dos Santos 1969 and 1970. The former defines dependence as:

> a conditioning situation in which economies of one group of countries are conditioned by the development and expansion of others. A relationship of interdependence between two or more countries or between such countries and the world trading system becomes a dependent relationship when some countries can expand through self-impulsion while others, being in a dependent position, can only expand as a reflection of the expansion of the dominant countries, which may have positive or negative effects on their immediate development.
>
> (Dos Santos, 1969, reprinted in Bernstein, 1973: 76.)

This definition is elaborated in Amin (1976), in the course of his further development of the theme that there is a single world capitalist system which derives the momentum of its development from the centre. The centres of world capitalism are in principle capable of autarkic development, fully independent of the periphery, whereas the reverse is not the case. Autocentric accumulation at the centre is possible provided that wages increase at a given and calculable rate which permits the realisation of steadily expanding value through the expansion of consumption. True, expanding wage demand may also give rise to another problem, that of finding sufficient outlets for an expanding quantum of reinvestible capital without a significant fall in the rate of profit. However, monopoly capitalism has also found ways of counteracting this tendency through the non-productive use of the surplus on such items as welfare services, advertising and the military. These outlays, as Baran and Sweezy had earlier shown, serve simultaneously to expand consumption and to reduce the reinvestible surplus. Thus surplus realisation in, and appropriation from, the periphery are not logically essential conditions for development at the centre.[3]

However, in practice, because initially:

> real wages at the centre did not increase sufficiently, a form of expansionism was necessary which conferred certain functions upon the periphery [provision of a market for manufactures and supply of low-cost raw materials]. Since the last decades of the nineteenth century, however, real wages at the centre have increased at a faster rate, and this has caused the expansionism of the capitalist mode to assume new forms (imperialism and the export of capital) and has also given the periphery new functions to perform.
>
> (Amin, 1976: 76.)

Yet these new functions are still not essential to the survival of capitalism, for while they help to counteract the tendency of the rate of profit to fall, monopoly capitalism has, as we have just seen, also found ways of counteracting this tendency at the centre.

Thus, the periphery is not essential to the development of capitalism at the centre. There is no true interdependence between centre and periphery, in the sense of being different, complementary, but equal in importance one to the other. None the less the centre has found it convenient to exploit the periphery in order to aid its own capitalist accumulation. Over time it has done so in a variety of ways, modifying the modes of production in the periphery and creating various forms of dependency relation between the latter and the centre, such that the periphery in contrast has lost the possibility of autarkic capitalist development.

The neo-Marxists on dependent capitalist development

Three common themes of neo-Marxist dependency analysis are as follows:

1. The dominant forms of economic dependence in the periphery have changed over time in response to changing economic conditions at the centre (an application of Frank's concept of continuity in change).
2. The condition of dependency is sustained through the voluntary collaboration of the dominant class interests in the periphery.
3. An inherent feature of dependent underdevelopment or development

(the two concepts are interchanged quite loosely) is the restriction of mass incomes and, hence, of the expansion of the domestic market in the periphery.

The most notable change between neo-Marxist underdevelopment theory of the 1960s and neo-Marxist dependency analyses of the 1970s is the explicit acknowledgement that some economic development (albeit never very clearly defined) has occurred, and is occurring, in the periphery. Capital accumulation, expansion of wage labour relations, expansion of output in any sector and in particular development of industry are all variously taken in different writings as indicators of such development. A rise in mass incomes is no longer apparently regarded as an essential feature of some forms of development, although the perpetual exclusion of the masses from dependent development is one reflection of its failure to bring 'true' national development.

The above issues are analysed largely within the neo-Marxist perspective that had already emerged in the 1950s and 1960s. The 1960s perspective is, however, modified with varying degrees of success in the work of different writers, to take account of two of the dominant criticisms levelled against Frank (1967), namely that his analysis ignored the relations of production in the periphery, and that he wrongly defined capitalism in terms of exchange relations.

The following sections review in more detail selected neo-Marxist contributions to the analysis of dependency.

Frank on the 'Lumpenbourgeoisie'

As Frank pointed out in 1977, it was in *Lumpenbourgeoisie, Lumpendevelopment*, first published in 1970,[4] that for the first time he brought the concept of dependence to the forefront of his analysis of change in the periphery. This study is primarily a response to Marxist criticism of Frank's earlier work for the lack of any substantive analysis of class relations in the periphery. Here Frank attempts to meet that criticism at least with respect to the local bourgeoisie. The focus of Frank's analysis is now on the manner in which the dominant bourgeoisie in Latin America 'accepts dependence consciously and willingly but is nevertheless moulded by it' in ways which lead to the sustained extraction of surplus from the region and, hence, its underdevelopment.

Frank (1977) claims that *Lumpenbourgeoisie, Lumpendevelopment* constitutes 'a swan song in the dependency concert'. Although, he adds, 'some new stars in Latin America are still singing variations on the theme (and reflections thereof have only recently begun to be recorded or played back in other parts of the world).' *Lumpenbourgeoisie, Lumpendevelopment*, however, does little more than restate themes already present in Frank (1967), albeit with a more specific focus on the role of local bourgeoisie in the periphery in the generation of dependence.[5]

Frank's later (1978) study *Dependent Accumulation and Underdevelopment* also makes little addition to his earlier theoretical perspective. This work is largely a historical and descriptive account of the incorporation of the different parts of the periphery into the world economy. Like Amin, Frank's analytical method is one of theoretical dialectic interspersed with empirical data, but with the emphasis much more heavily geared towards the latter. The two distinctive theoretical contributions in Frank (1978) are, firstly, his thesis that the reasons for the different impact of *colonialism* on the one hand, and *colonisation* of parts of the new world on the other, lie in the different conditions (natural resource endowment, population density and mode of production, the last albeit never clearly defined) found in the new territories, and, secondly, his reassertion of the significance of the role played by commercial relations in the development of central and peripheral capitalism.

Dos Santos' contribution to dependency theory

Two much more succinct and clearly-focused attempts to provide a statement of the core elements of a theory of dependency are to be found in Dos Santos, 1969 and 1970.

The impetus to develop a dependency theory comes, for Dos Santos, from the crisis of structuralist development theory – a crisis demonstrated by the limits to, and disillusion with, import-substituting industrialisation.[6] Import-substitution, rather than leading to greater independence of foreign trade and increased national autonomy, has led to increased dependence on foreign trade, capital and technology. 'Control of the economy as a whole has still continued to pass to foreign hands.' While the notion of development has lost much of its credibility, 'the concept of dependence has appeared to offer a possible, if partial, explanation of these paradoxes, seeking to explain why Latin American development has differed from that of today's advanced countries' (Dos Santos, 1969). Dos Santos argues that dependence is not a purely external phenomenon. It can become manifest in its various forms only because of the collaboration of domestic dominant classes with the metropolitan bourgeoisie. Hence analysis of a national situation of dependence requires the analysis also of its own specific *domestic* characteristics and movement. In making this point Dos Santos (1969) appears to align himself with the intellectual position on dependency studies adopted by Cardoso and Faletto (see p. 213–15 below), but he then switches to the search for a general theory of dependence to complement the theory of imperialism.

Neither Lenin (1917), nor Bukharin (1966) and Rosa Luxembourg (1964) . . . nor the few non-Marxist writers like Hobson (1965) . . . approached the question of imperialism from the point of view of the dependent countries. Although dependence has its place in the general framework of a theory of imperialism, it also possesses a force of its own which entitles it to a specific place in the general process which is itself influenced by it.

(Dos Santos, 1969, reprinted in Bernstein, 1973: 73.)

Dos Santos 1969 and 1970 both argue that Latin America has passed through a series of stages of dependence. In Latin America three stages or forms of dependence may be distinguished – the mercantile dependence of the colonial era, the financial-industrial dependence that was consolidated at the end of the nineteenth century, and the technological-industrial dependence of the post-war era, 'based on multinational corporations which began to invest in industries geared to the internal market' (Dos Santos, 1970, reprinted in Livingstone, 1981: 144). These various relations of dependence each place fundamental limits on the scope for development.

In the last of these three stages, with which Dos Santos is chiefly concerned, three aspects of dependence combine to constrain economic development in the periphery:

1. Since industrial development in the periphery is dependent on exports to earn the foreign currency for purchase of essential inputs, the first consequence of *contemporary dependence* is the need to preserve the traditional export sector. This 'limits economically the development of the internal market by the conservation of backward relations of production and signifies, politically, the maintenance of power by traditional decadent oligarchies' (*ibid.*). In countries where the export sector is controlled by foreign capital it also signifies substantial profit repatriation and enhanced political dependence.

2. Not only is industrial development strongly conditioned by the balance of payments, but the latter has an inherent tendency towards deficit due to the relations of dependence themselves. Thus trade relations take place in a highly monopolised international market, which tends to lower the price of raw materials and to raise the prices of industrial products. Moreover, modern technology also tends towards replacement of natural raw materials with synthetics, thus reducing demand at the centre for the periphery's exports. In addition, foreign capital retains control over the most dynamic sectors in the periphery and repatriates high profits. 'Foreign financing' – and financial dependence – thus become necessary both to cover the existing balance of payments deficit and to provide the foreign exchange for further development.

3. Meanwhile, industrial development is also strongly conditioned by the technological monopoly exercised by imperialist centres – by the cost of this technology and by the tendency to obtain it in the form of investment by foreign firms. Use of this technology in the labour abundant economies of the periphery results in the super-exploitation of low-wage labour, in limited labour absorption, continuing mass deprivation and restricted development of the domestic market.

If it is possible to demonstrate, and Dos Santos suggests it is, that each stage of dependence is reinforced by a necessary coincidence between dominant local and foreign interests, then it follows that the only way to break out of dependence is radically to change the internal structure that reinforces it and to establish popular revolutionary governments which open the way to socialism.

Amin on dependent – or 'extraverted' – development within the world capitalist system

From the late 1960s the analytical work of three leading neo-Marxists (Frank, Amin, Wallerstein) came to be dominated by the theme that there is a single world capitalist system which derives its momentum from the development of the capitalist mode of production at the centre. This in turn impinges upon, and transforms, the economies of the periphery with the collaboration of the dominant classes in the latter. This theme is elaborated in, for example, Amin (1974 and 1976)[7] and in Frank (1978), the text of which was written chiefly in 1969–70 with revisions in 1972–73. Frank's text makes it clear that he was in contact with Amin while preparing this study, but that he had not seen Amin's finished texts. None the less there is a high degree of complementarity in the approach of the two writers, with Frank focusing more directly on patterns of change in the periphery while Amin gives more space to the evolution of the capitalist mode of production at the centre, and a critical review and, in most cases, rejection, of various aspects of economic theory which claim explanatory power in relation to different aspects of the trends and relationships that he examines (e.g. international trade theory, monetary theory, theories of the trade cycle). Both Frank and Amin incorporated references to dependence into their studies. Here the discussion focuses on the theoretical contribution of Amin, and since Amin (1976) provides some explicit emphasis on dependency reference will be made to this.

While Frank's (1978) account of dependent development is basically descriptive, Amin offers a more penetrating analysis of the role of the periphery within the world capitalist system. He too uses a stage approach, similar to that used by Dos Santos and Frank, although with slightly different dating. He also incorporates a fourth stage of dependence in the periphery, not specified by the other two.

Amin's analysis explicitly allows for the continuing existence of different modes of production in the periphery following the contact with capitalism, so he is able to explore the manner in which metropolitan capitalism both uses, and generates changes in, these modes.

Elements of the role of the periphery in the centre's development, as identified by Amin, have already been noted on p. 201. In each of the main eras of world capitalist development, the centre, although in theory capable of autarkic development, has in practice used the periphery to further its own economic expansion. In each of the first three phases changes were imposed on the periphery which led to economic development (in one or more of the senses noted on p. 202). However, this development was 'extraverted' – i.e. caused from without – and dependent in various ways on the centre – on its demand for raw materials, its supply of producer goods and technical skills, and, especially since 1880, its supply of finance capital. Such development led to various changes in the structure of production in the periphery and in the structure of production relations, but neither were of a kind capable of leading to self-sustaining development. For example, foreign capital investment in primary production during the era of monopoly capitalism has often been associated with a high level of development of the productive forces, combined with the proletarianisation of labour. Yet the very dependence on foreign technology, combined with repatriation of profits and production for foreign markets, ensures that this development of the capitalist mode does not provide the basis for sustained capitalist development in the periphery.

On the subject of the fourth stage of world capitalist development, and of dependent development in the periphery, Amin makes the following observations. Since World War II two changes have occurred to further modify centre-periphery relations – the development of transnational corporations and a technological revolution which transfers the centre of gravity of the industries of the future toward new branches (atomic power, space research, electronics), while rendering obsolete the classical modes of accumulation, characterised by increasing organic composition of capital.

> The 'residual factor' – 'grey matter' – has become the principal factor in growth, and the ultra-modern industries are distinguished by an 'organic composition of labour' that accords a much bigger place to highly skilled labour.
>
> (Amin, *op.cit.*: 189.)

In the future, Amin suggests, there will probably be an increasing transfer of traditional heavy industry to the periphery in line with new patterns of specialisation at the centre. Amin argues that the newly industrialising countries (NICs) are at the vanguard of this process (Amin, 1976: 211–213).

However, this new form of specialisation is unlikely to absorb the bulk of the labour force in the periphery. It is in the interests of the centre that this should not happen, since it is the excess labour supply that keeps wages in the periphery low, thus helping both to sustain the rate of profit on capital exported to the periphery and to keep down the cost of goods exported to the centre. Dependent development *entails* the marginalisation of the masses and, along with this, a widening variation in productivity between sectors in the periphery. Meanwhile the centre will continue to appropriate surplus from the periphery in the forms both of repatriated profits and unequal exchange.

Such are the consequences of what Amin terms 'extraverted' or dependent development. Only a socialist development strategy, implying rejection of the laws of profitability governed by existing income distribution and prices, can generate a pattern of development geared to meeting mass needs while simultaneously beginning to break the ties of centre-periphery dependence.

Sutcliffe on prospects for independent industrialisation in the periphery
Sutcliffe's 1972 analysis of the defining characteristics of, and scope for, independent industrialisation in the periphery has much in common with the work on dependency of Dos Santos, Frank, and Amin. Sutcliffe proposes four criteria for *independent* industrialisation: production should be oriented principally to the domestic market; investment funds should be raised locally or, at least, locally controlled; there should be a diversified industrial structure; and there should be 'independent technological progress'. In the periphery, the prospects for independent industrial development

> are limited by the relative backwardness of the underdeveloped countries, by [foreign capital's] monopolistic control based on technological superiority, and by the pumping of surplus out of underdeveloped countries by repatriation of profits and by unequal exchange.
>
> (Brewer, 1980: 290.)

Neo-Marxist dependency analyses: recapitulation
As the foregoing examples illustrate, neo-Marxist dependency analyses reflect an evolution of the neo-Marxist perspective of the 1960s. The concepts of dependent or extraverted development enable neo-Marxists to acknowledge that capital accumulation and output expansion have occurred in the periphery, while emphasising the distorted and undesirable features of this process. This is contrasted with the more complete self-sustaining and equitable expansion path which could, it is held, be achieved by pursuing autarkic, socialist development. There is a continuing presumption amongst members of this school that the dominant class alliances in the periphery (*comprador* trading bourgeoisie, local monopoly capitalists, landowners and the state bureaucracy) will, in alliance with metropolitan capital, continue to prevent the full development of the periphery.

STRUCTURALIST PERSPECTIVES ON DEPENDENCY: SUNKEL AND FURTADO

The attempts in the late 1960s and early 1970s by some members of the structuralist school to reformulate the thought of ECLA along dependency lines coincided closely with the burgeoning of the neo-Marxist literature on dependency. Furthermore both developments were initially prompted by the same phenomenon – the dramatic slowdown in capitalist economic growth in Latin America in the early 1960s, together with what were seen to be a series of undesirable consequences of that growth which had occurred.

To structuralists such as Furtado and Sunkel, a range of factors demanded analysis and explanation.

> The process of import-substituting industrialisation which ECLA recommended seemed to aggravate balance-of-payments problems . . . foreign investment

was not only in part responsible for that . . . but it did not seem to be having other positive effects that ECLA had expected; real wages were not rising sufficiently quickly to produce the desired increase in effective demand – indeed, in several countries income distribution was worsening; the problems of unemployment were also growing more acute . . . industrial production was becoming increasingly concentrated in products typically consumed by the elites, and was not having the 'ripple effect' upon other productive sectors of the economy, particularly the agricultural sector.

(Palma in Seers, 1981: 578.)

In the early 1970s Furtado and Sunkel, who had both been leading members of the ECLA structuralist school, sought to explain these phenomena in terms of theoretical models whose *primum mobile* was a particular aspect of dependence – cultural dependence in the one case and, in the other, dependence on foreign investment. Both explanations also reflect the influence of neo-Marxist theory as articulated in the 1960s.

Furtado on the consequences of cultural dependence

In a paper presented in 1973 to the Centre for Latin American Studies at Cambridge University, Furtado suggested an explanatory model of underdevelopment that assigns the key causal role to cultural dependence. His thesis can be summarised as follows.

Technical progress in those countries that led the industrial revolution opened the way to significant increases in labour productivity in other areas too, through geographical specialisation. Some of the extra surplus so generated may have left the economies concerned (being appropriated by foreign merchant and/or producer capitalists), but likewise some of the surplus was appropriated domestically. It is in the disposition of this surplus that Furtado now finds the key to explain underdevelopment.

The surplus remaining in the country was basically used to finance a rapid diversification of the consumption habits of the ruling classes through the import of new products. It was this particular use of the additional surplus that gave rise to the social formations that we now identify as underdeveloped economies.

(Furtado, 1973: 2.)

The sequence through which this process occurred was as follows. 'Consumption dependence' deterred capital investment by lowering the propensity to save. Moreover as the supply of new consumer goods from the 'central' countries expanded, so the consumption aspirations of the élites in the periphery rose too. In the absence of a corresponding process of capital accumulation and technical progress in the periphery, privileged groups there have sought to raise their incomes and consumption through expanding the *volume* of traditional exports and/or increasing the *rate of exploitation of labour* (thereby increasing income inequalities within the economy).

When domestic consumer goods production is established in the periphery it is largely to meet this élite demand. Consequently the technologies to produce the goods demanded have to be imported (since suitable domestic technologies are not available). Penetration by multinational corporations is bound to be very rapid, argues Furtado, specifically because of the sophistication of the technology generally required (Furtado, *op.cit.*: 9). Meanwhile these capital-intensive technologies generate employment for a privileged minority who receive wages well above those in the subsistence sector. Thus this pattern of consumption and production causes slow growth of modern sector employment, growing income inequality and mass marginalisation. This in turn slows the expansion of the domestic market and the scope for further investment.

Balance of payments difficulties increase *in tandem* with expanding industrialisation, due to the latter's high import content and to external surplus appropriation, and they too contribute to the slowing-down of industrial growth. New attempts to overcome balance of payments constraints through 'exports of cheap labour embodied in industrial products produced by foreign firms for foreign markets' are still in the making. These attempts, however, cannot eliminate underdevelopment defined in the orthodox structuralist sense (see p. 49) precisely because outward-orientated industrialisation can only succeed if labour is cheap (cf. Amin (1976) summarised on p. 207).

By 1973 Furtado had switched to the view that attempts to break out of this impasse through regional integration (a policy advocated by the 'classical' structuralists, including Furtado himself) are only likely to be at best medium-term palliatives. They may provide some one-off expansion in investment opportunities, but will then once more encounter domestic market and balance of payments constraints. Elsewhere, in an earlier discussion of dependency, Furtado (1970) also expresses doubts concerning the potential contribution to development of two other 'structural reconstruction policies', economic planning and agrarian reform – the former due to the inelasticity of the fiscal sector (for political reasons) and the latter largely due to the influence of the élite in watering down reform design and implementation.

In Furtado (1973) it is possible to recognise both the influence of Nurkse's emphasis on international demonstration effects[8] and the continuing influence of 'classical structuralist' concepts, yet his formulation of a dependency interpretation of underdevelopment clearly incorporates significant breaks with earlier structuralism. The interaction of the external and internal pressures generating underdevelopment is now seen to offer far less scope for the promotion of genuine development in the periphery. In his specification of the dominant aspects of contemporary dependency Furtado has much in common with the neo-Marxists. However, he does not join the neo-Marxists in advocating social revolution and withdrawal from the international capitalist system. Rather, he confines himself to an analysis of the problem, without suggesting solutions.

Sunkel on the impact of transnational corporations in the periphery

A similar pessimism and a similar affinity with neo-Marxism are also manifest in Sunkel (1973). The affinity is already made clear in Sunkel's definition of dependency.

> Development and underdevelopment should be understood as partial but interdependent structures, which form part of a single whole. The main difference between the two structures is that the developed one, due basically to its endogenous growth capacity, is the dominant structure, while the underdeveloped structure, due largely to the induced character of its dynamism is the dependent one. This applies both to whole countries and to regions, social groups and activities within a single country.
>
> (Sunkel, 1973: 136.)

Sunkel seeks to demonstrate the nature of the induced dynamic experienced by dependent structures, emphasising in particular its contemporary linkages to transnational capitalism and the consequences of these linkages. Transnational capitalism, he argues, is generating the break-up of national economic, social and cultural identity within the dependent economies. Increased international integration leads to increased national disintegration.

Sunkel's analysis focuses chiefly on the period of import-substituting industrialisation and its consequences. Since the mid-1950s the essential foreign resources for industrialisation in the periphery have been supplied increasingly through direct investment by transnational corporations with head offices in the centres of world capitalism, where strategic decisions are made, and new technologies developed. It is now the transnationals, who, through their control of technology, product design and marketing skills determine the predominant patterns of international economic change, creating thereby a new international division of labour. The bargaining strength of the transnational corporations (TRANCOs) *vis à vis* underdeveloped countries who need their capital, technology, markets and entrepreneurship has enabled them to strike very favourable deals with national governments. Conjointly these factors have contributed to undermining national economic autonomy in the Third World. While TRANCOs do promote some industrialisation in the periphery, given their chosen patterns of global specialisation this industrialisation will always be limited, and such as to lock Third World countries both into technological dependency and technological backwardness relative to the centres of world capitalism. Yet simultaneously TRANCO activities reduce the scope for indigenous accumulation to overcome these disadvantages, both through the generation of net capital outflows from Third World countries and through the active promotion of consumerism (with the consequent lowering of the national savings rate).

Meanwhile the transnational corporations have had a widespread negative impact on other aspects of national economic development in the periphery. Their investment strategies generate both increasing international inequality and increasing internal polarisation within the periphery: concentration of industrial location; limited modern sector employment; increasing rural-urban migration leading to expansion of urban slums; increased mass immiseration due to the undercutting of traditional employment by the products of the modern sector; increased income only, or largely, for the middle and upper income groups who tend to benefit from the additional investments in the modern sector. The demand patterns of these latter groups, largely focused on consumer durables, in turn contribute to the capital-intensity and low employment creation of modern sector investment.

Sunkel also makes no attempt to offer policy solutions. He confines himself to outlining the new world economic system as he sees it, and its impact in the periphery – a system dominated by a few hundred transnational corporations.

These ideas are further developed, culminating in an attempt to categorise a variety of types of impact of transnational capitalism in peripheral countries, according to the conditions prevailing in the latter, in Sunkel and Fuenzalida (1979). However, this later study was apparently influenced in part by the work of Cardoso and Faletto (see pp. 213–15 below) and finishes by echoing their plea for more individual country studies.

While Furtado (1973) and Sunkel (1973) have much in common with neo-Marxism, both diverge from the 1970s approach of the leading neo-Marxists in the relative narrowness of their analytical focus. Whereas by this time the latter were concerned to theorise the evolution of the world capitalist system as a whole – including the periphery as an integral yet distinctive part of this system – Furtado and Sunkel remain concerned specifically with the problems of the periphery.

Seers on the fruitful but incomplete nature of dependency theories

Meanwhile, other structuralists have also taken on board the dependency concept while going much less far towards adopting a neo-Marxist perspective than either Furtado (1973) or Sunkel (1973) appear to have done. Amongst these other analyses, Seers (1981b) shows how a focus on dependency can throw light on issues relevant to the selection of national development policies but ignored by some of the dominant intellectual perspectives in development economics. For Seers, however, a focus on dependency is potentially additive rather than substitutive.

Seers (1981b) argues that dependency theories make possible lines of analysis that cannot be derived from other branches of development theory because they are based on variables that the latter ignore. This applies, for example, to the analysis of the scope for delinking Third World economies from international capitalism (by, for instance, expropriating foreign capital or controlling its entry, reducing imports, and internal redistributive measures). Here dependency theories suggest a focus on variables such as the national origins of both finance capital and capital equipment and technology, the national sources of key imports, and the habituation of both the élite and the modern sector labour force to foreign styles of consumption and foreign technologies – all variables which, according to Seers, are clearly relevant but which are ignored by other theoretical perspectives.

However, Seers goes on to argue that dependency theorists have overlooked a number of other factors which are also important determinants of a government's room for manoeuvre. These include demographic and geographic factors such as population size, degree of ethnic and linguistic homogeneity in the population, natural resource endowments, and physical location. Some of these factors, such as low population size, or location, may increase international dependency. However, whereas dependency theorists argue that dependency is a consequence of the world capitalist system, in so far as demographic and geographic variables generate dependency, they would do so under any economic system.[9]

While Seers identifies additional factors which may to varying degrees accentuate international dependency, he is none the less critical of those theorists who argue that international dependency inevitably determines domestic policy. Such theorists are overly deterministic (Cardoso and Faletto, see p. 215, and Palma make the same point). In Seers' view such theorists ignore the role of political leadership in policy determination.

> The motivation, willpower, judgement and intelligence of actual or potential political leaders evidently differ significantly. The importance of these personal characteristics follows from the very multiplicity of constraints which have been described. . . It requires rare skills not merely to frame an optimal set of delinking policies but to mobilise an adequate coalition of diverse political forces to support it; to present it persuasively to the world outside; to explain to the domestic public why it is all that can be achieved; and of course to implement it. (Conventional historians may not have been so wrong in focusing attention on the talents of monarchs and prime ministers!)
>
> (Seers, 1981b: 11,12.)

CARDOSO AND FALETTO: THE SCOPE FOR 'DEPENDENT DEVELOPMENT' AND THE IMPORTANCE OF COUNTRY-SPECIFIC STUDIES

We now turn to the third category of dependency studies identified in Palma (1979) – those which emphasise the diversity of dependency experiences, the need to study specific situations of dependency and the impossibility of generating a fruitful general theory of dependency, at least at this stage of our knowledge. Palma identifies the founders in the 1960s of this branch of dependency studies as Cardoso and Faletto. He also identifies other contemporary supporters of the approach, including Laclau, Pinto, and Palma himself.

It is clear from the substance of Cardoso and Faletto (1979) that these analysts were, from the mid-1960s, developing in parallel to Warren, and apparently initially independently, since they do not cite him, a somewhat similar, thought not identical, perspective on capitalist development in the periphery.[10] The intellectual inspiration that Cardoso and Faletto acknowledge is chiefly Marxist, but it also draws on elements of structuralism – a concept that features frequently in their vocabulary.

Cardoso and Faletto (1979) was written in the mid-1960s, and first published in Spanish in 1971, in reaction to Frank's neo-Marxism, of which it contains a strong critique. However, by the 1970s, dependent development was acknowledged by the neo-Marxists, and this third approach to dependency has certain elements in common with the approaches already reviewed, most notably the following perceptions:

1. There is one integrated world capitalist system.
2. Economic and political conditions in the Third World are determined by the interaction of internal and external factors.

Cardoso and Faletto also have much in common with the neo-Marxists both in their definition of dependence and their specification of its external causes. Dependence they define (from an economic viewpoint) as a situation in which 'the accumulation and expansion of capital cannot find its essential component inside the system' (Cardoso and Faletto, 1979: xx). They too identify various stages and forms of dependency, which they characterise in terms of the composition and ownership of production in the periphery. These forms include export enclaves under foreign ownership, dependency where the production system is nationally controlled and contemporary dependent industrialising economies controlled by multinational corporations, in which, unlike the export enclaves, industrial production is for the domestic market. Meanwhile Cardoso (1974) also concurs with Sunkel in arguing that contemporary dependency has fractured any pre-existing national cohesion in the periphery.

However, while the dependency analyses reviewed so far suggest that change in the periphery is predominantly externally determined, this third approach gives greater emphasis to the scope for internal generation of change. For Cardoso and Faletto a basic assumption underlying their analysis is that social structures are not immutable:

> It is necessary to recognise from the beginning that social structures are the product of man's collective behaviour. Therefore, although enduring, social structures can be, and in fact are, continuously transformed by social movements. Consequently, our approach . . . emphasises not just the structural

conditioning of social life, but also the historical transformation of structures by conflict, social movements, and class struggles.

(Cardoso and Faletto, 1979: x.)

Like other dependency theorists, Cardoso and Faletto are primarily concerned with contemporary dependency and its consequences, and they apply this perspective to its analysis. Thus Cardoso (1974) observes that 'the new forms of dependency will undoubtedly give rise to novel political and social adaptations and reactions inside the dependent countries'. These are likely to be nationally divisive in nature. In contemporary situations of dependency not only is part of the national bourgeoisie likely to be the direct beneficiary of foreign investment in the periphery, but the beneficiaries of the latter include all economic groups that benefit from the eventual atmosphere of prosperity derived from dependent development (as is easily demonstrated in Brazil or Mexico). The process includes

> not only part of the 'middle-class' (intellectuals, state bureaucracies, armies, etc.) . . . but even part of the working class. Those employed by the 'internationalised' sector structurally belong to it . . . Analysis which is based on the naive assumption that imperialism unifies the interests and reactions of dominated nations is a clear oversimplification of what is really occurring. It does not take into consideration the internal fragmentation of these countries and the attraction that development exerts in different social strata, and not only on the upper-classes.
>
> (Cardoso, 1974: 93, 4.)

For Cardoso and Faletto the diversity of conditions – economic, social and political – in the periphery make it impossible to generalise concerning either the impact of dependency relations on peripheral economies *or the likelihood of their continuing.*Peripheral economies are diversified not only in terms of resource endowment and timing of integration into the international system but in terms of

> the different moment at which sections of local classes allied or clashed with foreign interests, organised different forms of state, sustained distinct ideologies, or tried to implement various policies or defined alternative strategies to cope with imperialist challenges in diverse moments of history.
>
> (Cardoso and Faletto, *op.cit.*: xvii.)

All these factors, but, in particular, the level of economic development, the nature and extent of support for the ruling class alliance and the degree of nationalist sentiment within this alliance make it impossible to generalise concerning the future direction and impact of dependency relations.

Cardoso and Faletto concur that, in the contemporary world, peripheral economies, even where they are no longer restricted to the production of raw materials, remain dependent in a very specific form: 'their capital-goods production sectors are not strong enough to ensure continuous advance of the system, in financial as well as in technological and organisational terms' (*ibid*: xxi). Acquisition of these resources generally entails entry into relationships of dependency with the centre. *However, the extent and durability of the relationship so generated varies.* Just as the client of a banker tries to break free of that dependency relationship through productive use of the resources borrowed, so dependent countries may try to do the same thing – with varying degrees of success. 'Successful attempts are not an automatic output of the game. More often, rules of domination are enforced'. Yet success is possible, and its attainment depends heavily both on levels of economic development and on the balance of political forces in individual countries of the periphery.

This is qualitatively different from the neo-Marxist conclusion that 'full' development in the periphery is only possible under socialism, with the explicitly-drawn implication that socialist revolution is therefore necessary at this juncture.

Meanwhile, given the variety and degrees of dependency, Cardoso and Faletto conclude that the most useful contribution that *'dependistas'* can make is to promote the study of different dependency situations and, through these, the more detailed characterisation of different forms of dependency. Only thus can appropriate recommendations, both for economic change and political action, be generated, and only thus can 'realistic' paths towards an ultimate transition to socialism be constructed.

WARREN ON THE ELIMINATION OF DEPENDENCY

Warren (1980) notes the differences of emphasis in Cardoso's work on dependency as compared with the neo-Marxist perspective outlined above. However, he did not acknowledge a full compatibility of perspective between himself and Cardoso and Faletto, emphasising that Cardoso still appeared to accept the neo-Marxian interpretation of underdevelopment and hence, he assumed, the analytical framework of neo-Marxism (Warren, 1980: 162). However, the balance of the argument in Cardoso and Faletto (1979) suggests that this assumption was an oversimplification (see, for example, their 'Preface', already cited, and their pp. 16–28).

Meanwhile, Warren's own view that the perpetuation of the dependency of the periphery is far from inevitable is outlined in his 1973 critique of Sutcliffe (1972). After listing Sutcliffe's four criteria of independent industrialisation – production mainly for the home market, diversified production including capital goods, local financial control, indigenous technological innovations – Warren argues that by all four criteria there is evidence of increasingly independent development in the Third World.

Firstly, manufacturing development has been based predominantly on the home market. Secondly, a considerable number of underdeveloped countries can now boast some development of heavy industry including even iron and steel, petrochemicals, shipbuilding, lorry-making, aircraft industries, loco-motives and other railway equipment, cement, electrical machinery, machine tools, heavy non-electrical machinery and so on.

Third, with respect to control of foreign finance, Warren focuses on the increasing control exercised by Third World countries over foreign firms with respect to such issues as profit-sharing, supply sourcing, the structure of ownership and export development. He argues that in all respects there is evidence of increasing control exercised by Third World countries.

Fourth, Warren argues that a range of processes that have been, and are, occurring in the Third World are contributing towards progress in the acquisition of an indigenous technological base. These include the devel-opment of education and research, the spread of a growing range of capital and intermediate goods industries, the regulation of foreign investment in order to ensure that it involves transfer of required technologies, policies of training local personnel to fill high level technical and managerial positions in foreign firms, and the universal, rapid and irreversible trend towards the processing of mineral and fuel resources within underdeveloped countries which involves complex advanced technologies for many products.

However, Warren also goes beyond Cardoso and Faletto in suggesting that while there is growing evidence of deepening capitalist industrial devel-opment in the Third World, the notion of 'independent industrialisation' itself remains highly ambiguous.

> The increase in economic interdependence within the capitalist world and the collaboration of ruling, exploitative classes throughout the world against socialism and the masses, both mean that the issue would be more accurately posed in terms of equality between previously unequal 'partners' in an increas-ingly interdependent relationship.
>
> (Warren, *op.cit.*: 33.)

A DEPENDENCY PARADIGM?

This chapter has discussed how a range of perspectives have been brought to bear on the phenomenon of dependency, designed to explain its forms, its causes, its significance, and its relationship with the processes of under-development and development.

The different approaches to dependency analysis that have been identified are as follows:

1. An incorporation of dependency analysis into the evolving neo-Marxist analytical framework.
2. A move towards adoption of a similar perspective by some 'disaffected' structuralists.
3. A critical but positive assertion of the value of the study of dependency (economic, cultural, political) and its significance for economic policy

and performance in the periphery, but as an *addition* to elements in the exisiting stock of economic theory, not a substitute (Seers, 1981b).

4. An assertion of the diversity of individual political and economic situations of dependency, and of the need for further country studies before any but a few preliminary generalisations can be made concerning this phenomenon.

Among those who find the concept of dependency significant, there are various interpretations of its form and significance. These range from those who argue that this is a distinctive and permanent characteristic of the periphery, leading inevitably to its blocked development, through to those who argue that dependency affects all countries – developed and less developed – in varying degrees (see pp. 218–19) and/or that this is not an immutable condition for all countries in the periphery, even while they remain part of the international capitalist system. Given the outstanding differences between these perspectives, it scarcely makes sense to speak of a dependency paradigm.

CRITICISMS OF DEPENDENCY STUDIES

The purpose of this section is to provide a brief review of the main criticisms that have been levelled against dependency studies and theories, i.e. against the stress on *dependency* in the analysis of the causes and nature of underdevelopment and development. Although others are also critical of the dependency approach (see e.g. Little, 1982: Ch. 12 and Lal, 1983), the main critiques of dependency studies and theories have tended to come from analysts who are sympathetic, in the words of one critic, 'to many of the fundamental tenets of the dependency school' (Lall, 1975: 798). Indeed some critiques stem from within the 'dependency school' broadly defined, being focused upon the work of other branches (e.g. Cardoso and Faletto, 1979, and Palma, 1981).

Some of the earliest critiques of dependency analysis focused on the meaning and validity of the concept itself (Lall, 1975, Seers, 1979). Subsequent criticism has also focused both on claims for the general validity of dependency theories (Cardoso and Faletto, Palma) and on the specific inability of certain dependency approaches to account for the growth performance of the newly industrialising countries (e.g. Leudde-Neurath, 1980; Browett, 1985).

Dependency – the validity of the concept

A number of critics, including Lall and Seers, have argued that it is impossible to draw a hard and fast line between economies that are dependent and those that are not. Rather, international dependence effects all economies to varying degrees. This line of criticism can be levelled against all branches of dependency studies.

In his critique, Seers identifies three key resources which are needed by all national economies, and in growing amounts in those in which output and/or average living standards are expanding. These are oil, cereals and technology. No country, Seers argues, is capable of truly autonomous economic development in that it can supply all its own needs for all three of these resources. Rather, countries can be ranked from least dependent to fully dependent according to whether they are net importers of one, two or all three of these items. For selected country examples see Table 7.1. The test of the significance of this categorisation would come, says Seers, in periods of economic crisis, specifically in periods of disruption to international trade, when the more dependent economies (according to this definition) would suffer the most.

Seers' critique thus ends positively, with an attempt to give greater operational precision to the dependence concept by focusing on *degrees of dependence* rather than on a clear-cut dichotomy between economic independence and dependence.

Lall's position, on the other hand, is less positive. Focusing primarily on the first two categories of dependency studies, his argument is that the

Table 7.1 Illustrative profiles of dependence on key inputs

	(1) Oil	(2) Cereals	(3) Technology
A Least-dependent countries (net importers of only one key input)			
USA	×		
Soviet Union		×	
China			×
B Some semi-dependent countries (net importers of two key inputs)			
(i) Net exporters of technology			
Japan	×	×	
East Germany	×	×	
West Germany	×	×	
(ii) Net exporters of oil			
Iran		×	×
Kuwait		×	×
Nigeria		×	×
(iii) Net exporters of cereals			
Argentina	×		×
Thailand	×		×
C Some dependent countries (net importers of all three key inputs)			
Brazil	×	×	×
Cuba	×	×	×
Portugal	×	×	×

Source: reproduced from Seers in Villamil 1979: 104.

concept of dependency cannot be given any operational precision of a kind that is analytically useful as an explanation of underdevelopment.

Lall argues that if a 'concept' of dependence is to have explanatory power in relation to underdevelopment, then it must satisfy two criteria:

1. It must lay down certain characteristics of dependent economies which are not found in non-dependent ones.
2. These characteristics must be shown to affect adversely the course and pattern of development of the dependent countries.

Lall then works systematically through the main characteristics of dependence, economic and non-economic, that are identified by the 'dependency school', and concludes that in all cases either instances of such dependence are to be found also among those countries that are generally agreed to constitute the centre of the capitalist system, or they are not in fact characteristic of all underdeveloped economies.

As Seers suggests focusing on *degrees* of dependency, so Lall advocates the notion of a pyramidal structure of social, political and economic dominance pervading the world economy, but with no clear cut-off between dependent and independent countries.

Others, too, have questioned the validity of the notion of dependence as used in dependency theories, for reasons similar to those raised by Seers and Lall. Thus Brewer (1980: 178) criticises Dos Santos' definition of dependence (see p. 200 above) on the grounds that it wrongly asserts that the dominant countries enjoy independent (self-sustaining) development. 'I do not believe that any part of the world economy can now be regarded as independent, and the historical record seems to me to confirm this view (consider, for example, the effects of the 'oil crisis' of the 1970s).'

Criticisms of general theories of dependency

Critiques of general theories of dependency have generally focused on the work of the neo-Marxist school, particularly Frank and Amin, but also relate in part to the pessimistic dependency analyses of structuralists such as Furtado and Sunkel.

Gabriel Palma takes the neo-Marxists to task for the development of theories which, in their argument that dependency generates the perpetuation of underdevelopment (Frank) or blocked growth (see e.g. Amin, 1976: 291–2), are mechanico-formalistic, leading to conclusions that are inevitable, static and ahistorical. These are criticisms which, as we have already seen in the preceding chapter, can be levelled against much of neo-Marxist theory including those earlier analyses of Baran (1957) and Frank (1967) which do not make notable use of the dependency concept.

Brewer (1980) has also criticised the neo-Marxist dependency theorists for providing an analysis of the consequences of a given pattern of international specialisation which fails to provide a satisfactory analysis of its *causes*. Brewer argues that Amin, like Emmanuel, fails to explain why, in the age of multinational corporations and high capital mobility, international special-isation based on technology – as opposed to specific natural resource endowments – should continue. In the present stage of development there are very large wage differentials between centre and periphery, while multi-national firms have great experience of transferring technology, so why do they not concentrate investment and production in the periphery until both the productivity gap and the wage differential between centre and periphery have been eliminated?

Alternatively, however, one can argue that the perpetuation of depend-ency, and of the associated productivity gap between centre and periphery, does not have to be explained, because there is no such universal contempor-ary perpetuation of the dependency of the periphery. This is the position taken by Warren (1973) in his critique of Sutcliffe.

Dependency analyses and the NICs

A further empirical criticism of dependency theories is that they fail to account for the rapid growth performance and economic transformation of the newly industrialising countries during the 1960s and 1970s. Browett (1985) points out that the conclusions of the dependency analyses of Frank and Amin rule out a priori the possibility of independent, self-sustained, balanced (i.e. non-specialised) growth in the periphery, with the benefits extending to the mass of the population.

In contrast, the perspective on dependence adopted by Cardoso and Faletto and by Warren permits an alternative interpretation of the prospects for the NICs from that offered in Amin's interpretation of the fourth, prospective, stage of the development of the world capitalist system. Amin predicts a continuation of dependent development in which the periphery will continue to lag behind the centre, with the composition of its industrial production being determined by the centre, and the inevitable continuation of mass marginalisation (see pp. 206–7). The perspectives of Cardoso and Faletto and of Warren allow of the possibility that at some point some of the NICs may 'catch up' with the capitalist economies of the centre (and become incorporated into the latter). That is to say, they may achieve comparable levels of labour productivity, comparable degrees of industrial diversification and full incorporation of their labour forces into a modern economy, dominated by capitalist production relations and offering a wage comparable to that at the centre. Browett too questions Amin's conclusion, albeit in rather general terms, quoting Smith's (1982) observation that many NICs have not only grown fast, but 'have a home-grown bourgeoisie . . . consider-able internal dynamism and technical progress'.

Meanwhile, however, Leudde-Neurath (1980) provides a more detailed array of the countervailing empirical evidence, derived from South Korea. Leudde-Neurath cites, *inter alia*, the South Korean government's stringent control of foreign investment, Korea's increasing sophistication in the procurement and absorption of new technology, her embarkation at the outset of the 1980s on a major programme to expand local research and development, the very high percentage of national ownership of new investment ('94 per cent of the cumulative total between 1959 and 1978'), the high share of investment in GDP, the high share of local financing of this investment and the rise in farm incomes and real wages in the period 1962–1978. On the basis of the evidence, Leudde-Neurath concludes that South Korea's development cannot be regarded as a simple reinforcement of dependency according to Frank's and Amin's version of the latter.[11]

Transnational corporations and dependency

Transnational corporations are ascribed, both by neo-Marxists and some structuralists, a major causal role in the contemporary generation of dependency. This is not the place to review the massive literature on transnational corporations. It is, however, relevant that recently at least one leading early critic of transnationals has revised his original analysis, arguing that the trend of experience and opinion in the Third World is towards a changed and, on balance, more favourable estimate of the impact of transnationals in host countries. This, he suggests, applies particularly with respect to technology transfer and its various ramifications, while there has also been a downward revision of estimates of the extent of transfer pricing. (See Lall, 1984.)

CONCLUSION

There are two categories of dependency analysis: those that aim to generate a generally valid theory of dependency, its nature and consequences, and those that do not. In the first category lie the contributions of the neo-Marxist school and of the disillusioned structuralists. With respect to the former, Dos Santos' hopes for a new theory of dependency to match the theory of imperialism can hardly by said to have been fulfilled. What the leading neo-Marxists have effectively done is to take up this concept and incorporate it into their analytical work in order to facilitate the acknowledgement that some 'development' has occurred in the periphery, albeit partial and distorted. At the same time these theorists have elaborated and reinforced the core propositions of neo-Marxism according to which the full development of the periphery will continue to be blocked as long as the latter remains within the world capitalist system. Dependency is found to be quite a useful concept in the elaboration of these analyses, but it does not hold centre stage in the manner anticipated by Dos Santos. Meanwhile the disillusioned structuralists who have attempted to generate general theories of dependency also seem to have taken their inspiration partly from neo-Marxism, but the neo-Marxism of the 1960s, with its specific focus on the periphery, rather than the neo-Marxism of the 1970s with its broader analytical and empirical focus on the development of the world capitalist system as a whole.

For many, a continuing weakness of neo-Marxist theory, both before and since its explicit emphasis on dependency, remains the rigid conclusion that there is no prospect for full national capitalist economic development in the periphery. It is this same pessimism, combined with the contemporary advocacy of an alternative, more open and pragmatic approach to the study of dependency, that seems to be chiefly responsible also for the failure of the Sunkel/Furtado attempts to reformulate structuralism in dependency terms to achieve widespread acceptance. The chain of causality that they identify is also seen to be rigid and determinist.

In contrast, the approach to dependency studies advocated by Cardoso and Faletto has been much more widely accepted amongst radical political economists. Cardoso and Faletto, however, emphasise that they do not subscribe to attempts to generate a new theory of dependent capitalism (Cardoso and Faletto, 1979: xxiii) – a view which is likewise held by others who support their approach (see e.g. Palma in Seers, 1981a, Leudde-Neurath, 1980, Seers, 1981b and Smith, 1980).

NOTES

1. Villamil (ed.), 1979: 1.
2. In this chapter the last six out of sixty-five pages are devoted to 'extraverted accumulation and dependence', though even here Amin's focus is on the former.
3. Amin (1976) omits mention of the other source of demand noted in Amin (1974) – that generated by industry itself for producer goods.
4. Subsequent references are to the English language (1972) edition.
5. These points are effectively acknowledged by Frank himself in his 'Mea Culpa' printed at the front of *Lumpenbourgeoisie, Lumpendevelopment.*
6. Dos Santos, like Frank up to this stage, focuses his analysis chiefly on Latin America.
7. First published in French in 1973.
8. See Chapter 3, p. 55.
9. Cardoso and Faletto also note the existence of, but do not analyse, dependent relationships between socialist countries.
10. Like Warren, Cardoso and Faletto define development specifically as *capitalist* development, of which they observe:

> This form of development, in the periphery as well as the centre, produces as it evolves, in a cyclical way, wealth and poverty, accumulation and shortage of

capital, employment for some and unemployment for others. So, we do not mean by the notion of 'development' the achievement of a more egalitarian or just society. These are not consequences expected of capitalist development, especially in the periphery.

(Cardoso and Faletto, *op.cit.*: xxiii.)

11. Cf. Little, 1982: 263. Little, discussing this issue from a neo-classical perspective, makes a number of the same points.

REFERENCES

Amin, S., *Unequal Development*, (Harvester Press, 1976; originally published as *Le Développement inégal*, Les Editions Minuit, 1973).

Amin, S., *Accumulation on a World Scale*, (Monthly Review Press, 1974).

Baran, P., *The Political Economy of Growth*, (Monthly Review Press, 1957).

Baran, P. and Sweezy, P., *The Theory of Capitalist Development*, (Monthly Review Press, 1966).

Bernstein, H. (ed.) *Underdevelopment and Development*, (Penguin, 1973).

Brewer, A., *Marxist Theories of Imperialism*, (Routledge and Kegan Paul, 1980).

Browett, J., 'The newly industrialising countries and radical theories of development', *World Development*, (Vol. 13, No. 7, July 1985).

Bukharin, N. (1915), *Imperialism and the World Economy*, (Martin Lawrence, 1929, and M. Fertig, New York, 1966).

Cardoso, F. H., 'Dependency and development in Latin America', *New Left Review*, (1974).

Cardoso, F. and Faletto, E., *Dependency and Development in Latin America*, (University of California Press, 1979; first published in Spanish in 1971).

Dos Santos, T., 'The crisis of development theory and the problem of dependence in Latin America', (1969); translated and reprinted in *Underdevelopment and Development*, ed. Bernstein, H., (Penguin, 1973).

Dos Santos, T., 'The structure of dependence', *American Economic Review*, (1970), reprinted in *Development Economics and Policy*, ed. Livingstone, I., (Allen and Unwin, 1981).

Frank, A. G., *Capitalism and Underdevelopment in Latin America*, (Monthly Review Press, 1967; revised edition 1969).

Frank, A. G., *Lumpenbourgeoisie:Lumpendevelopment*, (Monthly Review Press, 1972; first published in Spanish in 1970).

Frank, A. G., 'Dependence is dead, long live dependence and the class struggle', *World Development*, (Vol. 5, No. 4, April 1977).

Frank, A. G., *Dependent Accumulation and Underdevelopment*, (Macmillan, 1978).

Furtado, C., 'Underdevelopment and Dependence: The Fundamental Connections', Seminar Paper, (Centre of Latin American Studies, Cambridge University, 1973).

Furtado, C., *Economic Development of Latin America: Historical Background and Contemporary Problems*, 2nd edition, (Cambridge, 1976).

Lal, D., *The Poverty of 'Development Economics'*, Hobart Paperback 16, (Institute of Economic Affairs, 1983).

Lall, S., 'Is dependence a useful concept in analysing underdevelopment?', *World Development*, (Vol. 3, Nos. 11 and 12, November/December, 1975).

Lall, S., 'Transnationals and the Third World: changing perceptions', *National Westminister Bank Quarterly Review*, (May 1984).

Lenin, V. (1917), *Imperialism, The Highest Stage of Capitalism*, (Progress Publishers, Moscow, 1975).

Leudde-Neurath, R., 'Export orientation in South Korea: how helpful is dependency thinking to its analysis?', *IDS (Sussex) Bulletin*, (Vol. 123, No. 1, Dec. 1980).

Little, I.M.D., *Economic Development: Theory, Policy and International Relations*, (Basic Books, 1982).

Livingstone, I. (ed.), *Development Economics and Policy*, (Allen and Unwin, 1981).

Luxemberg, R. (1913), *The Accumulation of Capital*, (Routledge and Kegan Paul, 1963, and Monthly Review Press, 1964).

Palma, G., 'Dependency and development: a critical overview', in ed. Roxborough, I., *Theories of Development*, (Macmillan, 1979).

Seers, D., 'Patterns of dependence', in ed. Villamil, J., *Transnational Capitalism and National Development: New Perspectives on Dependence*, (Harvester, 1979).

Seers, D. (ed.), *Dependency Theory: A Critical Assessment*, (Frances Pinter, 1981a).

Seers, D., 'Development options: the strengths and weaknesses of dependency theories in explaining a government's room to manoeuvre', IDS, Sussex, *Discussion Paper*, (No. 165, September 1981b).

Smith, S., 'The ideas of Samir Amin: theory or tautology', *Journal of Development Studies*, (Vol. 17, No. 1, 1980).

Smith, S., 'Class analysis versus world systems: critique of Samir Amin's typology of underdevelopment', *Journal of Contemporary Asia*, (Vol. 12, No. 1, 1982).

Sunkel, O., 'Transnational capitalism and national disintegration in Latin America', *Social and Economic Studies*, (1973).

Sunkel, O. and Fuenzalida, E., 'Transnationalization and its national consequences', in *Transnational Capitalism and National Development: New Perspectives on Dependence*, ed. J. Villamil, (Harvester, 1979).

Sutcliffe, R., 'Imperialism and industrialisation in the Third World', in Owen, R. and Sutcliffe, R., (eds.) *Studies in the Theory of Imperialism*, (Longman, 1972).

Villamil, J. (ed.), *Transnational Capitalism and National Development: New Perspectives on Dependence*, (Harvester, 1979).

Warren, B., 'Imperialism and capitalist industrialisation', *New Left Review*, (1973).

Warren, B., *Imperialism: Pioneer of Capitalism*, (Verso, 1980).

8 · THE MAOIST PARADIGM[1]

REASONS FOR STUDYING THE MAOIST PARADIGM

The paradigm to which we turn in this chapter is unique amongst those reviewed in this book for two reasons. Firstly, it was developed with the problems and potentialities of one particular country in view – the People's Republic of China. Secondly, it is a paradigm not simply of economic development, but of a conjoint and interlinked process of social, political, ideological and economic development, perceived in terms of progress towards the goal of material abundance in an egalitarian society.

Neither those who articulated the paradigm in China, nor the western scholars who reproduced it, had as their prime intention the provision of a universally-valid set of values, beliefs and theoretical relationships concerning economic development, applicable to all less developed countries. The question therefore arises as to why scholars outside China should study what, following convention and the name of one of its primary articulators, is referred to here as the 'Maoist' paradigm, particularly since this perspective did not command universal support, even in China, either during the Maoist era, or, as is well known, subsequently.

Various factors render the Maoist development perspective of general interest. Of these the most noteworthy are the following:

1. At the methodological level it provides an important exemplar of the application, elaboration and development of certain general tenets of Marxism-Leninism in relation to the transition to socialism in one particular backward economy.
2. The paradigm is more than an exemplar. It offers a theoretical perspective in which the basic tenets of Marxism-Leninism are elaborated and developed in a manner which in certain respects is markedly different from the earlier Stalinist interpretation.[2]

3. Certain elements of the Maoist perspective have exerted an influence outside China, at both a theoretical and a practical level.

4. The paradigm presents an all-embracing view of social, political, ideological and economic change; other economic development paradigms have been criticised for ignoring non-economic factors.

5. In 1949 China was one of the poorest economies in the world in terms of per capita income, degree of industrialisation and various indicators of human welfare (including life expectancy and adult literacy). Her subsequent progress, both in structural transformation and in meeting basic needs has been remarkable, at least as much in the Maoist era as since, given the poverty of the base from which she started. While the leadership of China has, since 1978, been anti-Maoist, a major question mark attaches to whether it would have had the same freedom to manoeuvre if the preceding pattern and rate of change (1949–1976) had not been implemented.

6. The present and likely future size of the Chinese population and economy render the development path of this country of major international significance.

HISTORICAL AND ECONOMIC BACKGROUND

The Chinese Communist Party achieved overall political and military control of China in 1949. At this time the country had been subject to over a century of increasing foreign intervention linked to attempts to open up China to foreign trade and investment. It had also been subject to several decades of war and civil war.

Many accounts have been written of the degraded state of the Chinese economy in 1949, all giving a similar picture. Selden and Lippit (1982) summarise the situation as follows:

> In the aftermath of World War II and the Civil War, heavy industrial production had fallen to about 30 per cent of the previous peak level, and agricultural and consumer goods output had fallen to about 70 per cent of the previous peaks. Hyperinflation had ruined the value of the currency, and economic exchanges were increasingly reverting to barter. The fighting had left the transportation system a shambles, and the Soviet Union, which had declared war on Japan in the closing days of World War II, systematically looted Manchuria of its most modern equipment, removing in all approximately US $2 billon worth of heavy industrial equipment, or about half of the capital stock in what had been the leading centre of heavy industry in this predominantly agrarian nation.
>
> (Selden and Lippit, 1982: 4.)

To this account of the destruction of industrial capital may be added the badly damaged state of the irrigation and land drainage systems which normally played a crucial role in agricultural production.

Meanwhile, underlying the problems posed by the ravages of war and civil war were the more fundamental problems posed by the basic structure and resource endowment of the Chinese economy.

> An arable land area of perhaps 300 million acres had to provide food for a population of more than 500 million. Even before the war-induced declines in production, the entire modern sector had accounted for only seven per cent of national income and could scarcely provide the material inputs the modernisation of agriculture would require. As a result, traditional production methods prevailed in agriculture, labour productivity was low, and some 80 per cent of China's labour force was needed to provide food and other agricultural products. Transportation links were weak. Outside of Japanese-occupied Manchuria in China's northeast, industry had grown in only a few coastal treaty-port cities which were often more closely linked to foreign economies than to the interior.
>
> (*Ibid.*: 5.)

The available agricultural land per capita was less than half of that in India, and a much lower fraction of that in the Soviet Union (Magdoff, 1975). As in India and much of South Asia, climatic variations in China are severe and unpredictable. Her history has been punctuated by crop failures and famines due to both droughts and floods.

Within the rural sector there was a significant degree of inequality in the distribution of land and incomes, although estimates of the degree of inequality vary. Landlords and rich peasants constituted less than ten per cent of the rural population, but owned between forty-five and seventy per cent of the land.[3] Lippit (1974) suggests that, on a conservative estimate, prior to 1949, nineteen per cent of national income flowed to rural property owners – landlords, rich peasants and moneylenders.[4]

THE EMERGENCE OF THE MAOIST PARADIGM

When the Chinese Communist Party achieved power, two major tasks confronted it with respect to the management of the economy – rehabilitation and reconstruction of the capital stock and initiation of the process of socialist transformation.

With the exception of the implementation of land reform, in the early years after the revolution the Chinese followed a Soviet-style development strategy. Both lack of experience in national economic management and the international isolation of China after the revolution led the leadership to turn to the Soviet regime for support. Centralised, authoritarian socialism as developed first by Lenin and then Stalin, which included central planning of the economy, represented the only concrete model of a socialist state available to China.

> In the early stages of liberation we had no experience of managing the economy of the entire nation. So in the period of the First Five Year Plan we could do no

more than copy the Soviet Union's methods, although we never felt entirely happy about this.

(Mao Tsetung, 1977: 122.)

After post-war rehabilitation emphasis was laid upon the technical transformation and development of heavy industry, which received the lion's share of state investment funds. Most of the latter were extracted from agriculture, chiefly through the use of compulsory state buying quotas combined with manipulation of the terms of trade. Output in both sectors grew fast.

However, by the mid-1950s it was clear that the initial buoyant growth rate could not be maintained.[5] It had been due chiefly to local efforts in repair and reconstruction of rural infrastructure, including irrigation and drainage systems, and to the positive motivational effects of the early stages of redistributive land reform (see p. 239) – both one-off events that could not be repeated. Meanwhile China's population was rising at about two per cent per annum. The rural population, whose incomes were still low and on whom the revolution depended, could not be expected to tolerate a rising rate of resource extraction from agriculture to sustain heavy industrial growth while their own per capita incomes stagnated or fell. The Stalinist policy of primitive accumulation in agriculture (i.e. enforced extraction of the surplus without significant prior state investment in agricultural productive capital) apparently could not be continued. Instead, a new approach was needed which would maintain the development momentum.

In the formulation of this new perspective, a number of other factors were also influential in addition to the objective conditions outlined in the preceding paragraphs. Of these the most significant were the following:

1. The theoretical legacy of previous socialist theorists (most notably Marx and Engels, Lenin and Stalin).
2. The empirical experience of the Soviet Union in the first three decades after 1917.
3. The experience of the Chinese Communist Party in mass mobilisation and local administration in north China during the civil war.
4. The personality and background of Mao himself.

The theoretical heritage

While the Chinese leadership perceived the need for change in their development strategy, they also recognised, given the aims and character of the revolution, the importance of continuing to claim Marxist-Leninist inspiration for this strategy. However, as is well known, Marx had little to say concerning the process of socialist economic development, while Marx and Engels also anticipated that socialist revolutions themselves 'would dialectically and inexorably grow out of the contradictions of advanced capitalism' (Selden in Selden and Lippit, *op.cit.*: 35). Thus early Marxism alone could not provide the Chinese communists with a fully developed conceptual framework for the planning and implementation of the transition to socialism. Yet there are certain elements in the writings of Marx and Engels that were potentially relevant. These take the form of, on the one hand, core elements of Marxist theory and, on the other, more specific observations concerning the socialisation of production and the transition to a socialist economy. They include the following:

1. Marx's analysis of the relationship between the level of development of the forces of production and the relations of production.[6]
2. Marx's analysis of class struggle.

As we shall see, the interpretation of these two elements of Marxist theory as applied to socialist construction differs markedly in Stalinism and Maoism. In addition, the following elements are important:

3. Observations by Marx and Engels concerning the possibility that the pre-capitalist peasant communes in Russia might by-pass the capitalist phase of development and instead be transformed directly into socialist units of production.
4. Marx's observation in the *Grundrisse* that

   > The greater the extent to which production still rests on mere manual labour, on use of muscle power, etc., in short, on physical exertion by individual labourers, the more does the increase of the *productive force* consist in their collaboration *on a mass scale* were also potentially relevant.[7]

Meanwhile the Chinese communists could also draw on the evolution of Lenin's ideas on the planning and praxis of the transition to socialism, including the following aspects:

1. The evolution of his thought with respect to the collectivisation of agriculture (although Lenin's own transition to an emphasis on voluntarism and gradualism were closer to Chinese practice pre- rather than post-1955[8]).
2. Lenin's view that 'bourgeois right' (individual attachment to accumulation of private property) would continue to exist after the abolition of the bourgeoisie. This contains the seeds of the view developed by part of the Chinese leadership concerning the need for continuing class struggle against growing inequalities in income distribution.

Meanwhile the most important features of the Stalinist model (theory and practice), against elements of which there was now a growing reaction amongst parts of the Chinese leadership, were as follows:

1. The view that following the nationalisation of capitalist property all efforts in the transition to socialism should be concentrated upon the development of the productive forces.

2. The use of primitive accumulation in order to extract resources from agriculture.
3. The centralisation of national economic planning and management.
4. Emphasis on the importance of one-man management and the role of technical experts in the development of modern industrial plants.
5. Mistrust of the capacity of the peasantry to spontaneously and voluntarily socialise agriculture, matched in practice by the forced collectivisation of Soviet agriculture in 1929.[9]

A sixth element of Stalinism – assignation of priority to the development of heavy industry – remained an important feature of the Chinese approach, albeit within an overall framework that came to hold marked differences from Stanlinism.

The accumulated experience of the Chinese Communist Party in mass mobilisation and in local socialist administration

Apart from the Marxist-Leninist-Stalinist theoretical legacy, and the concrete example of Soviet development experience, the Chinese leadership was also able to draw on its own pre-1949 experience of mass mobilisation and of socialist administration in the north of the country. In many respects this experience provided the foundations of an alternative development model. Peck has summarised its distinctive features as

> self reliance, decentralisation, antagonism to bureaucratism and elitism, collective aims and discipline, non-material incentives, and the participation of the masses in all aspects of social and economic activity.
>
> (Peck, in Mao Tsetung, 1977: 14.)

Mao himself had been a notable contributor to the formulation of this approach.

The personality and background of Mao Tsetung[10]

Mao was born in Hunan in 1894, of peasant stock. He received limited formal education. However, he grew up in a province with a long intellectual tradition of pragmatism, giving equal emphasis to empirical investigation and abstract reasoning. Although an early member of the Chinese Communist Party, Mao would not have stood a chance of making a major career in the Party through conventional channels, for the latter was dominated by an urban-based, often foreign-educated intellectual élite. However, conditions in China, combined with the Party's decision to send Mao in 1927 to work in the countryside, generated the opportunities for his leadership potential to emerge.

In 1927 Mao was sent to organise the Autumn Harvest Uprising in Hunan and Kiangsi. The uprising was defeated and Mao retreated to the mountains to organise a local resistance movement.

This grassroots experience reinforced Mao's views that the survival of socialist revolution in China depended upon the Communist Party's ability to win the support of the peasant masses. At this time his ideas on the importance of listening to peasant demands and proposals, and of following the mass line, emerged. During the late 1920s and 1930s Mao was engaged in various debates and disputes over policy with the party leadership, frequently concerned with the degree of control to be exercised by the centre. He also sought to demonstrate the relative importance of the peasantry *vis-à-vis* the insignificant urban proletariat if a socialist revolution was to succeed in China.

During the 1930s Mao's ideas were increasingly vindicated, and his standing in the party grew. The late 1930s and early 1940s saw the emergence of a personality cult of Mao among the membership at large that continued after the revolution. Mao accepted this change, for it coincided with the period when he was arguing that the time had come to establish a unified leadership of the Communist Party given the effective collapse, in the early 1940s, of the alliance with the Guomindang, and the consequent need to wage war on two fronts – against both the Guomindang and the Japanese. At the centre, however, other leading members of the Party continued to insist on the existence of a collective leadership – a view which Mao did not actively dispute.

THE ARTICULATION OF THE MAOIST PARADIGM

From the mid-1950s, in the face of growing economic difficulties, and in the midst of lively debate amongst the Chinese leadership, a new development perspective began increasingly clearly to emerge as a major influence on policy formation in China. It was a perspective whose content and significance became increasingly clear through policy statements made, and policy action taken, at various points over the following two decades. As already noted, this perspective did not govern policy formation to the same degree throughout the whole of this period. It is, however, the perspective which exerted the strongest influence on state policy and praxis taking this period as a whole.

Summary of the Maoist paradigm

The essence of the Maoist paradigm was briefly summarised in Chapter 3 (pp. 74–5). This summary is elaborated here, before proceeding to a discussion of its key features.

1. The ultimate goal of economic development is to achieve material abundance with income differentials abolished and all productive property socially owned and operated.

2. To progress towards this goal it is necessary simultaneously to build up the economy's productive capacity and to socialise the production process, moving towards social ownership of the means of production, social control of production decisions and social control of the distribution of the product.

3. In the transformation to a high growth economy the building up of a modern heavy industrial sector must have priority.[11]

4. The rate of development of modern heavy industry will depend upon the extent of the surplus that can be mobilised to support industrial investment.

5. In a poor, underdeveloped economy this surplus can come from two main sources:
   (a) retained profits of such modern industry as already exists;
   (b) the extraction of surplus from the traditional sector through tax, pricing policy and voluntary savings mobilisation in people's banks.

6. The pace of social and economic transformation must be determined by the mass of the population. Given their extreme poverty, and also the political need for their support, the incomes of the masses cannot be reduced or even allowed to remain constant in order to enlarge the surplus. Rather, the welfare of the masses must rise in order to sustain their support.

7. In an underdeveloped economy such as China the masses are predominantly rural-based.

8. Consequently, while the development of large-scale heavy industry must be given first priority in state investment plans, a balance must be achieved between the development of heavy and light industry and agriculture. In any period it is necessary to search for that set of relative emphases in the mobilisation and allocation of investible resources between sectors which will maximise the rate of capital accumulation while providing also for a sufficient increase in mass welfare to maintain support for the revolution.

9. Light industry and agriculture play two key roles in this process:
   (a) they produce basic consumer goods;
   (b) expansion of these sectors can increase the overall rate of surplus accumulation because investments in these sectors have much shorter gestation periods and capital pay-back periods than modern, large-scale, heavy industry.[12]

10. A balance must also be achieved between investment in large-scale and small-scale industry. Although modern, capital-intensive, large-scale industry can achieve the highest levels of labour productivity, in the medium term not all the expansion of the output of either heavy or light industry need or should come from large-scale plant. Rather, the emphasis given in the expansion of production to different scales of

plant using different technologies should also be governed by the principle of maximisation of overall resource mobilisation given existing physical constraints (for example, in the transport network, and in the production capacity of large-scale state-owned industry). Wherever small quantities of appropriate resources are available, these should be mobilised to add to the total output, rather than being left idle.

11. The consequent expansion of small-scale industry can
    (a) expand the supply of consumer goods;
    (b) expand the supply of rural producer goods;
    (c) provide, out of profits, funds for agricultural construction;
    (d) make some contribution to the expansion of employment and facilitate the development of the technical and innovatory skills of the labour force;
    (e) help to raise rural incomes while also augmenting the surplus made available to the state for development of modern industry;
    (f) help to minimise the competition between the rural sector and modern industry for scarce state resources.

12. Output growth can also be accelerated through the mobilisation in the rural sector of seasonally slack labour for labour intensive capital formation.

13. Concerning economic equity and economic incentives:
    (a) economic and political equality between regions should be promoted by
       (i) allocating a greater share of industrial investment to backward regions;
       (ii) promoting regional self-sufficiency in basic industries and food-stuffs;
       (iii) giving greater power in decision-taking to the regions;
    (b) income differences between persons should be minimised as fast as possible, but not faster than the masses are prepared to accept. As a part of this process reliance on material incentives should be steadily reduced. Also, professionals should work among the masses, learn from them about their needs and use their skills towards helping to overcome concrete difficulties.

The following discussion focuses upon four elements of this perspective:

1. The key linkages between sectors and the significance of technological choice.
2. The importance of following the mass line.
3. The relative significance of the development of the productive forces, production relations, and the political and ideological superstructure.
4. The importance of continuing class struggle,

Intersectoral linkages, technological choice and the rural–urban distribution of industrial investment

Some of the ideas reviewed in this sub-section are to be found in the strategy statement prepared by Mao in 1956 entitled 'The Ten Great Relationships'. Of this statement Mao later observed that '[we] made a start in proposing our own line for construction'.[13] It was prepared at a time when, as we saw earlier, agricultural growth had slowed markedly, and in which the Chinese realised that new policy emphases were required to sustain economic development.

One such shift in policy emphasis was a recognition of the need for an increase in the share of agriculture and light industry in total investment.

> Heavy industries are the centre of gravity and their development should be given first priority . . . What will be needed is more investment in light industries and agriculture. Let its proportion rise. Will this change shift the centre of gravity? It will not be shifted; it will remain on heavy industries. The only difference is that both light industry and agriculture will receive a greater weight.
>
> What will be the result of this? The result will be a more extensive and better development of heavy industries, of the production of means of production.
>
> To develop heavy industries requires an accumulation of capital. Where does capital come from? Heavy industries can accumulate capital; so can light industries and agriculture. However, light industries and agriculture can accumulate more capital and faster . . . light industries can [also] meet the needs of the people's livelihood.
>
> (Mao Tsetung in Ch'en, 1969: 67, 8.)

'The Ten Great Relationships' identifies several policy instruments for the promotion of this shift in sectoral resource allocation. They include agricultural tax and price policy and the pattern of allocation of collective farm revenues (between recurrent production costs, management expenses, a sinking fund (to finance new investment) and the welfare fund. In practice, however, these policy instruments were complemented by the use of two others, introduced in the late 1950s, to raise capital accumulation in agriculture and light industry, and it is these that represent part of the innovatory element in the Chinese approach to resource mobilisation. They are large-scale labour intensive capital formation in agriculture through mobilisation of labour in the agricultural slack season, and the development of small- and medium-scale industry (heavy and light) in rural areas, producing both producer goods (for agriculture and small-scale industry) and consumption goods. Many small-scale industries were owned by the communes, and the financial surpluses that they generated were in turn used partly to fund agricultural accumulation.[14]

In contrast to Stalinist industrialisation strategy and in practice in contrast also to the large-scale, modern technology investment orientation of both the western version of the paradigm of the expanding capitalist nucleus and the structuralist paradigm, from the late 1950s the Maoist approach to economic development emphasised alongside state development of modern heavy industry the local mobilisation of slack resources for the development of small- and medium-scale light and heavy industry. This strategy was known in China as 'walking on two legs'.

This alternative view of industrial development represented a pragmatic reaction to conditions prevailing in China – to the scarcity of resources to finance state investment, to the vastness of the country and its poor infrastructure and to the scattered local availability of small deposits of natural resources and other materials that would be wasted if the only option were to transport them to large-scale plant. Such resources included small mineral deposits, scrap metal, farm and household waste, agricultural raw materials, etc., which, if combined with limited amounts of local labour, could be used to produce agricultural producer goods (tools, fertiliser), construction materials, energy and consumption goods.

Small- to medium-scale plants could produce steel, energy, cement, fertiliser and coal to supplement the output of large-scale plants, and the output could be used locally, largely to expand agricultural production. Meanwhile small-scale light industry could increase the supply of incentive goods in the rural sector. Walking on two legs would thus permit an acceleration in overall growth, including expanded production of agriculture and light industry, while minimising the need to increase state investment in these sectors.

Mao's statement on 'The Ten Great Relationships' also emphasised the importance of regional self-sufficiency in basic foodstuffs and industrial goods. (During the rest of the Maoist era all regions were required to aim for self-sufficiency in food-grains, while an attempt was made to build up a more even distribution of basic industry.) This emphasis on regional self-sufficiency was represented as an essential precondition for the decentralisation of economic and political power (see Mao Tsetung in Ch'en, 1969: 74–76). However, the dispersal of basic industry and essential food supplies also had an important strategic significance for a country of China's size (where individual regions may have a population and land area comparable to that of one of the larger countries in Europe). This emphasis on self-sufficiency is of little relevance to most developing countries and constitutes an element of the Maoist perspective that has had no notable influence outside China, either theoretical or practical.

The importance of following the mass line

Prior to 1949 Mao had written:

> all correct leadership is necessarily 'from the masses to the masses.' This means: take the ideas of the masses (scattered and unsystematic ideas), then go to the masses to propagate and explain those ideas until the masses embrace them as

their own, hold fast to them and translate them into action, and test the correctness of these ideas in action.

(Mao Tsetung, *Selected Works*, Vol. III: 119.)

In principle, following the mass line provides a criterion to guide not only the *pace* of change, but also the *pattern* of change. Reference to the latter principle has already been noted in the preceding section, with respect to the recognition of the need for increased investment in agriculture and light industry. However, following the mass line applies not only to the pace and pattern of output growth, but also to the pace of development of production relations – to the pace of change in the structure of control over the allocation of productive resources and the basis on which incomes are distributed.

In general following the mass line implies gradualism and voluntarism as opposed to rapid, authoritarian change coerced from the centre. In practice the dividing line between voluntarism encouraged by a degree of persuasion/manipulation from the centre on the one hand, and coercion on the other, can sometimes be a subtle one.

Finally, the application of this principle also presupposes the existence of criteria for identifying the masses. To this end Mao himself applied a simple class analysis, but, as we shall see, in the mid-1950s he also manipulated his definition in order to be able to justify policy that was unpopular with part of the masses (as previously defined).[15]

The relative importance of the development of the productive forces, the relations of production and the political and ideological superstructure

Between 1958 and 1962, probably between 1958 and 1960,[16] at the time of China's rift with the Soviet Union, Mao reconsidered two key Soviet texts on socialist economic development: *Political Economy: A Textbook* and Stalin's *Economic Problems of Socialism in the USSR*. In his critique of these texts Mao emphasises the need for continuing development of the political and ideological superstructure and production relations during the phase of socialist construction. These issues go beyond the sphere of economic development narrowly defined, but in the Maoist perspective they constitute an integral part of the process of socialist development.

Stalin took the view that with respect to the transition from capitalist to socialist production relations it was sufficient for the state to nationalise all private property. After this the development of the productive forces would carry forward the process of socialist construction. Mao expresses a different view. The development of the productive forces alone is not sufficient to sustain the process of socialist construction. It will not necessarily ensure a steady decline in individualistic attitudes and behaviour with respect to productive work; nor *a fortiori* will it automatically ensure the converse – the steady development of socialist consciousness, attitudes and behaviour on the part of workers, managers and the bureaucracy. It is therefore necessary deliberately to promote the development of production relations during the process of socialist construction *as well as* the development of the productive forces.

Mao argued that the relations of production should be given a broader interpretation than the Stalinist reference to ownership rights in productive property. Other important elements that he emphasised include the determination and form of the remuneration of labour, the balance between material and non-material incentives, and the relationship between cadres, managers, technicians and shop-floor workers.

The Maoist view also holds that the use of appropriate methods to eliminate the divisions between mental and manual labour can lead to an increase in both equity and economic efficiency, through more informed decision-taking and greater worker motivation, while helping to prevent the emergence of dominant bureaucratic and technocratic classes.

Meanwhile, in agriculture, the collective ownership of productive property is held to represent only a partial socialisation of productive property, inferior to ownership by the nation on behalf of the whole nation. Here and in industry progressive socialisation entails shifting from payment by task to payment by time worked (task and output being undifferentiated) and then payment according to need; in agriculture these changes are to be combined with progressive reduction of private plots and enlargement of the collective unit. Not only would concentration upon the development of the productive forces alone not necessarily ensure progress on these fronts, but it could impede it through encouraging individualism and through allowing technical cadres and the bureaucracy to accumulate excessive power and status.

Meanwhile, the sustained development of production relations is in turn dependent on, and promoted by, the development of the political and ideological superstructure. It is this that provides the appropriate inspiration, guidance and framework for the development of both production relations and productive capacity.

The need for continuing class struggle

By 'class struggle' in a socialist society, the Maoists in China had in mind a continuing struggle to maintain an equitable society avoiding excessive income differentials and, above all, the emergence of entrenched privilege and the abuse of power. In the context of socialised production this entails watchfulness against the emergence of class divisions between privileged party cadres, bureaucrats and technicians on the one hand, and the masses on the other.

In 'On the Correct Handling of Contradictions Among the People', written in 1957, and also in a talk to the third plenum of the Eighth Central

Committee held later that year, Mao argued the need for continuing class struggle in socialist society:

> survivals of bourgeois ideology, bureaucratic ways of doing things in our state organs, and flaws in certain of our state institutions stand in contrast to the economic base of socialism.
> (*Selected Readings from the Works of Mao Tsetung*: 463, reproduced by Peck in *Mao Tsetung*, 1977: 17.)

Only continued mass struggle could reduce the powerful hold of bourgeois ideology and the entrenchment of a self-interested bureaucracy.

Later in 1957 Mao added

> When we say that large-scale class struggle has fundamentally ended and that contradictions have been fundamentally resolved, we are speaking of the political system and the problem of ownership. But in building the superstructure, the question of ideology and political power in large measure has not been resolved.
> (Mao Tsetung, in Joint Publications Research Service, 1974: 73.)

THE POLICY IMPLICATIONS OF THE MAOIST PARADIGM

The Maoist perspective was not simply interpretative. It was intended to guide action, and its policy implications are wide-ranging. In the economic sphere they concern every sector of the economy, every aspect of productive activity and production relations. Amongst the most significant are the implications for land reform, the aggregate rate of investment, the sectoral composition of investment, industrialisation strategy, price policy, tax policy, technology, the ownership and management of production units and the relationship between mental and manual labour.

Some of these issues have already been touched upon. This section recapitulates their most salient features, while the next section reviews policy design in practice.

1. *Land reform* should tend towards the socialisation of production relations but should be based upon mass support and therefore be, if necessary, gradualistic.
2. The *aggregate rate of investment* should be maximised subject to the constraint that there must be a sustained increase in mass welfare adequate to sustain popular support for the economic development programme.
3. The *sectoral composition of investment* should be geared to achieving the objectives outlined in 2.
4. *Industrialisation strategy* should give primacy to the development of modern, state-owned heavy industry. However, to sustain pursuit of

this goal light industry, much of it initially small- and medium-scale, must expand output of mass consumption goods at a pace sufficient to maintain popular support.

5. *Technology* – to maximise the overall pace of output expansion the economy should walk on two legs, using large-scale capital-intensive technology in state-owned heavy industry, while small- and medium-scale industries (light and heavy) use more labour-intensive techniques.[17]

6. *Price policy and tax policy* should be designed to maximise surplus mobilisation for the state sector subject to the constraint that adequate incentives must be provided to expand agricultural output.

7. The *relations of production* should be progressively socialised, and the *class struggle* should be continued against newly emerging party, bureaucratic and technocratic élite elements in society.

POLICY IMPLEMENTATION: THE APPLICATION OF THE 'MAOIST' PERSPECTIVE

In the following paragraphs we briefly review examples of the application of the 'Maoist' perspective in policy implementation.

Land reform

Ex post facto land reform was represented by the Chinese authorities during the Maoist era as having been gradualistic and voluntaristic, the stages being as outlined below. However, while the reforms were indeed introduced sequentially, Selden has shown that in practice most peasants did not directly experience the complete sequence:

1. 1949–1950: poor and middle peasants encouraged to seize landlords' land and surplus lands of rich peasants for redistribution to individual households.

2. Building on traditional forms of cooperation in the Chinese countryside, redistribution was followed by formation of mutual aid teams (first temporary, then permanent) in which households pooled resources (tools, implements, draft power, occasional labour) but still cultivated land on an individual basis: some 65 per cent of peasants had joined mutual aid teams by mid-1955.[18]

3. Formation of elementary co-operatives in which land as well as other resources were pooled, but individual ownership rights maintained. Incomes were based partly on property ownership and partly on labour time committed to co-operative production in ratios ranging from 60:40 to 40:60, the ratios being manipulated in order to maximise local

support.[19] By mid-1955, 14 per cent of all rural households reportedly belonged to elementary co-operatives, the majority in North and North-East China.[20]

4. Between late 1955 and spring 1958 all peasant households were incorporated into advanced producer co-operatives, with common ownership of productive resources.[21] A typical co-operative contained several hundred households (usually the population of several neighbouring hamlets or of one larger village).

5. During the second half of 1958 the advanced co-operatives were in turn incorporated into larger units of collective economy and government – the communes.

In 1955 Mao revised his definition of the rural masses, excluding the 'well-to-do' middle peasants who opposed further collectivisation. Only thus was he able to claim that stages 4 and 5 had also entailed 'following the mass line', with the support of some 60 to 70 per cent of the rural population (Mao, quoted by Selden in Selden and Lippit, *op.cit.*: 66). However, even though many peasants did not experience the full sequence of stages in the transformation of production relations, and even though elements of the middle peasantry as well as rich peasants and landlords did not want collectivisation, the Chinese were far more successful than the Soviet Union in implementing a land reform that, particularly in the first three stages, was sensitive to the issue of voluntarism, and that carried the active co-operation of the majority of the population throughout.

The overall rate of accumulation

Mao argued that the share of investment in national income must not be so high as to prevent a steady increase in mass living standards. Despite this, savings were always highest when Maoist policies were being fully implemented. In theory this is reconcilable with the above-mentioned constraint if implementation of these policies also entails more effective resource mobilisation, appropriate allocation of investment, and high investment productivity. Assessments as to whether, and to what extent, these occurred, vary (see below).

The sectoral composition of investment

Assessments of the extent to which the Maoist perspective was applied to sectoral resource allocation vary. On the one hand statistics such as those cited by Ma Hong, 1983, have been widely quoted as suggesting that it was not:

During the First Five-Year Plan period, investment in heavy industry made up 38.7 per cent of total investments, a proportion which was already excessive.

But then the investment share of heavy industry continued to increase from 1958 to 1978 to 52.8 per cent of the total.

(Ma Hong, *op.cit.*: 24.)

On the other hand, however, Kojima Reiitsu has shown that in the Maoist era, the value of collective labour time committed to labour-intensive investment in the communes *exceeded* the value of investment in heavy industry. Critics who have ignored this crucial element of capital formation in Maoist development strategy provide a distorted picture of the overall allocation of investment.[22]

Industrialisation strategy

From the Great Leap Forward (1959–1961) onwards, 'walking on two legs' became a key feature of Maoist development strategy. Since then, small-, medium- and large-scale plants have provided varying shares of the output of different industries and, within individual industries, varying shares over time, depending upon their relative pace of development.[23] Many small- and medium-sized industries are located in rural areas and country towns. Regional dispersal of large-scale industry was also promoted in the Maoist era (see Riskin, 1987: 225–228).

Technology

State industry adopted modern technology, while, from the late 1950s, small- and medium-scale industries were encouraged to adopt technologies appropriate to local resource availabilities. Meanwhile, the same philosophy governed the pattern of development of other sectors too, most notably the health care sector, where the Chinese laid heavy emphasis on the expansion of medical auxiliaries – 'barefoot doctors' – to provide education in preventive medicine and basic curative care throughout the rural sector. In the Maoist era this programme generally operated at the level of the production brigade (a subsection of the commune usually covering a large village or cluster of small hamlets). Local individuals were trained as paramedics, the cost of their services being covered from a combination of small individual contributions, collective funds and state subsidy.[24]

Tax policy, price policy and the terms of trade between agriculture and industry

In the mid-1950s an agricultural tax was introduced that was designed to achieve a degree of equity between regions while simultaneously maximising the incentive to expand production and securing a steady income for the state. The tax was based upon current average annual land yields. It was estimated in the first instance as a percentage of the average yield, the rate being set higher in the more prosperous zones. The tax then remained almost constant in real terms for the rest of the Maoist era: there was no taxation of incremental agricultural output, and hence no tax-derived disincentive to expand production.[25]

Meanwhile, agricultural prices were also raised in the mid and late 1950s (1953–1959) and the terms of trade between agriculture and basic manufactured consumption goods were improved.[26] Recent criticisms levelled against agricultural price policy in China from the mid-1950s to the mid-1970s concern whether prices were raised enough. One criticism is that even though agricultural prices rose, they did not improve relative to agricultural producer goods.[27] The latter, however, were in extremely scarce supply in relation to the potential demand, and had to be rationed somehow. Keeping their price high permitted the realisation of greater value by the state to finance future accumulation. Selden and Lippit make the more general criticism that the improvement still left agricultural prices

> unduly low relative to industrial prices, whether considered historically, in terms of embodied labour contents, or in terms of the price relationships competitive labour markets would establish.
>
> (Selden and Lippit, *op.cit.*: 18.)[28]

However, it should be borne in mind that in the mid-1950s the Chinese were also using non-price incentives in combination with material incentives in order to expand production. The adequacy of price and tax policy is in principle best gauged in terms of actual output performance, although this criterion itself leaves scope for dispute. It is discussed further in the next section.[29]

The socialisation of the relations of production

During both the Great Leap Forward and the Cultural Revolution moves were made to advance the socialisation of production relations beyond the nationalisation of large-scale industry and the service sector and the creation of rural communes.

During the Great Leap attempts were made to reduce reliance on material incentives, to extend the sphere of communal living,[30] and to enlarge yet further the communes themselves. During the Cultural Revolution there were renewed attempts to reduce reliance on material incentives, in state-owned industry as well as the communes, and moves were also made towards breaking down divisions between mental and manual labour and between bureaucrats and technocrats and the masses. Examples of such attempts included the following:

1. In industry – the formation of joint management committees incorporating managers and worker representatives,[31] and the requirement that technicians and party cadres spend a certain amount of time each week working on the shop floor.[32]

2. In agriculture – the requirement that scientists working at agricultural research stations should spend, on a rotation basis, periods of up to a year working with a production brigade learning about the production problems faced by its members, and that they should apply this knowledge to the design of research programmes.[33]
3. In education – the requirement that all students enrolled in higher education should spend periods of time engaged in manual labour, working alongside ordinary workers and peasants.[34]
4. In the party – the requirement that party cadres should also engage in productive labour.[35]

Continuing class struggle

It was of course in the Cultural Revolution (1966–1976) that the need for continuing class struggle was most obviously carried through into practice. Apart from the widespread criticism of, and encouragement of self-criticism by, officials and functionaries such as party cadres, managers of state enterprises and educationists, two other important manifestations of the implementation of this policy were the allocation of substantial time to political education in all stages of the education system, and selection for higher education largely on the basis of political commitment rather than educational attainment.

CHINA'S ECONOMIC PERFORMANCE IN THE MAOIST ERA

Table 8.1 summarises estimates of China's growth performance in the Maoist era (extending in one case to 1982) taken from three different sources. The first two sets of estimates are taken from recent assessments of China's economic performance, while the third is drawn from a major appraisal of alternative data sources undertaken in the 1970s.

The first two sets of estimates in Table 8.1 for aggregate and sectoral growth are not incompatible given the different time series covered. One would expect the Hong estimates to be higher than those of Selden and Lippit both because of the earlier base year (1949), and because the terminal year is later, so that the accelerated growth performance of 1978–1982 is also incorporated. Meanwhile, Paine's upper series for industrial growth, based on official Chinese data, seem somewhat too high to be compatible with Hong's figures. The precise reason for discrepancy is not clear, but Paine herself emphasises the various methodological difficulties involved in aggregating the industrial output statistics, which involves transforming these from physical quantities into value added form. (Paine's lower estimate is based on official American estimates; see Joint Economic Committee, United States Congress, 1975.)

Table 8.1 Recent estimates of China's growth performance

Source	Period	Sector	Average annual growth rate	
			Aggregate growth rate	Per capita growth rate**
Ma Hong (1983: pp. 15–16)	1949–1982	Agriculture	4.4	
		Industry	12.9	
		GDP (industry and agriculture)	9.2	
		National income	7.1	5.1 (implied)
Selden and Lippit (1982: 19–20)	1952–1978	Agriculture	3.2	
		Industry	11.2	
		GDP	4.0–6.0	2.0–4.0
		National income	lower than GDP	
Paine (1976: 1360–1 and Table 1.5)	1949–1975	Industry*	12.3–13.1	
	1950–1975	Industry*	11.1–11.9	
	1952–1975	Industry*	8.9– 9.6	
	1950–1974	GDP		4.3–5.3
	1952–1974	GDP		3.3–4.5

Notes

* Lower figure taken from estimates by Field for United States Central Intelligence Agency; upper figure based on Chinese official series. For her discussion of the available agricultural statistics see Paine, *op.cit.*: 1358 and 1360.

** All performance estimates presented on a per capita basis are a function *inter alia* of the estimated rate of population growth. In China there is some uncertainty about this. However, a crude averaging of the various estimates suggests that the average rate of increase from 1949–1978 probably did not exceed two per cent per annum (see Paine, 1976: 1356; also Selden and Lippit, *op.cit.*: 20; and Nolan and White in Gray and White (eds.), 1982).

One interpretation of China's growth figures is that on a comparative basis they represent a remarkably good long-run output performance for both agriculture and industry, particularly given China's initial poor resource endowment in agriculture.[36] On the other hand, recent critics of the Maoist era have chosen to emphasise the variations in performance within this era. Although with agriculture growing at 4 per cent per annum and industry at 9.1 per cent per annum, growth in China during the second half of the Cultural Revolution decade was still above the average for low-income countries – and also above that for high-income market economies. Indeed, it is notable that GDP growth figures *per se* are not emphasised by critics of economic performance in the Maoist era.

Turning to the agricultural statistics, these represent a weighted average for different product categories. It is widely held that, after significant growth in the early 1950s, from 1957 to 1978 per capita output of foodgrains grew very little, output just keeping pace with population growth. On the other hand, certain product categories, most notably livestock production, have grown much more rapidly. While many recent studies criticise the stagnation or near-stagnation of per capita food grain output in the Maoist era, Paine takes the view that this can be explained in terms of attainment of self-sufficiency in food grains in relation to human consumption requirements.[37]

A further criterion for the assessment of China's economic development performance concerns the impact on inter-personal income distribution. In the 1970s a growing number of studies reported very favourably on China's success in combining growth with a reduction in inequality and absolute poverty. Since 1978, however, there has been a reappraisal of China's performance in these two respects. This reappraisal has not, however, generated a new consensus, and opinion remains divided on the progress made by the Chinese in the elimination of inequality and mass poverty between 1949 and 1976. The following quotation from Lippit (1982) is illustrative of a view widely held in the 1970s and still maintained by a significant proportion of sinologists:

> In contrast to the growing inequality in income which characteristically marks the early stages of capitalist development, China established a relatively high degree of equality soon after the success of the revolution and has sustained it since then. The single most important factor underlying income inequality in capitalist countries is the unequal ownership of property; the socialisation of industry and land reform in agriculture eliminated this factor in China. . .
>
> Although differences among peasants persisted (and still do), what is most striking is the narrowness of the differentials between the 'poor' and the 'rich', a narrowness which verges on the extraordinary whether contrasted with the income differentials which existed in pre-revolutionary China (see, for example, Fei and Chang, 1945) or in capitalist Third World countries today.
>
> In urban areas, the elimination of the private ownership of houses (now permitted again) and the more expensive consumer durables like automobiles provided a counterpart to the equalisation of incomes resulting from the socialisation of property. Although the highest-paid workers could earn as much as three times the income of the lowest-paid ones (and still can), this reflects in part differential wages over the working-life cycle. . . Further, most necessities (housing, utilities, medical care, public transport, and so forth) are heavily subsidised, so the difference in real incomes is much less than the difference in money wages would appear to indicate. . . In the elimination of poverty, too, the Chinese practice has been in accord with the socialist model. . . the relatively equal distribution of the national income and the heavy subsidies for essential living requirements like housing and medical care have virtually eliminated the types of extreme poverty that are everywhere visible in the capitalist third world.
>
> (Lippit in Selden and Lippit, *op.cit.*: 124–126.)

In contrast, others, both in China and outside, have more recently emphasised certain failures of the Maoist era with respect to the reduction of inequality and absolute poverty. Thus with respect to the former, Gray states that

> the gap between the average income of the urban minority and that of the rural majority is still such as would be considered a scandal in any country, far less [*sic*] in one committed for thirty years to socialism.
>
> (Gray, *op.cit.*: 292.)

Gray notes that inter-regional inequalities also remain substantial, while inequalities between neighbouring villages and between members of the same production team though less substantial were still notable at the end of the Maoist era. He also notes inequality between the terms of employment of permanent and casual workers in the urban sector (Gray, *op.cit.*: 297). Riskin, in an excellent survey of income distribution in China, confirms the high gap between rural and urban incomes (Riskin, 1987: 249).

Turning from inequality to absolute poverty, Ma Hong reports the existence in 1978 of 32.94 million agricultural households whose expenditures exceeded their incomes (Ma Hong, 1983: 22). At an average of just over three persons per household this amounts to some 100 million people apparently unable to meet their basic needs from their own income. This figure of some 100 million people, or ten per cent of the population, living in poverty is widely quoted both in and outside China.[38] However, in 1978 this represented 10 per cent of the population, a much lower proportion living below the poverty line than in most Third World countries (cf. Riskin, *op.cit.*: 250).[39]

Finally, there is a divergence between the favourable assessments of the mid-1970s and the more critical ones of the late 1970s and the 1980s with respect to the growth of consumption per capita in the Maoist era. Paine estimated this as having risen at three per cent per annum from 1950 to 1975.[40] However, it is now widely agreed that due to a combination of exceptionally high shares of investment in national income (Gray reports a peak of 36.6 per cent) and rising capital/output ratios, disposable income per capita rose hardly at all between 1957 and 1978.[41] This has been one of the main criticisms levelled against the Maoist era in recent years.

CRITICISMS OF THE MAOIST PARADIGM

The main categories of criticism

Criticisms of the Maoist era fall into two categories – criticism of the Maoist perspective, and criticism of actual policies and economic performance. While some of the latter reflect on the application of the Maoist perspective, others do not.

At each level – paradigm, policies and performance – the Maoist era has been criticised from a number of different perspectives: Stalinist, market socialist, and the perspective of capitalist ideology backed by neo-classical theory, *inter alia*. However, the seminal criticisms of both economic planning and administered prices from a neo-classical perspective remain those of Hayek and Von Mises which were first written in the 1920s and 1930s. In recent decades neo-classical theorists have shown relatively little interest in detailed critical appraisal of Maoism and the Maoist era as compared with the first two categories of critics both inside and outside China (and with other external critics who do not make their position clear but appear also to have sympathy with the notion of market socialism). The neo-classicals take it as a foregone conclusion that the Maoist perspective advocates both economic inefficiency and the infringement of individual political and economic freedom.

In what follows we shall focus chiefly on criticisms that stem from the first two perspectives, perspectives that have a sufficient shared element of beliefs and values with Maoism to take the Maoist perspective seriously, while also diverging from it in important respects.

Criticisms of the perspective itself

In the literature on Maoism three major criticisms of this perspective have been emphasised:

1. Overemphasis on the importance of continuing class struggle at the expense of development of the productive forces.
2. Overemphasis on the continuing development of production relations, likewise at the expense of development of the productive forces.
3. Overemphasis on the planned economy, and failure to supplement this adequately with a market dimension (point made by market socialists).
4. In addition, Maoism has also been criticised for excessive emphasis on self-reliance, both regional and national (see e.g. Ma Hong, 1983: 25).

Meanwhile, Maoism has also been criticised for internal inconsistency, represented in the economic arena by the expectation that decentralised planning and resource mobilisation can be promoted by centrally controlled party cadres and bureaucrats (Ellman, 1986: 423 *et seq.*) and in the political arena by the role assigned to the party in mobilising the masses for continuing class struggle against the bureaucracy and party cadres themselves. However, Riskin (1987) expresses the former point differently, emphasising that Mao reduced central control but put nothing in its place, i.e. he refused to accept the market as the alternative. Thus what the centre lost of its power to direct was simply transferred to the province and the county.

As noted above, a range of criticisms have also been levelled against actual policies and elements of development performance in the period 1949–1976. Two interesting points to note about these criticisms are that they are not always consistent with those just reviewed and that they also suggest the Maoist perspective was not always carried through in practice. These criticisms include the following:

1. Pursuit of high growth targets while ignoring the need to control economic efficiency.[42]
2. The placing (*in practice*, and despite the preoccupations expressed in 'The Ten Great Relationships') of undue emphasis on heavy industry at the expense of agriculture and light industry (see e.g. Ma Hong, *op.cit.*: 24).
3. Over-emphasis on new capital construction at the expense of the technological improvement of existing enterprises (*ibid.*).
4. Over-emphasis on production of primary and intermediate products in industry, with consequent stockpiling (*ibid.*: 25).
5. Over-emphasis on achieving high accumulation rates out of national income, at the expense of the people's necessary consumption (*ibid.*).
6. Loss of essential skilled manpower due to the disruption of the education system during the Cultural Revolution (see Gardner in Gray and White, 1982: 280).

Some of these criticisms – such as too heavy an emphasis on the expansion of production and construction of new capital, too high a share of investment in the national product, too high a share for heavy industry in aggregate investment, and too heavy an emphasis on production of primary and intermediate goods – do not immediately suggest underemphasis on the development of the productive forces, but rather the opposite. Indeed, only criticism 6 suggests such an underemphasis.

However, some of the criticisms listed in points 1–6 above also suggest that development of the productive forces may have been done inefficiently with rising fixed capital-output and input-output ratios, insufficient emphasis on the full utilisation of existing capacity and on the upgrading of existing capital stock, and insufficient attention to the matching of supply and demand. Possibly reduced emphasis on the needs for continuing class struggle and development of production relations would have been associated with greater attention to efficiency, but the chain of causality here is certainly not automatic, as the Soviet development experience testifies.[43] On the other hand, the third line of theoretical criticism of Maoism – that which emphasises the role of the free market in the promotion of economic efficiency – does appear at first sight to offer a credible explanation of the inefficiencies just noted.

Criticisms of Maoism reconsidered

There are, however, a number of further points to note with respect to the criticisms outlined in the preceding paragraphs. Firstly, the strength of the causality between emphasis on continuing class struggle and development of production relations on the one hand, and inefficiency in economic performance on the other, remains unclear. This partly depends on the scale on which, and intensity with which, the errors of over-emphasis and ignoring the 'mass line' were committed. Yet detailed information on these points is often lacking.[44]

Secondly, in some cases there may also have been both positive learning effects, and mobilising effects in the sphere of production, resulting from the continuing attempt to develop production relations, which, in the political climate prevailing since 1978, critics have chosen to ignore. (Such positive effects were emphasised by some of the outside observers who visited China during the Cultural Revolution, e.g. Bettelheim, 1974: 26, 27 and 81, and Robinson, 1976).

Closer examination of the individual criticisms of economic performance also reveals that some, due to their narrow focus, fail to take into account key features of Maoist economic theory and strategy. Thus, given effective pursuit of the Maoist strategy of walking on two legs, the rising shares of heavy industry in total investment and of total investment in national income would not necessarily have been inappropriate. For if in agriculture and light industry low capital-output ratios and short gestation and recovery periods for investment (which are emphasised in Maoist theory[45]) are combined with a sufficiently high profit rate, then these sectors could, in principle at least, generate such a rate of increase in *total* investible resources as to permit an increase in the *share* of investible resources allocated to heavy industry while still sustaining healthy rates of accumulation in agriculture and light industry. Likewise, high capital productivity of these sectors could in principle also provide for rising per capita consumption at rate x, and growth of total consumer goods output at $x + n$ (where $n =$ the rate of population growth) while permitting the growth of investment at a rate greater than $x + n$. This would automatically raise the share of investment in national income. While the logic of these criticisms can be queried, so in at least one case can their empirical accuracy (see p. 241).

Given the foregoing problems, it seems that the question of whether agriculture and light industry did or did not grow sufficiently fast during the period 1957–1976 must be judged not in terms of investment shares *per se*, but in terms of outcomes. More specifically, the issue is whether or not the material consumption of the masses grew sufficiently fast. However, while the question seems straightforward, the answer is not, for there are three alternative criteria for answering it. The first is instrumental, the second speculative, and the third based on political value judgement. Firstly there is the question whether mass living standards were high enough, and rising fast enough, to sustain the masses' political support and to provide sufficient work incentives to maintain rapid growth – points emphasised by Maoism itself. Looking at China's economic performance there is no clear-cut evidence that this was not the case, with the exception of the period of the Great Leap Forward.[46] Secondly, however, it is possible to speculate that growth would have been yet faster if mass consumption had risen faster. While it is true that the output growth rate rose after 1978 at a time when mass incomes and consumption also rose, it remains to be seen whether this higher growth rate can be sustained, particularly without rising social tension in the face of increasing inequality. (For example, the rapid growth rate in agriculture since 1978 can be explained by a combination of the one-off effects of decollectivisation and the consequent improvement of individual incentives, the 1978 price increases and a favourable climate in 1981–83. It may be much harder to sustain a similar rate over the long-term[47]).

Thirdly, there are political value judgements to be made concerning when and how fast mass living standards should rise during the socialist transition, and the role that individual material reward should play in socialist development. The Maoist perspective gives greater emphasis to non-material reward than do its critics in China and outside. However, these same critics, through selective use of statistics, may also have tended to underestimate the rise in mass welfare during the Maoist era. While food grain output per capita grew little, output of certain other food products, including pork and poultry meat, rose rapidly leading to some diversification in the popular diet[48] and an improvement in its quality. Food prices were subsidised. Social welfare provision also developed. Basic health care was improved in the rural and urban sectors, and there were low, subsidised prices for schooling, child care and medical care (Riskin, *op.cit.*), while pensions were established for permanent workers in state industry.

In a poor, underdeveloped economy the timing and rate of increases in mass consumption are key political and economic issues, as we have already seen in earlier chapters. The concern with mass welfare as an immediate policy issue that is expressed in the Maoist perspective is greater than in either the paradigm of the expanding capitalist nucleus or the 'classical structuralist' paradigm. This concern appears to have been carried through into development policy and performance in the form of emphasis on the provision of basic consumption needs and improvements in social welfare provisions (the latter being relatively labour-intensive services which made limited demands on scarce capital), while the rate of growth of consumption of non-essential consumption goods was tightly contained.

THE RELEVANCE OF THE MAOIST PARADIGM TO OTHER UNDERDEVELOPED COUNTRIES

In the mid-1970s interest developed outside China in the potential relevance of Chinese development theory and practice to other underdeveloped countries. For those impressed by China's performance there were three key questions:

1. Could China's development model be exported wholesale?

2. Could China's dominant development philosophy act as a guide to other underdeveloped countries, particularly those also attempting a socialist development path?
3. Could elements of Chinese development practice be replicated else-where?

The Chinese themselves led the field in answering the first question in the negative. Already in 1959 Mao, in his *Reading Notes on the Soviet Text*, quoted with approval the statement that every country 'has its own particular forms and concrete methods of constructing socialism'.[49] This view has been strongly supported by scholars outside China (see e.g. Eckstein, 1977).

Turning to the second point, Mao also argued, in this and other writings, that the development of socialism must address the integration of universal laws and concrete particulars. While the laws are general statements of ideology and theory, their application in particular circumstances requires, *inter alia*, both a pragmatic assessment of the physical resource base and its potential, and the mobilisation of the masses for the purpose of socialist construction. Mao saw some of his writing as contributing to a revised and improved statement of the universal laws, while development practice in China provided a concrete example of their application in particular circumstances. Other countries engaged in socialist construction might learn from both, taking the universal laws as a general guide to the formation of development strategy given their particular circumstances. However, they in turn might also add to or modify these laws should experience demonstrate the need to do so.

Meanwhile, the crucial questions remain: how relevant and how applicable are these general laws in other countries, both socialist and non-socialist? Furthermore, if relevant, can the manner of their application in China (acknowledged errors obviously excluded[50]) be replicated elsewhere, if not in total then at least in part? Possible reactions to these issues include the following:

1. Rejection of the general laws emphasised by Maoism as governing effective socialist construction. This is the line taken by the Tseng regime since 1978.
2. The view that the particular characteristics of China's cultural and political tradition render these laws, while applicable there, of little relevance elsewhere. Thus it has been suggested that the degree of responsiveness to patriotic and other ideological incentives, the discipline demonstrated in mass labour mobilisation, and a highly pronounced work ethic are patterns of behaviour more readily found in China than elsewhere (Eckstein, 1977: 314, 5).[51]
3. Countries attempting the transition to socialism may learn from the values and the general laws of Maoism, although they will wish to apply them at their own pace and in their own manner. Meanwhile, other

developing countries, both socialist and non-socialist, may adopt specific elements of Maoist praxis such as 'walking on two legs'.

Eckstein (1977), after offering an excellent analysis of the Chinese development model that evolved in the Maoist era, and of the manner of integration of its various elements, concludes that it is highly improbable that elements of Maoist development praxis can be separated out for replication elsewhere. The scale of China's natural and human resource endowment, her culture and specific political and economic system all render this impossible.[52]

However, Eckstein is unduly pessimistic, for elements of Maoist development ideology and praxis *have* exerted an influence outside China. Some of the proponents of meeting basic needs, discussed in the next chapter, cite China's relative success in the pursuit of growth with equity.[53] More specifically, the World Health Organisation has endorsed the ideas behind China's 'barefoot doctor' programme and is encouraging increased use of medical auxiliaries in the rural areas of other developing countries. Meanwhile labour-intensive rural capital formation, albeit wage-based, has received increased emphasis in a number of countries since the mid-1970s (including India, Bangladesh and Kenya[54]). In debates on the development of rural non-farm production and employment the Chinese experience of 'walking on two legs' is frequently cited. While the economic efficiency of particular lines of non-farm production developed in China have been questioned (for example the backyard steel furnaces[55] and, more recently, the biogas plants) the principle of mobilising slack labour and physical resources to produce both locally needed consumer goods and small-scale producer goods as well as handicrafts for export is now increasingly widely emphasised.[56] Also, the recent literature on farming systems research and rural poverty emphasises the need to go out and learn from farmers about the nature and rationale of their current production processes, and the most pressing constraints that they face, before designing research programmes – a practice that became official policy in China in the last decade of the Maoist era.[57]

SUMMARY AND CONCLUSION

The distinctive characteristics of the Maoist paradigm derive from a particular perception of the goal of development and of the development path by which this state is to be achieved. Key features of the paradigm are as follows:

1. The simultaneous pursuit of economic, social and political development towards the ultimate goal of communism.
2. Pursuit of this attempt under the guiding aegis of a single political party (the Chinese Communist Party).

3. Pursuit of an economic development strategy which assigns priority to development of heavy industry and is based on a pragmatic search for the appropriate intersectoral allocation of investment given this objective.
4. Within this perspective, a refusal to marginalise agriculture.
5. Exploitation of the potential contribution to development of both labour- and capital-intensive technologies, and of small- and large-scale production.
6. Recognition of the persistent need to sustain mass support partly through continuing improvements in material welfare.
7. Emphasis, especially in the early stages of development, on the promotion of self-reliance at all levels of economic activity.

The Maoist paradigm is, in all key respects but one, internally consistent. The problem of how to mobilise, on the one hand, and control on the other, mass vigilance against the entrenchment in power of a new bureaucratic and politically dominant class, insensitive to the needs of the masses, had still not been resolved at the time of Mao's death. Moreover, without mass enfranchisement it is difficult to see how this could be done. This, however, takes us beyond the confines of economic strategy and policy. With respect to these, the model is internally consistent and, at the same time, pragmatic in its search for the correct (and shifting) balance in sectoral resource allocation and choice of techniques. What the Maoist model is not, however, is an optimising model (but no economic model is when applied in the real world, and it is a delusion to think otherwise). In Maoist economic theory and policy, a crucial missing ingredient is, as in other planned economy models, a sound basis for ensuring enterprise efficiency. On the other hand, the Maoist paradigm, despite the micro-economic lacuna, proved remarkably successful as a basis for mass mobilisation for economic development in a low-income economy, combining economic growth and structural change with a relatively high degree of equity. To what extent this was due to the particular characteristics of China's cultural tradition, while it is a highly pertinent issue, is still a matter of debate.

APPENDIX

Summary of key policy changes in China since 1978

Since 1978, wide-ranging economic reforms have been introduced in China. Overall, the new economic policy mix contains elements of continuity (in, for example, the development of small-, medium- and large-scale industry), of accelerated – and more radical – change (in, for example, the opening-up of the economy to international trade, and foreign investment and credits) and dramatic breaks with the past. There has been a clear-cut rejection of the Maoist emphasis on the development of production relations – vividly illustrated in agricultural decollectivisation – combined with a switch to much greater reliance on individual incentives and growing emphasis on profitability as a gauge of economic efficiency. Administered decentralisation has also been replaced by attempts to achieve co-ordinated decentralisation through increasing reliance on the market (both free and restricted).

Meanwhile, the education sector has experienced a return to selectivity and emphasis on professional standards, and a downgrading of political education.

With respect to the development of production relations, key policy reversals include the following:

1. Increased emphasis on material incentives.
2. Disbandment of worker-management committees in industry.
3. The break-up of the communes and switch to direct contracts with individual households to fulfil state quotas for agriculture, and to an increased role for free markets for surplus agricultural produce.
4. Official sanction of the development of small-scale individual and co-operative enterprise in trade and production, in both urban and rural areas.

Analyses of these and other policy reforms are provided in a range of recent publications including Ellman (1986) and Riskin (1987). As Ellman emphasises, Maoism has been replaced not by a coherent new development perspective, but by the search for one. The principles of market socialism have not yet been fully established, either in China or elsewhere.

NOTES

1. I am indebted to Jack Gray for his helpful comments on this chapter.
2. The Stalinist perspective is not given comparable attention in this study because it has exerted much less direct influence on the development debate despite, indeed perhaps in part *because*, of the influence of Feldman's work on the design of the Mahalanobis model which governed the underlying strategy of India's second

five year plan (see the Appendix to Chapter 4, where certain parallels between some of the theoretical content of the Stalinist perspective and that of the paradigm of the expanding capitalist nucleus were also pointed out).

3. While the Chinese Communist Party had assumed that this group owned 70 per cent of agricultural land, Schran (1969) has estimated that they probably held about 46 per cent. See Schran, 1969: 14–17 and *State Statistical Bureau*, 1960: 128 cited in Schran, *op.cit.*: 14.

4. Lippit, 1974, cited in Selden and Lippit, *op.cit.*: 17.

5. From 1949 to 1952 grain output rose at over 7 per cent per annum and from 1952 to 1957 at 3.4 per cent (Selden and Lippit, *op.cit.*: 46).

6. Both defined on p. 19.

7. Marx, 1973, quoted by Selden in Selden and Lippit, *op.cit.*: 35. Emphasis in original.

8. Lenin 1959, quoted by Selden in Selden and Lippit, *op.cit.*: 37.

9. See Mao Tsetung, 1977, *passim*, including introduction by Peck.

10. Much has been written about the background of Mao and the evolution of his political thought. See for example Ch'en, 1969, Peck in Mao Tsetung, 1977 and Li Jui, 1977.

11. Heavy industries are those that produce capital and intermediate goods. Their main components are mining, cement production, power production, steel and machinery and petrochemicals.

12. Investment in a large scale heavy industrial project may take several years for construction and installation and several more before it begins to generate a surplus.

13. Mao Tsetung in *Peking Review* (Vol. 20, No. 1, January 1977: 11); reproduced by Peck in Mao Tsetung, 1977.

14. Jack Gray, personal communication, February 1988.

15. See Selden and Lippit, *op.cit.*: 66 and below p. 240.

16. See Peck *et al.* in Mao Tsetung, 1977: 30.

17. In contrast, Stalinist development policy concentrated upon the development of large-scale plant using modern technology. The theoretical justification underpinning this concentration lay in the greater scope for co-ordinated central planning that is thereby provided.

18. Selden in Selden and Lippit, *op.cit.*: 54.

19. *Ibid.*: 57.

20. *Ibid.*: 56.

21. *Ibid.*: 55.

22. Reiitsu in Selden and Lippit, *op.cit.*

23. See, e.g., Gurley, 1975; Sigurdson, 1975; Riskin, 1978; and the bibliography given by Gray in Gray and White, 1982: 333, footnote 2.

24. See Lampton, 1978.

25. See Schran, 1969: 149.

26. *Ibid.*

27. See Lardy, unpublished, cited in Selden and Lippit, 1982: 18.

28. See also Riskin, 1987: 242–248.

29. See pp. 249–50.

30. By, for example, expanded use of communal mess halls and children's nurseries; see Choh-ming Li in Schurmann and Schell, 1968: 201 and 206.

31. See Eckstein, 1977: 91.

32. See Robinson, 1976: 33.

33. See Sprague, 1975: 551.

34. See Gardner in Gray and White, *op.cit.*: 284.

35. Mao Tsetung, 1977.
36. See, e.g., Paine, *op.cit.* and Nolan and White in Gray and White, 1982: 178, 9.
37. See also Wortman 1975: 15, who supports Chinese and FAO estimates that the growth of food grain output from 1957–71 exceeded population growth, permitting attainment of self-sufficiency by the latter date.
38. See e.g. Ellman 1986: 426; Riskin 1987: 250.
39. In 1980, according to World Bank estimates, some 33 per cent of the Third World's total population (excluding China) were living in absolute poverty (World Bank 1981: 18). For India, estimates for the late 1970s range from 33 per cent (Sinha *et al.*, 1979: 19) to 40 per cent (Bardhan, 1984: 2).
40. Paine, *op.cit.*: 1349.
41. See Ma Hong, 1983: 22; Selden and Lippit, *op.cit.*: 19; and Gray in Gray and White, *op.cit.*: 297.
42. Ma Hong, *op.cit.*: 24; and Selden and Lippit, *op.cit.*: 19–21.
43. See. e.g., Nove and Nuti, 1972: Part IV.
44. For example, during the Great Leap not all communes moved equally far in the direction of distributing income on the basis of need. Furthermore it seems reasonable to suppose that factors which were variable between communes, such as leadership quality and sense of common purpose, may have made such experiments more acceptable in some communes than in others.
45. See p. 232.
46. While Mao's critics blamed him for the errors committed at this time, it is noteworthy that Mao also acknowledged these, both in the sphere of development of small-scale production technology and the premature transformation of production relations, urging that it was necessary to rectify these errors and learn from them.
47. Indeed, in 1985 agricultural output fell by almost seven per cent. See Ellman, 1986: 427 and 441.
48. See Paine, *op.cit.*: 1360.
49. Mao Tsetung, 1977: 35.
50. I.e. errors admitted and rectified by Mao and his colleagues, such as the errors of the Great Leap Forward.
51. Lardy, 1978: 186 *et seq.* also argues that specific historical and cultural elements that provide the foundations of China's development model considerably reduce its relevance elsewhere.

52. 'For instance, in the case of India, transferability may be impeded not only by its vastly different economic system but by the lack of linguistic unity, the persistence of the caste system and a number of other differences in the traditions.'

   Later, Eckstein observes

   'it is also very doubtful that the kind of spirit, motivation and social controls prevailing in China can be transferred to the entirely different systematic settings of other developing countries.'

   Eckstein, *op.cit.*: 316 and 317.

53. See, e.g., Singh, 1979.
54. See, e.g., Dandekar in Robinson (ed.), 1983, Vol. 2 and Ghai, Godfrey and Lisk, 1979.
55. Albeit now revived profitably by peasant private enterprise! (Jack Gray, personal communication, February 1988.)
56. See, e.g., UNIDO, 1978.
57. See Sprague, 1975: 551 and Wortman, 1975: 20.

REFERENCES

Bardhan, P., *The Political Economy of India*, (Blackwell, 1984).

Bettelheim, C., *Cultural Revolution and Industrial Organisation in China*, (Monthly Review Press, 1974).

Ch'en, J., (ed.), *Mao*, (Prentice Hall, 1969).

Choh-ming Li, 'Economic development', *China Quarterly*, (Vol. 1, January–March 1960); reprinted in *Communist China*, eds. Schurmann, F. and Schell, O., (Penguin, 1968).

Dandekar, K.,'Tackling unemployment in Maharastra through the employment guarantee scheme', in *Employment Policy in a Developing Country*, Vol. 2, ed. Robinson, A., *et al*. (Macmillan, 1983).

Eckstein, A., *China's Economic Revolution*, (Cambridge, 1977).

Ellman, M., 'Economic reform in China', *International Affairs*, (Vol. 62, No. 3, Summer 1986).

Fei Hsiao-Tung and Chang Chih-I, *Earthbound China*, (University of Chicago, 1945).

Gardner, J., 'New directions in educational policy', in *China's New Development Strategy*, ed. Gray, J. and White, G., (Academic Press, 1982).

Ghai, D., Godfrey, M. and Lisk, F., *Planning for Basic Needs in Kenya*, (ILO, 1979).

Gray, J., 'Rural enterprise in China, 1977–79', in *China's New Development Strategy*, eds. Gray, J., and White, G., (Academic Press, 1982).

Gray, J., 'Conclusion', in *China's New Development Strategy*, eds. Gray, J. and White, G.,(Academic Press, 1982).

Gurley, J., 'Rural development in China and the lessons to be learned from it', *World Development*, (Vol. 3, Nos. 7 and 8, July–August 1975).

Hayek, F., (ed.), *Collectivist Economic Planning*, (Routledge, 1935).

Joint Economic Committee, Congress of the United States, *China, A Reassessment of the Economy*, (US Government Printing Office, Washington, 1975).

Joint Publications Research Service, *Miscellany of Mao Tsetung's Thoughts (1949–1968)*, Part I, (National Technical Information Service, U.S. Dept. of Commerce, 20 February 1974).

Lampton, D., 'Development and health care: is China's medical programme exportable?', *World Development*, (Vol. 6, No. 5, May 1978).

Lardy, N., *Economic Growth and Distribution in China*, (Cambridge 1978).

Lenin, V., 'The tasks of the proletariat in our revolution' in *Alliance of the Working Class and the Peasantry*, (Foreign Languages Publishing House, Moscow, 1959).

Li Jui, *The Early Revolutionary Activities of Mao Tsetung*, (Sharpe, 1977).

Lippit, V., *Land Reform and Economic Development in China*, (Sharpe, 1974).

Lippit, V., 'Socialist development in China', in *The Transition to Socialism in China*, eds. Selden, M. and Lippit, V., (Sharpe, New York and Croom Helm, London, 1982).

Magdoff, H., 'China contrasts with USSR', *Monthly Review*, (1975).

Ma Hong, *New Strategy for China's Economy*, (New World Press, 1983).

Mao Tsetung, *Selected Works*, (Foreign Languages Press, Peking, 1965).

Mao Tsetung, *A Critique of Soviet Economics*, (Monthly Review Press, 1977).

Marx, K., *Grundrisse: Foundations of the Critique of Political Economy*, (Vintage, 1973).

von Mises, L., *Critique of Interventionism*, (Arlington House, 1977; first published in German 1929).

Nove, A. and Nuti, D. (eds.), *Socialist Economics*, (Penguin, 1972).

Nolan, P, and White, G., 'The distributive implications of China's new agricultural policies,' in *China's New Development Strategy*, eds. Gray, J. and White, G., (Academic Press, 1982).

Paine, S., 'Development with growth: a quarter century of socialist transformation in China', *Economic and Political Weekly*, (Vol. XI, Special Number, Nos. 31, 32 and 33, August 1976).

Peck, J., 'Introduction' in *A Critique of Soviet Economics*, Mao Tsetung, (Monthly Review Press, 1977).

Reiitsu Kojima, 'Accumulation, technology, and China's economic development', in *The Transition to Socialism in China*, eds. Selden, M. and Lippit, V., (Sharpe, New York and Croom Helm, London, 1982).

Riskin, C., 'Political conflict and rural industrialisation in China', *World Development*, (Vol. 6, No. 5, May 1978).

Riskin, C., *China's Political Economy: The Quest for Development Since 1949*, (Oxford, 1987).

Robinson, J., *Economic Management in China*, (Anglo-Chinese Educational Institute, Modern China Series No. 4, 1976).

Schran, P., *The Development of Chinese Agriculture, 1950–1959*, (University of Illinois, 1969).

Schurmann F. and Schell, O. (eds.), *Communist China*, (Penguin, 1968).

Selden, M., 'Co-operation and conflict: co-operative and collective formation in China's countryside', in *The Transition to Socialism in China*, eds. Selden, M. and Lippit, V., (Sharpe, New York, and Croom Helm, London, 1982).

Selden, M. and Lippit, V. (eds.), *The Transition to Socialism in China*, (Sharpe, New York, and Croom Helm, London, 1982).

Sigurdson, J., 'Rural industrialisation in China', *World Development*, (Vol. 3, Nos. 7 and 8, July–August 1975).

Singh, A., 'Basic needs approach to development versus NIEO', *World Development*, (Vol. 7, No. 6, June 1979).

Sinha, R., Pearson, P., Kadekodi, G. and Gregory, M., *Income Distribution and Basic Needs in India*, (Croom Helm, 1979).

Sprague, G.F., 'Agriculture in China', *Science*, (Vol. 188, 9 May 1975).

United Nations Industrial Development Organisation, *Industrialisation and Rural Development*, (UNIDO, New York, 1978).

World Bank, *World Development Report 1981*, (Oxford University Press, 1981).

Wortman, S., 'Agriculture in China', *Scientific American*, (Vol. 232, No. 6, June 1975).

9 · THE BASIC NEEDS PARADIGM[1]

The background to the emergence of the basic needs paradigm and its key features were both summarised in Chapter 3.[2] Part of the purpose of this chapter is to elaborate those summaries. However, it also aims to distinguish the main approaches to meeting basic needs that have emerged in the literature and to justify the classification of the more radical of these as representing a distinctive new perspective on development. For while the key features of the background to the emergence of meeting basic needs as a planning objective, and of the ensuing debate on its feasibility, are widely acknowledged, to affirm the existence of the paradigm itself is to court controversy. While Paul Streeten, one of the leading writers on basic needs, has noted the paradigm change implicit in a pure basic needs approach to development,[3] many writers on basic needs have chosen to focus simply on a basic needs *approach* in development planning and policy formation. The reasons for this include, as Streeten points out, a preoccupation among some of the proponents of meeting basic needs with minimising the extent to which the adoption of measures for doing so entails any change in previous approaches to development planning and policy formation.[4] This concern is, as we shall see, clearly apparent in some of the literature.

In this chapter it is argued that within the literature on meeting basic needs it is possible to identify two main perspectives on meeting basic needs, one of which is located in a new paradigm – a novel way in which development economists view the world. The other is explicitly reformist in character, and is not based on a paradigm switch. In the case of the former, there has been a significant shift not only in the perception of the nature of development, but in perception of the key parameters in the development process and in the theorisation of this process.

THE BACKGROUND TO THE EMERGENCE OF BASIC NEEDS CONCERNS

The redefinition of development

In earlier chapters we have noted the growing concern that emerged during the 1960s Development Decade with respect to the apparent absence of a trickle-down effect from economic growth.[5] This concern was voiced by, *inter alia*, Dudley Seers, first in his Presidential address to the Society for International Development in 1969 and again in a now widely quoted article published in 1972.

> The questions to ask about a country's development are therefore: what has been happening to poverty? What has been happening to unemployment? What has been happening to inequality? If all three of these have declined from high levels, then beyond doubt this has been a period of development for the country concerned. If one or two of these central problems have been growing worse, especially if all three have, it would be strange to call the result 'development', even if per capita income doubled.
>
> (Seers, 1972.)

Yet growth, Seers argued, was still a necessary precondition for sustained development – for how else could mass welfare continue to rise over time?

In the 1950s and 1960s Seers, like other structuralists, appears to have assumed that if a sustained process of modern sector growth and structural diversification could be established, this would lead to a steady incorporation of labour from the traditional sector into higher productivity and higher-wage occupations. In other words, he accepted the classical structuralist definition of development (see p. 49). It is important, therefore, not to underestimate the significance of this changed definition, introduced by someone who was in a position to influence both development theory and practice. (Seers was at the time Director of the Institute of Development Studies at Sussex, and in the early 1970s also played a leading role in three major ILO employment missions – to Sri Lanka, Colombia and Kenya).

It is difficult to avoid the conclusion that this new definition of development was stimulated in part by the ferment of debate in development economics in the late 1960s and early 1970s, not least at IDS, Sussex itself. This debate in turn was largely stimulated by the neo-Marxist school and other sympathetic radicals, chiefly among the younger, rising generation of students of development and underdevelopment, who were outspoken in their condemnation of what they saw as the inequity of contemporary patterns of change in the non-socialist Third World.

The growth-development divergence: the accumulating evidence

While the United Nations Research Institute on Social Development (UNRISD) had, from its foundation in 1962, been concerned with the generation of a range of social development indicators, it was only in the early 1970s that attention really focused on statistical measures of other aspects of development than economic growth. In 1973 Robert McNamara placed the weight of the World Bank behind the growing concern at the outcome of policies that focused chiefly on GNP increase while ignoring their distributional implications.

> Despite a decade of unprecedented increase in the gross national product of the developing countries, the poorest segments of their population have received relatively little benefit. Nearly 800 million individuals – 40 per cent out of a total of two billion – survive on incomes estimated (in US purchasing power) at 30 cents per day in conditions of malnutrition, illiteracy and squalor. They are suffering poverty in the absolute sense. . . Among 40 developing countries for which data are available, the upper 20 per cent of the population receives 55 per cent of national income in the typical country, while the lowest 20 per cent of the population receives 5 per cent . . . policies aimed primarily at accelerating economic growth, in most developing countries, have benefited mainly the upper 40 per cent of the population and the allocation of public services and investment funds has tended to strengthen rather than to offset this trend.
>
> (McNamara 1973: 10–11.)

At about this time several major studies concluded that the dominant trend is for economic inequality to increase as growth occurs in poorer countries. Adelman and Morris (1973), Paukert (1973) and Ahluwalia (1976) can all be interpreted as broadly confirming Kuznets' earlier hypothesis that income inequality increases (i.e. the Gini coefficient rises) during the early stages of economic growth.[6] However, these studies also showed that the predominant trend was not uniform across countries.

Adelman and Morris pinpointed certain factors which tend to mitigate the trend towards rising inequality, although in these cases it is the middle, rather than the lowest, income groups that benefit. Paukert's cross-section data revealed wide variations in degrees of inequality at different per capita income levels: so much so that some countries in the middle income (rising inequality) range not only fall below the mean inequality measure for their class, but for lower income classes as well. According to Paukert's data the trend towards rising inequality is not inevitable,[7] although he does not emphasise this. This point was, however, to be emphasised later in the decade and in the 1980s by advocates of meeting basic needs.

Meanwhile Adelman and Morris' findings (the results of a cross-section study of 43 developing countries) also led them to conclude that economic growth was not only associated with increasing inequality but with a worsening of absolute poverty, particularly in the early stages of economic development. Indeed,

> Even in the last phase of the stage before take-off, with relatively high levels of development and a capacity for more broadly based economic growth, the poorest segments of the population typically benefit from economic growth

only when the government plays an important economic role and when widespread efforts are made to improve the human resource base.

(Adelman and Morris, 1973: 181.)

However, these findings remain more controversial. They are not, for example, supported by Ahluwalia's 1976 study.[8]

New measures of development

Dissatisfaction with the rate of growth of GDP as a measure of development led to the search for alternative measures. One approach was based on an attempt to revise the conventional estimation of GDP growth in such a way as to either give equal weighting to a given percentage increase in income for all income groups, or give an explicitly greater weighting to a given percentage increase for the lower income groups. Both these possibilities were outlined by Ahluwalia and Chenery in Chenery *et al.* (1974).

Assuming a division by total income level into quintiles of the total population of any country, the rate of growth of income of each group, g_i,

can be taken to measure the rate of increase of its social welfare over the specified period. The rate of increase in welfare of the society as a whole can then be defined as a weighted sum of the rate of growth of income of each group:

$$G = w_1 g_1 + w_2 g_2 + w_3 g_3 + w_4 g_4 + w_5 g_5$$

where G is an index of the rate of growth of total social welfare and w_i is the weight assigned to group i.

A summary measure of this type enables us to set development targets and monitor development performance not simply in terms of growth of GNP but in terms of the distributional pattern of income growth. The weights for each income class reflect the social premium on generating growth at each income level. . . As the weight on a particular quintile is raised, our index of the increase in social welfare reflects to a greater extent the growth of income in that group. Thus if we were only concerned with the poorest quintile we would set $w_5 = 1$ and all other $w_i = 0$, so that growth in welfare would be measured only by g_5 . . .

In these terms the commonly used index of performance – the growth of GNP – is a special case in which the weights on the growth of income of each quintile are simply the income share of each quintile in total income. The shortcomings of such an index can be seen from the following income shares for the different quintiles, which are typical for underdeveloped countries.

Quintiles	1	2	3	4	5	Total
Share in total income	53%	22%	13%	7%	5%	100%

The combined share of the top 40 per cent of the population amounts to about three-quarters of the total GNP. Thus the rate of growth of GNP measures essentially the income growth of the upper 40 per cent and is not much affected by what happens to the income of the remaining 60 per cent of the population.

An alternative welfare principle that has considerable appeal is to give equal social value to a one per cent increase in income for any member of society. On this principle, the weights in equation 1 should be proportional to the number of people in each group and would therefore be equal for each quintile.

(Ahluwalia and Chenery, in Chenery *et al.*, 1974: 39, 40.)

However, while Ahluwalia and Chenery's proposals have been widely quoted in the literature, they have not been applied in practice, presumably due to the following factors:

1. The political difficulty of agreeing weightings.
2. Concern at the potential confusion that might arise in the comparison of various GDP estimates incorporating different weightings.
3. The fact that data by income group do not exist (or are difficult to obtain).[9]

One subsequent approach has been to seek to generate composite measures of development in which changes in each of three variables (growth inequality and absolute poverty) are measured separately. For example, inequality is usually measured in terms of the income shares of different deciles or quintiles or in terms of the Gini coefficient,[10] and absolute poverty in terms of the numbers living below some predetermined poverty line. This approach has allowed governments to continue to publish GDP growth data (conventionally estimated) even while many were still seeking to generate the relevant information to estimate the other performance measures.[11] However, in time dissatisfaction also grew with the focus on these two supplementary measures, partly because of lack of data on absolute poverty, partly because of problems in agreeing the cut-off income for estimating the number affected by absolute poverty and partly because this itself was increasingly perceived to be a multifaceted condition ill-expressed in a single figure. The early and mid-1970s also saw an upsurge in research on the impact on inequality and poverty of public sector policy and expenditure in different fields of social policy – most notably education and health.[12] The findings of such studies contributed to a growing emphasis on a range of specific basic needs which should be met for all before absolute poverty can be said to have been eliminated. In conjunction with this there has emerged a still broader range of development indicators (see pp. 267–9).

The search for a new development strategy

The recognition that successful pursuit of economic growth had often been associated with rising inequality, and possibly with rising absolute poverty too, led in the early 1970s to the search for a new development strategy. Presaged in the 1972 ILO report *Employment, Incomes and Equality: a Strategy for Increasing Productive Employment in Kenya*, one such strategy was articulated in the joint study by personnel of the World Bank and IDS Sussex entitled *Redistribution with Growth*[13] – the name given to the new strategy.

However, as noted in Chapter 3,[14] a key feature of both the above studies was their continuing acceptance of certain key assumptions of the paradigm of the expanding capitalist nucleus. Thus the most dynamic sector of the economy is the modern sector, and within this it is the rich, and presumably rich capitalists in particular, that are assumed to have the highest propensity to save and invest. Any redistribution of income from rich to poor is therefore bound to slow down economic growth.

The problem confronted in *Redistribution with Growth* is how to minimise the growth:equity conflict. The strategy recommended is continued pursuit of modern sector growth combined with limited resource redistribution (some two per cent of GNP annually) for investment in various forms designed to raise the productivity and incomes of the poor in both wage- and self-employment.[15]

The focus of *Redistribution with Growth* was on reducing inequality through raising the income share of the poorest 40 per cent. However, it was quickly recognised by some that a possible consequence of focusing on such a target was that policy-makers would concentrate upon raising incomes at the top end of the poverty range, while the worst-off experienced little or no improvement in welfare. Concern about this contributed directly to the focus on the need for a direct attack on severe deprivation that emerged in the development literature in 1975 and 1976.

Meanwhile a more dramatic break with previous thinking on development strategy came, also in 1974, with the publication of Lefeber's paper 'On the paradigm for economic development'. Lefeber broadened the discussion of income distribution in order to analyse its implications for the structure of demand and the incentive to invest in underdeveloped economies. A key proposition in Lefeber's paper is that Third World countries cannot replicate the growth path of the now industrially advanced ones because they do not have access to either the overseas investment outlets or the expanding external markets that were available to the latter. Likewise the outlets for migration which both helped to raise per capita income at home (as the labour supply contracted, the marginal product of those who remained rose), and to develop new export markets through settlement of resource-rich areas, are also not available.

Two consequences follow from the absence of these conditions which formerly favoured growth. Firstly, contemporary underdeveloped countries

will increasingly have to rely on their own capacity to generate savings and resources for development. This, of course, is no contradiction to development theory which, in any case, calls for a high average and marginal savings rate. But there is a paradox here. For unless there is export demand for the goods and services produced in an economy, the demand which motivates investment must come from domestic sources. Thus, on the one hand, there is need for increased savings and, on the other hand, for increased consumption or other forms of absorption.

(Lefeber in Mitra (ed.), 1974: 163.)

Lefeber accepts the traditional assumption concerning the relative savings propensities of rich and poor. His preoccupation is therefore to find ways of expanding mass demand in predominantly rural economies without lowering savings. To achieve this he advocates as a first step land redistribution and promotion of labour-intensive public works in the rural sector along Maoist lines; after this agriculture and industry must develop symbiotically.[16]

While Lefeber advocated a strategy based upon the Chinese model of agricultural collectivisation, Adelman (1975) argued for a similar strategy based upon a different model. She urged that Third World countries should switch to a 'strategy of depauperisation', which would provide the basis for rapid growth. The strategy would be implemented in three stages:

1. Radical asset redistribution, focusing on land.
2. Massive accumulation of human capital.
3. Rapid human-resource-intensive growth.

Adelman cites five countries as examples of this strategy: Israel, Japan, South Korea, Singapore and Taiwan.[17]

Priority for basic needs

In 1975 the Dag Hammarskjöld Foundation Report also urged that first priority in development policy and programmes should be assigned to meeting the basic needs of all, and, hence, the elimination of absolute poverty. These proposals were taken up and presented, with a more elaborate discussion of the policy implications, in the report of the ILO Director General to the 1976 World Employment Conference. It was now that the concept of 'basic needs' was brought to the forefront of the development debate. The report identifies four categories of basic needs and proposes the year 2000 as the target date for meeting these (ILO, 1978: 6). The four categories are:

1. The minimum requirements of a family for personal consumption – food, shelter, clothing.
2. Access to essential services, such as safe drinking water, sanitation, transport, health and education.
3. Availability of an adequately remunerated job for each person able and willing to work.
4. 'The satisfaction of needs of a more qualitative nature: a healthy, humane and satisfying environment, and popular participation in the making of

decisions that affect the lives and livelihood of the people and individual freedoms'.

(ILO, 1978: 7.)

For a few developing countries (e.g. China and Tanzania) these proposals represented endorsement of existing goals. In India, too, part of the planning community had been urging adoption of similar priorities, albeit with limited success.[18] However, for the majority of Third World countries implementation of the ILO proposals would require, in order to be effective, significant changes in government perspective and policy.

In the Programme of Action adopted by member governments of the ILO at the end of the World Employment Conference, emphasis was given to meeting the first two categories of basic need. However, the Programme also notes the importance of popular participation in decision-making concerning these policies, and that in all countries

> freely chosen employment enters into a basic-needs policy both as a means and as an end. . . It provides an income to the employed, and gives the individual a feeling of self-respect, dignity and of being a worthy member of society.
>
> (ILO, 1978: 182.)

It was unanimously agreed that all participating governments would seek to ensure the universal provision of all four categories of basic need by the year 2000. The values expressed in this agreement have provided the seeds of the first western paradigm geared to the explicit and integrated pursuit of economic, political and social development.

EARLY CRITICISMS OF PROPOSALS FOR MEETING BASIC NEEDS

The case for meeting basic needs presented by the Dag Hammarskjöld Foundation in 1975 and the ILO in 1976 was primarily a moral/ideological one. However, early criticisms of the proposal put pressure on its proponents to justify more fully both the arguments for doing so and the proposed means of achieving this. These criticisms are summarised at this stage because, being raised soon after the publication of the basic needs proposals, they helped to focus much of the subsequent debate. They were as follows:

1. The concept of basic needs lacks the operational precision needed in a planning objective.
2. The pursuit of a basic needs development strategy would conflict with growth maximisation and entail perpetuation of economic and technological backwardness.
3. In order to provide employment to the poor within a short time period, developing countries would become locked into perpetual emphasis on

primary production, using primitive, labour-intensive technology.
4. The public-sector resource cost would be prohibitive.
5. Emphasis on basic needs represents an attempt by the North to divert attention away from the South's requests for a number of other changes as part of the introduction of a new international economic order (NIEO).
6. The theoretical arguments adduced in favour of a basic needs strategy represent an intellectual miscellany drawn from various schools of economic thought and have no logical coherence.
7. Meeting basic needs in non-socialist underdeveloped countries is politically non-viable because the landowning classes and national *comprador* bourgeoisies will not release the necessary resources.

For all proponents of meeting basic needs it was necessary to demonstrate, in response to criticism 1, the feasibility of setting operational targets. The main tenor of the response to this criticism is therefore briefly reviewed in the next section.

BASIC NEEDS AS AN OPERATIONAL TARGET

The discussion of how performance in meeting basic needs can be assessed has generally started from acceptance of the proposition that the purpose of development is to provide everyone with the opportunity for a full life, and that meeting basic needs is an essential prerequisite for this. There is also broad consensus that certain basic physical, intellectual and psychological needs are common to all people, and that their fulfilment constitutes an essential precondition for a full life. The most important of these needs are for adequate nutrition, shelter, fuel, clothing, clean water, sanitation, health care, basic education, productive employment (for all willing and able to work) and popular participation in decisions concerning the provision of these needs. However, given the acceptance of a core list of basic needs, the interlinked questions remain of how performance in meeting these both can and should be assessed. Two issues that have been debated in this context are whether performance should be measured in terms of 'inputs' or 'outputs', and whether it is possible to identify a single indicator of basic needs performance.

Morris and Liser (1977) and Grant (1978) argue that certain variables are unambiguously sought as end results or *outputs* of the development process. They identify three:

1. Decreased infant mortality.
2. Increased life expectancy.
3. Increased literacy.

Most other development indicators such as nutrition, health services, etc., are, they claim, *inputs* into the attainment of these end results, and their use as development indicators is invalid because the input-output relationship is not constant.

However, an opposing view is that this conceptualisation of development is itself invalid because, platitudinous though it may seem to say so, development is a complex process in which many variables act and react upon one another. Even variables such as improved health and literacy which the Overseas Development Council team see as unambiguous end results are in fact inputs into further development – a healthy individual is more productive than an unhealthy one, a literate individual can assimilate and respond to functional information presented in a low-cost form unavailable to an illiterate. Meanwhile it is also questionable whether increased longevity should automatically be regarded as a welfare gain, since its value depends on the quality of life experienced.

None the less, a number of writers accept the input-output distinction and have moved a step further to consider whether one can identify a single indicator of basic needs performance that would be analogous to GDP as an indicator of aggregate ouput performance. Various proposals have been made. First, Morris and Liser proposed a Physical Quality of Life Indicator (PQLI) based on the three 'outputs' just specified – life expectancy at age one, infant mortality and literacy – and assigning equal weights to each. One potential attraction of the PQLI is that the necessary data are available for a large number of countries. However, it is subject to a number of conceptual weaknesses. As Streeten observes:

> The term 'quality of life' is perhaps a misnomer, since what is really being measured is effectiveness in reducing mortality and raising literacy. Life expectancy measures the length, not the quality of life . . . Most important, the weighting system of the PQLI is arbitrary, and there is no rationale for giving equal weights to literacy, infant mortality, and life expectancy at age one.
>
> (Streeten, 1981: 88.)

Stewart (1985) proposes an even simpler basic needs indicator, life expectancy at birth, which she justifies on the grounds that it is highly correlated both with infant mortality and literacy – hence it will stand as proxy for both of these. This indicator is however subject to the same criticism of life expectancy already noted.

Meanwhile, others have argued that the single variable with the most basic impact on the quality of life is per capita calory intake, and hence if a single variable is selected as a focal indicator of basic needs performance it should be this.

To date none of these proposals has achieved widespread acceptance as adequately encapsulating basic needs performance. Instead, the dominant trend is to use a limited but composite set of indicators along the lines proposed by Hicks and Streeten (1979).[19] These authors specify six essential

Table 9.1   The Hicks/Streeten list of suggested indicators of basic needs performance

Need	Performance indicator(s)
Health	Life expectancy at birth.
Education	Literacy; Primary school enrolment (as per cent of population aged 5–14).
Food	Calorie supply per head or calorie supply as a per cent of requirements.*
Water supply	Infant mortality (per thousand births); Per cent of population with access to potable water.
Sanitation	Infant mortality (per thousand births);** Per cent of population with access to sanitation facilities.
Housing	None.

Notes:
* Since 1979, uncertainties among nutritionists as to levels of calorie requirements have led FAO to drop the per cent of calories with respect to requirements as a published indicator of nutritional level and to refer simply to total calories available per caput (see FAO, *Fifth World Food Survey*, 1985).
** The infant mortality rate is suggested as an indicator for both water supply and sanitation.
Source: Hicks and Streeten, 1979: 578.

basic needs and then seek to identify optimal indicators of each, emphasising results (outputs) where possible. The resultant list of indicators is reproduced in Table 9. 2.

With respect to housing Streeten and Hicks observe that the only readily available indicator is people per room, 'but this does not really capture much of the quality of housing'. Others have suggested that square metres of floor space per person might be a preferable measure.

Cornia (1984) also distinguishes a third category of basic needs indicators. These are *process* indicators which measure the availability of public services. The types of measures used include the numbers reached by different services, staffing levels and levels of public expenditure. The main problem with process indicators is that usually they give no indication of the quality of service provided and hence of its impact. However, when analysed in conjunction with other indicators they do help to build up a fuller picture of what has been happening over time to basic needs provision (see Cornia, 1984).

An application of the general approach advocated by Streeten and Hicks can be found in the World Development Reports published annually by the World Bank. Many would concur that these measures provide a useful basis both for the assessment of individual country performance over time in meeting basic needs and for cross-country comparisons. However, as with GDP itself, there is an outstanding need to improve accuracy of estimation. The necessary yardsticks exist, but their application could be improved.

MEETING BASIC NEEDS: ALTERNATIVE APPROACHES

In its orginal formulation, meeting basic needs was advocated for its own sake: the provision of minimum levels of personal consumption and access to social services which should be universally regarded as a human right, essential to a decent life, represented a choice a priori, on ideological and humanitarian grounds. Today many proponents of meeting basic needs continue to regard this as a moral imperative (see, e.g., Streeten, 1981).

However, a number of the early criticisms of the 1976 ILO proposals (see pp. 266-7.) provided the impetus to strengthen the case for meeting basic needs in order to win over some of the sceptics. Essentially, two approaches were adopted.

In the literature on meeting basic needs, a division of opinion has emerged. Some writers concur with Minhas that

> The main problem is one of focusing efforts on the absolutely poor to increase their productivity and therewith their levels of living. The provision of minimal basic needs of social consumption through collective means is better seen as a useful supplement and incentive to the poorest to increase their efforts to help themselves to grow.

(Minhas in Hill (ed.), 1979: 92.)

Others argue that policy efforts should concentrate primarily on the provision of basic public services. While Streeten (1981) is at times ambiguous on this point, for much of this text he adopts the latter position. Improvement in the provision of basic public services to the poor is justified as investment in human capital, in an argument that harks back to the emphasis in Denison (1967) on the importance of the 'residual factor' in explaining growth rate variations between countries. In what follows, the latter approach is reviewed first.

The arguments for improved public services and investment in human capital

The 'improved public services' approach has generally sought to minimise the extent to which a focus on meeting basic needs requires radical policy change while, as just noted, emphasising the potentially positive effects on economic performance of improvements in a country's stock of human capital. The humanitarian aspect of such improvements is also reiterated. Advocates of this approach also seek to demonstrate that the public sector resource costs of meeting targets for basic provision of public services can be dramatically lowered by the following measures:

1. Targeting provision on those in need.
2. Use of more cost-effective techniques of provision (generally more labour-intensive and less capital-intensive[20]).
3. Mobilisation of local voluntary contributions in cash and kind to help

meet the costs of service provision (particularly through use of voluntary labour to construct basic facilities such as schools, dispensaries, etc.).

Streeten also argues that the cost sceptics ignore the complementarities and linkages between the different components of a basic services package – each individual component is made more cost-effective by the simultaneous provision of others. Thus a nutrition programme becomes more effective when the target group also benefits from improved water supplies, education and health care.

The supporting arguments for this approach are thus in various ways 'efficiency-oriented'. Investment in human capital, cost minimisation and cost-effectiveness are all strongly emphasised.

It is probably not insignificant that a number of the leading proponents of meeting basic needs who assign priority to public service provision have worked in association with the World Bank. From the Bank's point of view a basic needs programme that is politically uncontentious is clearly preferable to one that is; and land reform, which features as a key measure in the more radical approach to meeting basic needs (see below) is generally more contentious than developments in the provision of health care and education. Moreover, the Bank has a tradition of lending for public works, whereas it has only once done so to support land redistribution (from British colonials to Kenyan nationals at the time of Kenyan independence[21]). Furthermore this approach evolved rapidly at a time, in the early to mid-1980s, when the World Bank's Research Department under the direction of Anne Kreuger was focusing almost exclusively on improving efficiency in resource use in developing countries.[22]

Proponents of the improved public services/investment in human capital approach to meeting basic needs do not ignore the first and third category of basic needs (i.e. the need for improved employment and income opportunities for the poor in order to provide those basic needs that families usually supply themselves). Labour-intensive public works programmes and public sector investment in research and development of appropriate technology are both advocated (see e.g. Stewart in Cornia *et al.*, 1987: Chapter 10). However, the emphasis on meeting these needs is less strong in this approach than in the alternative, more radical, perspective to which we now turn. In general it is assumed that they will be met following investment in human capital.

The more radical basic needs perspective: the emergence of a new paradigm

By the mid-1980s the reformist, public service oriented approach to meeting basic needs was in the ascendancy, for two main reasons. Firstly, the approach is in tune with the neo-classical revival in development economics (which is discussed in the next chapter) and with related developments in

World Bank thinking and policy (see the previous section). Secondly, its flexibility in terms of scale and content can clearly be expected to increase its acceptability, at least in some degree, to a wide range of governments, and/or to any non-governmental organisations (NGOs) that these governments are prepared to tolerate.

However, in the late 1970s an alternative, more radical perspective on meeting basic needs emerged in the development literature. This differs from the approach just reviewed in the following respects:

1. Assignation of higher priority to meeting the first category of basic needs and, by implication, the third also (see p. 265.).
2. Consequently greater emphasis upon ensuring adequate access either to wage employment or to productive assets for self-employment on the part of the poor.
3. Emphasis on the positive implications for self-sustaining growth, structural change and reduced international dependency of meeting the first and third categories of basic needs.

It is probable that some who during the 1980s have emphasised the public services approach to meeting basic needs also accept the values, beliefs and logic of this more radical perspective, but do not emphasise it because contemporary political realities – the conservative tenor of leading governments in the West, the neo-classical revival in international funding institutions and the balance of power in most Third World governments – appear unfavourable.

THE BASIC NEEDS PARADIGM: AN ELABORATION

This perspective is characterised not only by the values incorporated in its interpretation of development but by a particular theorisation of the development process and its key causalities.

The basic needs paradigm may be summarised as follows:

1. Economic development consists not simply in growth, but in improving mass welfare with priority assigned to meeting the basic needs of all.
2. To achieve the latter the masses must have the right to participate in policy debate concerning the provision of basic needs.
3. A 'basic needs first' oriented development strategy will lay more effective foundations for sustained long-run growth than any other strategy.
4. This is primarily because of its impact on the structure of domestic demand and the associated inducement to invest.
5. Among the consequences that flow from the restructuring of domestic demand that is entailed in this strategy are an easing of both the domestic demand constraint and the balance of payments constraint to economic growth.[23]

6. Such a strategy also lays the foundations for sustained structural change, while helping to overcome the capital and foreign exchange constraints thereto.
7. A basic needs oriented strategy also generates faster, and more appropriate, development of human capital.

The arguments used to demonstrate a potential positive correlation between meeting basic needs on the one hand, and growth, structural change and greater self-sufficiency on the other, focus on the dominant constraints that confronted earlier strategies of import-substitution – foreign exchange shortages and inadequate domestic demand. Successful implementation of a set of policies which enable the poor to meet their basic consumption needs by raising their productivity and incomes will affect the structure of demand in ways that will induce an increase and a qualitative change in aggregate investment. Firstly, more equal income distribution in developing countries would generate a more homogeneous demand pattern, enlarging demand for a range of products, many of which can be produced in small and medium-scale plants. Thus market size would not restrain expansion of production. At the same time, by increasing total demand for a range of goods in mass demand, meeting basic needs could also encourage the expanded large-scale production of certain products, particularly where competitive labour-intensive products are not available – underutilised capacity in plant producing essential goods would be taken up, and unit costs would fall. Meanwhile the same change in demand structure would help to ease other production constraints, for it would tend to lower the overall foreign exchange and capital intensity of the goods and services demanded in the domestic market.

The increased demand would not only be for consumer goods. It would also be for capital and intermediate goods needed to produce mass consumption goods (Ghai, 1978: 18). In so far as these consumption goods can be produced economically by technologies which use capital and intermediate goods of relatively simple design, some of which can in turn also be produced on a small scale,[24] the changed demand structure is likely to induce expanded production in the capital and intermediate goods sectors as well. Here, too, both small-scale production by small firms and artisans and complementary large-scale production (e.g. from steel mills) is likely to expand. Thus the new structure of demand and investment would also contribute to structural change in production capacity and to greater self-sufficiency.

According to this interpretation, a basic needs development strategy provides the basis for the linked development of labour-intensive production in agriculture and in small-scale manufacturing and service enterprises and of large-scale modern industrial production, the latter of a widening range of goods starting with essential items for which there is no labour-intensive substitute. Large-scale modern industry will provide a growing share of the capital and intermediate goods requirements of the economy, as well as some mass consumption goods.[25] The modern industrial sector will also continue to process various primary products for export, as well as producing some manufactured exports. However, because modern industry is likely initially to employ only a small proportion of the total labour force, the early development and use of relatively labour-intensive means of production are seen as essential features of a basic needs strategy, not only for poverty reduction but to sustain long-term growth through expanding demand and, hence, the inducement to invest.

A significant proportion of new labour-intensive production would be developed in the rural sector. Not only do the majority of the poor in most developing countries live in the rural sector,[26] but there are also greater opportunities for the productive mobilisation of unemployed labour there, both for labour-intensive capital formation[27] and for labour-intensive recurrent production processes, especially in agriculture itself. The pattern of development of the rural sector, and the flow of goods that it supplies and demands, will therefore exert a significant influence on the pattern of development of the economy as a whole.

In many countries a redistributive land reform (either collective or individualistic) would be an essential precondition for a basic needs oriented development strategy.[28] In all countries, too, investment in rural infrastructure and services are essential. An anticipated spin-off would be a reduction in excess rural urban migration as rural incomes and welfare rise (Streeten, 1981: 24).

In the late 1970s and early 1980s proponents of meeting basic needs reinforced the arguments for a basic needs oriented development strategy by emphasising also that the deterioration in the economic position of the industrially advanced economies had severely reduced the opportunities for export-led growth, and that underdeveloped countries must look primarily to an expansion of their domestic markets to induce growth and structural change (Singh, 1979; Godfrey, 1978).[29] Indeed the view is still held by many that any major attempt by all or the majority of Third World countries to expand either primary or labour-intensive manufactured exports to the North would result in both deteriorating commodity terms of trade and increased protectionism in the North. While some countries in the South might experience improved *income* terms of trade, it is doubtful to what extent this would be possible for the South as a whole. A basic needs oriented development strategy would, it is argued, reduce (though not eliminate) dependence on exports to the North both as a means of expanding the market and as a source of essential resources. At the same time, however, a basic needs strategy can contribute to the growth of trade between underdeveloped countries both in agricultural goods and in more appropriate manufactured goods (Streeten, 1981: 24).

Meanwhile, on the supply side, a basic needs oriented strategy would promote the more effective mobilisation of local entrepreneurial and technical innovatory capabilities, not only because demand that can be met by small-scale enterprise is expanded, but because this strategy entails a more equal distribution of access to productive assets (see pp. 278–9). At the same time, expansion of small-scale production where the producer controls the full production process and there is a direct interface with consumers, increases the opportunity for adaptations in product design and production technology in economies still short of advanced skills in engineering and market research.

Expansion in opportunities for small-scale investment would also increase the productive mobilisation of significant untapped small-scale savings potential, for which in the past there have often been insufficient productive outlets (ILO, 1978: 52).[30] According to this perspective, other interpretations of the development process exaggerate the distinction between the savings propensities of the rich and of small-scale entrepreneurs. In practice the rich often have a high propensity to engage in luxury consumption, often undertake 'unproductive investments' (for instance land purchase or speculation in urban property) and often transfer savings abroad. In the past, on the other hand, small-scale entrepreneurs have been discouraged from fulfilling their full savings potential by policy and institutional bias and lack of adequate productive outlets for investment.

An underdeveloped economy with a strong mass market for consumer and small-scale producer goods, and with corresponding opportunities for small-scale as well as large-scale investment, is, after initial adjustments, likely to experience fewer permanent leakages from the circular flow of national income in the form of capital exports. It is also likely to be capable of sustaining a higher growth rate without running into balance of payments constraints than an economy with the less equal income distribution, and the demand structure biased towards import-intensive élite consumption, which are characteristic of most market economies in the Third World.

Meanwhile, higher incomes for the poor will enable them to make more effective use of public services as they become better nourished and have surplus cash to meet the complementary costs of using these services (transport to the dispensary, school uniforms and equipment, etc.). Improved education and health standards should contribute to further advances in labour productivity. Proponents of the basic needs paradigm also emphasise the significance of improved and expanded public service provision as a means of raising the health, productivity and welfare of the poor. However, this perspective pays greater attention to the positive interaction between improved incomes and consumption of the poor and the use and impact of these services than does the 'public sector investment in human capital' approach.

This perception of the development process is not one in which Third World countries are expected to remain locked into an economic structure dominated by primary production based on labour-intensive technologies (see Ghai, *op.cit.*). It is, however, one which assigns much greater weight to both of these in the early stages of development than has occurred in most Third World countries in recent decades, where capital-intensive import-substituting industrialisation based on, and promoting, unequal income and wealth distribution has been emphasised. It is, furthermore, these early stages of development that basic needs theorists emphasise. The precise direction to be taken by economic development in its more advanced stages is generally left open.

It is claimed that evidence of the viability of meeting basic needs in low-income countries in conjunction with rapid growth and structural change is already available. One frequently cited example is China (see e.g. Singh, 1979). Taiwan, and, to some extent, South Korea are also cited as instances of countries which have sustained good, long-term growth performances combined with the elimination of absolute poverty and attainment of relatively low levels of inequality. These country examples are important, for they have the advantages of representing both planned and market economies, both large and small countries, and, in some respects at least, countries with initially poor resource endowments, particularly in the case of China.[31] Other country successes cited include Cuba and also Sri Lanka from 1960 to 1977 (Streeten, 1981: 5, and Stewart, 1985).[32]

Meanwhile, cross-country regressions have been carried out to test the relationship between country performance in growth and basic need satisfaction. A number of them show favourable results. For example, Hicks (1979) found that 'countries which had done well on basic needs in 1960 had above average growth later during the period 1960–1973'.

THE THEORETICAL FOUNDATIONS OF THE BASIC NEEDS PARADIGM

The basic needs paradigm is based not so much on a new set of theoretical constructs as a reordering of old ones. The arguments that underpin the basic needs paradigm are innovatory because they turn old assumptions on their head (most notably with respect to the relative propensities to save and engage in productive investment of rich and poor), emphasise the crucial importance for growth of variables whose significance had previously been ignored or underestimated (notably, the level and *composition* of domestic demand and their determinants), and analyse systematically the implications of a changed structure of asset and income distribution for the patterns and pace of growth and structural change and for self-reliance. They have also contributed to the concept of human capital formation (as in part have the less radical proponents of meeting basic needs as well).

The other concepts and the analytical techniques used by the proponents of meeting basic needs are largely familiar. It is the manner in which they are combined, and their focus, that is distinctive. At the macro level the theoretical arguments that underpin the 'basic needs first' paradigm are predominantly structuralist. The focus is on the significance of the structure of asset distribution and of demand and production for the level of current employment and income distribution and for the rate and pattern of growth. This is combined with quite frequent use of elements of price theory at the micro level. Indeed, one of the distinctive features of the basic needs paradigm is the relatively even balance accorded to macro and micro issues.

THE POLICY IMPLICATIONS OF THE BASIC NEEDS PARADIGM

The basic needs paradigm has two main types of macro-economic policy implication. The first concerns the need to remove many of the price distortions generated by strategies of protected import-substitution. It reflects the wide recognition that government interventions in factor and product pricing (tariff structures, modern sector interest rates, minimum wages, the internal terms of trade between agriculture and industry) have often encouraged inefficient patterns of resource use, high on scarce factors and low on the abundant one – labour. These recommendations are not peculiar to the basic needs paradigm. However, their blending with the second set of policy implications (see below) is one of its distinctive features.

The second set of policy implications concerns the reform of economic structures – asset distribution, structures of demand and production, public services provision and institutional structures. Streeten (1981) and Stewart (1985) seek to justify in neo-classical terms the case for public sector intervention to modify the last two of these, basing their argument on the existence of externalities and market imperfections. The efficiency arguments for redistributive land reform which have been widely noted by proponents of meeting basic needs also command the support of some neo-classical economists.[33] However, so far as proponents of the basic needs paradigm are concerned the case for asset redistribution rests not simply on efficiency criteria but on the fact that this can both improve the immediate status of many poor households and lay the foundations for a development path capable of generating steady improvements in basic needs as well as continuing growth and structural change. The theoretical underpinnings of these policy recommendations lie in an explicitly value-laden normative economics where the fundamental values differ from those of the neo-classical school, but which also uses elements of price theory to demonstrate the potential efficiency gains of pursuing certain welfare objectives.[34]

The list in Table 9.3 summarises the main policy implications of the basic needs paradigm. There follows a brief comment on some of them.

Table 9.2   The main policy concerns of the basic needs paradigm

Policy concern	Main recommended policy instruments
1. Asset distribution	Land reform, creation of new productive assets.
2. Composition of demand	Income redistribution (via 1), price policy, taxation, rationing.
3. Composition of production	Income distribution, price policy, credit policy, investment licensing, public sector production.
4. Choice of technology (in agriculture, industry and services)	Farm size, price policy, R and D, investment licensing, credit policy, selective use of subsidies, public sector investment.
5. Institutional development (credit, marketing, research, extension)	Interest rate policy, public sector investment, retraining for extension personnel.
6. Popular participation in resource mobilisation and allocation	Promotion of local associations (self-help groups, credit and savings groups, etc.), district level planning, reductions in absolute poverty, inequality and sources of rural patronage.
7. Composition and distribution of public services	Public expenditure, popular participation in construction of capital assets (e.g. schools, dispensaries, choice of technology).
8. Scale of public services	Ditto, plus policy on fees and levies for use, and general tax policy.

Asset distribution

In some developing countries the structure of income and asset distribution is such that even substantial improvements in public services provision to the poor in addition, within budgetary constraints, to the expansion of labour-intensive public works, arguably could not be guaranteed to ensure adequate employment and income opportunities for the poor to enable them to meet the first category of basic needs. Where this is so, a redistributive land reform could often make a significant contribution towards enabling the poor to meet these needs. The extent of land reform's potential contribution to poverty reduction depends on the existing structure and distribution of land rights, the person:cultivable land ratio, the economic potential of the land available and the cost of exploiting this potential. In some parts of sub-Saharan Africa traditional land tenure systems still prevail which do not recognise individual freehold tenure (ownership rights are vested in a larger kin group, the lineage or clan) and person:cultivable land ratios are also low, although agricultural potential is often low too. Here the primary needs are for investments in agricultural research and rural infrastructure. In other areas, however, in Asia, Latin America and parts of Africa too, the scope for, and income generating potential of, land reform is widely recognised.

The argument for land reform does not rest solely on its equity impact. There is substantial evidence of an inverse relationship between farm size and productivity in developing countries which extends down to very small farm size ranges.[35] The greater efficiency of small farms is manifested both in more appropriate factor combinations (use of labour-intensive production methods) and higher returns to scarce factors (indicating greater intensity of resource use).

A redistributive land reform can, via its impact on income distribution, make a significant contribution to the restructuring of demand and investment opportunities – an outcome which is reinforced by any positive efficiency impact of land reform.

In those countries where there is a case for land redistribution, two key issues to be confronted are how much to compensate landowners, and in what form, and how to promote the diversification of landowner economic interests. In some cases one possibility may be to privatise, wholly or partly, selected state-owned productive assets, issuing shares in these as one component of a compensation package. Almost certainly, however, to stand any chance of acceptability compensation would have to be granted partly in the form of freely transferable foreign exchange (hence a potentially important role for foreign aid agencies) with acceptance that these funds might move out of the economy during the initial years of strategic reform.[36]

Meanwhile new asset creation – either large-scale public works or small-scale capital formation – can also be used to expand income-generating opportunities for the poor. Examples include both labour-intensive creation of new productive assets (for instance via land drainage, irrigation of arid lands or controlled forest clearance for agriculture) and assistance to the poor to acquire other productive assets (e.g. wells, stall-fed livestock and skills and tools for non-farm production).[37]

Composition of demand

The composition of demand is expected to change as a result of the change in asset and income distribution. Streeten (1981) argues that education and price policy can both be used to influence income allocation by the poor in order to enhance their performance in meeting basic consumption needs. Where basic consumer goods are subsidised, this may have to be matched by rationing, especially in the short run (Stewart, 1985: 47, 48), while the cost of subsidies will have to be covered by taxation of the rich (or by foreign aid).

Some writers have also observed that it will be necessary to ensure that the income benefits of productivity gains in agriculture are not negated by a decline in the terms of trade arising from low demand elasticities for the output of small farmers. According to Streeten this would be done by government intervention in marketing (Streeten, 1981: 43).[38] However, if surpluses are not to be accumulated the primary need would be not for price support but for suggestions for new crops and help in finding and promoting markets.

In practice, however, the risk of such low elasticities arising seems much greater with dualistic market structures and in the absence of land reform.

With a more homogeneous market structure food preferences would presumably be less varied and more closely matched to small farmer production patterns. Farmers would, however, have to diversify their production over time to match the changing demand patterns for food generated by rising incomes.

Composition of production

It is anticipated that the changed composition of effective demand arising from new structures of asset ownership and income distribution will induce appropriate changes in the composition of production. The elimination of price distortions in factor and product markets should serve to reinforce this trend (by, for example, increasing the costs of production of capital-intensive goods, and by raising, in many countries, prices for farm output). However, governments may also use both selective direct controls over private investment and investment by the state in order to promote changes in the composition of output.

Production technologies

In agriculture there exists a wide range of production technologies which do not affect product quality. Correct price policies, combined where appropriate with redistributive land reform, as in China, Taiwan or South Korea, would reduce the use of capital- and foreign-exchange-intensive technologies, releasing these resources for use in other sectors. With time, as surplus labour is absorbed by other sectors, increased capitalisation of agriculture will become necessary. Initially, however, labour-intensive technologies are advocated on equity and static efficiency grounds and because evenly distributed incomes and an effective mass demand for basic consumption and producer goods are needed to get sustainable industrial growth under way.[39]

In industry a spectrum of technologies for production of a given product, comparable to the range of choice that exists in agriculture, does not usually exist. Furthermore, in the manufacturing sector product quality is affected by choice of production technology. Consequently, if product characteristics are precisely specified, then product choice predetermines the choice of technology (Stewart, 1978: 23). In these circumstances policy recommendations for a basic needs oriented strategy emphasise the following factors:

1. Elimination of price distortions.
2. A changed demand structure geared towards basic consumption and producer goods, some of which can be produced competitively by labour-intensive methods.
3. Increased public sector research into the economics of alternative technologies and into the development of new or improved labour-intensive production processes (see e.g. ILO, 1978: 143; UNIDO, 1978; Singer, 1979b and 1982).

4. Licensing of investment in *certain branches* of manufacturing in order to protect users of labour intensive technologies from competition from more capital intensive production (see e.g. Streeten, 1981: 44; Minhas in Hill (ed.), 1979; Hunt, 1983 and 1984: chapter 5). Licensing is necessary not merely to counter the influence of élitist and imitative tastes on consumer choice (Minhas *op.cit.*: 89) but to counter market expansion by large firms for whom organisation of production in large numbers of dispersed, small-scale, labour intensive units is simply not feasible, however efficient the latter may be (Hunt, *op.cit.*).

Examples of products that are price-competitive when produced by relatively labour-intensive methods include such basic items as bread and sugar (see Kaplinsky, 1981, and Hunt, *op.cit.*). For certain labour-intensive products which are not fully competitive with the output of capital-intensive processes it may also be argued that requiring consumers to buy a product of a lower quality and/or at a higher price represents a form of compulsory saving (a reduction in the value of present consumption), which can be justified in terms both of present equity (increased employment creation) and the potential dynamic benefits that may stem from expanding mass incomes.

For some products and processes (e.g. some chemicals; high quality steel) capital-intensive technologies are the most appropriate. The release of scarce capital and foreign exchange from other branches will help to accelerate the development of production of these goods.

Meanwhile, in both reformist and radical approaches to meeting basic needs, it is argued that the technologies used in capital construction and recurrent provision of public services should reflect a country's factor endowments. For example, labour-intensive methods can be used in rural feeder-road construction, in building dispensaries, primary schools and community centres, and in laying water pipe-lines, while health care provision can rely heavily at grass roots level on paramedics (ILO, 1978: 58, 9).

Institutional development

Institutional development is needed to ensure the success of land reform (new credit and marketing outlets will be needed, and revision of extension coverage and content), to underpin sustained agricultural development, to promote, via research and pilot dissemination, the use of efficient labour intensive technologies in both agriculture and manufacturing, to mobilise labour for public works, etc.

Popular participation

Within the basic needs paradigm, popular participation is both an end in itself and a potentially important policy instrument for resource mobilisation. It also implies the creation of a more effective interest group to press for the interests of those who in principle should benefit from a basic needs programme. There are a wide range of possible participatory forms including producer co-operatives, service co-operatives, self-help groups, elected representatives to district planning committees, etc. All are likely to operate more effectively once members have not only a common interest but comparable social and economic status.

Public services

Popular participation in resource mobilisation and capital construction can accelerate the expansion of basic public services (Streeten, 1981: 40). In mixed economies a degree of rigorously implemented, but realistic, progressive taxation can also increase aggregate resource availability. Meeting basic needs entails a shift in the balance of location of public services towards rural areas and urban slums. In some cases it also entails a shift in the balance of their composition away from sophisticated services based on costly technology towards essential services based on simpler, lower cost technologies (e.g. in health care and housing).

THE FOREIGN AID IMPLICATIONS OF THE BASIC NEEDS PARADIGM

Fields in which the basic needs paradigm identifies a potentially important role for aid include the funding of public services, institutional development (research and development, small-scale credit provision, etc.) and compensation for land reform. While some of these are broad areas of which aid donors already have funding experience, a significant degree of innovation in aid provision is also implied.

One area in which foreign aid has been conspicuous for its absence is the provision of support for land reform via the funding of compensation.[40] Also, while donors have substantial experience in funding public services, they have far less experience in supporting the use of appropriate technologies in the provision of these services. However, exceptions – in this case more recent than that for land reform – do exist. For instance, the UK Government provides support to the Government of Kenya's Rural Development Fund (which is distributed to district administrators for funding small-scale projects) and to Kenya's rural feeder-road construction programme. WHO has considerable experience and expertise in the development of paramedical staffing of basic health care projects. A significant number of national and international small farmer oriented agricultural research programmes are also supported by foreign aid.

However, it is notable that a large proportion of the aid that has been committed to basic needs oriented projects has come from non-governmental organisations. In many ways the latter are better adapted to the relatively small-scale, local level mobilisation of people and resources that popular participatory self-sustaining development projects require. In the 1980s, emphasis on the role of NGOs in providing help to the poor, and in mobilising them for self-help, has also meshed with the contemporary international political and economic emphasis on public sector retrenchment. There are, however, limits to what the NGOs can achieve given their resources. (Host governments may also become preoccupied by the proliferation of large numbers of foreign-funded NGOs over which they have little control.)

Official foreign aid could, if the commitment were there, contribute to a range of these developments, both directly and indirectly: directly through funding for land reform compensation schemes, and through supporting the local costs of staff (re)training for public service provision and of institutional development; indirectly by providing medium-term budgetary and balance of payments support in periods of structural adjustment geared to the type of strategic changes that the 'basic needs first' perspective advocates.

CRITICISMS OF THE BASIC NEEDS PARADIGM

In the course of this discussion four criticisms levelled against proposals for giving priority to meeting basic needs have already been mentioned. These are as follows:

1. That the objective is operationally non-viable.
2. That the theoretical justification is incoherent.
3. That the public sector costs would be prohibitive.
4. That basic needs strategies would lock economies permanently into use of primitive labour-intensive production technologies focused on primary production for export.

By implication the discussion has also answered a fifth criticism. While some governments in the North and the South may have supported the 1976 ILO basic needs proposals for opportunistic reasons,[41] many contributors to the development debate do so for more positive ones. The next section considers a sixth criticism.

The political viability of basic needs strategies

Implementation of an effective strategy for meeting basic needs presupposes the existence of the political will to make the necessary changes. In this respect the literature on the basic needs paradigm reveals two main themes. One is the attempt to convert others both to the values (priorities) and to the perception of the development process which are adhered to by proponents of this paradigm. The other is to argue that the prospects for the emergence in capitalist or mixed economies of dominant political coalitions that favour the meeting of basic human needs is not as bleak as some would suggest. In relation to the latter, the relevant arguments were outlined by Bell in Chenery *et al.* (1974) in relation to redistribution with growth, and are in part reiterated by Streeten with respect to meeting basic needs. In both cases emphasis is placed on the possibility that influential interest groups may perceive it to be in their interests to reduce inequality or absolute poverty.

For example, an urban class alliance may override landlord resistance to land reform in the interest of lower food prices, while a range of producers and distributors for the domestic market might support the same measure in the interests of increased mass demand. In some instances capitalists may also support peasant demands for land reform if the resulting smallholder system promises greater political accommodation (see Bell in Chenery *et al.*, 1974: 54, and Streeten, 1981: 57, 58).

The key issue which is not considered by the 'political optimists' is whether alternative lines of action might promote the same interests equally effectively – at least in the medium term – while costing influential interest groups less, either in taxes, or temporary disruption to production, or perceived threats to their own property rights. With respect to meeting basic needs, even more than with respect to redistribution with growth, there is reason to suppose that such alternatives are often perceived to exist. This can be well illustrated with respect to the agricultural sector, to which a key role would be assigned. Faced with a choice between expanding urban food supplies via a radical redistributive land reform with the anticipated increase in farm efficiency (as advocated, for example, by Minhas in Hill, 1979, for India and by Hunt, 1984, for Kenya), or through intensifying existing farm development programmes with their typical orientation towards large farms and rich and middle peasant farms, it seems a fair guess that in future, as so often in the past, the latter would be preferred by the capitalist class and many elements of the *petite bourgeoisie.* Short-run disruptions to production can be avoided, as can the budgetary costs of compensation, let alone the risk of violence; at the same time the 'sanctity' of private property would be protected. Likewise, to take an example from the service sector, if the incidence of communicable diseases can be largely confined to the poor, this may also continue to be preferred as a lower cost alternative to their eradication.

Meanwhile those capitalists engaged in manufacturing for the domestic market, who might be expected to form an influential part of an alliance of class interests favouring land reform, could not be expected to support readily measures to remove cost biases in favour of large-scale, capital- and foreign-exchange-intensive manufacturing, or to license new investment in certain products in order to encourage small-scale production. To devise and implement a comprehensive basic needs oriented development strategy would require considerable political negotiation and bargaining, or else a more radical change in the political power structure.

Political commitment is a *sine qua non* for the implementation of a comprehensive basic needs oriented development strategy, and the lack of such commitment is the dominant impediment to its implementation. It is significant that in Taiwan and South Korea, two countries often cited for their success in meeting basic needs, land reform was initiated in the late 1940s by the American military govenment in response to mounting social unrest (due in Taiwan to the extreme insecurity of tenure, food shortages and the pressures imposed on the economy by the influx of 640,000 mainlanders, and in South Korea to peasant awareness of the prior land reform in the North).[42]

The opposition to the proposals for land reform that were generated within the Philippines Government in the mid-1980s, and the strength of that opposition despite President Aquino's popularity and the left-wing rebel threat, is illustrative of the problem that would be faced by many pluralistic governments in attempting to implement a comprehensive basic needs oriented development strategy.

The misconceived need for basic needs strategies

Meanwhile, some economists (e.g. Lal, 1983; Collier and Lal, 1986) argue that the basic needs approach is fundamentally misconceived for other reasons. They claim that the predominant evidence shows that in efficiently operating less developed market economies growth has brought a general increase in mass welfare as evidenced *inter alia* by the expansion of primary education, health care and small farmer cash-cropping. Inequality may have increased, but this provides a necessary incentive for individual enterprise. Government policy should be concentrated on improving market efficiency. In contrast, the structural changes and government intervention advocated by proponents of the basic needs paradigm would reduce output in both the short run and the long run due both to the initial disruption to the economy and the associated reduction in incentives.

SUMMARY AND CONCLUSION

The basic needs paradigm adopts a distinctive interpretation of the immediate objectives of development, with a strong emphasis being assigned to elimination of absolute poverty (meeting basic needs) as well as economic growth. Over the longer term, the importance of sustained progress on both fronts is also emphasised (the former both as an end in itself and as a means to growth). From this distinctive interpretation of development there flows a particular perception both of immediate policy priorities and of the type of development path which it is appropriate to pursue. The recommended strategy is based not on a heavy concentration on modern sector development but on a more evenly diffused, broad-based development to which the 'traditional' sector makes a substantial contribution via rising productivity, incomes and demand.

This strategy is one for which there is a significant potential role for foreign aid in the early stages in providing support for, *inter alia*, land reform, follow-up institutional developments to support agrarian reform, and the development of research and development in agriculture and small-scale manufacturing technology.

With respect to the theoretical justification of this development strategy, the emphasis is on domestic mass-demand-led growth which initially is to come not from expanded wage employment in the modern sector as from a broad-based expansion of mass incomes, largely in the traditional sector – an expansion which can probably only be achieved if promoted partly by restructuring the distribution of ownership of productive assets.

Proponents of the basic needs paradigm can argue that the development strategy which they advocate is both coherent and logically consistent. Since 1976 the components of this strategy, their interrelationship and the specific policy options for their implementation, have been analysed in increasing detail, albeit with continuing emphasis on the preliminary stages of strategy change and implementation. The focus remains on the meeting of those 'minimum levels of personal consumption and access to social services which should be universally regarded as essential to a decent life' (ILO, 1978: 7), and on the implications of meeting those for the structure and rate of economic growth. Detailed speculation on subsequent patterns of growth, structural change and country increase in basic needs standards has been avoided, although the experiences of Japan, Taiwan and South Korea and of some of the socialist countries, especially China and Cuba, have been noted.

Achievement of this preliminary stage, however, presupposes the existence of the political will to make the necessary changes, and this is far from guaranteed. At this stage, if confidence in the political viability of the strategy advocated is to be sustained, new examples of contemporary success in its implementation are needed. In this respect, the medium-term strategies pursued in countries such as Nicaragua, Zimbabwe and the Philippines will be of particular interest.

NOTES

1. I am indebted to Hans Singer, Barry Herman and Mohammed Ahmed for their comments on an earlier draft of this chapter.
2. See pp. 71–8.

3. See Streeten, 1981: 33.
4. *Ibid.*
5. See especially Chapter 3, p. 71.
6. See Kuznets, 1955: 18–19 and 24; and Kuznets, 1965: 206–219. For an explanation of how the Gini coefficient is calculated, see Killick, 1981: 110 or Atkinson, 1975: 45.
7. See Paukert, *op.cit.*: Table 6, pp. 114, 5.
8. See also Little, 1982: 211, 2 and Galenson, 1977. On the other hand, Griffin, 1978 (Chapters 6 and 7), gives evidence of persistent poverty in rapidly growing economies. Meanwhile Fields, 1980: 170–173, provides statistics of absolute poverty increase in India during the 1960s but of declines in several other countries. The experience of Brazil in the 1960s remains controversial; while Adelman and Morris argue that absolute poverty rose, others claim that the per capita income of the poor increased (Fields, 1980: 211; Little, 1982: 211; Streeten and Burki, 1978: 411).
9. Beckerman, 1977: 666, also points to the logical inconsistency of this approach if, as proposed, it is used to calculate welfare growth from a base year value of GDP that is conventionally estimated rather than calculated with the same weightings.
10. The Gini coefficient has the disadvantage that an apparent improvement in equity can be generated by a rise in the income share of the middle income groups combined not merely with a fall in the share of the upper income groups but with an either constant or falling share for the poorest. See Killick, 1981: 110 and 111.
11. World Bank, 1980, Table 24 (p. 156) reveals how few Third World countries had the relevant data at this time.
12. See e.g. Sharpston, 1972; Gish, 1973; and IBRD, 1974.
13. Chenery *et al.*, 1974.
14. See pp. 71–2.
15. For example, expanded technical education and small farmer credits; these are to be combined with the removal of any pre-existing policy, price and institutional biases against the informal sector, including over-valued exchange rates and low modern sector interest rates, both of which encourage the use of imported, capital-intensive production technology, and a range of public sector regulations which have operated to restrict the development of the urban informal sector. See Ahluwalia and Chenery in Chenery *et al.*, *op.cit.*; Rao in *ibid.*; and also ILO, 1972: Chapter 13.
16. Lefeber in Mitra, 1974: 174–176.
17. Minhas, 1974, makes similar proposals specifically for India.
18. See Minhas in Hill (ed.), 1979: 80–82; and Minhas, 1974 *passim*.
19. Reprinted in Streeten, 1981: Chapter 4.
20. See e.g. Mosley and Jolly in Cornia *et al.*, 1987.
21. In a programme jointly funded with the British Government and the Commonwealth Development Corporation; see Wasserman, 1976: 157–160.
22. Singer (1979a) notes the probable attraction to the Bank of the selectivity (targeting of supplementary services) that is emphasised by proponents of this approach.
23. I.e. the two constraints which the early structuralists expected import-substitution to overcome, but which it in fact exacerbated.
24. E.g. farm implements, brick or tube ovens for bakeries, etc.
25. Here there is a close parallel with the Chinese experience of 'walking on two legs.'
26. The ratios of rural to urban poor vary among less developed countries. In India, the percentage of rural poor out of the total poor at the end of the 1960s appears to have been in the order of 83 per cent, probably a fairly typical figure for the

larger Asian countries (Srinivasan and Bardhan, 1974: 122, 124, 168 and 257). In Kenya, recent estimates suggest a higher proportion of about 90 per cent rural, which is typical for much of sub-Saharan Africa (Crawford and Thorbecke, 1978). In the more urbanised Latin American countries the ratio is around 50 per cent.

27. For instance, in soil and water conservation projects, swamp drainage, irrigation systems and feeder-road construction. The scope for rural labour-intensive capital formation was demonstrated in China in the Maoist era. However, proponents of a basic needs first strategy emphasise that there is potential for labour absorption in these activities also in market economies (see below).

28. In arguing that land reform will promote growth proponents of this perspective emphasise not only the impact on mass incomes and demand, but also the supporting evidence with respect to the inverse relationship between farm size and efficiency under private ownership that is now available from various countries (see e.g. ILO, 1977; Bhalla, 1979; Hunt, 1984). The scope provided by collective ownership for mass labour mobilisation for rural capital formation, as demonstrated in China, is also noted.

29. See also Lefeber, *op.cit.*

30. Many of the foregoing points are also raised in Ghai, 1978, and Streeten, 1981: see especially p. 24.

31. However, it has also been observed that these countries have certain very important characteristics in common. They are all, like Japan, in the Far East which has one of the longest state traditions in the Third World and long traditions of literacy, efficient administration, hard working habits, entrepreneurship and commercial expertise.

32. In a piecemeal form, examples of the viability of individual basic needs orientated policies, projects and programmes are becoming available from a growing number of other countries too (see e.g. Goulet, 1979; Stewart, 1985).

33. See Little, 1982: 173.

34. Occasionally, the neo-classical notion of the diminishing marginal utility of income is also drawn upon to lend support to these welfare objectives, on the grounds that it follows from this concept that the marginal utility gains to the poor from direct resource redistribution must exceed the marginal utility losses to the rich. However, in the absence of generally agreed weights to be assigned to marginal variations in the income of different groups one cannot proceed far along this analytical path.

35. See e.g. Bhalla in Berry and Cline, 1979: Appendix A; Hunt, 1984: Chapter 7; Cornia, 1985.

36. For a further review of options for funding land reform compensation see Hunt, 1984: 282–287.

37. The scope for reliance on these measures in market economies is, however, limited by budgetary constraints (see, for example, Rudra, 1978, on the budgetary cost of labour-intensive public works in rural India).

38. See also Adelman, 1984: 945.

39. Cf. Adelman, 1984.

40. For one exception see p. 271; for further details see Wasserman, 1976.

41. Apart from diversion of attention from proposals for NIEO, other such reasons that have been identified include: in the North, the prospect of expanded supplies of cheap raw materials, and the potential gains to the North's exporters from increased political stability in developing countries (which it is assumed meeting basic needs would bring); in the South, *comprador* regimes may find it politically expedient to appear to be committed to meeting basic needs.

42. See Fei, Ranis and Kuo, 1979: 39; Brun and Hersh, 1976: 134.

REFERENCES

Adelman, I., 'Development economics: a reassessment of goals', *American Economic Review*, (Vol. 65, May 1975).

Adelman, I., 'Beyond export-led growth', *World Development*, (Vol. 12, No. 9, September 1984).

Adelman, I. and Morris, C., *Economic Growth and Equity in Developing Countries*, (Stanford University, 1973).

Ahluwalia, M., 'Inequality, Poverty and Development', *Jnl. of Development Economics*, (December 1976), reprinted in *Development Economics and Policy: Readings*, ed. Livingstone, I., (Allen and Unwin, 1981).

Ahluwalia, M. and Chenery, H., 'The economic framework', in Chenery, H. *et al.*, *Redistribution with Growth*, (Oxford, 1974).

Atkinson, A., *The Economics of Inequality*, (Oxford, 1975).

Beckerman, W., 'Some reflections on redistribution with growth', *World Development*, (August 1977).

Bell, C., 'The political framework' in Chenery, H., *et al.*, *Redistribution with Growth*, (Oxford, 1974).

Bhalla, S., 'Farm size, productivity, and technical change in Indian agriculture', in *Agrarian Structure and Productivity in Developing Countries*, eds. Berry, R. and Cline, W., Appendix A, (Johns Hopkins, 1979).

Brun, E. and Hersh, J., *Socialist Korea: a Case Study in the Strategy of Economic Development*, (Monthly Review Press, 1976).

Chenery, H., *et al.*, *Redistribution with Growth*, (Oxford, 1974).

Collier, P. and Lal, D., *Labour and Poverty in Kenya, 1900–1980*, (Clarendon Press, 1986).

Cornia, G., 'A summary and interpretation of the evidence', in Cornia, G. and Jolly, R., (eds.), *The Impact of the World Recession on Children*, (Pergamon, 1984).

Cornia, G., 'Farm size, land yields and the agricultural production function: an analysis of fifteen developing countries', *World Development*, (Vol. 13 No. 4, April 1985).

Cornia, G., Jolly, R. and Stewart, F., (eds.), *Adjustment with a Human Face*, Volume I, (Oxford, 1987).

Dag Hammarskjöld Foundation, *What Now? Another Development*, (Uppsala, 1975).

Denison, E., *Why Growth Rates Differ*, (Brookings, 1967).

Food and Agriculture Organisation, *Fifth World Food Survey*, (FAO, 1985).

Fei, J., Ranis, G. and Kuo, S., *Growth with Equity: The Taiwan Case*, (Oxford, 1979).

Fields, G., *Poverty, Inequality and Development*, (Cambridge, 1980).

Galenson, W., 'Economic growth, income and employment', (paper presented at the Conference on Poverty and Development in Latin America, Yale University, April 1977).

Ghai, D., 'Basic needs and its critics', *Institute of Development Studies Bulletin*, (Vol. 9, No. 4, June 1978).

Gish, O., 'Resource allocation, equality of access and health', *World Development*, (Vol. 1, No. 12, December 1973).

Godfrey, M., 'Prospects for a basic needs strategy: the case of Kenya', *Institute of Development Studies Bulletin*, (Vol. 9, No. 4, June 1978).

Goulet, D., 'Development as liberation: policy lessons from case studies', *World Development*, (Vol. 7, No. 6, June 1979).

Grant, J., *Disparity Reduction Rates in Social Indicators*, (Overseas Development Council, 1978).

Griffin, K., *International Inequality and National Poverty*, (Macmillan, 1978).

Hicks, N., 'Growth vs basic needs: is there a trade-off?', *World Development*, (Vol. 7, No. 11/12, 1979).

Hicks, N. and Streeten, P., 'Indicators of development: the search for a basic needs yardstick', *World Development*, (Vol. 7, No. 6, June 1979).

Hill, K.Q. (ed.), *Toward a New Strategy for Development*, Rothko Chapel Colloquium, (Pergamon, 1979).

Hunt, D., 'The limited scope for poverty reduction through non-farm employment,' in *Manchester Papers on Development*, (No. 7, May 1983).

Hunt, D., *The Impending Crisis in Kenya: The Case for Land Reform*, (Gower, 1984).

International Bank for Reconstruction and Development, *The Assault on World Poverty*, (Johns Hopkins, 1974).

International Labour Office, *Employment, Incomes and Equality: a Strategy for Increasing Productive Employment in Kenya*, (ILO, Geneva, 1972).

International Labour Office, *Employment, Growth and Basic Needs: A One-World Problem*, (ILO, Geneva, 1976; second edition, 1978).

International Labour Office, *Poverty and Landlessness in Rural Asia*, (ILO World Employment Programme, 1977).

Kaplinsky, R., *Alternative Techniques of Bread Production in Kenya*, (University of Sussex, D.Phil. thesis, 1981).

Killick, T., *Policy Economics: A Textbook of Applied Economics on Developing Countries*, (Heinemann, 1981).

Kuznets, S., 'Economic growth and income inequality', *American Economic Review*, (Vol. 65, 1955).

Kuznets, S., *Modern Economic Growth: Rate, Structure and Spread*, (Yale, 1965).

Lal, D., *The Poverty of 'Development Economics'*, (Hobart Paperback 16, Institute of Economic Affairs, 1983).

Lefeber, L., 'On the paradigm for economic development', in Mitra, A. (ed.), *Economic Theory and Planning*, (Oxford, 1974).

Little, I., *Economic Development: Theory, Policy, and International Relations*, (Basic Books, 1982).

McNamara, R., 'Address to the Board of Governors', Nairobi, Kenya, September 4, 1973, (World Bank Reprint).

Minhas, B., *Planning and the Poor*, (S. Chand and Co. Ltd., New Delhi, 1974).

Minhas, B., 'The current development debate', in Hill, K. (ed.), *Towards a New Strategy for Development*, (Pergamon, 1979).

Morris, M. and Liser, F., 'The PQLI: measuring progress in meeting human needs', (Communiqué on Development Issues No. 32, Overseas Development Council, Washington DC, 1977).

Mostey, W. and Jolly, R., 'Health policy and programme options: compensating for the negative effects of economic adjustment' in Cornia, G., Jolly, R. and Stewart, F. (eds.), *Adjustment with a Human Face*, (Clarendon Press, Oxford, 1987).

Paukert, F., 'Income distribution at different levels of development: a survey of evidence', *International Labour Review*, (1973).

Rao, D. C., 'Urban target groups' in Chenery, H., *et al.*, (eds.) *Redistribution with Growth*, (Oxford, 1974).

Rudra, A., 'Organisation of agriculture for rural development', *Cambridge Journal of Economics*, (Vol. 2, 1978).

Seers, D., 'Challenges to development theories and strategies', (Presidential address, Society for International Development World Conference, New Delhi, 1969).

Seers. D., 'What are we trying to measure?', *Journal of Development Studies*, (April 1972).

Sharpston, M., 'Uneven geographical distribution of medical care: a Ghanaian case-study', *Journal of Development Studies*, (Vol. 8, No. 2, January 1972).

Singer, H., 'Thirty years of changing thought on development problems', in Hanumantha Rao, C. and Joshi, P. (eds.), *Reflections on Economic Development and Social Change*, (Allied Publishers, 1979a).

Singer, H., 'Policy implications of the Lima target', *Industry and Development*, (No. 3, 1979b).

Singer, H., *Technologies for Basic Needs*, (ILO, Geneva, 1977; second edition, 1982).

Singh, A., 'The 'Basic Needs' approach to development, vs the new international economic order: the significance of Third World industrialisation', *World Development*, (Vol. 7, No. 6, June 1979).

Srinivasan, T. and Bardhan, P., *Poverty and Income Distribution in India*, (Statistical Publishing Company, Calcutta, 1974).

Stewart, F., *Technology and Underdevelopment*, second edition, (Macmillan, 1978).

Stewart, F., *Planning to Meet Basic Needs*, (Macmillan, 1985).

Stewart, F., 'Supporting productive employment among vulnerable groups,' in Cornia, G., Jolly, R. and Stewart, F., (eds.), *Adjustment with a Human Face*, (Clarendon Press, Oxford, 1987).

Streeten, P., *First Things First: Meeting Basic Human Needs in Developing Countries*, (Oxford, 1981).

Streeten, P. and Burki, S., 'Basic needs: some issues', *World Development*, (Vol. 6, No. 3, March 1978).

United Nations Industrial Development Organisation, *Industrialisation and Rural Development*, (United Nations, New York, 1978).

Wasserman, G., *Politics of Decolonisation*, (Cambridge, 1976).

World Bank, *World Development Reports*, 1978 – present, (Oxford, annually).

World Bank, *World Development Report, 1980*, (Oxford, 1980).

10 · THE NEO-CLASSICAL PARADIGM AND ITS ROLE IN DEVELOPMENT ECONOMICS

The neo-classical paradigm is summarised in Chapter 3, pp. 32–3. The reader may find it helpful to review that summary before proceeding with this chapter.

As Chapter 2 showed, the late nineteenth century heralded an era in which economic growth was increasingly taken for granted by the majority of economists. The main focus of attention shifted to the maximisation of efficiency in short-run resource allocation. This issue was explored using the approach of comparative statics, the methods of partial and general equilibrium analysis, and the techniques of marginal analysis. In other words, the focus was on exploring the impact of change in the value of some economic variable upon that of other variables in the system, on the assumption that consumers maximise utility and producers profit and that following the change both make marginal adjustments in resource allocation until they have returned to a maximising equilibrium. Markets were generally assumed to operate efficiently and smoothly, with prices being flexible in both directions.

The values and beliefs that underlay this analytical approach emphasised the merits of competitive private enterprise operating in free markets. Belief in the philosophy of *laissez-faire* and acceptance of the theory of comparative advantage were common characteristics of the neo-classical school in the late nineteenth century and the first half of the twentieth century.

This chapter is concerned specifically with the application of the neo-classical perspective to development economics. It begins by taking note of two early contributions to the development debate that were made explicitly from the perspective of a belief in free trade and *laissez-faire*. One of these, Bauer and Yamey (1957), also comes nearer than any other work on development economics written from this perspective to providing a general overview of the causes of, and constraints to, economic development.

Subsequent neo-classical contributions to development economics have been more fragmentary. Most substantive contributions to development theory written from this perspective have concentrated on particular issues, as have most neo-classical policy critiques. In the core of the chapter, therefore, a number of these issues are singled out for review. Although neo-classical theory is generally thought of as primarily 'micro-economic' in orientation, all of the issues that we shall review have, with one exception (cost-benefit analysis) a distinctly 'macro-policy' orientation.

The following discussion will seek to concentrate chiefly on the positive theoretical contributions of the neo-classical perspective rather than on critiques of other development theories and of development policies, some of which have already been noted in earlier chapters. However, since the critiques often prompted the positive contribution, it will be impossible entirely to avoid the former.

Meanwhile, in tracing the key theoretical contributions to come from the neo-classical perspective, a second theme will also be explored. This concerns the growing divergence of opinion amongst development economists whose work is generally classified as neo-classical, as to the degree of acceptable public sector intervention in the economy. In the development field this divergence emerged in the 1960s between those who continued to adhere to the philosophy of *laissez-faire* and the expanding school of neo-classical welfare economists who did not.

THE CONTRIBUTION OF THE NEO-CLASSICAL PARADIGM TO DEVELOPMENT ECONOMICS: THE OVERALL PERSPECTIVE

For those who have applied (and do apply) a neo-classical perspective to economic development, two overriding concerns have been to promote individual incentives and efficient resource use by improving the operation of the market system. These concerns with individual incentives and the importance of individual decision-taking within a freely-operating impersonal market system are closely linked to – the assumptions about individual economic behaviour already noted, combined with a fundamental belief in the primacy of the value of individual freedom – economic and political. A free enterprise market economy is seen as the economic counterpart to a multi-party democratic political system based upon a universal secret ballot. (Others, however, have questioned whether in countries as poor as many in the Third World these should be regarded as the overriding values determining the immediate goals of economic and political life.)

In the 1950s few leading contributions to the new 'sub-discipline' of development economics were neo-classical in perspective. There were, however, two notable exceptions: Viner's 1950 lectures delivered at the National University of Brazil (later published under the title *International Trade and*

Economic Development,[1] and *The Economics of Underdeveloped Countries*, published by Bauer and Yamey in 1957.

Written by economists who remained convinced of the general validity and relevance of the corpus of neo-classical theory to developing economies, these early essays represented in part a carefully-argued rejection of those innovations in the theory of economic development, and their policy implications, that were designed specifically to replace the neo-classical paradigm. Two themes are central to these contributions: the importance of restricting, rather than expanding, the role of governments in the promotion of national economic development, and the importance of promoting, rather than constraining, the expansion of free international trade.

Viner

Viner's 1950 lectures anticipated observations on each of these themes that have constantly recurred in later neo-classical writings. With respect to an extension of the economic role of governments, Viner's misgivings were various: lack of omniscience on the part of central governments;[2] lack of adequate technical expertise in economic management; corruptability of officials; the administrative delays and rigid adherence to the written rule that tend to characterise bureaucratic decision-taking; the diversion of private skills and time either to manipulation of officialdom and/or to avoidance of the rules; the lack of any compulsion or incentive for public sector efficiency. Viner articulates these concerns in a stringent critique of government promotion of import-substituting industrialisation.[3]

Meanwhile it is in his advocacy of an alternative development strategy (which, with its emphasis on agriculture, can be seen in some ways as an early precursor of Adelman's (1984) proposal for agricultural-development-led industrialisation), that Viner arguably made his main positive contribution to the development debate.

Firstly, there are a number of reasons, Viner argues, why statistics which purport to demonstrate lower per capita incomes in agriculture than in industry may be misleading (e.g. undeclared income from production of goods and services for own consumption by rural households, and higher urban living costs). Meanwhile, urban bias in government policies may be the prime cause of any such differences that do exist.[4] Instances of rich countries and regions with large agricultural sectors relative to the size of their total economy include Australia, New Zealand, Denmark, Iowa and Nebraska.

In response to advocates of government-promoted industrialisation, Viner propounds an alternative thesis in which the prosperity of agriculture determines average incomes both in agriculture and, largely via their impact on demand, in the economy as a whole.[5] Rising agricultural incomes provide the impetus for industrial development. Viner's argument for agriculture-based development meshed both with his advocacy of reduced government intervention in resource allocation and of specialisation according to comparative advantage.

Viner's foresight in anticipating issues that have been of enduring importance in development economics is also reflected in his discussion of the meaning of development. He asks whether this should take into account trends in mass poverty as well as average per capita income. Viner notes the lack of adequate statistical data on poverty trends and then goes on to observe that:

> There is a school of thought with respect to economic development which... believes that to subject a national programme of economic development to the requirement that it shall prevent an increase in the absolute extent of severe poverty may doom the programme to failure without lasting benefit to any sector of the population. They hold that in many cases all that is practicable, at least for some time, is to increase the national area of economic health and strength, perhaps relatively but at least absolutely, without preventing or even retarding, and possibly even while stimulating, the growth of the area of desperate poverty. Eventually, they contend, the prosperity will trickle down to the lower levels of the population, and the national resources will become abundant enough to make possible large-scale programmes to rescue them from their poverty, whereas a direct and immediate attack on mass poverty would result only in the squandering of the limited national resources on temporary palliatives, with increases in the number of the desperately poor as the only important result.
>
> (Viner 1953: 99–101.)[6]

Viner aligns himself with this school of thought and, on grounds of convention, practicality, and the potential conflict with growth, rejects the notion of a poverty-oriented measure of development.[7]

Bauer and Yamey

While Viner gave to development economics not only the first major neo-classical critique of government-promoted import substitution, but a positive view of the potential role of agriculture as a leading sector in economic growth, it was Bauer and Yamey who provided the first comprehensive analysis of the causes of economic backwardness and growth in under-developed countries from a perspective explicitly governed by the philosophy of domestic *laissez-faire* combined with application of the law of comparative advantage in foreign trade. We should, however, note Bauer and Yamey's own disclaimer. They do not aim to propose a *new* theory of development (Bauer and Yamey, *op.cit.*: 13), but rather to show how certain tenets of *existing* theory can be usefully applied to economically backward regions.

The discussion of their approach begins by quoting the authors on their interpretation of development – an interpretation which directly reflects the liberal philosophy of the neo-classical school.

> Our criterion for judging economic development is the widening of the range of alternatives open to people as consumers and as producers. The extent of the achievement of this goal is obviously not one which can be measured quantitatively. However, it corresponds broadly to an increase in the national income. Other things being equal, an increase in the goods and services available for consumption or investment improves the range of choice and of opportunities in economic life.
>
> (Bauer and Yamey, 1957: 151.)

The authors also note that this proxy measure of development may sometimes fail, not for the distributional reasons emphasised by Seers and others,[8] but because growth may be achieved via compulsion and restriction of choice. Growth in national income generated by such means could not be defined as development. Meanwhile, the underdeveloped countries are characterised by 'poverty in income and accumulated capital and backwardness in technique' (Bauer and Yamey *op.cit.*: 4).

Later Bauer and Yamey also elaborate upon the value judgements and beliefs that underlie their analytical perspective.

> As we see development essentially as the widening of people's access to alternatives, our inclination is towards economic systems in which decisions about the composition of national output, including those affecting the distribution of resources between consumption and investment, are taken largely by the individuals participating in economic life, and against economic systems in which central direction and detailed economic decision-making by governmental bodies affect a large sector of economic activity. . .
>
> However, our preference for an economic system in which decision-making is widely diffused and co-ordinated by the market mechanism is not predicated solely on our criterion of development, nor on the political safeguards which the system provides. We consider that in general this system secures an efficient deployment of available resources, and also promotes the growth of resources. Its efficiency stems largely from two of its features: mobilisation of knowledge and provision of incentive.
>
> (Bauer and Yamey, *op.cit.*: 152–4.)

Bauer and Yamey believe that *laissez-faire* promotes three desirable goals: political freedom, economic freedom and economic efficiency.

Bauer and Yamey emphasise the great diversity of conditions – economic, political and cultural – that are prevalent in underdeveloped economies. Given this diversity (their book is rich in empirical illustrations) they aim to demonstrate the main respects in which generalised economic argument can be applied to the analysis of problems prevalent in these countries and to the formulation of economic policy. Their analytical approach reflects an amalgam of a classical preoccupation with the expansion of markets and the development of appropriate institutions, and a neo-classical preoccupation with allocative efficiency (Bauer and Yamey, *op.cit.*: pp. 8–12).

The two economists begin with a review of the key characteristics of underdeveloped countries that are relevant to economic growth – resource endowments, institutions, culture and political systems – and the diversity of each. Already, important conclusions emerge, some of which have become recurring themes in neo-classical analyses of underdevelopment. Among the latter are the following:

1. 'The availability of naturally-occurring material resources do not immutably determine the economic development of a country.' (Bauer and Yamey, *op. cit.*: 46.) This point, already made by Viner, who cites the case of Switzerland,[9] is significant in neo-classical analyses of underdevelopment not only in its own right but because it is generally made, as in both studies just cited, as a prelude to a further observation.
2. It is not so much a country's natural resources endowment as its human resources, institutions, policies and political stability that determine its growth potential.
3. Economic rationality: certain institutions, customs and beliefs may tend to impede an economically efficient allocation of resources in under-developed economies – for example the extended family system (*ibid.*: pp. 64 *et seq.*), the caste system in India (*ibid.*: pp. 37,8) and the refusal of Hindus to slaughter cattle (*ibid.*: pp. 99, 100). However, within such cultural and religious constraints, producers and consumers behave with the same economic rationality (allocating resources so as to maximise profit and utility respectively) as in industrially advanced societies.[10] This too has since been a recurring theme in neo-classical writing on underdevelopment.

Neo-classical theorists frequently emphasise the economic rationality of producers and consumers in less developed countries as part of the case for 'getting the prices right' – itself a dominant theme in neo-classical writings on development (see e.g. World Bank, 1981; Lal, 1983). However, some neo-classical economists have also followed Bauer and Yamey in emphasising the particular significance of these and related points for policy towards peasant agriculture and small-scale industry. The related points in question concern the existence or otherwise of entrepreneurial capabilities and positive savings propensities among small-scale producers in the Third World. Bauer and Yamey were among the first to emphasise the entrepreneurial characteristics and positive savings propensities of most small-scale, traditional producers. Thus 'people in underdeveloped countries are generally well aware of such alternatives as are open to them as sellers or buyers'. Furthermore, 'many are prepared to take a long view and to postpone consumption for several years if the prizes are considered satisfactory.' (Bauer and Yamey, *op.cit.*: pp. 97 and 159.) The first of these points was taken up as a central theme in Schultz's 1964 analysis of agricultural development policy.[11] Subsequently (in the 1970s and 1980s) both points have been emphasised by McKinnon and others in discussions of interest rate policy for underdeveloped countries (see pp. 311–13.).

In the second half of their book Bauer and Yamey turn their attention fully to policy analysis. Firstly, certain other contemporary theories of under-development and development and their policy implications are vigorously rejected, both because of what are claimed to be errors in key assumptions and because of the interventionist policies that they have inspired.[12]

Bauer and Yamey's positive policy recommendations, and the type of development process for which they indicate a preference, are consistent with their theoretical perspective. Given private sector economic ration-ality, governments should concentrate on the performance of those tasks which are essential preconditions for the development of the private sector – maintenance of law and order, national defence, regulation of the money supply and the provision of minimum education and health services, for example (*ibid.*: p. 163). In addition governments have a role to play in disseminating technical information to small-scale producers, both agricul-tural and industrial (private enterprise may try to exercise monopoly control over such knowledge) and promoting institutional changes conducive to the development of private enterprise such as individual land tenure in place of communal tenure (*ibid.*: p. 253).

Like Viner, Bauer and Yamey see a leading role for the agricultural sector in the promotion of economic development.

> The leading industrialised countries of today were once predominantly agricul-tural, and . . . a prosperous and expanding agriculture formed the basis for the concurrent or subsequent establishment and expansion of manufacturing. The agricultural sector . . . provided a large part of the sustenance of the growing urban population. It also supplied a market for manufactured goods bought out of higher real incomes, a source of capital for industry (often through the medium of the capital accumulated by traders), and a source of foreign income to pay for imported capital goods for industry . . . paradoxically, the best way for government to foster industrialisation may be for it to use more rather than less of its resources to encourage the enlargement of agricultural output and the improvement of agricultural techniques.
>
> (Bauer and Yamey, 1957: 235, 6.)

Emphasis on the importance of the free market in promoting efficiency also leads Bauer and Yamey to various other policy recommendations, including the following:

1. Free movement of immigrants across national boundaries (immigrants often provide badly-needed entrepreneurial talents and occupational skills).
2. Use of regressive lump-sum taxation because it is non-distortionary, i.e. it does not tax the marginal return to effort.
3. Selective provision of international credit, which should be made available 'only to countries which agree to follow economic policies which are likely to conduce to the best use of the available capital, foreign or local' (*ibid.*: 145).

The subsequent contribution of neo-classical theory to development economics

Subsequent contributions to development economics by neo-classical economists have concentrated almost entirely on the more detailed exploration of particular theoretical and policy-related issues. It is to some of the most important of these that this discussion now turns.

Meanwhile, certain developments both in mainstream neo-classical theory and the development debate itself have led a majority of development economists who still regard themselves as working within the neo-classical tradition to qualify the support that they give to *laissez-faire*. This has generated, albeit to varying degrees between these theorists, a divergence from the conclusions reached by Bauer and Yamey on certain issues, notably income distribution and public sector involvement in production.

The abandonment of strict adherence to the principle of *laissez-faire* – justified theoretically in Bergson's enunciation of the 'social welfare function' and the need for government determination of this (see Bergson, 1964) – has important implications, for it enables the neo-classical welfare theorist to accept, and work with, public sector policy choices that the *laissez-faire* theorist should in principle reject, including choices concerning income redistribution and public sector engagement in production. The role of the neo-classical welfare theorist then involves determining the most efficient, least distortionary method of achieving government objectives, i.e. that method which interferes least with the smooth operation of market forces and private-sector economic incentives.

One possible interpretation of this division within the neo-classical school is that the abandonment of *laissez-faire* by the welfare theorists represents so radical a split that this should be regarded as having given rise to a totally distinct analytical perspective. In what follows, however, the author prefers to refer to two branches of the one neo-classical tradition. This is for two reasons. Firstly, a substantial common core still remains in the two approaches.[13] Secondly, as already noted, and as will be seen in what follows, the degree and range of state interventions that is regarded as acceptable by neo-classical welfare theorists varies. On this issue neo-classical welfare theorists do not in practice present a clear-cut alternative to the principle of *laissez-faire*, but gradations of divergence from it, combined with advocacy of the use of a stock of analytical techniques based upon standard neo-classical principles designed, as indicated in the previous paragraph, to minimise the distortionary impact of state interventionism.

SPECIFIC ISSUES IN THE NEO-CLASSICAL CONTRIBUTION TO DEVELOPMENT ECONOMICS[14]

The following seeks, through a focus on selected issues, to give the flavour of more recent neo-classical contributions to the development debate. The discussion turns first to international trade and national industrialisation. This is an area in which the neo-classical school has recommended a particular development strategy, that of export-led growth, and in which neo-classical welfare theorists have also contributed a set of 'distortion-minimising' principles as the basis for policy formation.

Trade and industrialisation

Background
It was noted earlier that it is a characteristic of neo-classical contributions to the development debate that the positive theoretical contributions are preceded by a critique of alternative theories and of the policies to which they have given rise. The present instance is a case in point. The neo-classicals have been leading critics of both the methodology and logic employed in structuralist analyses of trends in the terms of trade, and they have also been the leading critics of the policy instruments used to promote the import-substituting industrialisation for which these analyses were held to provide partial justification. These criticisms were reviewed in Chapter 5 (see pp. 147–8 and 152–3) and will not be reiterated again here. Rather, the discussion turns now to the principles that the neo-classical school argue should govern intervention in the economy in order to promote both trade and industrialisation.

Theoretical developments in the analysis of the welfare impact of government intervention
Neo-classical analyses of trade and industrialisation policy start from the proposition that 'countries can mutually gain from trade. For each country the opportunity to trade extends its choice – its frontier of consumption (and investment) possibilities' (Corden, 1974: 5). Neo-classical theorists, unlike the early structuralists and the neo-Marxists, continue to accept the principle of comparative advantage as a justification for free international trade. Not only does trade widen choice, it permits the exploitation of economies of scale and, through competition, promotes X-efficiency (Lal, 1983).[15]

Meanwhile, all neo-classical theorists concur that economies may be subject to various types of institutional and other factors which distort the efficient functioning of the market system. These may be categorised into two groups: those that are endogenous to the existing culture, society and economy (for examples see pp. 70, 93–4 and 297), and those that are created by government policies. Once distortions are recognised, should governments intervene to 'correct' (i.e. compensate for) or remove them? It is here that the *laissez-faire* and welfare branches tend to diverge. According to the former, government-created distortions should undoubtedly be removed; however, intervention to correct endogenous distortions is for the most part discouraged, on the grounds that such interventions are more likely to exacerbate the situation than the opposite. Welfare theorists, however, are less dogmatic on this issue. While they concur with the *laissez-faire* branch that the case for certain types of corrective action has been misjudged by other development economists, they are more ready to acknowledge that in some instances this may be justified and, to this end, they have sought to elaborate a set of guiding principles to ensure effective intervention. These principles are elaborated with specific reference to underdeveloped countries in Johnson (1965). Firstly, only distortions in the international market place (specifically a country's possession of monopolistic or monopsonistic power) justify the use of tariffs by that country. This is a reassertion of Bickerdike's theory of the optimum tariff which

> rests on the proposition that if a country possesses monopolistic or monopsonistic power in world markets, world market prices for its exports and imports will not correspond to the marginal national revenue from exports or marginal national cost of its imports.[16]

In this case, by appropriately chosen export and import duties, the country can equate the relative prices of goods to domestic producers and consumers with their relative opportunity costs in international trade (Johnson, 1965, reprinted in Bhagwati, 1969: 185,6).

In contrast, domestic distortions

> do not logically lead to the recommendation of protection, in the sense of taxes on international trade: instead they lead to the recommendation of other forms of government intervention which do not discriminate between domestic and international trade and which differ according to the nature of the distortion they are intended to correct.
>
> (ibid.)

The case for infant industry protection, for example, if it is valid, must derive from some aspect of the condition of the domestic economy, and therefore is an argument not for intervention in foreign trade, but for appropriate intervention at home. This is a key proposition of neo-classical welfare theory.

Johnson, however, like other neo-classicals, expresses scepticism concerning the strength of the case for government intervention to assist infant industries, particularly since it may be politically difficult to remove such protection (*ibid.*: 212). On this point Little, Scitovsky and Scott also argue that the case for infant industry protection is confused and exaggerated. Not all industries in an underdeveloped economy can simultaneously be infants – yet the notion lacks any clear statement of why and how the public sector should be able to single out the appropriate industries. In addition the infant industry argument fails to consider the possibility that agricultural 'infants' may sometimes be equally deserving of protection, and fails to take on board the need to set the costs of protection against the benefits that the same resources might have generated in other uses (Little, Scitovsky and Scott, 1970: 118–120).

A similar argument is made in relation to the linked problem of the absence of external economies such as developed transport and financial systems and developed industrial skills.[17] The lack of these is faced by producers in all sectors, and does not, it is argued, constitute a case specifically for the promotion of the industrial sector, nor of particular industries within this sector (see e.g. Bauer and Yamey, *op.cit.*: 244, 5).[18]

In the instances so far cited there is broad agreement between members of the two branches of the neo-classical school. In other cases, however, this is not so. Neo-classical welfare theorists acknowledge a possible case for intervention in circumstances where the *laissez-faire* branch deny this. A case in point is the possibility of wage cost distortion, the private supply price – and, hence, hiring cost of labour – in many developing countries being above the true social opportunity cost for the reasons outlined in Lewis (1954), which are acknowledged also by the neo-classical school.

The correction of domestic distortions: an illustration of analytical method
Neo-classical welfare theory seeks to offer guidance both on the appropriate degree of government intervention to correct for particular domestic distortions, and the form it should take, and on, if not optimal, then at least appropriate, tariff structures and tariff reform programmes.

An illustration of the analytical method proposed by neo-classical welfare theorists for dealing with domestic distortions – i.e. for identifying the appropriate form of compensatory intervention for a distortion – is provided in Corden (1974). The method is summarised in the following paragraphs using an example which applies not to distorted wage costs (for these the recommendation would be for a subsidy per person employed) but to a case where unspecified external economies are generated by the production of the product for which it is considered that compensation is justified.

Figure 10.1 describes the demand and supply conditions for a good that can either be produced at home or imported. In the diagram the quantity of a particular importable product is shown along the horizontal axis, and its price along the vertical one. The domestic demand curve for the product is *DD'*, the foreign supply curve is *PP'*, and the supply curve of the domestic import-competing producers is *GG'*. However, while *GG'* indicates the marginal private cost of production for various levels of output, the social cost is assumed to be less.

We can imagine that external economies of some kind attach to production of this product. The value of these benefits should be subtracted from the costs from a social point of view. Hence we obtain a curve showing the marginal social cost of production at various output levels, namely *HH'*.

(Corden, 1974: 9.)

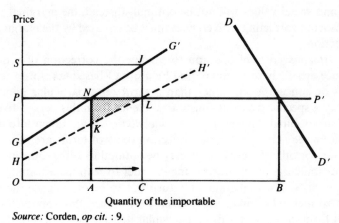

Figure 10.1

The general characteristic of *HH'* is that it is below *GG'*. Corden continues:

> The marginal social cost of production is equal to the marginal cost of imports at output *OC*. This is greater than actual output in the absence of intervention. Hence intervention, designed to increase output or protect the industry, is required. But this intervention should not, ideally, alter the level of consumption.
>
> The aim would be achieved by a subsidy on output at the rate *PS* per unit, or alternatively, the *ad valorem* rate *PS/OP*. It would raise the price received by producers and lead them to raise output to *OC*. The marginal private cost of production would become *CJ*. The total cost of the subsidy to the Treasury would be *PSJL*. Consumers would continue to pay a price of *OP* for the product.
>
> (*Ibid.*: 10.)

Corden then goes on to ask, 'In what sense is this subsidy "optimum"? And what are the nature and size of the gains that it brings about?' In answering these questions he observes that three important assumptions are involved.

1. Financing the subsidy through taxation is non-distortionary.
2. There are no tax collection or subsidy disbursement costs.
3. Any income redistribution that occurs in implementing the subsidy is socially acceptable.

Johnson also makes these assumptions, but, unlike Corden, he does not explore systematically the implications of dropping them.[19]

Corden's conclusions on these issues can be summarised as follows. Subsidies must be financed. However, there is no practical way of collecting taxes that does not entail costs. In practice taxes generate two types of cost, distortion costs and collection costs,[20] while subsidies also entail disbursement costs. Consequently, in reality full correction of a divergence between private and social values will not be optimal. Instead, the marginal value of the gains from correcting a divergence must be equated by the marginal costs of correction.

The *distortion costs* of taxation to finance the correction of a domestic divergence are likely to be minimised by a broad-based tax, for example on incomes or consumption, rather than a tariff on a particular good which taxes only a specific group of consumers. Hence from this perspective tariffs remain sub-optimal. However, once *collection costs* are taken into account the position *may* change, for the collection costs of tariffs are generally far lower than for other taxes. Thus it may be optimal to allow some increase in the distortion costs of revenue raising in order to reap the advantage of low collection costs; taxes on trade may turn out to be on balance the socially lowest cost method of financing a subsidy. However, this approach remains different from the use of tariffs on particular items in lieu of a subsidy. Trade taxes on a range of products are less distortionary than those on one or on a few, so a subsidy financed by a general tariff would still appear preferable to a specific tariff in lieu of a subsidy.

Yet when subsidy disbursement costs are also taken into account, then if these are high, it becomes possible that a specific tariff may become a preferable (first-best) form of compensation for a domestic divergence. Corden suggests that this may occur if small-scale industry is to be subsidised, or if an all-embracing subsidy on manufacturing employment is proposed (Corden, *op.cit.*: 48–50).

Meanwhile, the correction of a divergence, by whatever means, is likely to affect income distribution, in ways that may be either desirable or undesirable. If they are undesirable, then the resulting income distribution will also need to be at least partially corrected. Now a more complex trade-off is involved: since resource mobilisation to correct for income distribution will not be costless, the marginal gains for correcting the divergence must be set against the marginal costs of correcting the ensuing income distribution as well as the marginal other costs of correcting the divergence.

Corden further observes that in practice political exigencies may inhibit the financing of subsidies in the optimum manner. Tariffs or quotas are 'covert' subsidies, not always recognised as such, and usually not subject to scrutiny in the annual budget. While they may be imperfect and distortionary, they may be politically the least controversial method of providing some compensation for domestic divergences.

Welfare theory and tariff reform

Part of the interest of Corden's analysis is in the implication, once a fuller approximation of reality is introduced into the analysis, that tariffs may not necessarily be a socially inefficient means of correcting domestic distortions: it depends upon economic and political circumstances. However, Corden also sustains the view, with other welfare theorists, that existing tariff structures are themselves frequently distorted (with rates diverging wildly and apparently irrationally between products) and, hence, are the cause of sub-optimal resource allocation.

If it is possible to convince a government to reform at least part of a distortionary tariff structure, then modern welfare theory can provide guidelines on the tariff reform paths that are likely to generate an increase in overall efficiency and welfare, and those that will do the opposite (Corden, *op.cit.*: Chapter 13). It offers such guidance via the theory of the second best,[21] of which the theory of tariff reform is a specific application. Thus, for example, in a situation in which free trade would enable a country to maximise economic welfare, but where due to political constraints tariffs must remain on some commodities, full abolition of tariffs on others would be unlikely to lead to a second-best solution. Partial abolition would be preferable (Corden, *op.cit.*: 368).

However, a further complication is introduced by the fact that it is the effective rate of protection, i.e. the rate of protection *offered to domestic value added* by a given nominal tariff, which generates production distortions, and nominal tariff rates which generate consumption distortions. The search for an 'optimum' tariff structure therefore entails a trade-off between two sets of second-best structures – a set of effective rates, and a set of nominal rates. Probably the best that can be done is to search for a sensible rule of thumb to guide tariff reform (*ibid.*: 361–372).

Foreign trade and development strategy
Underlying the literature on optimal tariff structures and the correction of domestic market distortions there is, as noted earlier, a continuing emphasis on the principle of comparative advantage. As far as possible, governments should ensure that private producers face the correct set of relative prices and should then encourage specialisation according to comparative advantage. Since competition raises efficiency and specialisation enlarges markets (so lowering unit costs wherever scale economies exist) producers should be encouraged to compete in international markets rather than be protected from them. From the publication of Little, Scitovsky and Scott (1970) onwards, the neo-classical school has advocated a strategy of export-led growth.[22] Depending on a country's resource endowments, this may be based on either primary or manufactured exports or on a mixture of both (many developing countries had, by 1970, significantly expanded their manufacturing capacity, chiefly through government promoted import-substitution). If foreign competition forces the closure of some manufacturing industries which are unable to compete, this will be in the national interest.

The stabilisation programmes of the International Monetary Fund

The monetarist macro-economics which underpins the IMF view of the causes of balance of payments instability and domestic inflation in less developed countries also has its foundations in the standard neo-classical model of economic behaviour: a model in which all prices are assumed to be flexible (upwards and downwards), structural rigidities in both supply and demand are discounted, and competition (international as well as national) is regarded as a healthy stimulus to economic efficiency.

The monetarist view of the causes of balance of payments deficits and domestic price inflation in developing countries, as elsewhere, is as follows. In all countries with a central banking system, the authorities can vary the money supply independently of the demand for it. If the growth rate of the money supply in a particular country exceeds the growth rate of output and incomes, then the demand for goods and services will also grow faster than output. This leads to upward pressure on domestic prices and to pressure on the balance of payments. At the same time, declining real interest rates may lead to increasing capital outflows.

According to the mainstream monetarist perspective, the cure for both balance of payments deficits and for domestic price inflation lies primarily in curtailing the rate of growth of domestic demand by controlling the growth of the money supply. Since excessive money supply growth is generally due to governments' need to finance their own deficits – i.e. to finance expenditure programmes that exceed tax revenues plus borrowing – an important feature of monetary control is the reduction of the public sector deficit. This can be achieved via a reduction in public expenditure supported by improved tax performance. Since the latter is difficult to achieve in low-income countries, the emphasis is placed chiefly on the former. Meanwhile, to restore balance of payments equilibrium via reduced imports and increased exports it is also necessary to devalue the domestic currency. In addition, both in order to curtail aggregate domestic demand – via reduced borrowing and increased saving – and to reduce capital outflows, an increase in domestic interest rates is likely to be necessary.

IMF stabilisation programmes characteristically also include measures that focus on increasing the short-run efficiency with which existing resources are allocated. These are measures to reduce distortions caused by price and exchange-rate rigidities, monopolies, taxes, subsidies and trade restrictions (Khan and Knight, 1981: 713).

This perspective is, of course, in stark contrast to the structuralist view of the causes of, and the remedies for, domestic inflation and balance of payments crisis in developing countries, as this was enunciated in the 1950s and 1960s (see Chapter 5).

The 1970s and 1980s have greatly increased the scope for applied analysis of country experiences in the implementation of the policy reforms advocated by the neo-classical school, and implemented during this period usually at the instigation of the IMF. While failures to attain desired objectives are acknowledged, these are ascribed by neo-classical analysts to attempts to introduce large changes too fast (thereby creating political tension and rising uncertainty in the private sector), and/or to failure to implement the complete package of reforms. These studies are linked to a debate on the optimal timing of liberalisation programmes, a debate in which there is evidence of growing acknowledgment by some neo-classical/monetarist economists that structural rigidities impede the pace at which less-developed economies can respond to a shift in relative prices, and that, given balance of payments imbalances of the extent and magnitude that have occurred since the early 1970s, stabilisation programmes cannot any longer be expected to rely solely on short-run demand management (see Khan and Knight, *op.cit.*: 714). Instead a medium-term, staged programme should be adopted in planning reform.

Disequilibrium analysis and policy impact analysis

Since the late 1970s the neoclassical school has begun to focus on the modelling of a range of national *dis*equilibrium situations (i.e. those in which certain key prices, such as the foreign exchange rate or the interest rate are fixed at a non-market-clearing level, as well as those in which there are distortionary tariffs and quotas). The purpose is to explore systematically the welfare implications of various type of policy reform given these starting conditions. The December 1982 Special Issue of *World Development* ('Analysing disequilibrium in developing countries') outlines the direction being taken. So far these developments have generated innovations primarily in econometric method rather than in theory.

The New International Economic Order (NIEO)

Since the mid-1970s, neo-classical economists have also contributed to the debate on proposals by the 'Group of 77' for a New International Economic Order intended to offer more favourable trade and international financing prospects to developing countries, combined with greater control over the activities of multinational corporations in the Third World (see e.g. *UN Monthly Chronicle*, May 1974: 73). The neo-classicals have not been entirely dismissive of these proposals, but they have subjected them to wide-ranging criticism (see e.g. Bhagwati, 1977; Lal, 1983). For example, they argue that while a case can be made for Third World countries trying to raise primary product prices, in theory this should be done through export taxes (which, being passed back to the producer, would restrict supply by lowering producer prices) rather than through direct quantitative controls (i.e. production quotas) as proposed. Neo-classical economists argue that in this instance, as in others, centralised non-price controls would promote inefficiency and should be replaced by measures that influence via market prices the allocative decisions of individual consumers and producers. (In practice, however, the neo-classicals also assert that the scope for such policy intervention to raise primary product prices, which depends on all exporting countries agreeing to participate, and on the existence of price inelastic demand in importing countries, is limited; see Henderson and Lal, 1976; and Lal, 1983: 50, 51.)

Social cost-benefit analysis

Another major focus of the contribution of neo-classical welfare economics to development economics has been upon the underlying theory, and upon the techniques and application, of social cost-benefit analysis. This is in keeping with both the micro-economic orientation of the neo-classical paradigm and its emphasis upon the role of prices in resource allocation.

Cost-benefit analysis is in itself a *technique*, not a body of theory, the purpose of which is to provide a set of theoretically sound and systematic rules and procedures to guide public-sector investment decisions. However, its theoretical basis, from which the rules are derived, is neo-classical welfare economics.[23] The perceived need for this technique derives from the view that public sector investment decisions should do the following:

1. Take into account the full range of social costs and benefits that the project would generate within the national economy, whether or not these accrue to the investing institution, and whether or not they are incorporated in market transactions.
2. Value inputs at their marginal social opportunity cost, and outputs at their marginal social value.
3. Discount the future stream of appropriately valued costs and benefits at the social rate of discount.

It is chiefly the greater problems that are perceived to be associated with 2 in underdeveloped economies, that has led to the elaboration of principles, rules and procedures of cost-benefit analysis specifically for these regions. The aim is to take account of the wide range of factor and product price distortions that exist there, whether endogenous or government generated. In addition, cost-benefit analysis has been perceived as a medium for the pursuit of certain policy targets which cannot be reached via the use of more conventional policy instruments (see below).

Since the late 1960s various sets of cost-benefit rules and procedures for underdeveloped countries have become widely known and used. However, those developed by Little and Mirrlees (1974) and by UNIDO (1972) constitute the two basic sets of guidelines from which others have subsequently been derived.[24] Both aim to ensure fulfilment of the three criteria listed above, although they differ in the procedures used for valuing project inputs and outputs, and in the emphasis given to externalities.[25] Both also adopt the position that if governments in underdeveloped countries are unable, for political or other reasons, to achieve the desired rate of savings and/or the desired pattern of income distribution through the use of more conventional policy instruments, then the choice of public investment projects should also be geared to achieving these ends. Project costs and benefits should be weighted to take into account their impact on savings and income distribution.[26]

Central to each approach is the agreed need to compute a set of shadow prices which will reflect the true social value of all resources. Fundamental to the estimation of shadow prices for commodities is the prior estimation of shadow prices for two key resources: labour and foreign exchange. To indicate the issues involved, the latter will be discussed first. To keep the discussion simple reference will be made solely to the methodologies advocated in the Little–Mirrlees and UNIDO guidelines.

The starting-point is the proposition that, for individual countries, free trade is normally welfare-maximising.[27] In conditions in which free trade does not exist, domestic and foreign prices for tradeable goods diverge. (Tradeables are goods which either *are* traded or *could be*, i.e. transport costs are not prohibitive.) In such cases of price divergence, neo-classical welfare theorists argue that it is international price relatives, which are given for any national economy, and represent the international purchasing power earned or saved by domestic production of a tradeable good or service, that represent the true marginal social value of tradeables. Foreign exchange so earned or saved can be allocated according to society's preferences, but the greater the amount of foreign exchange at its disposal, the better off a society will be. By estimating shadow prices for project appraisal such that these prices directly reflect international price relatives, it is argued that the public sector can nudge the economy nearer to a free-trade equilibrium in which net foreign exchange availability is maximised. This can be done either by pricing all tradeables at border prices (as advocated by Little and Mirrlees),[28] or by estimating a shadow price for foreign exchange which is then applied to project inputs and outputs – to the full value of tradeables and to the tradeable inputs in non-tradeables (as advocated by UNIDO).[29]

With respect to the shadow-price of labour, the two sets of guidelines follow the same principles. These are threefold. Firstly, this shadow price should reflect the true opportunity cost to society of employing different types of labour (skilled and unskilled). The main component of this cost is the social value of the output foregone as a result of employing labour on the new project. Additional costs, similarly valued, include those of moving labour to the project site and any increase in essential living costs (housing, etc.) associated with residence at or near the site.

For unskilled labour whose supply price is determined for institutional reasons by average per capita income in the traditional sector, the social opportunity cost of hiring labour (i.e. labour's exisiting marginal value product, appropriately shadow priced) is likely to be below the actual wage. However, the operators of the project have to pay the actual wage. This leads on to the second principle underlying labour valuation: where the actual wage exceeds the social opportunity cost of labour, the difference represents a net increase in private consumption (assuming all wage income is consumed). Where savings are sub-optimal, any such increase in consumption in principle represents a cost to society, whose social value should be estimated and included in labour costs. To do this the market value of the main items in the consumption packages of the income groups affected should be converted to accounting prices. Using a weighted index based on the share of different items in the package, the shadow cost of the extra consumption can then be estimated.

Thirdly, however, since society may actually wish to see some increase in the consumption standard of wage-earners, the *positive* value attached to this consumption increase on income distribution grounds must also be estimated. This can be done by applying predetermined weights to the consumption gain (according to the existing consumption level of the gainers), where the weights reflect the social value attached to a consumption increase of different income groups relative to an increase in savings. The value of this distributional benefit is then deducted from aggregate labour costs (opportunity cost, movement and rehousing costs, and consumption costs) in order to obtain the net shadow wage.

Similar principles to those just described would also be applied in valuing consumption gains that arise on the benefit side of a project – for example when the increased output is expected to lead to a reduction in prices for one or more commodities, and hence to a real disposable income gain for consumers. Furthermore, if it is expected that part of the income increase will be saved then, under the suboptimal savings assumption, this would normally be given a higher weight than the part to be devoted to consumption, except, possibly, in the case of very poor households.

Of the third key shadow price that is advocated for use in cost benefit analysis, the accounting rate of interest (ARI), less needs to be said. In principle this should reflect the scarcity value of finance capital to the public sector, given the projects it might finance, their respective internal rates of return, and the finance capital available for funding them. 'The right ARI is the one that passes just the right volume of projects' (Little and Mirrlees, *op.cit.*: 291) – i.e. that volume which just uses up the available investible resources, so that the social internal rate of return on the marginal project exactly equals the accounting rate of interest.

As Corden points out,

A problem which sometimes tends to get neglected in the shadow-pricing approach is the problem of implementation: a project may not be profitable when internal costs and benefits are evaluated at market prices but would be profitable when the full social costs and benefits are evaluated on the basis of shadow prices – and vice versa.

(Corden, 1974: 390–392.)

Thus the market price calculation of private profitability must also be made. This will indicate how much subsidisation or protection will be required in the first case, and the need to ensure that the project is not undertaken in the second. In the latter case, if the project so appraised would otherwise be undertaken in the private sector, then either a system of investment licensing or imposition of a tax that makes the project prohibitive may be called for (*ibid.*).

It has been suggested that cost-benefit analysis, like the theory of tariff reform, is an exercise in the theory of second best, i.e. it attempts to bring about allocative improvements in a 'sub-optimal' economic system in which distortions, externalities and monopolies prevent attainment of a Paretian optimum via the operation of the market system.[30]

Macro-economic policy in developing countries: further issues

Monetary policy

Chapter 5 has shown that one of the factor price distortions identified by neo-classical critics of government-promoted import-substitution concerns the price of capital. Since the early 1970s the implications of capital price distortions for resource allocation, growth and income distribution, and the analysis of appropriate directions for policy reform, have become the subject matter of a separate branch of the contribution of neo-classical theory to development economics. The main theoretical contributions in this field are associated with the names of Shaw and McKinnon.

Shaw (1973) develops three linked themes:

1. For efficiency and growth, prices matter as much in financial markets as in markets for real goods and services.
2. Maintenance of below-equilibrium-price real interest rates in the formal sector of developing countries leads to 'financial repression'. That is to say, the development and diversification of the financial sector, through which in principle increasing savings should be mobilised and allocated, are discouraged.
3. 'Financial deepening' – the increase and diversification of a country's financial assets, linked to a widening in the range of their users – is an essential precondition for economic development.

McKinnon (1973) takes this analysis further, basing his argument partly on a new theorisation of the relationship between self-finance, credit and real capital formation in developing countries. The essence of his argument is as follows.

Low real interest rates in the formal financial sector alongside high informal sector interest rates charged by private money lenders lead both to inefficient allocation of finance capital and to a reduction in the overall rate of capital formation. Capital is allocated inefficiently for three main reasons:

1. Low real interest rates encourage risk-minimisation by lenders, combined with attempts to minimise administrative costs. The latter leads to a preference for large loans, and the former to a preference for

known borrowers with a good credit-rating, such as multinational corporations, the government sector, and established indigenous firms specialising in import-export or highly protected manufacturing (McKinnon, *op.cit.*: 68).

2. Acceptable borrowers are encouraged by low real interest rates to borrow up to the point where the internal rate of return on investment is equal to the low borrowing rate, and private individuals are also encouraged by low borrowing charges to make unproductive investments (for example in imported consumer durables). At the same time potentially higher return, but riskier, small-scale investments are not financed (see below).

3. Low real interest rates also encourage the use of relatively capital-intensive techniques and reduce absorption of the relatively abundant resource – labour.

Meanwhile the overall rate of capital formation is reduced, for two main reasons:

1. Low real interest rates reduce the mobilisation of financial savings, and, hence, the stock of finance capital available for lending.

2. Large numbers of small-scale investments which could be expected to generate internal rates of return above the formal sector interest rate but below that charged by private moneylenders are not financed. Provision of credit to such small-scale entrepreneurs would also call forth additional self-finance for these investments, but as long as they do not have access to credit this does not occur.

McKinnon argues that many small-scale entrepreneurs are ready to achieve quite high rates of saving and investment out of low incomes, but are frustrated by the indivisibility of many potentially high-return investments (e.g. sinking a tube-well, purchase of a dairy-cow) whose cost exceeds the attainable level of self-finance. As a result, potential savings in cash and kind from the individual's own resources are not realised. In this case provision of supplementary credit would act as a complement to self-finance, and not a substitute as is normally assumed in monetary theory (McKinnon, *op.cit.*: 57).

McKinnon, like Shaw, concludes that most developing countries would benefit from an increase in formal sector real interest rates. This would lead to the following:

1. Increased mobilisation of financial savings.

2. Elimination of formal sector loans with low real returns.

3. An incentive (resulting jointly from the consequent increase in savings deposits and reduction in inefficient large-scale borrowing) for financial institutions to diversify their activities, by looking for smaller scale, higher-risk borrowers.

4. Due to 3, a reduction in any monopoly rent element in the charges of private money-lenders.
5. Due to 3 and to higher interest rates, increased mobilisation of deposits from small-scale savers previously outside the formal sector.
6. Encouragement of local entrepreneurship.
7. An increase in labour intensity in production technology.
8. A geographically more diffused pattern of investment.
9. As a result of 7 and 8, a more equitable pattern of development.
10. A reduction in inflationary pressures due, on the one hand, to increased savings and, on the other, to more, and more productive, capital formation and, consequently, a faster rate of increase in real output.

McKinnon favours the trade liberalisation policies advocated by the mainstream neo-classical critics of protected import-substituting industrialisation. However, in the McKinnon/Shaw perspective it is not export-led growth *per se* but 'a vigorous capital market, centred on the monetary system, (that) can be a more efficient engine of economic development' (McKinnon. *op.cit.*: 132).

Poverty and income distribution
The main propositions on income distribution that have emerged from the neo-classical perspective may be summarised as follows:

1. Inequality is a source of economic incentive.
2. However, the distribution of income generated by the operation of market forces may not be the socially desired distribution.
3. Where this is so it is up to governments
   (a) to establish what is the socially optimal distribution – this forms part of the social welfare function which every government needs to specify in order to guide rational policy formation;[31]
   (b) to decide whether to intervene to achieve the socially desired distribution; however 'if [non-distortionary] lump-sum taxes and subsidies cannot be used in practice, the costs of distortion from using other fiscal devices . . . will have to be set against the benefits from any gain in equity' (Lal, 1983: 88).[32]

However, beyond this there is a divergence of opinion among neo-classical economists as to both the desirability and the appropriate form of policy action with respect to income distribution. Some, such as Bauer and Lal, argue that governments should not intervene to redistribute income because the distortion costs (leading to output foregone chiefly due to reduced incentives to save and invest) will exceed the welfare gains (see also the efficiency arguments for non-intervention in David, 1986: 28–29). Instead, governments should concentrate upon providing the conditions for more efficient resource allocation and accelerated private sector growth. This will lead inevitably to expanding self- and wage-employment opportunities and to rising real wages. Others, including the cost-benefit theorists whose work was discussed on pages 308–11, favour redistribution to the poor. They argue that members of developing countries' governments may also favour this, although political constraints may prevent them from taking the more obvious forms of policy action on this front; hence the need to evaluate and select public-sector investment projects (and those private-sector projects over which the public sector has influence), taking into account their impact on income distribution.

Land reform

The variation in attitude among neo-classical economists to policy interventions which are specifically equity-oriented may in part be a reflection of the fact that the neo-classical preoccupation with equity is largely reactive rather than purposive. (Neo-classical theory is primarily concerned with efficiency. It was the neo-Marxist school, supported by some structuralist economists, who first placed distributive issues high on the agenda of development economics.) This variation is also found in the stance taken by neo-classical economists on land reform.

In no case has advocacy of land reform been a central theme in neo-classical writing on development, and attitudes towards this issue range from strongly negative to lukewarm. The arguments levelled against redistribution focus on:

1. The negative effects on confidence in private property rights and the incentive to invest.
2. The negative effects on present and future output arising from lack of knowledge, expertise and finance capital among land recipients.[33]
3. The insufficiency of land for redistribution.
4. Difficulties of implementation (Bauer and Yamey, *op.cit.*: 97).
5. The proposition that if there are inefficiencies (as opposed to inequities) arising from the existing land distribution the solution lies in government promotion of more efficient capital and land markets (Collier and Lal, 1986).

On the other hand, some neo-classicals have been impressed by the results of empirical studies indicating an inverse relationship between farm size and efficiency in a number of developing countries. They feel constrained from making asset redistribution a key policy issue on feasibility grounds – the prohibitive costs of compensation, and the political constraints to expropriation (e.g. Timmer *et al.*, 1983: 285). Some of this group would also favour redistribution on equity grounds (see e.g. Little, 1982: 173), were it deemed feasible.

Two types of land reform have, however, met with the approval even of the 'hard-liners'. These are the individualisation of communal tenure – regarded as necessary in order to permit the expansion of successful farm enterprises, to provide security for credit, to discourage over-grazing and to encourage long-term investment in land (Bauer and Yamey, *op.cit.*: 52 and 174) – and the consolidation of fragmented holdings (*ibid.*: 177–80; see also McKinnon, 1973: 28).

Other recent neo-classical contributions to the development debate

Other recent neo-classical contributions to the development debate include Schultz' reassertion of the importance of investment in human capital (see for example Schultz, 1979) and Stiglitz' attempt to found a 'new development economics' on further theoretical exploration of the nature and implications of the rationality of small-scale producers (see Stiglitz, 1986).

FOREIGN AID

Foreign aid is also an issue on which a range of opinions have been expressed by the neo-classicals. Some have also shifted their position over time. The strongest opposition to aid, consistent, one might argue, with firm adherence to a philosophy of *laissez-faire*, was first expressed by Bauer in the late 1960s and early 1970s. In a position analagous to that which opposes government intervention in the domestic economy, Bauer likewise opposes provision of assistance by foreign governments, albeit for different reasons. The latter include the fact that aid inflows help to sustain the avoidance of necessary policy reforms in the recipient country, and that aid encourages the view that the rich countries should carry the moral responsibility for the poor countries' underdevelopment as well as a significant share of the cost of relieving it (Bauer, 1976: 100–102; see also Bauer and Yamey, 1981).

An intermediate view is that of Lal (1983), who argues that while financial aid is likely to be counter-productive, technical assistance has positive value.

The majority view, however, espoused by most neo-classical welfare economists who have written on aid, is that financial aid also has a potential positive value, and that the problem is to ensure that this potential is realised. This was the reasoning that underlay the development of the cost-benefit methodologies reviewed on pp 305–7. More recently the view adopted by this group is that there is a major role for aid not only in assisting specific projects but in providing general support for stabilisation and structural adjustment programmes. This aid should be provided on conditions that are designed to ensure its efficient use (as perceived by the donors). As a corollary it should not be provided to all potential recipients, but only those who accept these conditions. (This view in fact coincides with that expressed in Bauer and Yamey, 1957, before Bauer moved to a more radical position.)

RECENT CRITICISMS OF APPLICATIONS OF THE NEO-CLASSICAL PARADIGM IN DEVELOPMENT ECONOMICS

The criticisms levelled against the neo-classical paradigm have been pitched at various levels, focusing on various elements of the paradigm. These elements have included the values and beliefs it embodies, its assumptions concerning the key features of economic systems, the preoccupation with identifying the conditions for economic equilibrium (and the associated emphasis on a particular analytical method and body of technique), and the almost exclusive focus on short-run allocative issues.

Values and beliefs

While much has been written by economists in criticism of the neo-classical perspective in general, and of its various applications to development economics in particular, relatively little has been written in the form of a critique that explicitly addresses the values and related beliefs that this perspective embodies. In development economics in particular this issue has more often been addressed indirectly via the positive statement of an alternative set of values and beliefs governing an alternative interpretation of, and theorisation of, development.

It is in fact impossible to 'debate' the values and beliefs that underlie any social theory, with a view to reaching a choice by rational criteria. People may be *persuaded* to modify their values and beliefs, but not logically convinced. (It is for this reason that in the 1970s and 1980s those anxious to see greater resources committed to poverty reduction committed part of their efforts to disseminating evidence both of the extent of poverty itself and of the cost-effectiveness of certain measures in relieving it.)

The key elements of the values and beliefs that are embodied in the neo-classical perspective, and which have been either explicitly or implicitly questioned by many who have espoused other intellectual frameworks for the analysis of social change, are as follows:

1. A belief that economic inequality is a major source of incentive.
2. Attachment of a very high value to personal freedom – economic as well as political.
3. An associated belief that the free market generally allocates resources more efficiently than can be achieved by government intervention.

With respect to the first of these, a further basis for the unwillingness of some to give as much weight to this point as do the neo-classical school is the belief that inequality may also be a source of inefficiency (both static and dynamic) as well as inequity (the former may occur, for example, with unequal land distribution, while dynamic inefficiencies may also be generated by the structure of demand generated by highly skewed income distribution in some developing countries).

Secondly, for many economists who do not espouse the neo-classical perspective, a key issue is precisely the extent to which individual freedom and individualism should be assigned primacy in economic life.

Thirdly, critics also argue (see e.g. Toye, 1987) that there is no objective reason for supposing that markets, which in the contemporary world are necessarily imperfect, are invariably better mediators of resource allocation than imperfect governments.

Neo-classical assumptions concerning the key features of economic systems

The basic assumptions of neo-classical partial and general equilibrium models are well known – utility and profit maximisation by consumers and producers respectively, perfect competition (with the subsidiary assumptions that this entails), etc. Some of these will be referred to again in the next section. However, before proceeding to review the criticisms that have been levelled against the neo-classical preoccupation with the conditions for economic equilibrium, it may be helpful to note the reply offered by neo-classical theorists to the argument that their basic assumptions are unrealistic.

Neo-classicals have offered two main replies to this criticism. The first, to be found in Friedman (1953), is that in a theoretical model the primary issue is the accuracy of its predictions, not the realism of its assumptions. The second is that the model and its findings are not intended so much to represent reality as to act as a benchmark to guide policy formulation (see Lal, 1983). It may be helpful to bear these responses in mind in the following discussion.

The irrelevance of equilibrium economics

Neo-classical theory has been criticised as irrelevant to the analysis of actual economic systems for reasons which relate both to the assumptions of the theory and its focus. Early criticisms (prior to the emergence of development economics) emphasised the following aspects:

1. Excessive abstraction from reality in order to achieve a specious general validity.
2. Failure to retain within that abstraction key features of the real world which are crucial in explaining the functioning of actual economic systems in diverse concrete situations.[34]

Meanwhile, as shown in Chapter 3, many early development economists were also strongly critical of the neo-classical representation of economic systems as tending towards equilibrium – or, on a slightly less harsh interpretation, the persistent fascination with the conditions that would lead to equilibrium, both in different sectors and in the economy as a whole.[35] Part of the emphasis on this issue undoubtedly derives from the preoccupation of these critics with the identification of strategies to generate long-run economic change of a kind that would radically transform the less-developed economies. Clearly the notion of equilibrium seems logically irrelevant to such a preoccupation. Meanwhile more specific reasons, such as the significance of externalities (pecuniary as well as real) were also put forward for questioning its relevance.

Subsequently, Kaldor has taken up the theme of the irrelevance of equilibrium economics not only for development economics but for economic analysis in general. Kaldor (1972) starts from the proposition that the assumptions needed to generate equilibrium solutions are generally either untestable (utility maximisation) or unreal, and then focuses his attention on one of these, that of constant returns to scale. Kaldor argues that if increasing returns are widespread in the real world there can be no tendency towards equilibrium, and asserts that they are indeed widespread, largely for the reasons identified by Adam Smith. With increased scale, complex processes can be broken up into simple processes and then mechanised, while specialisation also increases opportunities for 'learning by doing'. In addition, 'plant costs per unit of output necessarily decrease with size in any integrated process operation . . . simply on account of the three-dimensional nature of space.' (Kaldor, 1972: 1242, 3.)

In place of an irrelevant notion of general equilibrium, Kaldor proposes the reinstatement of the 'theorem of endogenous and cumulative change', pioneered by Adam Smith in the first three chapters of the *Wealth of Nations*, elaborated by Allyn Young in 1928 (see Chapter 2, pp. 12–13), and revived in the 1950s by the development economist Gunnar Myrdal, who called it 'the principle of cumulative causation'. Disequilibrium is not generated exogenously by, for example, inappropriate policies, but is *endogenous* to the economic system, and policies that assume otherwise are likely to be inappropriate. Only in the consideration of short-run problems where certain resources may justifiably be taken as given, does Kaldor concede that equilibrium analysis may have a potential relevance as a predictive device and potential guide to policy.

Livingstone (1978) has indicated further ways in which the dynamic logic of economies of scale generates phenomena of policy importance for developing countries, including both the inherent tendency towards monopoly that is associated with scale economies, and the emergence of multinational corporations partly in order to exploit scale economies in international markets. Given the widespread prevalence of these phenomena, 'the viewing of a monopoly situation as a correctable deviation from the 'norm' of perfect competition is problematic, as indeed is the whole concept of an 'optimum' allocation of resources'. (Livingstone, 1978: 40.)

Neither Kaldor nor Livingstone advocates the wholesale rejection of the analytical concepts and methods employed within the neo-classical school. Rather, it is the central focus of the paradigm that they reject – the notion that it is appropriate to analyse the functioning of economic systems, and to formulate policy, particularly long-run policy, in terms geared towards the attainment of welfare-maximising equilibria.

Both these critics, among others, also reject certain more specific assumptions about the characteristics of market economies which are essential building blocks in neo-classical theory, including the predominance of perfect competition and also, more specifically, the pervasiveness of profit maximisation as the governing objective of firms.[36] In later work Kaldor also develops his critique of the neo-classical emphasis on the allocative role of markets. In Kaldor (1985) he argues that neo-classical theory over-emphasises the role of prices as guides to output; most firms are price-makers not price-takers, and in manufacturing industry it is quantity variations (in stocks and order books), not price variations, that are the dominant determinants of output change. Moreover, while most firms set their own prices, they do not do so on the basis of marginal cost.

The adoption of a different set of assumptions concerning the objectives of firms, the dominant characteristics of production technology, and the dynamic of market systems would still entail the use of a number of familiar tools and concepts associated with neo-classical theory to analyse the functioning of economic systems. Witness, for example, the role played by the concept of demand elasticity in Young's analysis and in Kaldor's elaboration thereof, and the roles of demand and supply elasticity in structuralist analyses of underdevelopment. (See also Livingstone, *op.cit.*: 45–7 on this point.) Use of these concepts implies a continuing need for analysis of the influence of prices on the supply of and demand for both factors of production and commodities. However, recognition of the influence of prices on resource allocation does not entail either assigning to prices the *degree* of relative importance that they assume in the neo-classical paradigm, nor making the assumption that price changes generate precise profit- and utility-maximising responses. Rather the degree, nature and causes of price-responsiveness become themselves a subject for study.

Others, meanwhile, have criticised neo-classical theory for the manner in which it ignores those broader issues of political economy which in practice both determine much of the nature of economic interaction in the private sector and influence government policy formation (see e.g. Dobb, 1940: 131–133).

However, an alternative perspective on this omission argues that the neo-classical paradigm is itself geared to the validation and reinforcement of a particular politico-economic structure.[37]

Specific criticisms of the contributions of neo-classical theory to development economics

The foregoing has focused on the overall perspective of the neo-classical paradigm and its basic assumptions. This section reviews how both these and other criticisms have been applied to particular elements of the paradigm's contribution to development economics. It will concentrate chiefly on the neo-classical contribution to the debate on trade and industrialisation and to the development of the technique of cost-benefit analysis by neo-classical welfare theorists.

International trade and industrialisation

First there is the question of the universal validity of the theory of comparative advantage. It has been shown that this theory, and its policy conclusions, were rejected by a wide range of development economists: Arthur Lewis, Singer, Prebisch, Nurkse, Myrdal and Emmanuel, to name the most notable.[38] While their reasons for doing so varied, they had in common the view that the theory's conclusions were derived from premises that did not adequately reflect the real world. They believed that these premises ignored trends in the income elasticity of demand for primary and manufactured goods in the developed countries (Singer, Prebisch in his later work, Nurkse); they ignored the combined implications of trade union bargaining strength and oligopolistic pricing for the ability of developed countries to retain, rather than pass on in lower prices, the benefits of productivity gains in manufacturing production (Prebisch, 1949; Emmanuel, 1972); and they ignored the inability of less developed countries to retain the value of *their* productivity gains in primary production due to the depressant effect of excess labour supply on real wages (Lewis, 1954; Emmanuel, 1972). Meanwhile the Hecksher-Ohlin version of the theory of comparative advantage is also criticised for the assumption that all goods are technology-specific, whereas for primary production this is not so (nor is it for some manufactures). This undercuts the Hecksher-Ohlin conclusion that all countries can gain from trade if they specialise in those products to which their factor endowments are best suited; another technology may be more competitive.

The strategy of export-led growth, which the principle of comparative advantage is held to underpin, has also been criticised on empirical grounds, for lack of realism in two senses: incorrect interpretation of historical experience and unrealistic assumptions concerning the feasibility of exports acting as an engine of growth for a large number of low- and middle-income countries.

It is argued that the main country experiences used to justify the concept of non-interventionist export-led growth, based on specialisation according to comparative advantage, have been misinterpreted. In reality the countries cited (Taiwan and South Korea are two leading examples) have experienced various forms of government intervention in the economy, including a prior phase of import-substituting industrialisation, while exports have also been actively promoted by the public sector, especially in South Korea. (Furthermore, Korea's export-led growth itself both has been and is combined with a particular form of import-substitution. Export promotion has entailed subsidisation of manufactured exports with an initially high import content, followed by deliberate promotion of domestic production of the imported inputs.)[39] Meanwhile both Brazil and Mexico – also often cited by neoclassicals as countries that have made a successful transition to export-led growth – both provide instances of import-substituting industries that subsequently, as they gained in efficiency, became successful exporters (as also occurred in the United States and West Germany in the nineteenth century, and in Japan in the twentieth).

Secondly, it has been argued that the proponents of export-led growth ignore the fallacy of composition. If all Third World countries simultaneously seek to promote the expansion of manufactured exports they will inevitably encounter a new wave of protectionism on the part of the industrially advanced countries (Streeten, 1982; Cline, 1982).[40] Meanwhile the terms of trade effects of export expansion for a number of important primary products are bound to be adverse (Godfrey, 1985).

Godfrey (1985) argues that the blanket recommendation of primary export expansion according to existing comparative advantage should at least be replaced by advocacy of primary export diversification, i.e. of the search for new lines of comparative advantage in primary exporting as well as manufactured exports. Some critics however go further and argue that particularly in the early stages of development, and particularly in conditions of international recession, developing countries must generate the engine of growth at home (see e.g. Adelman, 1984). Furthermore, in most countries policy instruments largely eschewed by the neo-classicals (land reform and income distribution) have a crucial role to play in laying the basis for an initially *domestic demand-led* process of combined economic expansion and structural diversification (see both Adelman, 1984, and the arguments reviewed in Chapter 9).

The neo-classical underpinnings of IMF stabilisation programmes

In recent years one of the areas in which the neo-classical perspective has made the greatest impact both upon the Third World and upon the development debate is through the implementation of IMF stabilisation programmes. The neo-classical underpinnings of the monetarist approach to the balance of payments were outlined on pp. 305–6. Here we summarise the main criticisms that have been levelled against this approach, initially from a classical structuralist perspective but subsequently also by dependency theorists and proponents of meeting basic needs. These are as follows:

1. The approach attacks the symptoms but not the causes of instability.
2. The inevitable short-run effects of the recommended policy measures are further price inflation, industrial recession and increased unemployment.
3. The recommended policy measures do not guarantee significant improvement in the balance of payments.
4. These programmes hit the poor hardest.

The first of these points (symptoms versus causes) was elaborated in Chapter 5 (see pp. 137 and 140; see also Amin, 1976: 126–131). With respect to the first set of predicted consequences, the main arguments are, firstly, that the devaluations recommended in IMF stabilisation programmes will raise import prices, while the removal of food price controls (advocated by the IMF as part of the general elimination of price distortions) will raise food prices. The consequent increases in the prices of producer goods and money wages combined with the recommended domestic demand deflation will severely squeeze profits in the modern sector, leading to recession and unemployment combined with spiralling inflation as firms and workers try to maintain real profits and wages. Secondly, the domestic currency devaluation advocated by the IMF will not necessarily have a significant positive effect on the balance of payments if international demand elasticities for developing countries' exports and the latters' demand for imports are both low (if the Marshall-Lerner condition is not met the effect will be negative). Finally those hurt most by the joint impact of public sector credit restrictions, food price increases and rising unemployment are the poor, who are least able to afford the rising prices and who often also bear the brunt of cut-backs in public sector health and education expenditure. Meanwhile, whether the agricultural sector can respond to agricultural price increases will depend on whether essential institutional reforms (not part of IMF stabilisation programmes) have been undertaken (see e.g. Killick *et al.*, 1984a and b; Kydd, 1986; and Baer and Welch, 1987).

An essential feature of these criticisms is the view that the neo-classical assumptions of relatively high price elasticities, and of significant short-run real wage flexibility, which underpin the monetarist policy recommendations, are both invalid in developing countries.

Cost-benefit analysis
Criticism of cost-benefit analysis has focused both on the degree of emphasis given to the role of prices in determining welfare maximising patterns of resource allocation, and on the ability of governments to determine the

correct prices for this purpose in the face of various distortions. In relation to both issues critics have focused both on the underlying theory and its practical implications.

One of the best critiques of the theoretical basis of cost-benefit analysis prepared primarily with developing economies in mind is Kornai (1979). His criticisms focus first on the four key assumptions underlying cost-benefit analysis:

1. That economies can be guided to some uniquely optimal allocation of resources.
2. That this can be achieved through establishing the correct set of relative prices.
3. That governments have the knowledge to do this.[41]
4. That they have a common will to do this, i.e. there is a unique social welfare function (Kornai, 1979).

Many economists have questioned the notion of a unique social welfare function (which expresses the agreed economic objectives of society) – invariably on grounds of realism. There is no such thing as *the* social interest, rather every society is formed of a series of overlapping interest groups based on class, age, geographical regions, race, religion and occupation. In reality, public sector resource allocation must be based not on 'common interest' but on compromise – the particular compromise reached being largely a function of power relationships. As these change, so will the nature of the compromise. One possible response to the problem is to argue that the social welfare function reflects the preferences of the government in power. However, this raises the question of whether even particular governments have an internally consistent, stable, unanimously weighted set of economic and social objectives. In practice, argues Kornai, they do not. Coexistent priorities are often conflicting, and resolved by succumbing to the current most intensive pressures. Furthermore, decentralised production decisions within the public sector are frequently based not on social profit-maximisation but on the self-interest of the decision-maker and those in a position to influence him/her. In the case of public sector investment decisions, those with a personal interest in the outcome will try to influence both the prior economic calculations of the cost-benefit analyses which are supposed to determine whether particular projects are undertaken, and the actual decision itself – irrespective of the final calculation.

Meanwhile, the fact that production functions are often concave, not convex, due to economies of scale, inhibits the determination of a unique set of equilibrium prices even if there were a clearly defined social welfare function (which patently there is not).

If the underlying axioms of cost-benefit analysis are dubious, so, argues Kornai, is the manner in which the results of such analyses are presented.

Firstly, there is the question of whether it really helps decision-taking to try to present the predicted outcome of a project in a single figure when many separate and important issues are at stake.

> A physician would never think of expressing the general state of health of a patient by one scalar indicator. He knows that good lungs are not a substitute for bad kidneys. The physician thinks about health as a vector and not as a scalar. Why cannot the economist also shift at last to that way of thinking?
>
> (Kornai, *op.cit.*: 88.)

Likewise the desirability of trying to attribute a monetary value to all costs and benefits is open to question.

Cost-benefit analysis as designed for developing countries has also been further criticised for its judgemental content, for its capacity to lead to *inefficient* resource allocation and for lack of political realism.

The judgemental/normative content of cost-benefit analysis. Whereas cost-benefit analysis has been presented as an exercise in positive economics, several critics have noted its normative content. Value judgements are recognised in the choice of income distribution weightings, and, in practice, in the choice of the accounting rate of interest (Streeten and Stewart, 1972; Fitzgerald, 1977). Although some proponents of cost-benefit methods emphasise that the results of cost-benefit analyses should be presented in such a way that these value judgements are left to politicians (see e.g. UNIDO, 1972: Chapter 18), in reality this will not always be practicable.

It has been argued too that value judgement underlies the choice of international price relatives for valuing project inputs and outputs (see Rudra, 1972). Exponents of cost-benefit analysis reply to this criticism with the argument that use of these prices means only that they are taken as given. 'They represent a set of constraints subject to which a country must pursue its own objectives.' (Corden, 1974: 399.) This, however, is problematic. Normally, when economists think in terms of constraints, they do so either in terms of physical resource constraints, as in linear programming, or of a budget constraint. It is true that using international price relatives in public sector projects should contribute to an efficient allocation of foreign exchange, as well as to improved generation of foreign exchange earnings, in conditions where foreign exchange itself is a scarce, sometimes limiting, resource. The problem, however, remains that taking a particular *set of price relatives* to represent a *constraint* necessarily also implies a judgement about the relative value to society of different goods (see also Lall, 1976: 188).

The contribution of cost-benefit analysis to inefficient resource allocation. Meanwhile, cost-benefit analysis, while purporting to increase efficiency in resource allocation, may actually do the opposite, for the following reasons. Whatever distortions, endogenous or exogenous, enter into the setting of domestic price relatives, the fact of the matter is that, at any moment in time, it is these which will reflect the current marginal valuation of goods and services by consumers (always assuming individual utility maximisation), and it is these also that 'do begin to reflect the local opportunity cost of resources used in production' (Streeten and Stewart, *op.cit.*: 79). In these circumstances it can never be certain that public sector resource allocation decisions based on a different set of price relatives will lead to an improvement in welfare. A similar point applies where different interest rates guide investment decisions in the public and private sectors.

At a practical level, there is also the problem of accurately predicting international prices, given the possible actions of competing suppliers, importing countries' protection decisions, foreign devaluations, etc. (Streeten and Stewart, *op.cit.*: 84).

The lack of political realism in cost-benefit analysis. Finally, we may note one further criticism. It may be asked (see e.g. Stewart, 1978: 164) whether public sector project choice can really have more than a putative 'window-dressing' effect on either income distribution or employment, or any significant effect on the savings rate. If governments really want to influence these variables and the foreign balance also, then they should act directly upon the appropriate policy instruments including taxes, tariffs, interest rates and the exchange rate (Stewart, 1978: 164). In this respect both Stewart and Fitzgerald (*op.cit.*) apply to cost-benefit analysis a criticism that has been levied against neo-classical price theory in general – that it either abstracts from, or reflects a naïve interpretation of, real world political economy and, in particular, the role of class interest in the formulation of policy (cf. Dobb, 1940).[42]

The critics' reply to Friedman and Lal

It would appear from the foregoing review of criticisms of the neo-classical perspective that a significant number of economists working within other intellectual perspectives do not accept the basic counter-arguments of Friedman and Lal outlined at the beginning of this section. The inadequate representation of the determinants of the direction and momentum of economic change in developing countries in the basic neo-classical model of market equilibrium means that the model, *pace* Friedman, has limited predictive value except, as Kaldor observes, in the case of short-run change in particular markets. Likewise, the critics also hold that this inadequate representation of reality means that neo-classical theory cannot necessarily be assumed to act as a useful benchmark to guide policy formation.

SUMMARY AND CONCLUSION

In recent decades two branches of the neo-classical school have contributed to the development debate: the *laissez-faire* branch (whose leading exponent is Peter Bauer) and the more numerous body of neo-classical welfare theorists. In principle this is a difference of major philosophical and practical importance. In reality, however, differences between these theorists are very often more of degree than of total espousal or rejection of *laissez-faire*, and there is still a significant common core of value, belief, theory and analytical method that is espoused by the neo-classicals in general. This core includes the following features:

1. A belief that economic inequality is an important source of incentive.
2. A belief that, for the most part, unimpeded operation of the market will maximise efficiency and economic welfare.
3. A continuing conviction in the mutual benefits to be obtained from free international trade.
4. A belief in a 'minimalist' intervention role for government, although the exact range of interventions that are regarded as acceptable varies.
5. A continuing focus on relatively short-run allocative issues.
6. A continuing fascination at the level of theory with general and partial equilibrium analysis, albeit also with particular divergences therefrom.
7. Assignation of particular importance to prices not as one theoretical variable, or policy instrument, among a number, but as the most important means by which economic information is conveyed and the dominant guide according to which resources are, and should be, allocated.

For critics of this perspective, its weaknesses include a failure to analyse the dynamics of long-run change, inadequate acknowledgement of the cumulative disequilibria that are inherent in dynamic economic systems, failure to recognise the potential risks, and costs, of continuing specialisation in international trade according to static comparative advantage, and inconsistency regarding the role of government in the setting of policy objectives. On this last point, neo-classical welfare theorists argue that once the social welfare function has been articulated economists can formulate a set of price relatives that will guide resource allocation so as to maximise social welfare. Yet it is remarkable how often members of this same school choose to emphasise the inefficiency of policy choices that give a relatively high role to industrialisation, to regional or personal equity or to deliberate modification of trade patterns. On the one hand, it is up to governments to choose their priorities; on the other, neo-classical economists still criticise these in terms of the traditional perspective of their paradigm.

Critics of this perspective also question the relative weight assigned to the values it embodies, and the effectiveness of the 'basic model' in interpreting the real world, due *inter alia* to the inaccuracy of the starting assumptions, the ease with which key factors may be omitted in the neo-classicals' successive approximations to reality, the misrepresentation of the dominant tendencies in actual economic systems and 'political naivety'. However,

> that does *not* mean that they reject all the insights provided by neoclassical economists, and especially the powerful concept of opportunity costs, nor does it mean that they outlaw the use of the price system.
>
> (Stewart, 1985: 284.)

Instead they hold that the use of elements of price theory does not automatically entail full acceptance of all the assumptions peculiar to the neoclassical paradigm. It does not entail, for example, acceptance of the precise assumptions that are necessary for partial and general equilibrium analysis. As Kornai, Kaldor and others have shown, firms may have other goals than profit maximisation, use other criteria than marginal revenue and marginal cost in setting output levels, often set their own prices, but do not use marginal costs to do so, and do not know their own demand curves. Yet the setting of prices (by firms and by governments) and reaction to price changes (by firms and consumers) are part, albeit only part, of the economic picture, and no economist can afford to ignore these.

NOTES

1. Haberler's article 'Critical observations on some current notions in the theory of economic development', published in *L'Industria*, 1957, and reprinted in Meier, G. (ed.), 1970, is also noteworthy.
2. A theme first developed by Hayek and von Mises in the 1930s.
3. This also anticipates later criticisms of the terms of trade argument for import substitution. See Viner, *op.cit.*: 112–114.
4. Viner, *op.cit.*: 51, 2.
5. *Ibid.*: 49, 50.
6. While the conclusions reached by the two economists are radically opposed, the style and wording of the paragraphs that precede this quotation are remarkably similiar to those of the key questions concerning welfare trends raised in Seer's later paper on the meaning of development (Seers, 1972, quoted in Chapter 9, p. 260).
7. It is notable that Viner, non-interventionist though he may be, acknowledges the possibility, and desirability, of large-scale programmes of poverty alleviation at a later date.
8. See pp. 260–2.
9. Viner, *op.cit.*: 103.
10. Prior to the preparation of this book, Bauer had carried out research and policy analysis in Malaya and West Africa on small-farmer cash-crop production. In both cases he had been impressed by the entrepreneurial dynamism of small-scale farmers.
11. See also Stiglitz, 1986.
12. The theories criticised are those that were reviewed in Chapter 3, pp. 52–63.
13. See e.g. pp. 301–2.
14. The issues discussed in this section are each components of the 'neo-classical counter-revolution' in development economics. For a more comprehensive analysis of the neo-classical revival, see Toye, 1987.

15. For an explanation of X-efficiency see Leibenstein, 1978.
16. Since the monopolist faces a downward-sloping demand curve, marginal revenue is always below price and conversely for the monopsonist (who faces an upward-sloping supply curve).
17. The absence of external economies is sometimes used as part of the argument for infant industry protection.
18. See also Corden, 1974: Chapter 9.
19. Corden thus follows a precedent that was set by Meade (1955) but rejected by Johnson, and also by Bhagwati and Ramaswami (1963) in their analysis of domestic distortions.
20. Non-distortionary poll taxes are, observes Corden, merely a useful theoretical fiction (albeit one much used by earlier neo-classical theorists); see Corden, *op.cit.*: 43.
21. The central proposition of the theory of second-best is that

    if there is introduced into a general equilibrium system a constraint which prevents the attainment of one of the Paretian conditions, the other Paretian conditions, although still attainable, are, in general, no longer desirable.
                                        (Lipsey and Lancaster, 1956–7: 11.)

22. See, for example, Kreuger (1985) and World Bank (1987).
23. See Prest and Turvey (1965) for a review of the basic theory underlying cost-benefit analysis.
24. See e.g. Squire and Van der Tak (1975), and Gittinger (1982).
25. Little and Mirrlees are inclined to ignore these on the grounds that externalities are often extremely difficult to measure, and that they do not usually vary significantly between projects.
26. On the other hand, Gittinger's rules for agricultural project appraisal ignore these objectives.
27. The one exception is the orthodox optimum export tax or import tariff that a large country might impose to improve its terms of trade.
28. Except for items where the border price is believed to vary significantly with the amount bought or sold, in which case the marginal import cost, or marginal export revenue is estimated.
29. Little and Mirrlees estimate the shadow price of non-tradables by breaking these down into their two basic components: tradables and domestic labour inputs which are also shadow priced (see next paragraph).
30. See Little and Mirrlees, *op.cit.*: Chapter XIX.
31. See Bergson, 1964.
32. Alternatively, it is acknowledged that in reality lump-sum taxes and subsidies also generate both 'deadweight' distortion costs and collection costs (Corden, *op. cit.*: 43), in which case the principle just enunciated applies in their case also.
33. A point which does not seem consistent with the emphasis on the efficiency of small farmers noted above (see p. 297).
34. See e.g. Clapham, 1922, and Dobb, 1940.
35. See Chapter 3, p. 52 Bauer and Yamey were in partial sympathy with this criticism (see Bauer and Yamey, *op.cit.*: 9–10 and also 12). Here, as elsewhere, Bauer and Yamey show themselves as more in tune with the *laissez-faire* tradition reflected in the earlier work of Hayek and von Mises than with the continuing refinement of partial and general equilibrium analysis that has tended to characterise the other branch of the neo-classical school (see Hayek, 1945).
36. Livingstone is among those who argue that sales maximisation is a more common objective.

If the motivation underlying sales maximisation is general, then equilibrium is not likely to be the result at all, but a progressively changing market structure quite inconsistent with the basic model of competition: but much nearer to reality.

(Livingstone, *op.cit.*: 38.)

See also Leibenstein (1978) on this issue.
37. For further general criticisms of neo-classical theory not pursued here, see Diesing, 1982: Chapter 2.
38. See Chapters 4, 5 and 6.
39. Hans Singer, seminar at IDS, Sussex, November 1987.
40. The authors of the 1987 World Bank Development Report offer a four-part reply to this criticism: industrial country capacity to absorb new imports may be under-estimated; 'the idea that a large number of countries might suddenly achieve export-to-GDP ratios for manufactures like those of Hong Kong, Korea or Singapore is highly implausible'; export-oriented countries produce different products and inter-industry trade 'is likely to be important'; and 'the first wave of newly-industrialising countries is already providing markets for the labour-intensive products of the countries that are following' (World Bank, 1987: 81). It is notable, however, that two of the counter-arguments are speculative, while the second is based on logical error (it is not the export:GDP ratio that is at issue but the absolute level of exports). Furthermore sceptics might also query whether the first wave of NICs can supply a sufficiently large market for the followers if large numbers of countries join the latter group.
41. Ironically, an analogous last criticism is also levelled against proponents of development planning by members of the neo-classical school; see Lal, *op.cit.*
42. The urban riots that have broken out in some countries in response to IMF cost-of-living increases resulting from IMF programmes have given sustenance to those who criticise not only monetarists, but the neo-classical school in general, for political naïvety. There is little point in requiring governments to implement policies that could lead to their own demise. (See *The Economist*, May 9–15, 1987 and the *Guardian*, November 1987 for divergent accounts of a case in point.)

REFERENCES

Adelman, I., 'Beyond export-led growth', *World Development*, (Vol. 12, No. 9, September 1984).
Amin, A., *Unequal Development*, (Harvester, 1976).
Baer, W. and Welch, J., 'Editors' introduction', *World Development*, (Vol. 15, No. 8).
Bauer, P. T., *Dissent on Development*, student edition, (Weidenfeld and Nicolson, 1976; first edition 1971).
Bauer, P. T. and Yamey, B., *The Economics of Underdeveloped Countries*, (Cambridge, 1957).
Bauer, P. T. and Yamey, B., 'The political economy of foreign aid', *Lloyds Bank Review*, (1981).
Bergson, A., *Essays in Normative Economics*, (Harvard, 1964).
Bhagwati, J. (ed.), *The New International Economic Order: The North-South Debate*, (MIT, 1977).
Bhagwati, J. and Ramaswami, V., 'Domestic distortions and the theory of optimum subsidy', *Journal of Political Economy*, (February 1963).
Clapham, J., 'Of empty economic boxes', *Economic Journal*, (September 1922).

Cline, W., 'Can the East Asian export model of development be generalised?', *World Development*, (February 1982).
Collier, P. and Lal, D., *Labour and Poverty in Kenya, 1900–1980*, (Clarendon Press, 1986).
Corden, W. M., *Trade Policy and Economic Welfare*, (Oxford, 1974).
David, W., *Conflicting Paradigms in the Economics of Developing Nations*, (Praeger, 1986).
Diesing, P., *Science and Ideology in the Policy Sciences*, (Aldine, New York, 1982).
Dobb, M., *Political Economy and Capitalism: some Essays in Economic Tradition*, (Routledge and Kegan Paul, 1940).
Emmanuel, A., *Unequal Exchange*, (New Left Books, 1972).
Fitzgerald, E., 'The public investment criterion and the role of the state,' *Journal of Development Studies*, (Vol. 13, July 1977).
Friedman, M., *Essays in Positive Economics*, (University of Chicago, 1953).
Friedman, M., *Capitalism and Freedom*, (University of Chicago, 1962).
Gittinger, J.P., *Economic Analysis of Agricultural Projects*, (Johns Hopkins, 1972; revised edition 1982).
Godfrey, M., 'Trade and exchange rate policy in Sub-Saharan Africa', *IDS Bulletin*, (Vol. 16, No. 3, July 1985).
Haberler, G., 'Critical observations on some current notions in the theory of economic development', *L'Industria*, (No. 2, 1957); reprinted in Meier, G. (ed.), *Leading Issues in Economic Development*, (Oxford, 1970).
Hayek, F. (ed.), *Collectivist Economic Planning*, (Routledge, 1935).
Hayek, F., 'The use of knowledge in society', *American Economic Review*, (Vol. 35, September 1945).
Heckscher, E., 'The effect of foreign trade on the distribution of income', *Ekonomisk Tidskrift*, 1919, reprinted in Ellis, H. and Metzler, L., eds., *Readings in the Theory of International Trade*, (Blakiston, 1949).
Henderson, P. and Lal, D., 'UNCTAD IV, The Commodities Problem and International Economic Reform', *ODI Review*, (No. 2, 1976).
Johnson, H., 'Optimal trade intervention in the presence of domestic distortions', in Baldwin, R., *et al.* (eds.), *Trade Growth and the Balance of Payments*, (Chicago, 1965); reprinted in Bhagwati, J. (ed.), *International Trade*, (Penguin Modern Economics Readings, 1969).
Kaldor, N., 'The irrelevance of equilibrium economics,' *Economic Journal*, (December, 1972).
Kaldor, N., *Economics without Equilibrium*, (M. E. Sharpe and University of Cardiff Press, 1985).
Khan, M. and Knight, M., 'Stabilisation programs in developing countries: a formal framework', *IMF Staff Papers*, (1981).
Killick, T. (ed.), *The Quest for Economic Stabilisation: The IMF and the Third World*, (Heinemann, 1984a).
Killick, T. (ed.), *The IMF and Stabilisation: Developing Country Experiences*, (Heinemann, 1984b).
Kornai, J., 'Appraisal of project appraisal', in Boskin, M. (ed.), *Economics and Human Welfare: Essays in Honour of T. Scitovsky*, (Academic Press, 1979).
Kreuger, A., 'Import substitution versus export promotion', *Finance and Development*, (June 1985).
Kydd, J., 'Changes in Zambian agricultural policy since 1983: problems of liberalisation and agrarianisation', *Development Policy Review*, (September 1986).
Lal, D., *The Poverty of 'Development Economics'*, Hobart Paperback 16, (Institute of Economic Affairs, 1983).

Lall, S., 'Conflicts of concepts: welfare economics and developing countries', *World Development*, (Vol. 4, No. 3, March 1976).

Leibenstein, H., *General X-Efficiency Theory and Economic Development*, (Oxford, 1978).

Lewis, W. A., 'Economic development with unlimited supplies of labour', *Manchester School*, (May 1954); reprinted in Agarwala, A. and Singh, S., eds., *The Economics of Underdevelopment*, (Oxford, 1958).

Lipsey, R. and Lancaster, R., 'The general theory of second best', *Review of Economic Studies*, (Vol. XXIV, 1956–1957).

Little, I., *Economic Development: Theory, Policy and International Relations*, (Basic Books, 1982).

Little, I. and Mirrlees, J., *Project Appraisal and Planning for Developing Countries*, (Heinemann, 1974).

Little, I., Scitovsky, T. and Scott, M., *Industry and Trade in Some Developing Countries*, (Oxford, 1970).

Livingstone, I., 'After divorce: the remarriage of economic theory and development economics', *Eastern Africa Economic Review*, (1978).

McKinnon, R., *Money and Capital in Economic Development*, (Brookings, 1973).

Meade, J., *Trade and Welfare*, (Oxford, 1955).

von Mises, L., 'Economic calculation in the socialist commonwealth', in Hayek, F. (ed.), *Collectivist Economic Planning*, (Routledge, 1935).

Myrdal, G., *Economic Theory and the Underdeveloped Countries*, (Duckworth, 1957, Methuen, 1963).

Ohlin, B., *Interregional and International Trade*, (Harvard, 1933).

Prebisch, R., 'The economic development of Latin America and its principal problems', *Economic Bulletin for Latin America*, (Vol. VII, No. 1, February 1962; first published 1949).

Prest, A. and Turvey, R., 'Cost-benefit analysis: a survey', *Economic Journal*, (December 1965).

Rudra, A., 'The use of shadow prices in project evaluation: a critique', *Indian Economic Review*, (Vol. 82, 1972).

Schultz, T., *Transforming Traditional Agriculture*, (Yale, 1964).

Schultz, T., 'Investment in population quality throughout low-income countries', in Hauser, P. (ed.), *World Population and Development: Challenges and Prospects* (Syracuse, 1979).

Seers, D., 'What are we trying to measure?', *Journal of Development Studies*, (Vol. 8, No. 2, April 1972); reprinted in Bastor, N. (ed.), *Measuring Development*, (Frank Cass, 1972).

Shaw, E., *Financial Deepening in Economic Development*, (Oxford, 1973).

Smith, A., *Wealth of Nations*, (Pelican, 1974).

Squire, L. and van der Tak, H., *Economic Analysis of Projects*, (Johns Hopkins, 1975).

Stewart, F., 'Social cost-benefit analysis in practice: some reflections in the light of case studies using Little–Mirrlees techniques', *World Development*, (Vol. 6, No. 2, February 1978).

Stewart, F., 'The fragile foundations of the neo-classical approach to development', *Journal of Development Studies*, (Vol. 21, No. 2, 1985).

Stiglitz, J., 'The new development economics', *World Development*, (Vol. 14, No. 2, February 1986).

Streeten, P., 'A cool look at 'outward-looking' strategies for development,' *The World Economy*, (Vol. 5, No. 2, September 1982).

Streeten, P. and Stewart, F., 'Little–Mirrlees methods and project appraisal', *Bulletin of the Oxford University Institute of Economics and Statistics*, (Vol. 34, 1972).

Timmer, C. P., Falcon, W. and Pearsons, S., *Food Policy Analysis*, (Johns Hopkins, 1983).

Toye, J., *Dilemmas of Development*, (Blackwell, 1987).

United Nations, *United Nations Monthly Chronicle*, (No. 5, May 1974)

United Nations Industrial Development Organisation, *Guidelines for Project Evaluation*, (UNIDO, New York, 1972).

Viner, J., *International Trade and Economic Development*, (Clarendon Press, Oxford, 1953).

World Bank, *Accelerated Development in Sub-Saharan Africa*, (Oxford, 1981).

World Bank, *World Development Report 1987*, (Oxford, 1987).

World Development, 'Analysing disequilibrium in developing countries', Special Issue, (Vol. 10, No. 12, December 1982).

Young, A., 'Increasing returns to scale and economic progress', *Economic Journal*, (Vol. XXXVIII, No. 152, December 1928).

11 · CONCLUSION

Since the 1940s the study of economic development has generated a diversity of interpretations of the process of economic change in less developed economies. It is hardly surprising that both students and development practitioners who have to work within the context of the continuing debate in development economics periodically ask whether consensus – or synthesis – is possible. The study and analysis of development issues would certainly be simpler if it were.

An essential first step in establishing what scope for consensus exists is to identify the key features of the different perspectives that dominate the debate. This is what this book has sought to do so far. Now this concluding chapter seeks to identify the main areas of consensus or compatibility on the one hand, and of incompatibility on the other, between these different perspectives.

In order to proceed it is essential first to confront the view that different intellectual frameworks or paradigms (in the Kuhnian sense from which the usage of the term in this book derives[1]), are by definition mutually incompatible. This is, for example, the position taken by Foster-Carter (1976). If correct, it implies that the question of compatibility does not arise. However, so rigid a position can be questioned on several grounds. Firstly, a paradigm may fail to work as an explanatory and predictive device for two main reasons, mis-specification or omission – because it is based on what others regard as false premises or because it has omitted one or more crucial variables and relationships. Where two paradigms are based upon conflicting premises there is no scope for synthesis without destroying one or both, but where a second paradigm is developed in order to handle an important relationship or relationships omitted by the first then the possibility of synthesis does at least merit consideration.[2] In what follows we shall consider examples of both causes of divergence between different perspectives.

Meanwhile, Foster-Carter, again claiming to follow T. S. Kuhn, suggests that different paradigms, in the social sciences as in the natural sciences, use completely different concepts, to the extent that they may be said to use a different language. This assertion is paradoxically both helpful and unhelpful. It is helpful because it does pinpoint part of the distinction between paradigms, but unhelpful because it is an exaggeration. While there are major conceptual distinctions between analytical frameworks, there are also some elements of conceptual overlap, and in attempting to make comparisons this overlap is also of interest. (Indeed Kuhn himself, in a reply to his critics, explicitly rejects the above interpretation as too extreme; see Kuhn, 1970: 198, 9).

PARADIGM COMPATIBILITY AND INCOMPATIBILITY

The discussion now turns to the main issue: the extent of compatibility or incompatibility of the different paradigms reviewed in earlier chapters. The first part of the discussion will concentrate on the five new perspectives on development and underdevelopment that have emerged since the 1940s. It will then consider the relationship between these and the two pre-existing analytical approaches that have been applied to the analysis of economic development – the neo-classical and the Marxist. It will be helpful to proceed by taking pairs of paradigms, focusing on one and then comparing it with the others.

The paradigm of the expanding capitalist nucleus

As Chapter 4 showed, at the core of this perspective is the argument that developing countries should concentrate upon expanding their modern sector using largely capital-intensive technology, with the impetus coming, as Rostow and Lewis originally proposed, either from state capitalism or private capitalism, growth being maximised in part by restraining the real income and consumption of peasants and wage-earners. This perspective on the development process is clearly not compatible with two of the three other paradigms of development discussed in this book, the Maoist and basic needs paradigms, for these both interpret the nature of development differently and assign a very different role to the peasantry and other small-scale producers. The dominant differences are not differences of omission (though these also exist), but fundamental differences in values, belief and interpretation of empirical reality. Thus the following points can be made:

1. For the paradigm of the expanding capitalist nucleus, growth (and development) require, until the take-off into self-sustained growth is completed, increasing inequality in income distribution. For the other two, development requires a lowering of income inequality.

2. For the one paradigm, the only class with a high enough marginal propensity to save to allow it to play a significant part in saving and capital accumulation is the capitalist class. For the other two, other lower-income producers may also demonstrate a high marginal propensity to save and invest, including peasants and artisans – either collectively (as in the Maoist paradigm) and/or individually (as in the basic needs paradigm).

3. Not surprisingly, the policy conclusions are also different. For example, the paradigm of the expanding capitalist nucleus, as it was developed, came to emphasise the importance of the use of capital-intensive techniques in view of their perceived impact on income distribution and savings. The Maoist and basic needs paradigms give much greater emphasis to the importance of using in addition, in labour-abundant economies, relatively small-scale, labour-intensive techniques, due to their contributions both to equity and to growth: the latter via the expansion of the domestic market, their potential for calling forth additional savings and mobilising other, otherwise slack, resources, and also their potential contribution to skill formation.

Both the Maoist and basic needs paradigms have a significant number of elements in common with the Bukharinite view of the optimal socialist development path as this was articulated in the Soviet Union in the 1920s: witness the latter's emphasis on the importance of raising peasant welfare and mass consumption, and of designing an industrialisation programme closely linked to the needs of the agricultural sector for producer and consumer goods. This too may be contrasted with the similarities previously noted between the paradigm of the expanding capitalist nucleus and the socialist development path identified in the work of Preobrazensky and Feldman (see the Appendix to Chapter 4).

When applied to market economies, the paradigm of the expanding capitalist nucleus is also incompatible with neo-Marxism, which denies the possibility of capitalist development in the periphery.

On the other hand, the relationship between this perspective and the structuralist paradigm was, at least initially, of a different order. The intellectual framework of the structuralist school that evolved from the 1940s to the early 1960s can perhaps best be described as a massive qualification rather than a total rejection of the paradigm of the expanding capitalist nucleus. (Hence the tendency of some, such as Foster-Carter, to lump the two together.) Amongst points omitted or downplayed in the paradigm of the expanding capitalist nucleus, the structuralists emphasised the following:

1. The important distinction between an internal supply-side, and an external demand-side, growth dynamic.

2. The diverse and strong *external linkages* of the modern capitalist nucleus in developing countries.
3. The negative implications for growth of adverse trends in the net barter terms of trade of primary products.
4. The significance of the small size of the domestic market.

The structuralists criticised those development economists who ignored the significance of the international economic relations of underdeveloped countries, and they rejected the optimism of the paradigm of the expanding capitalist nucleus that from an initially small capitalist enclave there can be a steady growth in capital stock, labour productivity and total output, provided that labour costs are kept down. However, their aim was to identify the structural changes and economic policies that would make such growth possible.[3]

Following from their analysis of the structure and terms of international trade, the structuralists were more specific about the necessary *composition of production*, and hence investment, in the capitalist sector. Their prime concern was with the development of an industrial sector, as opposed to the expansion of capitalist mining or farming, whereas the paradigm of the expanding capitalist nucleus was different between these. Industrial development in turn would require the following:

1. Emphasis upon economic protection.
2. The formation of customs unions by small countries to enlarge market size and to facilitate the creation of backward linkages to intermediate and capital goods production.

In one respect there is an apparent incompatibility between the two paradigms. This concerns the policy recommendations for modern sector wages policy, and the logic underlying these. On the one hand, we have the recommendation that wages should be contained (and, as a corollary, trade unionism restrained) in order to sustain capitalist profits and, hence, the rate of investment. On the other, we have the contrary recommendation that wages in the modern sector should be allowed to rise, and trade unionism encouraged, in order to promote the expansion of the domestic market and the inducement to invest. Producers may be compensated via other policy instruments (e.g. tariffs, tax concessions) for the divergence of market labour costs from their true social opportunity cost.

However, it is noteworthy that Marxism recognises both these sets of logic, concluding that capitalists must seek to resolve this contradiction by allowing wages to move in response to the relative strengths of these two needs. (This 'resolution' applies to an economy in which a large proportion of the domestic market consists of the consumption demand of wage-workers, rather than of non-wage, small-scale family enterprise. However, in the latter case, control of price movements for peasant output might in principle have the same effect.)

The structuralist paradigm

This section considers the 'classical' structuralist paradigm itself. The previous section has shown that this, with its focus on the two constraints largely ignored by the paradigm of the expanding capitalist nucleus (domestic market size and the international economic context) in many respects complements the latter. Yet, apparently paradoxically, some have also noted parallels between this paradigm and the neo-Marxist one in particular the common focus on the international context, and the common use of an historical approach to analyse this. It is true that both paradigms embody an historical analysis of the causes of underdevelopment, in each case concluding, *inter alia*, that the Third World cannot replicate the development experience of the industrially advanced countries. However, the variables emphasised in reaching his conclusion, and the logic of the respective arguments, diverge.

In reality the apparent complementarity of neo-Marxism and 'classical structuralism', as this evolved from the 1940s to the mid-1960s, is relatively superficial. Not only does the more specific focus of the two perspectives diverge, as is reflected in their central concepts – the nature of class control over the surplus on the one hand and the structural characteristics of production on the other – but the conclusions reached are, as has been shown in earlier chapters, radically opposed. Underlying these differences are different perceptions of the role of the capitalist class, domestic and foreign, in the development process: negative in the one case, and positive in the other.

It is this last point that undercuts any possibility of complementarity between the two perspectives. Whereas at one level there does appear to be scope for synthesis through the combined application of the key concepts of each – structure, class and surplus – in practice complete synthesis is blocked by the neo-Marxist paradigm's rigid view of the class structure in underdeveloped economies, and of its implications for development. This perspective, in other words, is, like its counterparts, based not only on the use of particular concepts, but on a specific interpretation of the nature of the real world – an interpretation which is not compatible with that of the classical structuralist school.

However, while neo-Marxism is not fully compatible with structuralism, the central conceptual elements of the two perspectives are, as just noted, potentially complementary. Thus the incorporation of class analysis into a structuralist perspective previously focused upon the generation of normative recommendations for policy permits the analysis also of the actual determinants of policy, not just in terms of *ad hoc* necessity, but of underlying class interest – thus promoting a potentially more profound analysis of the reasons for divergence between recommendations and reality. On the other hand, neo-Marxism is capable of incorporating, and has incorporated, the concept of economic structure, and its empirical significance, into its analytical framework.

For the structuralist paradigm, incorporation of class analysis does not necessarily undercut the aforementioned scope for synthesis with the (more simplistic) expanding capitalist nucleus perspective. Rather, structuralism so extended would analyse a more complex 'middle ground' between the simplistic optimism of the paradigm of the expanding capitalist nucleus and the equally simplistic pessimism of neo-Marxism concerning the prospects for capitalist development.

Thus far, however, nothing has been said about the continuing validity or otherwise of the classical structuralist interpretation of development (see p. 49) and its implications for the choice of development strategy. The relationship between the 'classical structuralist' paradigm and the basic needs and Maoist paradigms will be reviewed in the light of this focus in particular.

Given that the Maoist perspective is concerned with development of a planned economy, with state ownership of modern industry and a large role for administered prices, whereas the focus of structuralism is on a mixed economy with a large private sector, any potential interest in comparing the two can only be limited, and lies in the structural characteristics of the development path envisaged (i.e. the envisaged pattern of change in the sectoral composition of output and the linkages that are emphasised between sectors). Here there is a divergence in the proposed path of modern industrial development, between the backward-linked path emphasised for market economies, and the forward-linked path, starting with the development of basic heavy industry, emphasised by both the large planned economies, the Soviet Union and China. In the specific case of the Maoist perspective, however, there is also a further divergence in the relative emphases given to agriculture and to small-scale, labour-intensive industry of all types (light and heavy, producing consumer and producer goods). Since, however, in these respects there is a coincidence of perspective between the Maoist and basic needs paradigms it seems more appropriate to turn to the latter, which is held to apply also to market economies, and consider the relationship between it and 'classical' structuralism.

The basic needs paradigm takes as given the need for structural change and diversification of production in the periphery. It also takes as given the need for economic growth, and it follows the structuralist paradigm in emphasising both the inadequacy of the domestic market and the balance of payments as key constraints upon growth and diversification. It differs from early structuralism precisely because it emerged partly in response to an awareness of the problems generated by the import substitution strategies of the 1950 and 1960s: low modern sector employment growth; growing income inequality; apparently growing numbers in absolute poverty; worsening balance of payments problems; and the continuing failure of the domestic market in most countries of the periphery to justify investment in more than a limited range of modern industries. In response to some of these issues, the basic needs paradigm differs from the structuralist in that it embraces a broader definition of development, giving much greater weight to the elimination of absolute poverty. Furthermore, in response to the afore-mentioned problems, the basic needs paradigm generates a different set of policy conclusions from those associated with the 'classical structuralist' paradigm, reached by a deductive logic which now starts from a different set of premises.

Thus preoccupation with development based on modern technology is now replaced by a more detailed analysis of issues of technological choice and an emphasis on the need, for various reasons, to promote greater use of more labour-intensive technologies in some branches of production. Based partly on the Chinese development experience, it is argued that this can in fact lead to a speedier development of capital and intermediate goods production (small-scale and large-scale combined) than under the traditional approach to import-substitution. The issue of productive asset distribution, particularly land, and its implications for equity, for the structure of produc-tion and employment opportunities and for the structure of demand is now also brought to the fore.

In many respects these differences represent a response to perceived weaknesses and lacunae in the classical structuralist paradigm, while also deriving inspiration from, and generalising from, certain elements of Maoism, most notably with respect to technological choice. Structuralist economists who have espoused the basic needs approach not surprisingly tend to emphasise the evolutionary relationship between structuralism and the basic needs approach (see e.g. Singer, 1979). They have, however, abandoned a number of those features of the original structuralist paradigm which represented common ground with the paradigm of the expanding capitalist nucleus. Structuralism may synthesise, with little modification, with the latter paradigm or, with greater modification, with the basic needs paradigm, but not with both.

The basic needs and Maoist paradigms

The focus of this discussion now shifts specifically to the basic needs paradigm. Since the relationship between this and both the expanding capitalist nucleus and structuralist paradigms has already been discussed, it remains to consider the relationship with the neo-Marxist and Maoist perspectives. As applied to market economies, there is a clear-cut incom-patibility with the former which denies the political viability of basic needs strategies in this context. On the other hand, as emphasised in earlier chapters (8 and 9) and as noted briefly in the previous section, there is a high degree of complementarity with the Maoist approach to development. In-deed basic needs theorists see the latter as a specific instance of the pursuit of a basic needs oriented development strategy implemented in the context of the transition to socialism.

Turning to Maoism, we have already considered its relationship to three of the other four perspectives. With respect to the neo-Marxist paradigm, it is the only perspective with which the latter is potentially compatible precisely because Maoism generated a socialist development strategy implemented following political revolution, which is what the neo-Marxist school advocates. It should, however, be noted that the neo-Marxist school has devoted very little attention to the analysis of socialist development strategy *per se*, focusing its attention instead on the constraints to the development of peripheral market economies within the international capitalist system.

Recapitulation

To recapitulate, then, development economics has generated three new perspectives from which to analyse the determination of development strategy and policy in market, or mixed, economies. It has generated a perspective that denies the possibility of capitalist development in the periphery and it has generated the theorisation by western academics of the intellectual framework that dominated policy formation in the Maoist era in China (that theorisation being based on Chinese sources and praxis). Of the three perspectives geared to the determination of strategy and policy in market or mixed economy developing countries, the recommendations stemming from each are for varying degrees and types of policy intervention to achieve various ends. With this last point in mind, the discussion will now consider the relationship between each and the neo-classical perspective, bearing in mind also the latter's partial separation into two branches which was noted in the previous chapter.

The neo-classical paradigm

It would be convenient to be able to conclude that while the development paradigms reviewed in this book offer alternative perspectives on long-run strategy, neo-classical theory provides the necessary guide to short-run resource allocation. In practice, however, matters are not so straightforward, for the development paradigms reviewed above all also generate a range of policy conclusions which are applicable in the short-run. It is therefore necessary to consider the compatibility of the neo-classical paradigm with the three paradigms of economic development that claim general applicability to market economies.

The neo-classical paradigm and the paradigm of the expanding capitalist nucleus

The paradigm of the expanding capitalist nucleus, unlike the structuralist paradigm, is, in its western version, indifferent as to the allocation of investment between sectors. It takes the view that this should go where the return is highest, whether this be in agriculture, mining, or some branch of industry. Here there is a correspondence with the neo-classical view that investment allocation should be determined by market forces. On the other hand, however, there are a number of respects in which the former perspective diverges from the neo-classical. These concern key assumptions about economic phenomena, the key causal factors in the expansion of aggregate output and, following from these analytical differences, aspects of macro-economic policy.

Elements of incompatibility

1. The neo-classical paradigm assumes full employment of all resources; the paradigm of the expanding capitalist nucleus emphasises the possibility, in underdeveloped economies, of substantial un- or under-employment of labour.

2. The paradigm of the expanding capitalist nucleus attaches first priority in the promotion of economic development to an increase in the rate of savings and investment. Neo-classical economists dispute this; they argue that the first priority should be to promote increased efficiency in the allocation of *existing* productive resources.

3. The paradigm of the expanding capitalist nucleus recognises the potential of both private and state capitalist accumulation (however, in the western version there is a clear bias towards the private sector). The *laissez-faire* branch of neo-classical theorists are opposed to direct state involvement in production on efficiency grounds, but some neo-classical welfare theorists recognise some role for the state in this area.

4. The paradigm of the expanding capitalist nucleus acknowledges a role for deficit financing (with concomitant price inflation) as a means of accelerating the mobilisation of slack resources for investment. Monetarist economists, whose theoretical foundations are neo-classical, acknowledge no such role.

5. The paradigm of the expanding capitalist nucleus incorporates an argument for tariff protection in order to compensate producers in developing countries for distortions in the labour market (which generate modern sector wages in excess of the social opportunity cost of labour); it also acknowledges a role for tariff protection in expanding domestic demand for the output of infant industries. Neo-classical welfare theorists have argued that while wage-cost distortion exists, tariffs are a sub-optimal, distortionary means of compensating producers for this, and that the case for infant industry protection remains dubious (see Chapter 10, pp. 301–2). The *laissez-faire* branch recognises neither argument for intervention.

The neo-classical paradigm and the structuralist paradigm
The structuralist paradigm takes as its starting point the structure of the international economy and the typical internal structure of underdeveloped economies, both of which are ignored by the neo-classical paradigm.

Elements of incompatibility

1. Within the structuralist paradigm the theory of comparative advantage is rejected; the neo-classical paradigm favours free trade.
2. Within the structuralist paradigm, the deliberate state promotion of a strategy of structural change via the development of diversified modern industry is an essential precondition of development.
3. The policy instruments for the promotion of 2 above include the use of tax, credit and exchange rate policy, tariff protection and the allocation of public sector infrastructure investment, i.e. policies that alter both relative prices of inputs and outputs and relative rates of post-tax profit. Such wide-ranging interference with market forces is in direct contradiction to the neo-classical paradigm.
4. In principle, at least, structuralists argue that economic development entails land reform. This too falls outside the neo-classical perspective and is opposed by many neo-classicals (as an intervention with private property rights which would reduce confidence and incentives and deter private investment in productive capital).
5. The structuralist paradigm provides an explanation of the causes of inflation and of balance of payments crisis in developing countries which is in direct opposition to that of the neo-classical/monetarist school.

The neo-classical paradigm and the basic needs paradigm
At one level it is possible to observe an apparent link between the basic needs and neo-classical paradigms. This overlap occurs not so much at the level of the basic analytical models, which are designed for different purposes, but at the level of policy recommendation. For example, for obvious reasons the proponents of meeting basic needs would recommend a change in policies which under-price capital or foreign exchange. However, despite this convergence of view on certain policies, the two paradigms are not consistent.

Elements of incompatibility. The basic needs paradigm incorporates the following:

1. A preoccupation with the distributional aspects of development.
2. Advocacy of income and asset redistribution both to achieve distributional goals and to promote growth and structural change.
3. Recognition of price manipulation, rationing and investment licensing as possible policy instruments for meeting basic consumption needs.

4. Thus an acceptance, indeed emphasis upon, the need for various forms of state intervention in resource allocation and in the operation of the market in order to ensure an equitable foundation for sustained growth and structural change.

It is of course true that elements of price theory and the associated concepts and analytical method, commonly associated with the neo-classical paradigm, are used also by proponents of the three other perspectives that we have just reviewed, most notably in the case of the basic needs paradigm. However, as in the physical sciences, so in economics, common elements of analytical technique and method are sometimes utilised by proponents of more than one paradigm. The fundamental distinctions lie, as just noted, in the specification of the scope and nature of the problematic, and, linked to this, in value judgement, belief and interpretation of the real world.

Marxism and different development perspectives

There are two alternative views on the relationship between Marxism and the study of development. One interpretation of Marxism is that in essence it is an analytical method rather than a body of theory reflecting a particular intellectual framework or perspective.[4] The second is that Marx set out to apply this method to the analysis of the essential nature of the capitalist mode of production and its process of evolution. It is with this second interpretation that this book is concerned. According to this interpretation, Marxism can provide an intellectual framework, including a core body of theory, for the study of economic change and of capitalist development in less developed economies – albeit a body of theory which requires elaboration to take account of factors that were not analysed by the early Marxists, for example, the role of the state in the early stages of economic development (see e.g. Warren, 1973 and 1980). Marxism, however, does not provide an intellectual framework for the determination of development strategy or policy. It seeks, rather, to interpret the inner momentum of capitalism, and, in the light of this, the processes of economic and political change in the periphery, with the central focus being the emergence and expansion of the capitalist mode of production. Most Marxists have chosen to confine their analytical work to the above issues, explicitly delimiting their field of enquiry to the growth of capitalism (see e.g. Warren, 1973, quoted on p. 196 above).

The very fact that Marxists acknowledge the possibility of capitalist development in the periphery renders their intellectual perspective incompatible with neo-Marxism. Underlying this difference is the fact that despite any apparent verbal similarity, their conceptual framework, analytical purpose and interpretation of economic change in the periphery differ fundamentally from those of neo-Marxism.

As for the three market economy oriented development paradigms reviewed in this book, these, with their focus on the identification of development strategy and policy, have a different focus from Marxism, and the latter offers no basis, in itself, for discriminating between them. Rather, it offers the prediction that as the capitalist class comes to dominate the formation of state policy it will implement those policies which it perceives to further its own interests.

THE CONTEMPORARY DEBATE ON DEVELOPMENT THEORY AND POLICY

Contemporary development economics does not reflect a unanimity of analytical perspective. Today, just as in the past, differences in values, in beliefs, in interpretations of economic reality and in specification of key causal relationships are reflected in a diversity of viewpoints. However, just as has been the case at any point over the last three to four decades – a remarkably short period of time in the field of economic development, given the changes that it has generated, both empirical and intellectual – there are today, in the late 1980s, certain perspectives that dominate the development debate.

Without question the perspective that has 'made the running' in the debates of the 1980s has been the neo-classical-cum-monetarist: the international debt crisis, and the consequent need of many developing countries to turn to the International Monetary Fund and the World Bank for assistance, has ensured this.

Meanwhile the mainstream structuralist school, once the focus of swingeing critique from the neo-classicals, and more recently the subject of the diatribes of Deepak Lal (1983), has largely reversed roles, turning its attention to the critique of neo-classical proposals for export-led growth and of monetarist proposals for structural adjustment.

In this context, in the mid- and late 1980s, proponents of the more radical approach to meeting basic needs – as articulated in the basic needs paradigm – have been relatively quiescent.[5] Rather, the dominant emphasis of proponents of meeting basic needs has been upon lines of argument and policy analysis that are most likely to meet some support from neo-classical welfare economists: the moral case for absolute poverty reduction, the efficiency arguments for investment in human capital, and the efficiency arguments both for reappraisal of the technologies used in public service provision and for selective targeting of certain services. Finally, the efficiency arguments for encouraging small-scale farmers and urban informal sector producers are also emphasised (see e.g. Cornia *et al.*, 1987: Chapter 16). In this approach the arguments for restructuring agricultural asset distribution and for selective intervention to influence the pattern of industrial investment are downplayed. It is possible, however, that the more radical perspective on meeting basic needs may experience a revival in the future, for example if the guerilla wars cease in countries such as Nicaragua and Mozambique while leaving the present regimes in power, or if the pressure of circumstances – economic and political – forces some of the poorest countries to recognise that there is no realistic alternative to a basic needs strategy.

Meanwhile, there is a steady flow of Marxist-inspired analysis and critique both of the theoretical debate on economic development and of policy praxis. Neo-Marxism, however, appears to be in abeyance, having culminated in the publication in the 1970s of several attempts by leading members of the school to theorise the development of the world capitalist system as a whole.

THE CURRENT DEBATE ON THE FUTURE OF DEVELOPMENT ECONOMICS

How do these findings relate to the current debate on the condition and future of development economics? This debate has raised a number of important issues, including the following:

1. The question of whether development economics has justified, and does justify, its position as a distinct branch of economics.
2. The relative dearth of new concepts, ideas and theories in the 1970s and 1980s as compared with the previous two decades.
3. Various proposals as to what should now be considered the key objectives, causal factors and policy concerns in economic development.
4. Attempts to pinpoint, for purposes of analysis and policy prescription, the main categories of developing countries.
5. Discussion of the scope for eclecticism in the choice of analytical concepts and tools.

The following sections briefly consider each of these issues as they relate to the discussion so far. In doing so reference will be made in particular to four key contributions to this debate: Schultz, 1980; Sen, 1983; Lewis, 1984; and Livingstone, 1986.

The identity of development economics

'Standard economic theory is just as applicable to the scarcity problems that confront low-income countries as to the corresponding problems of high-income countries' (Schultz, 1980: 640). The argument that it has been a major mistake to presume that standard economic theory is inadequate for understanding low-income countries and that a separate economic theory is needed has been made forcefully by the neo-classical school (see also Lal, 1983). As such, it is not necessary to discuss this further here, since the main issues have already been considered in Chapter 10. However, the reassertion of this proposition in the 1980s, combined with the *de facto* revival of the influence of neo-classical economics, has helped to stimulate a certain degree of soul-searching among development economists as to what are the defining characteristics of their discipline. Various suggestions have been made.

On the one hand, Sen (1983) suggests that development economics may be defined in terms of a given body of beliefs and themes. Lewis, on the other hand, suggests that it is definable in terms of its subject matter – i.e. the problems confronted – and the tools used to analyse these. It is interesting that Sen expresses some misgivings about using the former definitional approach rather than the latter (Sen, *op.cit.*: 745), for in practice it leads him, as it had led others before him (see e.g. Seers, 1979), to a partial definition of the discipline in terms of some of the main themes which were generated in the theoretical work of the 1940s and 1950s. For Sen these defining characteristics are the 'major strategic themes' of industrialisation, rapid capital accumulation, mobilisation of under-employed manpower, and planning and an economically active state. This definition permits Sen to argue that while these themes can be justified in terms of their significance for economic growth, they constitute too narrow a delimitation of the subject. Growth does not equal development, and the future focus of the discipline should be upon the latter, which Sen interprets as the expansion of peoples' 'entitlements' and 'capabilities'. 'Ultimately, the process of economic development has to be concerned with what people can or cannot do' (Sen, *op.cit.*: 754). This leads Sen to the endorsement of what is effectively a comprehensive basic needs oriented development strategy. Yet, by the 1980s, most would argue that such advocacy was itself already part of the received subject matter of development economics (whether or not they agreed with the proposal).

Lewis' alternative definition of development economics in terms of its subject matter (an approach also followed in Livingstone, 1986) avoids this problem. It is also consistent with dominant convention in the definition of scientific and social scientific disciplines. Thus 'development economics deals with the structure and behaviour of economies where output per head is less than 1980 US $2,000' (Lewis, 1984: 1). Of the tools used to study these structures and behaviour, some are held in common with orthodox (i.e. neo-classical) economics, for example supply and demand analysis, while others have been generated within the discipline.

What Lewis and Sen have in common, however, is the conclusion that the issues raised in development economics are sufficiently distinctive for this to be recognised as a separate branch of political economy that has contributed significantly to the discipline of economics, and can continue to do so.

Furthermore, both see much of this contribution as lying in the sphere of analysis of long-run economic change.

The dearth of new ideas and theories

Some development economists in recent years have bemoaned the lack of new ideas generated in the 1970s and 1980s as compared with the preceding two decades (see e.g. Hirschman, 1981). While some have sympathised with Hirschman's diagnosis, it has also provoked other reactions, ranging from Lewis' sanguine assertions that a period of consolidation may be necessary, and that, in any case, 'a brilliant new idea . . . may just be about to erupt', to the recognition of the enduring nature of some of the early theoretical contributions (see Sen, *op.cit.*; also Livingstone, *op.cit.*: 13 on the enduring contribution of the Latin American structuralists). Others, meanwhile, are less preoccupied precisely because they feel able to pinpoint the key issues that should be at the forefront of the contemporary debate. It is to selected instances of such contributions that the discussion now briefly turns.

Recent theoretical contributions to the development debate

Some of the recent theoretical contributions to the development debate have already been reviewed in earlier chapters. It is not intended to recapitulate that review here. Rather, it is sufficient to note that if development economics has not recently proved as fruitful of new ideas as in the 1950s and 1960s, nor has it proved totally barren. In the sphere of development strategy three distinctive themes have been contributed in recent years. One is the neo-classical revival of focus upon investment in human capital, as epitomised in Schultz, 1980. In neo-classical hands this is not simply a reformist basic needs approach (see Chapter 9), but also the lynchpin for a fresh reiteration of more familiar theories. The poor are just as rational economic actors as the rich; as their skills and opportunities are increased so will their productivity; the freeing of markets and removal of price distortions will contribute directly to the latter and indirectly to the former (Schultz, *op.cit.*). This neo-classical perspective on the development of human capabilities may be directly contrasted with that of Sen. He is representative of those who continue to consider that a much greater degree of state intervention is required in order to ensure a steady increase in the capabilities of the poor than is acceptable to most neo-classicals – intervention both to ensure more equal access to means of livelihood and to ensure universal coverage in the provision of basic services (see also Lewis, *op.cit.*: 6).

A third theme in the recent debate, asserted but not yet fully developed, concerns the need to differentiate between types of developing country before any significant discussion of development strategy can occur. A recent contribution to this theme is to be found in Livingstone (1986). Factors that are pertinent to the determination of development strategy, and that vary between countries, are location, natural resource endowments and economic, social and political conditions (Livingstone, 1968: 26). They include structural factors such as the size of the domestic market, and natural resource-cum-structural factors, such as the richness of the agricultural sector and the potential for mineral production. Livingstone seemingly takes his cue from Lewis in arguing that the countries with the poorest development prospects are 'semi-arid, resource-poor, landlocked countries with military dictatorships'; these 'will need more than development economists to change this' (Livingstone, *op.cit.*: 26; see also Lewis, *op.cit.*: 5). Meanwhile Livingstone is also among those that suggest that the imperatives, economic and political, for a development strategy 'emphasising labour-absorption, income-distribution and basic needs' are greatest in the poorest developing countries. (Livingstone, *op.cit.*: 27.)

In the field of short- to medium-term policy design a lively debate also continues, a significant portion of which is on the issues of stabilisation and structural adjustment. Here neo-classical proposals have been criticised from a range of perspectives, including both classical structuralist and basic needs oriented viewpoints.

THE SCOPE FOR ECLECTICISM IN THE ANALYSIS OF UNDERDEVELOPMENT AND DEVELOPMENT

Is it essential that all development analysis should take place from within a clearly identifiable analytical perspective? Those who are sceptical of the need to make any such firm commitment may take heart from the fact that two distinguished development economists have recently endorsed a much more eclectic analytical procedure (Lewis, *op.cit.* and Livingstone, *op.cit.*). While Lewis and Livingstone differ in the basic building blocks which they advocate should be used in economic theorising about growth and development, both are agreed that they may be drawn from diverse bodies of theory (including, in Lewis' case, diverse disciplines). Thus Livingstone states that he would emphasise the significance of externalities in economic development (see Chapter 3, p. 52), the need for a historical perspective that recognises the particular problems and opportunities faced by late comers, Emmanuel's theory of unequal exchange, the significance of the fact that technological progress is biased towards the factor endowments of the developed countries and 'the role of investment, which together with the system of international trade, provides the two components of dependency theory' (Livingstone, *op.cit.*: 15–17).

Livingstone's argument is that the five preceding points constitute points of convergence in development economics, irrespective of the perspectives from which the subject is approached and the terminologies used. Consensus on these issues is indicative of proven empirical relevance, and therefore they may be taken as the starting point for future analysis. To this starting point, Livingstone adds one further item, 'the capacity to respond' to available market opportunities. Livingstone asserts that this varies between countries, so lending some support to the neo-classical doctrine of internal causes of development and underdevelopment. Thus, too, the eclecticism of the analytical base is further extended.

It is possible that the foregoing points constitute a basis for future consensual analysis in development economics. Yet, for the present, this must remain an open question. This is for a number of reasons. Firstly, to give this consensual perspective more coherence, the interlinkages – particularly the causal interconnections – between the different points raised need to be spelt out. Secondly, in terms of the component elements through which other analytical perspectives have been analysed, this proposal is incomplete. It is not simply that there may be other important empirical elements on which there is also consensus to add to the picture, nor that there is no clear overall picture of causality, but also that there is no clear statement of what is the desideratum – how is development itself to be defined or perceived? Furthermore, if this can be agreed, can the priorities, and the most effective means of fulfilling these also be agreed? Alternatively, does consensus depend on agreement that governments should set the priorities, while economists advise on the policy options for fulfilling them? This, of course, is the position taken by neo-classical welfare theorists. However, today it commands support in other circles also (see e.g. Preston, 1987). There is indeed much to be said in favour of the view that it is not for social scientists to set government objectives! Yet it is a view that may raise two problems. One which has been discussed in recent years in relation to both the physical and the social sciences concerns whether one can reasonably expect social scientists not to hold certain views on the desirable direction for a society to take. Once a person holds values about the desired nature of the human condition, surely the former is inevitable, and effectively everyone holds such values. Furthermore, if such views are held, are they not likely to influence an individual's professional work? (See e.g. Preston, 1982; Diesing, 1982; Rose *et al.*, 1984 on this issue).

Secondly, however, is it really possible to develop social scientific theories without specifying the goal(s) to be achieved? In practice, neo-classical theorists have handled this issue by specifying their assumptions about the goals of individual firms and consumers, and the (assumed to be desirable) implications of the pursuit of these goals for society as a whole. Others, however, have questioned both the general validity of the former assumptions and the social desirability of the outcome of unfettered pursuit of both these and other objectives by individual consumers and producers (the contrasting viewpoints are expressed in Schultz, 1980 and Sen, 1983).

This is the limit to 'consensual eclecticism': there cannot be full consensus without agreement also on the desired goals of development and, hence, on the values and beliefs that are a key component of any analytical perspective.

Whether such consensus is possible is for the reader to judge. A relatively optimistic view on this issue is to be found in Leeson (1988), based upon the observed trends towards market socialism in centrally-planned economies. It remains, however, important not to confuse growing consensus over the role of the market in stimulating efficiency in resource use with consensus over other economic objectives, and the most appropriate means of achieving these, preferably while sustaining or raising efficiency.

NOTES

1. See Chapter 1.
2. In the case of young sciences, where different intellectual perspectives have been proposed and are competing for 'paradigm status', Kuhn himself recognised this possibility (see Kuhn, 1970: 18).
3. When one has identified the important area of complementarity and compatibility between these two paradigms it becomes easier to understand why there are some important texts (theoretical and applied) published in the 1950s and 1960s (e.g. Nurkse's work on balanced growth and some five years plans) which are difficult to classify because the ideas expressed seem to straddle both.
4. Ken Cole, personal communication, March 1988.
5. The change of regime in China and the rejection of many elements of Maoism, coinciding with the neo-classical revival more generally, has undoubtedly undercut this perspective.

REFERENCES

Cornia, G., Jolly, R. and Stewart, F., (eds.), *Adjustment with a Human Face*, Vol. 1, (Oxford, 1987).

Diesing, P., *Science and Ideology in the Policy Sciences*, (Aldine, New York, 1982).

Foster-Carter, A., 'From Rostow to Gunder Frank: conflicting paradigms in the analysis of underdevelopment', *World Development*, (Vol. 4, No. 3, March 1976).

Hirschman, A., *Essays in Trespassing: Economics to Politics and Beyond*, (Cambridge, 1981)

Kuhn, T. S., *The Structure of Scientific Revolutions*, second edition, (University of Chicago, 1970).

Lal, D., *The Poverty of 'Development Economics'*, (Hobart Paperback 16, Institute of Economic Affairs, 1983).

Leeson, P., 'Development economics and the study of development' in *Perspectives on Development*, eds. Leeson, P. and Minogue, M., (Manchester, 1988).

Lewis, W. A., 'The state of development theory', *American Economic Review*, (Vol. 74 No. 1, March 1984).

Livingstone, I., 'The further development of development economics', University of East Anglia School of Development Studies, Discussion Paper No. 198, (November 1986).

Preston, P., *Theories of Development*, (Routledge and Kegan Paul, 1982).

Preston, P., *Rethinking Development*, (Routledge and Kegal Paul, 1987).

Rose, S., *et al.*, *Not in Our Genes*, (Penguin, 1984).

Schultz, T. W., 'The economics of being poor', *Journal of Political Economy*, (August, 1980).

Seers, D., 'The birth, life and death of development economics', *Development and Change*, (10, (1979), pp. 707–719).

Sen, A., 'Development: which way now?', *The Economic Journal*, (Vol. 93, December 1983).

Singer, H., 'Poverty, income distribution, and levels of living: thirty years of changing thought on development problems', in *Reflection on Economic Development and Social Change*, eds. Rao, C. H. H. and Joshi, P. C., (Martin Robertson, 1979).

Warren, B., 'Imperialism and capitalist industrialisation', *New Left Review*, (No. 81, September/October 1973, pp. 3–44).

Warren, B., *Imperialism: Pioneer of Capitalism*, (Verso, 1980).

INDEX